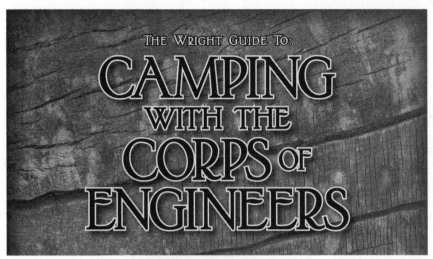

The Wright Guide To:

CAMPING WITH THE CORPS OF ENGINEERS

10th Edition
by Don Wright

D0881674

THE WRIGHT GUIDE

P.O. Box 2832
Elkhart, IN 46515-2832
1.800-272.5518
(NOT FOR RESERVATIONS)

www.rverbookstore.com
rverbookstore@gmail.com

Like Us On Facebook!
http://www.rverbookstore.com

THE WRIGHT GUIDE TO:

CAMPING
WITH THE
CORPS OF
ENGINEERS

FIELD EDITORS:
Forrest and Carol Byron

CONTRIBUTING EDITORS:
Allen Downs and Ted Houghton

The Wright Guide To:
Camping with the Corps of Engineers
10th Edition
ISBN 0-937877-58-6
Printed in the United States of America

OCLC 8/19/2015

P.O. Box 2832
Elkhart, IN 46515-2832
1.800-272.5518
(NOT FOR RESERVATIONS)
www.rverbookstore.com
rverbookstore@gmail.com

CONTENTS

INTRODUCTION

The information in this book is derived from many sources, including information provided by district and project office input. Some information came from personal visits, camping and people who have used the facilities. We wish to thank those U. S. Army Corps of Engineers personnel and other individuals who have contributed to making this book a success. Included herein are listings on hundreds of projects and campgrounds.

The Corps of Engineers is a Corps of the United States Army under the Department of Defense. As such, it operates much the same as any other government agency – in constant change. This is due to many factors, including but not limited to the following: size of the Corps, direction from congress and higher U. S. army commands, leeway granted the project officers by their district officers, size of the area utilized, budget concerns, safety, weather and other uses in the area. Since the 2001 terrorist attack and the continuing threats, many changes have been instituted by the government to protect the dams and facilities, and as a result, you may expect to be checked for identity and/or searched prior to participating in dam tours or other related facilities.

When using this book, please be remember that facilities are subject to change at any time. Campgrounds may be closed due to flooding, low flow augmentation releases, excessive soil erosion, insufficient funding, usage or personnel to supervise usage and other reasons. New campgrounds may be opened without notice. Additionally, areas which require a fee part of the year may not have some amenities such as water or electric available during the free or reduced fee season. Therefore, particularly when you are going to be traveling some distance, it is imperative that you call the campground or project office prior to departure for information necessary to meet your needs. Prices change, free parks may be closed or converted to fee parks, or parks may be consigned to other agencies (state, county, city, etc.) or leased to concessionaires.

Known fees are listed and subject to change without notice. Fees may be collected by roving patrol, ranger, gate attendant or self deposit (honor system). Also note that the symbols for some amenities, such as electric and water hookups, do not mean all sites have those amenities, but rather at least some are available. Other symbols for amenities such as golf courses, laundry facilities, marinas, etc., may be there as an indication that they are located nearby.

Your interest and assistance in providing us with updated information will be appreciated. Thanks to those who have provided information in the past. Please forward to The Wright Guide, P. O. Box 2832, Elkhart, IN 46515-2832. 1-800-272-5518. We have always found that the majority of Corps of Engineers Campgrounds are well maintained and administered. Hoping you will find them the same and get lots of use from this publication. Happy Camping.

GENERAL INFORMATION

The U. S. Army Corps of Engineers is the nation's leading federal provider of high quality outdoor recreation opportunities for the public. The Corps operates more than 2,500 recreation areas and leases an additional 1,800 sites. The Corps hosts 360 million visits a year at its lakes, beaches and other areas with estimates that 25 million americans visit a Corps project at least once a year.

General regulations for the Corps of Engineers recreational facilities are contained in Title 36, U. S. Code. You may procure a copy at most Corps facilities.

Unless otherwise noted, for information on group camping areas and pavilion rentals, contact the project office.

Most projects will accept payment by personal check requiring such information as phone number, driver's license number and address. Many, including the National Recreation Reservation Service accept Visa, MasterCard, American Express and Discover.

Many campgrounds and projects have much to offer that is not listed under the camping information. The listed information is taken from that received from the districts and projects, some more detailed than others. Common amenities usually not listed are fire rings, lampposts, tables, grills and public telephones. Contact the project you plant to visit to obtain a complete listing. You may want to visit the district websites listed on the address page.

Golden Age and Golden Access Passports are no longer issued, but they are still honored by the Corps of Engineers.

America the Beautiful - The National Parks and Federal Recreational Lands Senior Pass. You must be a citizen or permanent resident of the United States of the age 62 or older. This pass provides for access to and use of federal recreation sites that charge entrance standard amenity fees. It also provides a 50% discount on some expanded amenity fees such as camping, boat launching, etc. These passes must be obtained in person at National Parks Service, National Forest Service, U.S. Fish and Wildlife, Bureau of Land Management and Bureau of Reclamation recreation sites that charge fees. Identification is required to verify proof of age and residency. A $10 fee is charged for this pass, and it is good for your lifetime.

America the Beautiful - The National Parks and Federal Recreation Lands Access Pass. This pass must be acquired from the same entities listed under the senior pass information above. You will be required to provide proof of residency and have documentation issued by a federal agency such as the Veteran's Administration, Social Security Disability Income or Supplemental Income, or document issued by a atate agency such as a vocational rehabilitation agency, or a statement issued by a licensed physician. This pass provides the same discounts listed under the senior pass. There is no fee and the pass is good for your lifetime.

America the Beautiful - The National Parks and Federal Recreational Lands Annual Pass. This pass is not honored by the Corps of Engineers.

Corps of Engineers Day Pass - Anyone may purchase this pass from any Corps of Engineers site charging day use fees. You may also purchase it through the mail from Corps projects or district offices. These discounts for entry and camping apply to the card-holder and those accompanying them in a private noncommercial vehicle, which includes recreational vehicles.

Concessionaires normally do not offer the discount, but some honor them. Ask! A few state parks systems honor the passes; most don't.

Pets are permitted at most Corps campgrounds. They must be in the camper, vehicle, pen or on a leash no longer than 6'. Owners are requested to clean up after their pets. Pets are not allowed on beach areas where swimming is designated nor in rest rooms/showers, etc. Additional pet requirements and restrictions may apply at individual campgrounds and parks.

For the National Recreation Reservation Service (NRRS), call toll free, 1-877-444-6777, TDD 877-833-6777, or use the website, www.recreation.gov. Have the following information available when you call to place the reservation: Name of campground and project (lake, river, etc.), camp site number if possible or the type of site desired, arrival and departure dates, name, address and phone number, vehicles, trailers, tents and other equipment you will be bringing, license numbers of all vehicles you will be bringing, Golden Age/Access Passport Number or America the Beautiful Senior or Access Pass(if you have one), and your credit card number (Visa, MasterCard, American Express or Discover) to pay for the reservation stay. Many campground reservations required a 2 or 3-day minimum stay on weekends. Additionally, most projects require a cancellation fee when making the reservation.

Some campers may desire to contract as a gate attendant. Contact the district in the area you desire. Additionally, the Corps of Engineers has a volunteer program available for those who wish to help in many different areas. Call 1-800-865-8337, or visit the website, www.orn.usace.army.mil/volunteer/

Due to circumstances surrounding the World Trade Center building terrorist attack and continued terrorist threats, security at Corps projects has been enhanced. Some amenities and tours (such as dams and power plants) may not be available. Contact the project for further information.

REMEMBER TO WEAR YOUR LIFE JACKETS WHEN ON THE WATER.

ALABAMA

STATE INFORMATION:

CAPITAL: Montgomery
NICKNAME: Yellowhammer State
STATEHOOD: 1819 - 22nd State
FLOWER: Camellia
TREE: Longleaf Pine
BIRD: Yellowhammer

STATE TIDBITS:

• Alabama workers built the first rocket to put humans on the moon.

• Baseball player Henry Louis (Hank) Aaron was born in Mobile in 1934.

• The word Alabama means tribal town in the Creek Indian language.

WWW.ALABAMA.TRAVEL

Toll-free number for travel information:
1-800-ALABAMA

ALABAMA LAKES

To find campgrounds operated by the U.S. Army Corps of Engineers, match the lake's numbers on the preceding map page with numbered lake entries on the following pages. Campgrounds are listed alphabetically under the appropriate lakes. The following Alabama impoundments have Corps of Engineers campgrounds.

Claiborne Lake. 3 miles NW of Claiborne off US 84 on the Alabama River, NE of Mobile in southwestern Alabama. 5,900 acres.

Coffeeville Lake. 3 miles SW of Coffeeville off US 84 and N of Mobile in west-central Alabama near the Mississippi state line. 8,800 acres.

Dannelly Reservoir. Encompasses 105 miles of the Alabama River starting NW of Camden.

Demopolis Lake. Just N of Demopolis at the confluence of the Black Warrior and Tombigbee Rivers. It is W of US 43 and S of Tuscaloosa in west-central Alabama.

Holt Lake. NE of Tuscaloosa and NW of Peterson on the Black Warrior River.

Tennessee-Tombigbee Waterway. The waterway is a navigable link between the lower Tennessee Valley and the Gulf of Mexico, stretching from Demopolis to Pickwick Lake in the NE corner of Mississippi.

Walter F. George &
George W. Andrews Lakes. Together, they make up 45,000 acres of impoundment on the Chattahoochee River at the Alabama-Georgia state line.

Warrior Lake. This 7,800-acre lake is six miles SE of Eutaw off SR 14 and SW of Tuscaloosa.

West Point Lake. 35 miles along the Chattahoochee River, SW of Atlanta and I-85 on the Alabama/Georgia state line near West Point, Georgia.

R.E. (Bob) Woodruff Lake. SE of Selma off US 80, five miles N of Benton, eight miles W of Montgomery on the Alabama River.

❶
CLAIBORNE LAKE
ALABAMA RIVER
GPS: 31.62, -87.55

This 5,900-acre lake with over 60 miles of shoreline is 3 miles NW of Claiborne off US 84 on the Alabama River, NE of Mobile in southwestern Alabama. It is the most primitive of the river's three lakes (including Dannelly Reservoir and Woodruff Lake). The lakes project starts near Watumpka and flows into the Tombigbee River near Jackson. Day use parks include Bells Landing -- boat ramp, hiking (closed to camping); Clifton Ferry -- boat ramp, picnicking; Cobbs Landing -- boat ramp; Damsite East Bank -- boat ramp, fishing pier, shelter, playground, hiking/biking trail; Holleys Ferry -- boat ramp, shelter, hiking trail. Alcohol prohibited. Site Manager, Alabama River Lakes, 1226 Powerhouse Road, Camden, AL 36726. (334) 682-4244.

DAMSITE WEST BANK RECREATION AREA

From Claiborne, 5 mi NW on SR 48; 3 mi N, on W side of dam. All year; 14-day limit. 2 free primitive sites. Tbls, pit toilets, cfga, drkg wtr. Hiking trails, boating(l), fishing.
GPS: 33.2112343, -88.2903121

HAINES ISLAND RECREATION AREA

From Monroeville, 8 mi N on SR 41; 10 mi W on CR 17, then 2 mi on gravel rd following signs; secluded, along S shore of Majors Creek/Alabama River. All year; 14-day limit. 12 free primitive sites; 40-ft RV limit. Toilets, tbls, cfga, no drkg wtr, playground, picnic shelter. Nature trails, hiking, swimming, boating(l), fishing. 390 acres. Ferry.
GPS: 31.72577, -87.46929

ISAAC CREEK CAMPGROUND

From Monroeville, 8 mi N on SR 41 to CR 17 W; 10 mi W on CR 17 following signs; just N

of Lock & Dam Rd at E shore of Majors Creek/Alabama River. All year; 14-day limit. $20 base at 50-amp elec sites ($10 with federal senior pass), $22 at premium waterfront sites ($11 with senior pass). 47 sites; RV limit in excess of 65 ft; 4 pull-through sites. Fish cleaning station, picnic shelter, tbls, flush toilets, showers, cfga, drkg wtr, playground, coin laundry, dump. Multi-use court, boating(ld), fishing, hiking. (251) 282-4254. NRRS.
GPS: 31.62222, -87.55028

SILVER CREEK RECREATION AREA

From Claiborne, 8 mi NW on US 84 to just S of Whatley; 5 mi N on CR 35 to town of Vashti; 0.25 mi E on CR 39, then E on Silver Creek Rd, following signs SE to park; at E shore of lake/Majors Creek. All year; 14-day limit. 8 free primitive sites on 45 acres for self-contained RVs under 21 ft. Group camping, firewood. Tbls, toilets, cfga, no drkg wtr. Hiking trails, boating(l), fishing.
GPS: 31.6696, -87.568000

❷
COFFEEVILLE LAKE
BLACK WARRIOR AND TOMBIGBEE RIVERS WATERWAY
GPS: 31.745, -88.1431

This 8,800-acre lake is the third largest of the Black Warrior/Tombigbee system; it has 97 miles of shoreline. It is 3 miles SW of Coffeeville off US 84 and N of Mobile in west-central Alabama near the Mississippi state line. Non-campers are charged day-use fees at Service Park. Demopolis Site Office, Black Warrior-Tombigbee River Lakes, 384 Resource Management Drive, Demopolis, AL 37632. (334) 289-3540.

LENOIR LANDING PARK

From jct with US 84 about 5 mi E of Silas (W of Coffeeville), 3 mi N on CR 21; 3 mi NW on CR 14 to town of Womack Hill; 0.5 mi N on CR

25; 3 mi N on CR 23, then 2 mi S on paved rd to landing, following signs; at W shore of river. All year; 14-day limit. Free primitive sites. Tbls, firewood, picnic shelter, cfga, drkg wtr, pit toilets. Boating(l), fishing. ORVs prohibited. **GPS: 31.859663, -88.154447**

OLD LOCK 1 PARK

From jct with US 43 at Jackson, about 7 mi N on SR 69 to town of Mays Crossing, then left (SW) about 5 mi on access rd to park at Tombigbee River oxbow. All year; 14-day limit. 10 free primitive tent sites. Picnic shelter ($25), tbls, flush toilets, cfga, drkg wtr. Boating(l), fishing. ORVs prohibited. **GPS: 31.573673, -88.033705**

SERVICE PARK CAMPGROUND

From Coffeeville, 4 mi W on US 84, across bridge, then access right following signs. All year; 14-day limit. 32 sites with 50-amp elec/wtr; 2 tent only sites. Tent sites with elec/wtr, $16 ($8 with federal senior pass). RV elec/wtr sites $22 ($11 with senior pass). RV limit in excess of 65 ft; 10 pull-through; 1 handicap. Tbls, flush toilets, cfga, drkg wtr, dump, showers, playground, coin laundry ORVs prohibited. Non-campers charged $5 dump fee, $3 boat & entry fee ($30 annually). (251) 753-6935. NRRS. **GPS: 31.754463, -88.147988**

❸
DANNELLY RESERVOIR
WILLIAM DANNELLY LAKE
R.F. HENRY LOCK & DAM
ALABAMA RIVER
GPS: 32.11. -87.39

This 24 square mile lake encompasses 105 miles of the Alabama River starting NW of Camden. It is one of three impoundments in the Alabama River Lakes system, the other two being Claiborne and Woodruff Lakes. Parks with day use facilities include Old Cahawba Historical Site (state operated) -- visitor center, boat ramp, picnicking, overlook, hiking trail; Damsite East Bank -- fishing pier, picnicking; Damsite West Bank -- picnicking; Bogue Chitto Creek -- boat ramp; Bridgeport Beach -- showers, shelter, playground, beach, hiking; Bridgeport Ramp (city operated) -- picnicking, boat ramp, primitive camping; Ellis Landing -- picnicking, boat ramp; Gees Bend -- fishing dock, boat ramp, shelter, playground; Shell Creek -- boat ramp, picnicking; Steeles Landing -- boat ramp, picnicking, playground, water trail; Training Dike -- shelter, playground; Portland Park (county operated) -- boat ramp, primitive camping, picnicking. Gulletts Bluff and Black Creek Parks are operated by Wilcox County. A visitor center is open daily at the Millers Ferry resource office. Resource Manager, William B. Dannelly Lake, 1226 Powerhouse Road, Camden, AL 36726-9109. (334) 682-4244.

CHILATCHEE CREEK

From Camden, NW on SR 28; NE on SR 5; 9 mi SE on CR 29, then E on access rd. 3/1-11/12; 14-day limit (only primitive camping available 11/13-3/1). 6 primitive non-elec sites, $12 ($6 with federal senior pass); $20 at elec/wtr sites ($10 with senior pass), $22 at waterfront sites ($11 with senior pass). 33 elec/wtr sites; RV limit 65 ft; 3 pull-through sites, handicap sites with 50-amp elec/wtr. Picnic shelter, fish cleaning station, tbls, flush toilets, cfga, drkg wtr, showers, dump, playground, coin laundry. Boating(l), fishing, hiking trail. (334) 573-2562. NRRS. **GPS: 32.14139, -87.27417**

ELM BLUFF

From Camden, 18 mi NE on SR 41 to near town of Elm Bluff, then 2 mi NW on CR 407; right (N) on access rd; at S shore of Alabama River/Majors Creek. $10. All year; 14-day limit. 10 primitive sites. Tbls, toilets, cfga. Boating(l), fishing. **GPS: 32.164461, -87.115273**

MILLERS FERRY CAMPGROUND

From Camden, 12 mi NW on SR 28 through town of Millers Ferry, then right (N) before

Lee Long Bridge on access rd to campground (also called East Bank Park); at E shore of reservoir. All year; 14-day limit. Elec/wtr 50-amp sites, $20 base, $22 at 29 waterfront sites ($10 & $11 with federal senior pass). 42 sites; RV limit in excess of 65 ft; 6 pull-through, 12 handicap sites. Picnic shelter, tbls, flush toilets, cfga, drkg wtr, dump, coin laundry, beach, playground, showers, fish cleaning stations. Boating(ld), fishing, swimming, multi-use courts. 334-682-4191. NRRS.
GPS: 32.117257, -87.389867

SIX MILE CREEK PARK

From Selma at jct with US 80, 9 mi S on SR 41; 1.6 mi W (right) on CR 139 (signs); 0.7 mi N on CR 77. About 4/1-9/1; 14-day limit. 31 elec/wtr sites, $20 ($10 with federal senior pass). RV limit in excess of 65 ft; 3 handicap sites. 2 picnic shelters, fishing pier, tbls, flush toilets, showers, cfga, drkg wtr, dump, playground, coin laundry. Boating(l), fishing, basketball, tennis. (334) 875-6228. NRRS.
GPS: 32.328990, -87.010238

❹
DEMOPOLIS LAKE
BLACK WARRIOR &
TOMBIGBEE WATERWAY
GPS: 32.54, -87.87

A 10,000-acre lake just N of Demopolis at the confluence of the Black Warrior & Tombigbee Rivers, it extends 48 miles upriver on the Black Warrior and 53 miles up the Tombigbee. It is W of US 43 and S of Tuscaloosa in west-central Alabama. Campground checkout time 3 p.m. Boat ramps are at Arcola, Belmont, Backbone Creek, Lock 6, Runaway Branch and Spillway Falls Parks. Other day-use facilities include Bigbee Bottom and Lower Pool hiking trails. Demopolis Site Office, Demopolis Lake, 384 Resource Management Drive, Demopolis, AL 36732. (334) 289-3540.

BELMONT PARK

From Belmont at jct with CR 23, E on CR 22, then NE on Belmont Park access rd. All year; 14-day limit. Free primitive sites. Picnic shelter ($25), pit toilets, tbls, fire ring, lantern pole, drkg wtr. ORVs prohibited. Boating(l), fishing. Non-campers pay $3 day use fee at boat ramp.
GPS: 32.55, -87.87

LOCK 5 PARK

From Cedarville, 2 mi W on CR 16 to split with Owl Rd; continue SW to park; on Big German arm of lake. All year; 14-day limit. Free primitive sites. Picnic shelter, toilets, lantern poles, fire rings, drkg wtr. Boating(l), fishing. ORVs prohibited. **GPS: 32.59, -87.74**

RUNAWAY BRANCH II PARK

From Birdeye at jct with CR 25, S on US 43 (Demopolis Hwy) toward Demopolis; 1 mi W on CR 11; S on Runaway Park II access rd. All year; 14-day limit. Free primitive sites. Picnic shelter, lantern posts, fire rings, pit toilets, drkg wtr. Boating(l), fishing. ORVs prohibited.
GPS: 32.555088, -87.844459

FORKLAND CAMPGROUND

From Demopolis, 9 mi N on US 43; at Forkland, 1 mi SW (left) on CR, following signs. All year; 14-day limit. 10 sites with 30-amp elec/wtr, $20 ($10 with federal senior pass); $22 at 32 50-amp elec/wtr sites ($11 with senior pass). RV limit in excess of 65 ft; 13 pull-through. Tbls, flush toilets, cfga, drkg wtr, showers, dump, playground, coin laundry. Boating(ld), fishing. Picnic shelter with elec, $25; nature trail. ORVs prohibited. Non-campers pay $3 entry & boat ramp fee ($30 annual). (334) 289-5530. NRRS.
GPS: 32.626672, -87.884510

FOSCUE CREEK CAMPGROUND

From Demopolis, 3 mi W on US 80 (signs); 2 mi N (right) on Maria Ave. S of confluence of Black Warrior & Tombigbee Rivers. 54

sites with 50-amp elec/water $22 ($11 with federal senior pass); 48 full hookups, $24 ($12 with senior pass). RV limit in excess of 65'; 2 pull-through, 9 handicap, full hookups. Tbls, flush toilets, showers, cfga, drkg wtr, dump, coin laundry, playground, amphitheater. Boating(ld), fishing, waterskiing, ball field, hiking trail. 3 group shelters, $25-$35. Non-campers pay $5 for dump station, $3 for entry & boat ramp ($30 annually). Group camping. (334) 289-5535. NRRS.
GPS: 32.512060, -87.871528

❺ HOLT LAKE
BLACK WARRIOR & TOMBIGBEE WATERWAY
GPS: 33.31, -87.40

This 3,200-acre lake is 6 miles NE of Tuscaloosa and NW of Peterson. It is 18 miles long on Black Warrior River. ORVs prohibited. In addition to campgrounds, facilities include Beech Tree Hollow hiking trail; Gobbler Ridge hiking/biking trail, Holt Visitor Center (Mon-Fri with interpretive center), Lock 15 Park boat ramp, Rock Quarry swimming beach, and boat ramps, shelter, playground, beach and hiking trails at Rocky Branch Park. Resource Manager, Holt Lake, 11911 Holt Lock and Dam Rd, Peterson, AL 35478. (205) 553-9373.

BLUE CREEK PARK

From Tuscaloosa, 13 mi N on SR 69; just S of Windham Springs, 7.5 mi E & SE on CR 38; 1 mi S on Goodwater Rd; 2 mi S on Blue Creek Rd; at W shore of Holt Lake near confluence with Blue Creek. All year; 14-day limit. 18 free sites. Lantern poles, fire rings, drkg wtr (well pump). Boating(ld), fishing, waterskiing.
GPS: 33.43688, -87.37980

BURCHFIELD BRANCH (OLD LOCK 16) PARK

Follow I-20 exit 86 at Tuscaloosa to Brookwood, then 1 mi E on SR 16; 16.6 mi NW on CR 59; veer left 0.1 mi on Ground

Hog Rd; 1.2 mi left at stop sign on Lock 16 Rd; 3.9 mi left at grocery store to park. All year; 14-day limit. 36 sites with 50-amp elec/wtr & 1 tent site with elec. Tent site $16 ($8 with federal senior pass). $22 at internal RV/tent elec/wtr sites, $24 for premium water view locations ($11 & $12 with senior pass). RV limit in excess of 65 ft; 2 pull-through sites, 24 handicap sites. Tbls, flush toilets, showers, cfga, drkg wtr, dump, coin laundry, playground, beach. Biking, swimming, waterskiing, fishing, boating(ld). Picnic shelter $35. Non-campers pay $4 day use fee, $5 for dump station, $3 for boat ramp ($30 annually), $1 per person for beach. (205) 497-9828. NRRS. **GPS: 33.441738, -87.373087**

DEERLICK CREEK CAMPGROUND

12 mi NE of US 82 near Tuscaloosa on Rice Mountain Rd. Open 3/1-11/29; 14-day limit. 46 elec/wtr 50/amp sites (6 tent only). $16 at tent sites ($8 with federal senior pass); $22 base at RV/tent sites, $25 for premium water view locations ($11 & $12.50 with federal senior pass). RV limit 40 ft; pull-through sites, 1 handicap site. Tbls, flush toilets, cfga, drkg wtr, showers, beach, coin laundry, playground. Basketball, paved biking trail, boating(ld), swimming, waterskiing, hiking trails, amphitheater, horseshoe pits. Picnic shelter with elec, $25. Non-campers pay $4 day use fee, $5 for dump station, $3 for boat ramp ($30 annually). (205) 759-1591. NRRS.
GPS: 33.254333, -87.434049

❻ TENNESSEE-TOMBIGBEE WATERWAY
GPS: 33.56, -88.51

The Tennessee-Tombigbee Waterway is a navigable link between the lower Tennessee Valley and the Gulf of Mexico. Stretching 234 mi from Demopolis, AL, to Pickwick Lake in the NE corner of Mississippi, this man-made 44,000-acre channel has a series of ten locks and dams forming ten lake pools, providing navigation to the Gulf of Mexico. Off-road vehicles prohibited. Tom Bevill Visitor Center at Carrollton, AL (205-373-8705 is open daily except on some federal holidays; it is an 1830-1850 era antebellum style center with a restored 1926 stern-wheeler "U.S. Snagboat Montgomery" interpretive exhibits, artifacts, group tours. Campground checkout time 3 p.m. $3 daily or $30 annual fees charged at Corps boat ramps. Alabama's Gainesville Lake has boat ramps at Cochrane Recreation Area and Vienna, Ringo Bluff, S.W. Taylor, Riverside, Sumter and Heflin Access Areas. Picnic shelters available at Cochrane & Sumter. West Damsite & Heflin Access have fishing docks. Alabama's Aliceville Lake's boat ramps are at Raleigh Ryan Access Area and Pickensville Recreation Area. Picnic shelters at Pickensville, Raleigh Ryan and Tom Bevill Visitor Center. Resource Manager, Waterway Management Center, 3606 W Plymouth Road, Columbus, MS 39701. (662) 327-2142. See Mississippi entries.

COCHRANE RECREATION AREA GAINESVILLE LAKE

From Aliceville, 10 mi S on SR 17 (signs); 2 mi W of Huyck Bridge (signs); turn right, then 2 mi on access rd; on W bank of Gainesville Lake. All year; 14-day limit. 60 wtr/elec sites, $16 base, $18 at premium locations ($8 & $9 with federal senior pass). RV limit in excess of 65 ft; 3 handicap sites. Tbls, flush toilets, cfga, drkg wtr, showers,, beach, playground, dump, coin laundry. Boating(ld), fishing, waterskiing, swimming, basketball. Picnic shelter, emergency night exit, handicap fishing area. (205) 373-8806. NRRS 3/1-9/15.
GPS: 33.083757, -88.270512

PICKENSVILLE CAMPGROUND ALICEVILLE LAKE

From SR 14 at Pickensville, 2.6 mi W on SR 86, on right; across waterway bridge, on right near Aliceville Lake along W shore of waterway. All year; 14-day limit. 176 elec/wtr sites (50 full hookups). $20 base, $24 at premium sites ($10 & $12 with federal senior

pass). RV limit in excess of 65 ft; 4 handicap sites with elec/wtr, 1 full-hookup handicap. Tbls, flush toilets, cfga, drkg wtr, showers, dump, playground, beach, coin laundry, picnic shelters, fish cleaning stations. Boating(ld), fishing, waterskiing, swimming, hiking trails, handicap accessible fishing area, multi-use court. Visitor center. (205) 373-6328. NRRS 3/1-10/31. **GPS: 33.239890, -88.2299544**

SUMTER RECREATION AREA GAINESVILLE LAKE

From Gainesville, SW on SR 116; N on CR 85; E on access rd to W shore of Tombigbee River. All year; 14-day limit. Primitive undesignated sites; day use fee may be charged. Pit toilets, cfga, drkg wtr, shelter, showers. Boating(l), fishing. Boat ramp. Fishing.
GPS: 32.871072, -88.186977

❼ WALTER F. GEORGE
& GEORGE W. ANDREWS LAKES
GPS: 31.6267. -85.0633

Together, these lakes make up 45,000 acres of impoundment on the Chattahoochee River at the Alabama-Georgia state line, adjacent to Ft. Gaines, Georgia, W of Albany, Georgia and N of Dothan, Alabama. Sometimes referred to as Lake Eufaula, the lakes extend 85 miles and have 640 miles of shoreline. $4 day use fees are charged non-campers ($3 at boat launches) or $30 annually. Eight county and municipal parks are on the lakes. Campground checkout time 3 p.m. Off-road vehicles prohibited. For picnic shelter reservations, call 229-768-2516. Alabama day use parks include Franklin Landing -- boat ramp; Abbie Creek -- boat ramp, shelter, picnicking, drinking water; Chenneyhatchee Creek -- boat ramp; Highland Park -- shelter ($75), boat ramp, playground, picnicking, drinking water, swimming area, fishing pier, hiking trail; Hatchechubber Creek -- shelter ($35), boat ramp, playground, picnicking, drinking water. Former Corps camping area, Coheelee Creek, now leased to

Blakely-Early County; free camping. Resource Manager, Walter F. George Lake, Rt. 1, Box 176, Ft. Gaines, GA 31751-9722. (229) 768-2516/(334) 585-6537. See Georgia listings.

BLUFF CREEK CAMPGROUND

From Phenix City, 18 mi S on US 431; 2 mi S on SR 165; E (left, following signs) across railroad to park. All year; 14-day limit. 71 elec/wtr sites, $24 ($12 with federal senior pass). RV limit 40 ft; 6 pull-through sites. Tbls, flush toilets, cfga, drkg wtr, showers, dump, coin laundry, playground, fish cleaning station, picnic shelter. Boating(ld), fishing, swimming. Picnic shelter, fish cleaning station. (334) 855-2746. NRRS 3/7-10/5.
GPS: 32.184993, -85.011714

HARDRIDGE CREEK CAMP

From Ft. Gaines, Georgia, 3 mi W across river; 1 mi W on SR 46; 3 mi N on SR 97, E at sign. All year; 14-day limit. 76 sites. 50 elec/wtr sites, $24 ($12 with federal senior pass); 15 full hookups, $26 ($13 with senior pass). Double sites $52. RV limit 30 ft. Tbls, flush toilets, cfga, drkg wtr, showers, dump, coin laundry, picnic shelter, beach, playground. Boating(ld), fishing, swimming, waterskiing. (334) 585-5945. NRRS during 1/1-10/2.
GPS: 31.642723, -85.099690

WHITE OAK CREEK RECREATION AREA

From Eufaula, 8 mi S on US 431; 2 mi SE (left) on SR 95; E (left) at sign prior to the White Oak Creek bridge. All year; 14-day limit. 129 elec/wtr sites, $24 ($12 with federal senior pass). RV limit 40 ft; 5 pull-through sites. Tbls, flush toilets, cfga, drkg wtr, showers, dump, coin laundry, beach, fish cleaning station, picnic shelter. Boating(ld), fishing, swimming, hiking trails, waterskiing. (334) 687-3101. NRRS. **GPS: 31.776120, -85.154160**

❽ WARRIOR LAKE
BLACK WARRIOR & TOMBIGBEE WATERWAY
GPS: 32.52. -87.88

This 7,800-acre lake with 77 miles of shoreline is 6 miles SE of Eutaw off SR 14 and SW of Tuscaloosa. Public use areas include Finches Ferry (boat ramp, picnic shelter ($25), playground); Lock 7 boat ramp; Lock 8 boat ramp, picnic shelter ($25), playground, and Selden Damsite Park boat ramp. $3 daily fees at boat ramps ($30 annually). Mound State Monument on bluff overlooking lake. Demopolis Site Office, Demopolis Lake, 384 Resource Management Drive, Demopolis, AL 36732. (334) 289-3540.

JENNINGS FERRY CAMP

From Eutaw, 5.7 mi E on SR 14, across Warrior River Bridge; at N shore of river. All year; 14-day limit. 52 elec/wtr sites (50-amp), $22 ($11 with federal senior pass). 65-ft RV limit; 8 pull-through. Tbls, flush toilets, cfga, drkg wtr, playground, showers, dump, coin laundry. Boating(l), fishing, hiking trails, walking trail. Non-campers pay $5 for dump station, $3 for boat ramp (205) 372-1217. NRRS. **GPS: 32.806701, -87.812090**

❾ WEST POINT LAKE
GPS: 32.9183. -85.1883

This 25,900-acre lake is 35 miles along the Chattahoochee River, located SW of Atlanta and I-85 on the Alabama/Georgia state line near West Point, Georgia. It has 525 miles of shoreline. Four county and municipal parks are on the lake in addition to six Corps-operated campgrounds. Resource Manager, W Point Lake, 500 Resource Manager Drive, W Point, GA 31833-9517. (706) 645-2937. See Georgia listings for more details.

AMITY CAMPGROUND

From Lanett, 7 mi N on CR 212, 0.5 mi E on CR 393 (signs). About 3/8-9/8; 14-day limit. 92 elec sites. 3 non-elec tent sites, Tents $16 ($8 with federal senior pass); elec/wtr RV sites, $25 ($12.50 with senior pass). Tbls, flush toilets, cfga, drkg wtr, showers, dump, playground, coin laundry. Ball field, tennis, basketball, boating(l), waterskiing, hiking trail, interpretive trail. Amphitheater. (334) 499-2404. NRRS. **GPS: 32.97083, -85.22222**

⑩
WOODRUFF LAKE
MILLERS FERRY LOCK & DAM
ALABAMA RIVER
GPS: 32.3233, -86.7833

This 20 square mile lake is SE of Selma off US 80, 5 miles N of Benton, 8 miles W of Montgomery. It is one of three impoundments on the Alabama River system project, the others being Claiborne Lake and Dannelly Reservoir. Day use facilities include Benton Park -- picnicking, boat ramp; Damsite East Bank -- fishing pier, shelter; Damsite West Bank -- fishing pier; Holy Ground Battlefield Park -- showers, boat ramp, fishing pier, shelter, playground, beach, hiking trail, interpretive trail, overlook; Swift Creek -- boat ramp; project visitor center -- picnicking, shelter; Jones Bluff -- boat ramp, picnicking, shelter, hiking trail. Site Manager, Alabama River Lakes, 8493 US 80 W, Hayneville, AL 36040. (334) 872-9554/8210

GUNTER HILL CAMPGROUND

From Montgomery at I-65 exit 167, 9 mi W on US 80; 4 mi N (right) on CR 7 (signs) into campground; at shores of Antioch Branch & Gun Island Chute. All year; 14-day limit. 142 elec/wtr sites, $18 ($9 with federal senior pass), $24 full hookups ($12 with senior pass). RV limit in excess of 65 ft. 10 handicap, primitive sites available. Tbls, flush toilets, cfga, drkg wtr, coin laundry, pay phone, 4

playgrounds, dump, 2 group shelters, beach. Store. Multi-use courts, biking, boating(ld), fishing, swimming, waterskiing, hiking trail. (334) 269-1053. NRRS. **GPS: 32.366261, -86.457971**

PRAIRIE CREEK
RECREATION AREA

From jct with US 80 just E of Benton 5 mi N on Benton Rd; at 3-way split just S of Edsons, take center rd 0.8 mi N; right (E) on Jones Buff Rd, then left on Prairie Creek Rd into campground; at E shore of river. All year; 14-day limit. 55 elec/wtr RV sites, $18 base at elec tent sites, $20 for elec/wtr, $24 at premium waterfront locations ($9. $10 & $12 with federal senior pass). 7 tent sites, $16 base, $18 at premium locations ($8 & $9 with senior pass). RV limit 35 ft; 2 pull-through, 2 handicap. Tbls, flush toilets, cfga, drkg wtr, showers, picnic shelter, fish cleaning station, coin laundry, dump, playground, beach. Hiking trail, basketball, swimming, waterskiing, boating(ld), fishing, canoeing. (334) 418-4916. NRRS. **GPS: 32.336496, -86.770234**

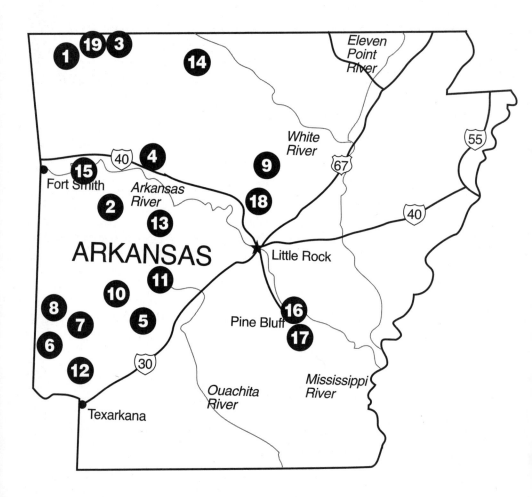

Eleven Point River

White River

Fort Smith

Arkansas River

ARKANSAS

Little Rock

Pine Bluff

Ouachita River

Mississippi River

Texarkana

ARKANSAS

STATE INFORMATION:

CAPITAL: Little Rock
NICKNAME: The Natural State
STATEHOOD: 1836 - 25th State
FLOWER: Apple Blossom
TREE: Loblolly Pine
BIRD: Mockingbird

STATE TIDBITS:

• Famous singer Johnny Cash was born in Kingsland.

• Milk is the official state beverage. It was designated in 1985.

• The Ozark National Forest covers more than one million acres.

WWW.ARKANSAS.COM

Toll-free numbers for travel information:
1-800-NATURAL

ARKANSAS LAKES

To find campgrounds operated by the U.S. Army Corps of Engineers, match the lake's numbers on the preceding map page with numbered lake entries on the following pages. Campgrounds are listed alphabetically under the appropriate lakes. The following Arkansas impoundments have Corps of Engineers campgrounds.

Beaver Lake. Nine miles NW of Eureka Springs on U.S. 62, 186 miles NW of Little Rock in northwestern Arkansas. It is the source of the White River.

Blue Mountain Lake. 1.5 miles SW of Waveland on SR 309 off SR 10, 5 miles E of Blue Mountain and 101 miles NW of Little Rock.

Bull Shoals Lake. 15 miles W of Mountain Home on SR 178 and SE of Brandon, Missouri, in north central Arkansas near the Missouri state line.

Dardanelle Lake/Winthrop Rockefeller Lake. At 34,300 acres, Dardanelle Lake is adjacent to the SW side of Russellville, E of Fort Smith

and N of Dardanelle on SR 22. Rockefeller Lake begins below Dardanelle Dam and extends 2.8 miles SE to Arthur V. Ormond Lock & Dam near Morrillton.

DeGray Lake. 8 miles NW of Arkadelphia and W of I-30 exit 78 off SR 7.

DeQueen Lake. 4 miles NW of DeQueen off U.S. 71 and 96 mi SW of Hot Springs (N of Texarkana) near the Oklahoma state line.

Dierks Lake. 72 miles SW of Hot Springs and N of Texarkana, E of DeQueen and 5 miles NW of Dierks in southwestern Arkansas.

Gillham Lake. 6 miles SW of Gillham, 15 mi N of DeQueen, E of U.S. 71 and SW of Little Rock near the Oklahoma state line.

Greers Ferry Lake. N of Heber Springs on SR 26, 65 mi N of Little Rock.

Lake Greeson. 6 miles N of Murfreesboro on SR 19, 69 miles NE of Texarkana on the Little Missouri River.

Lake Ouchita. 13 miles NW of Hot Springs on US 270 and SR 277, 67 miles SW of Little Rock.

Millwood Lake. 9 miles E of Ashdown on SR 32 and 28 miles N of Texarkana on the Little River.

Nimrod Lake. 8.3 miles SE of Ola on SR 7 and 66 miles NW of Little rock in north-central Arkansas.

Norfork Lake. 4 miles NE of Norfork on SR 177 near the Missouri state line and SE of Branson, Missouri.

Ozark Lake. SW of Ozark, 39 miles E of Fort Smith.

Wilbur Mills Pool, Arkansas River. Lock 2, from Mills Pool to the confluence of the Arkansas River.

Pools 3 & 5, Terry Dam, Arkansas River. From Pine Bluff to Little Rock on the Arkansas River.

Toad Suck Ferry, Murray L&D, Arkansas River. Pools of the Arkansas River from Little Rock to Dardanelle.

Table Rock Lake. In north-central Arkansas S of Branson, Missouri, on SR 165 W of U.S. 65.

Little Rock District - A fee may be charged for use of the dump station by non-campers. An extra fee may be charged for sites with water hookups.

❶
BEAVER LAKE
GPS: 36.4167, -93.8483

This 31,700-acre lake has 487 miles of shoreline. It is 9 miles NW of Eureka Springs on US 62, 186 mi NW of Little Rock in northwestern Arkansas. It is the source of the White River. Trout fishing, scuba diving, river rafting, nature trails. Eleven developed Corps campgrounds have 673 campsites. 7 parks contain year-around commercial marinas. $4 day use fees ($3 at Starkey Campground (annual passes $30). Campground checkout time 3 p.m. Alcohol prohibited. Campgrounds

with winter camping may have reduced amenities. 22 boat launches, 8 hiking trails. Dam Site campground beach open only to campers; park's day use beach open to all. Winter camping prohibited at Dam Site Lake, Indian Creek, Lost Bridge South, War Eagle, Starkey and Rocky Branch; $4 day use fee charged at those parks in winter. Visitor center. Resource Manager, Beaver Lake, 2260 N 2nd Street, Rogers, AR 72756. (479)636-1210.

DAM SITE LAKE PARK

From Eureka Springs, 4.5 mi W on US 62 (signs); 3 mi S (left) on SR 187, then right into campground, following signs; at end of peninsula, E shore of lake. 4/1-10/31; 14-day limit. 48 elec sites: $18 for 30-amp, $19 for 50-amp ($9 & $9.50 with federal senior pass). Tbls, flush toilets, cfga, drkg wtr, showers, beach, playground, picnic shelter ($75 plus $4 vehicle use fee). Boating(l), fishing, swimming, hiking, waterskiing, canoeing. Non-campers pay $4 day use fee for dump, beach, boat ramp.(479) 253-5828. NRRS. **GPS: 36.4203, -93.85541**

DAM SITE RIVER PARK

From Eureka Springs, 4.3 mi W on US 62 (signs); 2.5 mi SW (left) on SR 187; before crossing dam, turn left (E) on Dam Site River Rd, below dam (signs) to pay station (see GPS below). 3 camping loops -- Riverview, The Pines & Parker Bottoms. 4/1-10/31; 14-day limit. 59 elec sites (12 with 50-amp elec/wtr): 30-amp elec, $20; 50-amp elec/wtr, $23 ($10 & $11.50 with federal senior pass). Winter camping at 37 sites in 2014-15 were $14 for 30-amp elec, $16 for 50-amp elec/wtr; showers, wtr & dump available to all Beaver Lake winter campers. RV limit in excess of 65 ft. Tbls, flush toilets, cfga, drkg wtr, showers, dump, playground, beach. Boating(l), canoeing, fishing, waterskiing, hiking, swimming. River rafting trips available nearby. Non-campers pay $4 day use fee for boat ramp, picnicking, dump station, beach. (479) 253-9865. NRRS. **GPS for pay station: 36.42194, -93.84583**

HICKORY CREEK PARK

4 mi N of Springdale on US 71; 7 mi E on SR 264; 1 mi N (right) on Cow Face Rd (CR 602, signs); E (left) on Hickory Creek Rd. 4/1-10/31; 14-day limit. 61 elec sites (50-amp), $21 ($11.50 with federal senior pass). During 11/1-3/31 in 2014-15, 11 sites open for $15 (dump, pit toilet, elec, wtr services but no showers; $7.50 with senior pass). 50-ft RV limit. Tbls, flush & pit toilets, cfga, drkg wtr, dump, showers, playground, beach, 2 picnic shelters ($25 & $75 plus $4 vehicle day use fee). Non-campers pay $4 day use fee all year for dump station, picnicking, beach, boat ramp. Marina. (479) 750-2943. NRRS.
GPS: 36.238519, -94.038076

HORSESHOE BEND PARK

From Rogers at jct with US 71, 5 mi E on SR 94 (signs). 4/1-10/31; 14-day limit. Non-elec sites, $16 ($8 with federal senior pass); 188 elec sites (30-amp), $20 ($10 with federal senior pass); double sites $36. During 11/1-3/31 of 2014-15, 35 sites open, $14-$16 (dump, elec, pit toilets, wtr services but no showers); $7-$8 with senior pass). RV limit in excess of 65 ft. Tbls, flush & pit toilets, cfga, drkg wtr, showers, dump, playground, beach, picnic shelters ($75 plus $4 vehicle day use fee). Boating(ld), fishing, swimming, waterskiing, hiking. Non-campers pay $4 day use fee for boat ramp, beach, dump station. (479) 925-7195. NRRS. **GPS: 36.283971, -94.024022**

INDIAN CREEK PARK

2 mi E of Gateway on US 62; 4 mi S (right) on Indian Creek Rd (CR 89), following signs. 5/1-9/30; 14-day limit (no winter camping). 33 elec 30-amp sites, $20 ($10 with federal senior pass). Tbls, pit & flush toilets, cfga, drkg wtr, showers, dump, beach, playground, picnic shelter. Boating(l), fishing, hiking swimming, waterskiing, volleyball court. Non-campers pay $4 day use fee for boat ramp, dump station, beach, picnicking. 479-656-3145. NRRS.
GPS: 36.418675, -93.887486

LOST BRIDGE NORTH PARK

6.2 mi SE of Garfield on SR 127; follow signs, turning on 127 Spur, then left on Marina Rd. 4/1-9/30; 14-day limit. 48 elec sites (30-amp), $20 ($10 with federal senior pass). During 10/1-3/31 of 2014-15, 34 sites open for $14 (elec, wtr services, dump, no showers; $7 with senior pass). 60-ft RV limit; 9 pull-through sites. Tbls, flush & pit toilets, cfga, drkg wtr, dump, playground, beach. Boating(l), fishing, swimming, hiking, waterskiing Non-campers pay $4 day use fee for boat ramp, picnicking, beach, dump station. Youth group camping area, $40. (479) 359-3312. NRRS.
GPS: 36.413119, -93.894750

LOST BRIDGE SOUTH PARK

5 mi SE of Garfield on SR 127, following signs; right (SE) on CR 913 to park. 5/1-9/30; 14-day limit (no off-season camping). 36 elec (50-amp) sites, $19; $20 for elec/wtr ($9.50 & $10 with federal senior pass). 55-ft RV limit. Tbls, flush toilets, cfga, drkg wtr, dump, beach, playground, picnic shelter. Boating(ld), fishing, hiking, swimming, waterskiing, biking. Non-campers pay $4 day use fee for boat ramp, beach, picnicking, dump station. (479) 359-3755. NRRS. **GPS: 36.396924, -93.903794**

PRAIRIE CREEK PARK

3.3 mi E of Rogers on SR 12; 1 mi N on North Park Rd. 4/1-10/31; 14-day limit. $20 base for 30-amp RV/tent sites, $21 for 50-am, $22 for wtr/50-amp ($10, $10.50 & $11 with federal senior pass). During 11/1-3/31 of 2014-15, 8 elec sites $15-$16 (dump, wtr services, no showers; $7.50-$8 with senior pass). 112 total elec sites; RV limit in excess of 65 ft; 3 pull-through sites. 1 RV & one tent or 3 tents per site. Tbls, flush & pit toilets, cfga, drkg wtr, dump, coin laundry, playground, beach, 7 picnic shelters ($25, $60, $75 & $200); also 300-person Grand Shelter with full kitchen, serving station, restrooms, PA system, stereo. Boating(ld), fishing, hiking, waterskiing, swimming, volleyball, interpretive trail. Non-

campers pay $4 day use fee for boat ramp, picnicking, beach, dump station, shelters. (479) 925-3957. NRRS (4/1-10/31)
GPS: 36.347694, -94.056144

ROCKY BRANCH PARK

11 mi E of Rogers SR 12 (signs); 4.5 mi NE on SR 303 (signs) to paved access rd on left. 4/1-LD; 14-day limit (no off-season camping, but $4 day use fees charged). 44 elec sites, $20 for 30-amp, $21 for 50-amp ($10 & $10.50 with federal senior pass). Tbls, flush toilets, cfga, drkg wtr, showers, dump, beach, playground, 2 picnic shelters ($75 plus $4 vehicle day use fee). Boating(ld), fishing, swimming, hiking, waterskiing. Non-campers pay day use fee for picnicking, boat ramp, beach, dump station. (479) 925-2526. NRRS.
GPS: 36.338454, -93.937998

STARKEY PARK

4 mi W of Eureka Springs on US 62 (signs); 4 mi SW on paved SR 187; 4.3 mi W (right) on CR 2176 (Mundell Rd, signs). 5/1-LD; 14-day limit; no off-season camping. 23 elec 30-amp sites (7 with full hookups). $20 base, $22 full hookups ($10 & $11 with federal senior pass). Tbls, flush toilets, cfga, drkg wtr, showers, dump, beach, playground, picnic shelter ($75 plus $4 vehicle day use fee; call office for reservations). Change shelter at beach. Boating(l), fishing, hiking trails, swimming, waterskiing. Marina. Non-campers pay $4 day use fee for dump station, boat ramp, beach, picnicking.(479) 253-5866.
GPS: 36.389549, -93.876607

WAR EAGLE PARK

12 mi NE of Springdale on SR 68 to Nob; 3 mi NW on paved access rd. 5/1-LD; 14-day limit (no off-season camping, but some day use areas open). 26 elec sites (30-amp), $20 ($10 with federal senior pass). Tbls, flush toilets, cfga, drkg wtr, dump, playground, showers, beach, picnic shelter ($75 plus $4 vehicle day use fee; for reservations call office). Boating(l),

fishing, swimming, hiking trails, waterskiing. Day use fee for boat ramp, beach, dump station, picnicking. (479) 750-4722.
GPS: 36.21853, -94.01606

❷
BLUE MOUNTAIN LAKE
GPS: 35.1017, -93.6433

This 2,910-acre lake is 1.5 mi SW of Waveland on SR 309 off SR 10, 5 mi E of Blue Mountain and 101 mi NW of Little Rock. It was built for flood control of the Petit Jean River and lower Arkansas River valleys. Some campground amenities are reduced, along with fees, during the November through February off-season. Formerly free camping areas are now available only for day use, but primitive camping by permit is allowed in 7 designated areas; call 479-947-2372 for exact locations and details. Lick Creek Park's campground is closed due to budget constraints; restrooms and group shelter also closed. Both of the lake's current campgrounds provide boat launching ramps & fish cleaning stations. Day use fees are charged for boat ramps and other recreational facilities. Boat ramps are at Lick Creek, Hise Hill and Ashley Creek day use parks. Visitor center, interpretive programs. Permits required for metal detecting activities. Park Manager, 10152 Outlet Park Rd, Blue Mountain Lake, Havana, AR 72842. (479) 947-2372.

OUTLET PARK

From jct with SR 109 about 1 mi S of Waveland, 1 mi W on CR 32, then 1 mi S on CR 540 (Outlet Park Rd) to park at N shore of Petit Jean River. All year; 14-day limit. 38 sites, most elec/wtr. During 3/1-10/31, 30-amp elec/wtr, $16; 50-amp elec/wtr, $18 ($8 & $9 with federal senior pass). During 11/1-2/28, 30-amp elec/wtr, $14; 50-amp elec/wtr, $16 ($7 & $8 with senior pass). 3 multi-family sites at fees twice the per-site rate. RV limit in excess of 65 ft. Tbls, flush & pit toilets, cfga, drkg wtr, showers, dump, fish cleaning station, beach, playground, pay phone. Boating, fishing,

swimming, hiking trails. (479) 947-2101. NRRS (3/1-10/31).
GPS: 35.099162, -93.645157

PRIMITIVE CAMPING

7 free primitive camping areas are available by permits from the lake office. All have 28-day limits. They include Big Island Primitive Camping Area -- boat-in access from Waveland Park boat ramp to Big Island (GPS: 35.106, -93.676); Persimmon Point Camping Area 1 -- at NW shore of lake, S end of Persimmon Point Rd (GPS: 35.093, -93.736); Persimmon Point Camping Area 2 -- just S of Hog Thief Rd on Persimmon Point Rd, then E to lake on access rd (GPS: 35.105, -93.74); Persimmon Point Camping Area 3 -- just S of Hog Thief Rd on Persimmon Point Rd, camp on the left (GPS: 35.108, -93.743); Persimmon Point Camping Area 4 -- just S of Hog Thief Rd on Persimmon Point Rd, camp on the right (GPS: 35.107, -93.746); Lease Three Primitive Camping Area -- S & W of Waveland on Hwy 309, then S on CR 28, W on CR 31, N on County Line Rd & E on access rd to area across bay from Lick Creek boat ramp (GPS: 35.09, -93.698); The Slide Primitive Camping Area -- S & W of Waveland on Hwy 309, then N on Mountain View Lane to S shore of lake, or boat-in from lake. **GPS: 35.101, -93.675**

WAVELAND CAMPGROUND

From jct with SR 109 about 1 mi S of Waveland, 1 mi W on CR 32 to jct with CR 540; continue W on Waveland Park Rd to lake's E shore above dam. All year; 14-day limit. 51 elec/wtr sites. During 3/1-10/31, 30-amp elec/wtr $16; 50-amp elec/wtr $18 ($8 & $9 with federal senior pass). During 11/1-2/28, 30-amp elec/wtr $14; 50-amp elec/wtr $16 ($7 & $8 with senior pass). 40-ft RV limit. Tbls, flush & pit toilets, cfga, drkg wtr, dump, showers, pay phone, fish cleaning stations, beach, playground, amphitheater, picnic shelter ($25), change shelter at beach. Boating(l), fishing, hiking trails, ORV trails, swimming. (479) 947-2102. NRRS (3/15-9/15).
GPS: 35.106999, -93.656602

❸
BULL SHOALS LAKE
GPS: 36.3633, -925733

This 45,440-acre lake is 15 miles W of Mountain Home on SR 178 and SE of Brandon, Missouri, in north central Arkansas near the Missouri state line. It has more than 1,000 miles of shoreline. Off-road vehicles prohibited. Campground checkout time 3 p.m. Campsites that are free off-season may have reduced amenities. The Corps operates three developed campgrounds in Missouri and seven in Arkansas. In addition, free primitive camping (by permit) is available at Indian Point, Big Bend, Lowry, Yocum Creek and West Sugarloaf Parks. Day use fees are charged at swimming areas and the use of dump stations by non-campers. An extra fee may be charged for sites with water hookups. Visitor center. (870) 425-2700. Resource Manager, Bull Shoals Lake, 324 W. 7th St, Mountain Home, AR 72653. See Missouri listings.

BUCK CREEK CAMPGROUND

From Protem, Missouri, 5.5 mi SE on MO 125 (signs); in Arkansas at Little Buck Creek arm of lake. 5/1-9/30; 14-day limit. 2 non-elec sites, $14 ($7 with federal senior pass); 36 elec sites, $19 ($9.50 with senior pass); double sites $38. 40-ft RV limit. Tbls, flush & pit toilets, cfga, drkg wtr, showers, dump, playground, beach, picnic shelter ($20-$42). Marine dump station, change shelter. Boating, ball field, boating(ld), fishing, swimming. Peel Ferry (state's last ferry) leaves from park at SR 125, crosses lake to Missouri. (417) 785-4313. NRRS.
GPS: 36.489187, -92.796128

DAM SITE PARK

From Bull Shoals, 1 mi SW on SR 178 (signs); on bluff overlooking lake. 4/1-9/30; 14-day limit. 35 elec sites, $18 ($9 with federal senior pass). 40-ft RV limit. Tbls, flush toilets, cfga, drkg wtr, showers, dump, beach, playground, picnic shelter. Boating(l), fishing, waterskiing.

No reservations. (870) 445-7166. Note: Campground still closed for 2015 due to budget; check current status with lake office before arrival. Lease arrangement with city or state considered. **GPS: 36.37389, -92.57417**

HIGHWAY 125 PARK

14 mi NW of Yellville on SR 14, then 13 mi N on SR 125. 4/1-10/31; 14-day limit. 38 elec sites, $19 base, $20 for premium locations ($8.50 & $10 with senior pass). 45-ft RV limit. Tbls, flush toilets, cfga, drkg wtr, showers, beach, playground, pay phone, picnic shelter ($19-$42). Marine dump station. Boating(ld), fishing, swimming, waterskiing. (870) 436-5711. NRRS. **GPS: 36.490274, -92.775936**

LAKEVIEW PARK

From Mountain Home at jct with US 62, 6 mi W to Midway on SR 5; 7.1 mi W on SR 178 (signs); N on Boat Dock Rd; on bluff overlooking lake. All year; 14-day limit. 78 elec sites (26 wtr/elec). Non-elec sites $16; elec sites $19; elec/wtr $20 ($8, $9.50 & $10 with federal senior pass). 40-ft RV limit; 1 RV & 1 tent or 2 tents per site. Tbls, flush toilets, cfga, drkg wtr, showers, beach, playground, pay phone, group shelters ($19-$42). Boating, ball field, swimming, fishing. Marina, store. (870) 431-8116. NRRS (4/1-10/31).
GPS: 36.371116, -92.549425

LEAD HILL CAMPGROUND

From Lead Hill at jct with SR 14, 3.5 mi N through Diamond City on SR 7 (signs). 4/1-10/31; 14-day limit. 75 elec, $18 base, $20 at premium locations ($9 & $10 with federal senior pass). 40-ft RV limit; 4 pull-through sites. Tbls, flush & pit toilets, cfga, drkg wtr, showers, dump, playground, beach, pay phone, group shelters ($18-$40). Boating(ld), fishing, swimming, ball field. Marine dump station, change shelter. 870-422-7555. NRRS.
GPS: 36.471939, -92.920046

LOWRY PARK

From Lowry, E on Shoals Lake Dr; just W of Tucker Hollow Park at lake. 3 free primitive sites with permit from lake office. Pit toilets, campfire areas, no drkg wtr. Fishing, boating. **GPS: 36.4717, -93.0543**

OAKLAND PARK

14 mi N of Mountain Home on SR 5; 10 mi W on SR 202. 5/1-9/15; 14-day limit. 32 elec sites, $19 ($9.50 with federal senior pass). 40-ft RV limit. Tbls, flush & pit toilets, cfga, drkg wtr, dump, showers, beach, playground, pay phone, picnic shelter($), change shelter at beach. Boating(ld), fishing, swimming. Marina. (870) 431-5744. NRRS (5/17-9/13).
GPS: 36.443350, -92.628801

TUCKER HOLLOW PARK

From Lead Hill at jct with SR 7, 7 mi NW on SR 14 (sign); 3 mi N on SR 281, then E; on bluff overlooking lake. 5/1-10/31; 14-day limit. 30 elec sites (50-amp at 15 sites), $18 base, $20 for 50-amp ($9 & $10 with federal senior pass). 40-ft RV limit. Tbls with canopies, flush & pit toilets, cfga, drkg wtr, showers, dump, playground, beach, 2 picnic shelters ($40), change shelter at beach. Ball field, basketball, swimming, boating(ld), fishing. Marina. (870) 436-5622. NRRS (5/1-9/30).
GPS: 36.475098, -93.008650

WEST SUGARLOAF RECREATION AREA

Near Lead Hill campground where West Sugar Loaf Creek empties into White River arm of lake; access from Diamond City or Lead Hill, AR. Free primitive camping by permit from lake office. Pit toilets, campfire areas, no drkg wtr. Boating, fishing.

❹
DARDANELLE LAKE
WINTHROP ROCKEFELLER LAKE
ARKANSAS RIVER
GPS: 35.25, -93.1667

34,300-acre Dardanelle Lake has 315 miles of shoreline and is adjacent to SW side of Russellville, E of Fort Smith and N of Dardanelle on SR 22. It is two miles wide in places and stretches 50 miles upstream to the Ozark-Jeta Taylor Lock and Dam; it has 315 miles of shoreline. Winthrop Rockefeller Lake (GPS 35.102, -92.59) begins below Dardanelle Dam and extends 2.8 miles SE to Arthur V. Ormond Lock & Dam near Morrilton. Visitor center off US 7 on Lock & Dam Rd at the project office, which is midpoint of the 450-mile McClellan-Kerr-Arkansas River Navigation System. Theme of visitor center is "Renaissance of a River," featuring interpretive exhibits. Swimming beaches at Piney Bay and Shoal Bay Parks. Disc golf at Old Post Road Park. Two national nature trails -- Bona Dea and Sanctuary and Bridge Rock Trails -- are on project lands. Sweeden Island Campground, closed by the Corps in 2013 as a budgeting measure, is now privately owned. Cane Creek Park and Delaware Park, also closed in 2013, are now operated under lease by the Arkansas Wildlife Federation. Resource Manager, Dardanelle Lake, 1598 Lock and Dam Road, Russellville, AR 72802-1087. (479) 968-5008.

CANE CREEK PARK

From Scranton, 3.5 mi NE on SR 197; 2 mi N on paved rd. 16 free primitive sites on 48 acres. Closed by the Corps in 2013 for budget reasons, this park is now operated by the Arkansas Wildlife Federation.
GPS: 35.388971, -93.501828

DELAWARE PARK

From Subiaco at jct with SR 22, 3 mi N on SR 197; 2.5 mi NE on SR 393. Closed by the Corps in 2013 for budget reasons, this park is now operated by the Arkansas Wildlife Federation.

OLD POST ROAD PARK

From Russellville at jct with US 64, 2.2 mi S on SR 7; 1 mi W on Lock & Dam Rd, then follow signs; overlooks N bank of Arkansas River. All year; 14-day limit. 40 elec sites, $20 ($10 with federal senior pass). RV limit in excess of 65 ft. Tbls, flush toilets, cfga, showers, drkg wtr, dump, playground, 8 picnic shelters ($35 & $50). Soccer field ($), tennis court ($), volleyball, softball field ($), boating(l), swimming, fishing. No day use fees. 479-968-7962. NRRS (3/1-10/31).
GPS: 35.246614, -93.161970

PINEY BAY PARK

From London, 4 mi E on US 64; 3 mi N on SR 359, then left following signs on Rd 2720 into park. 3/1-10/31; 14-day limit. 91 sites, 85 with elec. Non-elec sites, $16 ($8 with federal senior pass); elec sites $18 base, $20 for elec/wtr ($9 & $10 with senior pass). RV limit in excess of 65 ft. Tbls, flush toilets, cfga, drkg wtr, showers, dump, pay phone, beach, playground, amphitheater, picnic shelter ($50). Boating(l), educational programs, swimming, fishing, waterskiing. Day use fees for boat ramp, dump station, picnicking, beach. (479) 885-3029. NRRS. **GPS: 35.398229, -93.316047**

RIVERVIEW PARK

1 mi N of SR 7 in Dardanelle on Second St; veer right on Dardanelle Dam Rd to park access rd, on right just below dam on the Arkansas River. 3/1-10/31; 14-day limit. 18 sites. 10 non-elec sites, $10 ($5 with federal senior pass); 8 elec sites, $18 ($9 with senior pass). Pit toilets, drkg wtr. Dump at Old Post Road Park on river's E shore. Tbls, pit toilet, cfga, drkg wtr, picnic shelter ($50). Fishing.
GPS: 35.246644, -93.174276

SHOAL BAY PARK

About 2 mi N of New Blaine on SR 197, following signs; at Little Shoal Creek arm of lake. 3/1-10/31; 14-day limit. 82 elec sites (62 elec/wtr), $16 base, $20 for elec/wtr ($8 &

$10 with federal senior pass). 50-ft RV limit; 2 pull-through sites. Tbls, flush & pit toilets, cfga, drkg wtr, showers, dump, playground, pay phone, beach, amphitheater, 2 picnic shelters ($50). Boating(l), fishing, swimming, interpretive trails, waterskiing, hiking. Day use fees for boat ramp, dump station, beach, picnicking. (479) 938-7335. NRRS (3/1-10/31)). **GPS: 35.306445, -93.428614**

SPADRA PARK

From I-40 exit 58 just S of Clarksville, about 1 mi S on SR 103 (through Jamestown), then 0.5 mi W & 0.5 mi S on Jamestown Rd; on bluff overlooking Arkansas River. All year; 14-day limit. 29 sites. 5 tent sites, $12 ($6 with federal senior pass); 24 elec RV/tent sites, $16 base, $18 for wtr/elec ($8 & $9 with senior pass. Tbls, flush & pit toilets, cfga, drkg wtr, showers, dump, playground, beach, picnic shelter ($50). Boating(l), fishing, swimming, hiking, waterskiing. (479) 754-6438. No camping reservations. Day use fee charged non-campers for boat ramp, dump station, picnicking, beach. **GPS: 35.424531, -93.477618**

❺
DEGRAY LAKE
GPS: 34.22, -93.11

This 13,500-acre lake with 207 miles of shoreline is 8 miles NW of Arkadelphia and W of I-30 exit 78 off SR 7. It is on the Caddo River and extends 27 miles upstream with 208 miles of shoreline. Visitor center, interpretive programs. DeGray has 20 recreation areas, 724 campsites, 18 boat ramps and 12 swimming beaches. $3 day use fees (or $30 annually) are charged ($1 per person or $4 vehicle at beaches). To reserve picnic shelters, call lake office. Day use facilities include: Highway 7 -- shelter, playground, swimming area; Lower Lake -- shelter, playground; Lakeview -- shelter; Caddo Drive -- shelter, beach boat ramp; Arlie Moore -- shelter, beach, 2 boat ramps, interpretive trail; Shouse Ford -- beach, boat ramp; Amity Landing -- boat ramp; Iron Mountain -- boat ramp; Point Cedar -- boat ramp; Ozan Point -- boat ramp; Spillway -- boat ramp. Resource Manager, DeGray Lake, 729 Channel Avenue, Arkadelphia, AR 71923. (870) 246-5501.

ALPINE RIDGE CAMPGROUND

From Alpine at jct with SR 8, 10 mi E on CR 22 (Fendley Rd) through Fendley on SR 346; 1 mi NE on Cr 418 to campground at W shore of lake (in foothills of Ouachita Mountains). All year; 14-day limit. 49 elec sites. High demand locations $18 during 3/1-10/31; all other sites $12 ($9 & $6 with federal senior pass). All sites $12 during 11/1-2/28 ($6 with senior pass). 40-ft RV limit. Tbls, flush toilets, cfga, drkg wtr, showers, dump, playground, beach. Swimming, boating(l), fishing. NRRS during 5/1-LD. **GPS: 34.258890, -93.229433**

ARLIE MOORE CAMPGROUND

2 mi S of Bismarck on SR 7; left (W) for 2 mi on Arlie Moore Rd to E shore of lake. All year; 14-day limit. 19 elec tent sites, $12 ($6 with federal senior pass). 38 elec RV/tent sites & 30 elec RV sites, $18 at high-demand locations, $12 at other locations during 3/1-10/31 ($9 & $6 with senior pass). All sites $12 during 11/1-2/28 ($9 with senior pass). 30-ft RV limit. Tbls, flush toilets, cfga, drkg wtr, dump, playground, amphitheater, beach, picnic shelter. Boating(l), swimming, hiking, fishing. NRRS during 5/1-9/30. **GPS: 34.274231, -93.196797**

CADDO DRIVE CAMPGROUND

From Bismarck, 3.5 mi SE on SR 7; 1.5 mi W on Caddo Dr; 1 mi S on Edgewood Dr (CR 12); 1 mi W on Lakefront Dr, following signs; at E shore of lake. 3/1-10/31; 14-day limit. 27 elec tent sites, $12 ($6 with federal senior pass). 30 RV/tent sites & 15 RV sites (all with elec), $12. 40-ft RV limit; 2 pull-through sites. Tbls, flush toilets, showers, cfga, drkg wtr, playground, beach, picnic shelter. Boating(l), fishing, swimming, horseback riding, hiking trails. NRRS during 5/1-LD. **GPS: 34.260537, -93.187628**

EDGEWOOD CAMPGROUND

From Bismarck, 4.8 mi SE on SR 7; 3 mi W on Edgewood Rd, then right for 0.5 mi on unpaved access rd. 3/1-10/31; 14-day limit. 4 elec tent sites, $12 ($6 with federal senior pass). 10 elec RV sites & 35 elec RV/tent sites, $18 at high-demand locations, $12 at all others ($9 & $6 with senior pass). Double sites $24. 30-ft RV limit; 9 pull-through sites. Tbls, flush toilets, cfga, drkg wtr, dump, showers, beach, playground. Boating, fishing, swimming, horseback riding. Boat rentals nearby. NRRS during 5/1-LD. **GPS: 34.254421, -93.184870**

IRON MOUNTAIN CAMPGROUND

From I-30 exit 78 about 3 mi N of Arkadelphia, 2.5 mi N on SR 7; left onto Skyline Dr for 2.5 mi, then right on access rd to SW shore of lake. 3/1-11/30; 14-day limit. 30 RV/tent sites with elec & 39 RV sites with elec, $12 ($6 with federal senior pass). 30-ft RV limit. Tbls, flush toilets, cfga, drkg wtr, showers, dump, playground. Boating(l), fishing, hiking trails. NRRS during 5/1-LD. **GPS: 34.22694, -93.127780**

LENOX MARCUS AREA

3 mi W of Bismarck on SR 84; 1 mi SW on CR 4; 1 mi S on Peach Dr; 0.5 mi E on Ozark Loop; 1.5 mi S on CR 295 (Walnut Dr) to N shore of lake. Free. All year; 14-day limit. Open camping, 200 remote acres. Pit toilets, cfga, drkg wtr, tbls. 30 picnic sites. **GPS: 34.26700, -93.21710**

OZAN POINT CAMPGROUND

From SR 8 at Alpine, 3 mi E (through town of Fendley on CR 22; 2 mi SE on gravel CR 241; at E shore of lake. 3/1-10/31; 14-day limit. $6 at 50 small primitive tent sites. Flush toilets, tbls, cfga, drkg wtr. Boating(l), fishing. **GPS: 34.241723, -93.208716**

POINT CEDAR CAMPGROUND

From SR 84 at Point Cedar, 3 mi S on Shouse Ford Rd (CR 5); right on Chinook Trail, then veer right onto Chinook East for 0.25 mi to

campground; at N shore of Cox Creek arm of lake. 3/10-11/30; 14-day limit. 62 sites, $6. 40-ft RV limit. Flush toilets, tbls, cfga, drkg wtr. Boating(l), fishing. 50 acres. **GPS: 34.280220, -93.294965**

SHOUSE FORD CAMPGROUND

From SR 84 at Point Cedar, 3 mi S on Shouse Ford Rd; 1 mi E on Chinook Trail (CR 980); NE on Chinook Ct to campground at confluence of Point Cedar Creek & Cox Creek arms of lake. All year; 14-day limit. 81 elec sites, $18 for high-demand locations, $12 all other sites during 3/1-10/31; all sites $12 during 11/1-2/28 ($9 & $6 with federal senior pass). 40-ft RV limit. Tbls, flush toilets, showers, cfga, drkg wtr, dump, playground, beach, amphitheater. Boating(l), fishing, swimming, hiking trails, horseback riding. NRRS 5/1-LD. **GPS: 34.289098, -93.273674**

⑥
DEQUEEN LAKE
GPS: 34.0983, -94.3817

This 1,680-acre lake is 4 miles NW of DeQueen off US 71 and 96 miles SW of Hot Springs (N of Texarkana) near the Oklahoma state line. It is on the Rolling Fork River; it has 32 miles of shoreline. Day use areas: Glen Canyon -- boat ramp, fishing pier, picnicking; Oak Grove Landing -- boat ramp, fishing pier, picnicking, beach, hiking trail; Overlook -- hiking trail; Rolling Fork -- boat ramp, fish cleaning station, picnicking, beach; Story Creek - boat ramp, picnicking, playground, beach. Non-campers pay day use fees for use of dump stations, swimming areas. Fee for reserving picnic shelters (870-386-7511). Resource Manager, DeQueen Lake, 706 DeQueen Lake Road, DeQueen, AR 71832. (870) 584-4161.

BELLAH MINE CAMPGROUND

From Gillham, 1.5 mi S on US 71; 5.3 mi W on Bellah Mine Road (CR 35/2430), veering right at split, then left on park rd before bridge over Mill Creek. (signs); at NW shore. All year; 14-day limit. 24 elec/wtr sites. During 3/1-10/31, $13 base, $15 at premium locations ($6.50 & $7.50 with federal senior pass); $10 rest of year ($5 with federal senior pass). RV limit in excess of 65 ft. Tbls, flush toilets, cfga, drkg wtr, showers, dump, picnic shelter ($25). Boating(l), fishing, canoeing, waterskiing. (870) 386-7511. NRRS (515-9/15). **GPS: 34.128823, -94.388469**

OAK GROVE CAMPGROUND

From DeQueen, 3 mi N on US 71; 5.5 mi W on DeQueen Lake Rd (CR 100), then 0.3 mi N on CR 227, following signs right into campground just W of dam. All year; 14-day limit. 36 elec/wtr sites. During 3/1-10/31, $13 base, $15 at premium locations ($6.50 & $7.50 with federal senior pass); $10 rest of year ($5 with senior pass). RV limit in excess of 65 ft; 7 pull-through sites. Tbls, flush toilets, cfga, showers, drkg wtr, dump, playground, beach. Boating(l), fishing, swimming, amphitheater, picnic shelter with wtr/elec ($25). (870) 642-6111. NRRS (3/15-9/15). **GPS: 34.097253, -94.394510**

PINE RIDGE CAMPGROUND

From DeQueen, 3 mi N on US 71; 5.5 mi W on DeQueen Lake Rd (CR 100), then 2 mi N on CR 227 & CR 226; right (E) on Ridge Park Rd into campground. All year; 14-day limit. 28 non-elec sites, $9-$10 ($4.50-$5 with federal senior pass). During 3/1-10/31, 17 elec/wtr sites $13 base, $15 at premium locations ($6.50 & $7.50 with senior pass); $10 rest of year ($5 with senior pass). RV limit in excess of 65 ft; 4 pull-through sites. Tbls, flush toilets, cfga, showers, drkg wtr, dump, fish cleaning station, store, picnic shelter ($25). Boating(l)(, fishing, waterskiing. 870-584-4161. NRRS during 5/15-9/15. **GPS: 34.098906, -94.413028**

⑦
DIERKS LAKE
GPS: 34.145. -94.10

This 1,360-acre lake is 72 miles SW of Hot Springs and N of Texarkana, E of DeQueen and 5 miles NW of Dierks in southwestern Arkansas

on the Saline River. The Corps owns about 33 miles of lake shoreline. 4 picnic shelters equipped with lighting, grills and electricity can be reserved from the lake office. Day use fees of $4 ($30 annual pass) are charged at Jefferson Ridge, Blue Ridge and Horseshoe Bend swimming areas. Visitor center. Resource Manager, Dierks Lake, 246 Jefferson Ridge Rd, Dierks, AR 71833. (870) 286-2346.

BLUE RIDGE CAMPGROUND

From Dierks, 3 mi NE on US 70; 4 mi NW on SR 4; 2.6 mi W on paved Blue Ridge Rd. All year; 14-day limit. 22 elec/wtr sites, $13 during 3/1-10/31 & $8 rest of year ($6.50 & $4 with federal senior pass). Tbls, flush toilets, cfga, drkg wtr, dump, beach, fish cleaning station. Boating(l), swimming, fishing, waterskiing. **GPS: 34.193053, -94.095910**

HORSESHOE BEND CAMP

From Dierks, 2 mi W on US 70; 4 mi NW on Lake Rd, then right on access rd, following signs; below dam at Saline River. All year; 14-day limit. 11 elec/wtr sites, $11 ($5.50 with federal senior pass). Tbls, flush toilets, cfga, drkg wtr, dump, picnic shelter ($25), change shelter at beach. Bank fishing, swimming, canoeing. (870) 286-3214). **GPS: 34.141824, -94.093502**

JEFFERSON RIDGE CAMP

2 mi W of Dierks on US 70; 1 mi N on Lake Rd; 4 mi W on CR 80 (Thirty Thousand Rd); right (N) for 0.5 mi on Greens Chappen Rd, then left (E) 2 mi on Jefferson Ridge Rd to campground; at W shore of lake. All year; 14-day limit. 85 elec/wtr sites, $13 base, $15 at premium locations during 3/1-10/31 ($6.50 & $7.50 with federal senior pass); $7.50 rest of year ($3.75 with senior pass). RV limit in excess of 65 ft; 41 pull-through sites. Tbls, flush toilets, showers, cfga, drkg wtr, dump, amphitheater, fish cleaning station, 2 playgrounds, beach, picnic shelter ($25). Boating(l), fishing, swimming, hiking, canoeing. Marina. 870-286-3214. NRRS during 5/15-9/15. **GPS: 34.152989, -94.110394**

⑧ GILLHAM LAKE
GPS: 34.15. -94.10

This 1,370-acre lake is 6 mi SW of Gillham, 15 mi N of DeQueen, E of US Route 71 and SW of Little Rock near the Oklahoma state line. It is on the Cossatot River, which is a popular canoe stream for about 16 mil S of the dam. Non-campers pay day use fees for use of dump stations, 5 boat ramps and one swimming area. The 2-mile Cook Creek Walking Trail begins at the entry road to Big Cook Creek Park. The lake has designated picnicking areas reservable shelters at three parks. The swimming area is at Big Coon Creek. The Cossatot River can be canoed 16 miles from below the dam to US 71. Resource Manager, Gillham Lake, 706 DeQueen Lake Rd, DeQueen, AR 71852. (870) 584-4161.

BIG COON CREEK CAMP

From jct with US 71 just N of Gillham, 1 mi E on CR 41; left (NE) on CR 236 (becoming Polk Rd 246) for 4 mi; left (N) on Polk Rd 474 about 1 mi to campground N of dam. All year; 14-day limit. 31 elec/wtr sites. During 3/1-10/31, $13 base, $15 at premium locations ($6.50 & $7.50 with federal senior pass); $10 rest of year ($5 with senior pass). RV limit in excess of 65 ft; 2 pull-through sites. Tbls, flush toilets, cfga, showers, drkg wtr, dump, playground, fish cleaning station, amphitheater, beach. Swimming, fishing, boating(l), canoeing, hiking, waterskiing, nature trails. (870) 385-7126. NRRS (5/15-9/15). **GPS: 34.221677, -94.24293**

COSSATOT REEFS CAMP

From jct with US 71 just N of Gillham, 1 mi E on CR 41; left (NE) on CR 236 (becoming Polk Rd 246) for 4 mi; follow Gillham Lake Rd 0.1 mi E, then 0.5 mi S & E on Reefs Park Rd to campground; at W shore of Cossatot River. All year; 14-day limit. 28 elec/wtr sites During 3/1-10/31, $13 base, $15 at premium locations ($6.50 & $7.50 with federal senior pass); $10 rest of year ($5 with senior pass). 2

walk-to tent sites, $9 base, $13 elec ($4.50 & $6.50 with senior pass). RV limit in excess of 65 ft. Tbls, flush toilets, cfga, showers, drkg wtr, dump, playground, beach, amphitheater, fish cleaning station, picnic shelter ($25). Boating(l), fishing, canoeing, swimming, hiking trail, waterskiing, basketball, nature trails. (870) 584-4161. NRRS (5/15-9/15). **GPS: 34.205698, -94.227891**

LITTLE COON CREEK CAMP

From Gillham, about 6 mi N on US 71 to town of Grannis; 5 mi E on Polk CR 3 (Frachiseur Rd), following signs to park (1 mi NW of Big Coon Creek Park) near W shore of lake. All year; 14-day limit. 10 elec/wtr sites. During 3/1-10/31, $13 ($6.50 with federal senior pass); $10 rest of year ($5 with senior pass). Group picnic shelter ($25). No reservations. **GPS: 34.231561, -94.249126**

⑨ GREERS FERRY LAKE
GPS: 35.525. -92.01

This 31,500-acre lake is N of Heber Springs on SR 25, 65 mi N of Little Rock. It is one of five multi-purpose projects in the White River Basin. Around the lake are 22 boat ramps and 9 private marinas ($3 day use fee charged at some ramps). Hiking trails include Buckeye Nature Trail, Collins Creek Trail, Josh Park Memorial Trail, Mossy Bluff National Nature Trail and Sugar Loaf National Nature Trail. Reservations for picnic shelters range from $30 to $175. Day use fees are charged non-campers at swimming areas. Campground checkout time 4 p.m. Visitor center with interpretive programs. Fish hatchery. Project Office, Greers Ferry Lake, P. O. Box 1088, Heber Springs, AR 72543-9022. (501) 362-2416.

CHEROKEE CAMPGROUND

From Drasco, 7.5 mi W on SR 92 (Greers Ferry Rd); 4 mi S on Brownsville Rd, through town of Brownsville; veer left onto Cherokee Park Rd to campground on N side of lower lake just

W of Silver Ridge Peninsula. 5/15-9/15; 14-day limit. 17 sites without hookups, $12 ($6 with federal senior pass); 16 elec sites $14 base, $16 at prime locations ($7 & $8 with senior pass). Tbls, pit toilets, cfga, drkg wtr, dump. Boating(l), fishing. No reservations. Closed to camping by budget cuts in 2014, but re-opened 2015. **GPS: 35.554535, -92.076110**

CHOCTAW CAMPGROUND

From Clinton, 5 mi S to Choctaw on US 65; 3.8 mi E on SR 330, following signs; on W end of upper lake. All year; 14-day limit. 146 sites. For 68 non-elec sites, $14 ($7 with federal senior pass). 78 elec sites, $17 base, $19 prime locations, $20 for wtr hookup or 50-amp elec ($8.50, $9.50 & $10 with senior pass). RV limit in excess of 65 ft. Tbls, flush toilets, cfga, drkg wtr, showers, dump, beach, playground, picnic shelter. Fishing, boating(ldr), swimming. Marina. NRRS (5/15-9/5). **GPS: 35.535212, -92.381372**

COVE CREEK CAMPGROUND

6.5 mi NE of Quitman on AR 25; 3.5 mi N on AR 16; 1.2 mi NE on paved Cove Creek Rd, following signs; on S end of lower lake. 5/15-9/15; 14-day limit. 65 sites. At 34 non-elec sites, $14 ($7 with federal senior pass). At 31 elec sites, $17 base, $19 prime locations ($8.50 & $9.50 with federal senior pass). RV limit in excess of 65 ft. Tbls, flush toilets, cfga, drkg wtr, showers, dump, beach, picnic shelter. No reservations. **GPS: 35.461234, -92.15328**

DAM SITE CAMPGROUND

From Heber Springs, 3.4 mi N on SR 25, following signs; on W side of dam. All year; 14-day limit. Non-elec sites, $14 ($7 with federal senior pass). Elec sites, $17 base; $19 at prime locations; $20 elec/wtr, $22 at 50-amp ($8.50, $9.50, $10 & $11 with senior pass). RV limit in excess of 65 ft. Tbls, flush & pit toilets, cfga, drkg wtr, dump, beach, playground, pay phone, picnic shelters (fees), marine dump station. Hiking, boating(ldr), swimming. Golf carts &

ATV or ORV prohibited. William Carl Garner Visitor Center (510-362-9067), marina. NRRS (5/15-9/6). **GPS: 35.523416, -91.999093**

DEVILS FORK CAMPGROUND

From jct of SR 92, half mi N on SR 16 at Greers Ferry; qtr mi N on SR 16, then NE on access rd following signs. All year; 14-day limit. 55 elec sites, $17 base, $22 for wtr or 50-amp ($8.50 & $11 with federal senior pass). RV limit in excess of 65 ft. Tbls, pit & flush toilets, cfga, showers, drkg wtr, beach, playground, pay phone, picnic shelter, change house, marine dump. Boating(l), fishing, swimming, hiking. Nearby Old Hwy 25 Campground's area B has 16 non-elec sites for group camping ($150 by reservation). NRRS (5/15-9/10). **GPS: 35.589918, -92.179509**

HEBER SPRINGS CAMPGROUND

2 mi W of Heber Springs on SR 110, 0.5 mi N on Park Rd, following signs; at SE shore of lake. 5/15-9/15; 14-day limit. 110 total sites. 12 non-elec sites $14 ($7 with federal senior pass); 98 total elec sites $17 base, $20 wtr/elec & 50-amp sites ($8.50 & $10 with senior pass). RV limit in excess of 65 ft. Tbls, flush & pit toilets, showers, cfga, drkg wtr, dump, playground, beach, picnic shelters ($30-$50), marina, store, pay phone. Boating(ld), swimming, fishing. 501-250-0485. NRRS (5/15-9/10). **GPS: 35.503845, -92.065950**

HILL CREEK CAMPGROUND

12 mi SW of Drasco (past Brownsville) on SR 92; 3 mi NW on SR 225 (signs); 2 mi S on access rd; at shore of upper lake (self-registration at GPS 35.609816, -92.147065). 5/15-9/15; 14-day limit. 16 non-elec sites, $14 ($7 with federal senior pass); 25 elec sites, $17 ($8.50 with federal senior pass). RV limit in excess of 65 ft. Tbls, flush & pit toilets, showers, cfga, drkg wtr, dump, beach, picnic shelters ($30-$50). Boating(ld), fishing, swimming. Marina. 38 acres. Info 870-948-2419. NRRS (5/15-9/10). **GPS: 35.612651, -92.148739**

JOHN F. KENNEDY CAMP

From Heber Springs, 4.4 mi N on SR 25; 1 mi E across dam; S side (following signs) on Hatchery Homes Rd, below dam on Little Red River (trout stream). All year; 14-day limit. 74 elec sites, $17 base, $19 at prime locations, $22 at 13 wtr/elec sites or 50-amp elec sites ($8.50, $9.50 & $11 with federal senior pass). RV limit in excess of 65 ft. Tbls, flush toilets, cfga, drkg wtr, showers, playground, pay phone, dump, fishing pier, picnic shelters ($40-$60). Boating (l), fishing. NRRS during 4/15-9/5. **GPS: 35.512797, -91.996320**

MILL CREEK RECREATION AREA

7 mi W of Greers Ferry on SR 92 (about 2 mi SW of Higden); 3 mi N on Mill Creek Rd, following signs; at S shore of upper lake. 5/15-9/15; 14-day limit. 39 sites without hookups, $16 ($6 with federal senior pass). Tbls, pit toilets, cfga, no drkg wtr. Boating(l), swimming, fishing. Closed to camping in 2014 by budget cuts, re-opened in 2015. **GPS: 35.581445, -92.218713**

NARROWS CAMPGROUND

From Greers Ferry, 2.5 mi SW on SR 16; across bridge, on N side (signs); near center of lake. 5/15-9/15; 14-day limit. 60 elec sites, $17 base, $19 at prime locations ($8.50 & $9.50 with federal senior pass). RV limit in excess of 65 ft. Tbls, flush & pit toilets, cfga, showers, drkg wtr, dump, pay phone, picnic shelters ($30-$50). Boating(l), fishing. Overflow area, marina. NRRS (5/15-9/10). **GPS: 35.562613, -92.198135**

OLD HIGHWAY 25 RECREATION AREA

From Heber Springs, 6.3 mi N on SR 25; 2.8 mi W on old SR 25 , following signs; on lakeshore 1 mi from dam. 5/15-9/15; 14-day limit. 36 non-elec sites, $14 ($7 with federal senior pass). 89 elec sites, $17 base, $19 at prime locations, $20 for wtr/elec or 50-amp elec ($8.50, $9.50 & $10 with senior pass). RV limit in excess of 65 ft. Tbls, flush & pit toilets, cfga, drkg wtr, showers, dump, playground, beach, picnic shelters ($30-$50). Fishing, boating(l), swimming. Group camping area (no elec) with 16 sites, $150. NRRS (5/15-9/10). **GPS: 35.538251, -92.017332**

SHILOH PARK

From Greers Ferry at jct with SR 92, 3.5 mi SE on SR 110 following signs; at mid-lake shore. 5/15-9/15; 14-day limit. Non-elec sites, $14 ($7 with federal senior pass). 60 elec sites, $17 base, $19 at prime locations ($8.50 & $9.50 with senior pass). RV limit in excess of 65 ft. Tbls, flush & pit toilets, cfga, drkg wtr, showers, dump, playground, beach, pay phone, picnic shelters ($30-$50). Boating(l), fishing, swimming. Marina. Group camping area (no elec) with 17 sites, $150. NRRS (5/15-9/10). **GPS: 35. 535457, -92.145746**

SUGAR LOAF CAMPGROUND

2.2 mi SW of Greers Ferry on SR 16, then 2 mi W on SR 92, following signs; 2.7 mi W on SR 337; at upper lake. 5/15-9/15; 14-day limit. Non-elec sites, $14 ($7 with federal senior pass). 56 elec sites, $17 base, $19 at prime locations ($8.50 & $9.50 with senior pass. RV limit in excess of 65 ft. Tbls, flush & pit toilets, shower, drkg wtr, cfga, pay phone, playground, beach, Picnic shelter, marina. NRRS (5/15-9/5). **GPS: 35.54583, -92.27222**

⑩
LAKE GREESON
GPS: 34.1483, -93.715

This 7,260-acre lake is 12 miles long. It is 6 miles N of Murfreesboro on SR 19, 69 miles NE of Texarkana on the Little Missouri River. It is surrounded by 15,842 acres of federally managed public lands. Visitors to 10 p.m. Visitor center. 31-mi cycle trail. Off-road vehicles permitted. Day use fees of $3 are charged non-campers at boat ramps, $3 per vehicle at beaches ($30 annually). The project has 30 miles of walking, nature & biking trails, including 20-mile Bear Creek Cycling Trail. For reservations at shelters, call 870-285-2151. Day use areas include Parker Creek -- beach; Dam Area -- beach, boat ramp, shelter, picnicking; Cowhide Cove -- beach; Kirby Landing -- beach; Self Creek -- beach, boat ramp, shelter, playground; Arrowhead Point -- beach; Riverside -- playground, shelter. Campsites that are free or open with lower fees in winter may have reduced amenities. Four private marinas are spotted around the lake. Resource Manager,0 Lake Greeson Field Office, 155 Dynamite Hill Road, Murfreesboro, AR 71958. (870) 285-2151.

ARROWHEAD POINT CAMP

9 mi W of Kirby on US 70; qtr mi S on access rd. All year; 14-day limit. 23 non-elec sites, $6 during 3/1-10/31 ($3 with federal senior pass); free off-season but reduced amenities. RV limit 35 ft. Flush & pit toilets, tbls, cfga, drkg wtr, beach. Boating(l), fishing, swimming, waterskiing. No reservations.
GPS: 34.24406, -93.801223

BEAR CREEK CAMPGROUND

1.5 mi SW of Kirby on SR 27; 1.4 mi W on CR 18 (Bear Creek Rd). All year; 14-day limit. 19 non-elec sites, $5 during 3/1-10/31 ($2.50 with federal senior pass); free off-season but reduced amenities. 35-ft RV limit. Pit toilets, tbls, cfga, drkg wtr. Boating(l), fishing, hiking, waterskiing. **GPS: 34.236341, -93.667603**

COWHIDE COVE CAMPGROUND

From Kirby at jct with US 70, 5.9 mi S on SR 27; 2.7 mi W on access rd; 2 camping sections -- one at end of Old Cowhide Cove Rd, second at end of New Cowhide Cove Rd. All year; 14-day limit. 2 tent sites, $10 during 3/1-10/31 ($5 with federal senior pass); $6 rest of year ($3 with senior pass). 48 elec sites (20/30-amp, no wtr hookups), $13 base, $15 at premium locations during 3/1-10/31 ($6.50 & $7.50 with senior pass); $14 off-season ($7 with senior

pass). RV limit 40 ft; 2 pull-through sites. Tbls, flush toilets, cfga, drkg wtr, showers, dump, beach, playground. Boating(l), fishing, swimming, waterskiing, hiking, interpretive trails. ORVs prohibited. NRRS (5/1-LD). GPS Old Cowhide Cove: **34.174040, -93.668758;** New Cowhide Cove: **34.173700, -93.680153**

DAM AREA CAMPGROUND

From Murfreesboro, 6 mi N on SR 19; right on Dynamite Hill Rd to E side of dam. All year; 14-day limit. 24 elec sites (20/30-amp, no wtr hookups), $18 during 3/1-10/31 ($9 with federal senior pass); $14 rest of year ($7 with senior pass). RV limit 60 ft. Tbls, flush toilets, showers, cfga, drkg wtr, playground, dump, picnic shelter. Boating(l), hiking, waterskiing.
GPS: 34.149793, -93.713384

KIRBY LANDING CAMPGROUND

From Kirby at jct with SR 27, 2.2 mi SW on US 70, then 1.2 mi S on access rd. All year; 14-day limit. 105 elec sites. $16 for 20/30-amp, $18 for 50-amp during 3/1-11/1 ($8 & $9 with federal senior pass); $14 off-season but reduced amenities ($7 off-season with senior pass). RV limit 45 ft; 23 pull-through sites. Tbls, flush toilets, showers, cfga, drkg wtr, dump, playground, beach. Interpretive trails, boating(l), fishing, swimming, ORV trails. Hiking, biking. NRRS (5/1-LD).
GPS: 34.23168, -93.69361

LAUREL CREEK CAMPGROUND

4 mi S of Kirby on SR 27; right (SW) on CR 660; then 2 mi W on gravel CR 16; at SE shore of lake. All year; 14-day limit. 24 sites, $5 during 3/1-10/31 ($2.50 with federal senior pass); free rest of year but reduced amenities. 20-ft RV limit. Pit toilets, tbls, cfga, no drkg wtr. Boating(l), fishing, hiking, waterskiing.
GPS: 34.185447, -93.708646

PARKER CREEK CAMPGROUND

6 mi N of Murfreesboro on SR 19; 3 mi NW of dam on paved Beacon Hill Rd, then E

following signs on access rd; at cove, W end of lake. All year; 14-day limit. 3 tent sites & 8 primitive RV/tent sites, $10 ($5 with federal senior pass); $6 during 11/1-2/28. 49 elec sites (20/30-amp), $13 base, $16 at premium locations during 3/1-10/31 ($6.50 & $8 with senior pass); $11 & $14 off-season ($6.50 & $7 with senior pass). No wtr mid-Sept to mid-Mar. 35-ft RV limit. Tbls, flush toilets, cfga, showers, dump, drkg wtr, beach, playground. Interpretive trail, hiking, fishing, boating(l), swimming, ORVs prohibited. NRRS (5/1-LD). **GPS: 34.159244, -93.733978**

PIKEVILLE CAMPGROUND

6 mi N of Murfreesboro on SR 19; 3 mi NW of dam on paved Beacon Hill Rd; 1 mi N on CR 630; 2 mi E on CR 247, then 2 mi E on gravel rd. All year; 14-day limit. 12 sites (1 for tents), $5 during 3/1-10/31 ($2.50 with federal senior pass); free rest of year but reduced amenities. 30-ft RV limit. Pit toilets, cfga, tbls, no drkg wtr. Fishing, boating. **GPS: 34.1669, -93.7365**

ROCK CREEK CAMPGROUND

From just E of Newhope at jct with SR 70, 0.5 mi S on CR 615, becoming Pine Mountain Rd (25000 Rd) eastward about 2 mi, veering right at Pine Mountain to continue SE on 25000 Rd about 3 mi; 1 mi S on Rock Creek Rd, then E on CR 628 to camping area at Rock Creek arm of lake. All year; 14-day limit. 14 free primitive sites. Pit toilets, cfga, no drkg wtr. Fishing. **GPS: 34.207836, -93.759930**

SELF CREEK/JIM WYLIE CAMP

7 mi W of Kirby on US 70 (1 mi W of Daisy), across bridge, then S on access rd. All year; 14-day limit. 76 sites. Tent sites & non-elec RV/tent sites, $10 during 3/1-10/31 ($5 with federal senior pass); $6 rest of year ($3 with senior pass). 10/30-amp elec sites, $13 base, $16 at premium locations during 3/1-10/31 ($7 & $8 with senior pass); $11 & $14 off-season ($5.50 & $7 with federal senior pass). 45-ft RV limit; 23 pull-through. Tbls, flush toilets, cfga, dump,

showers, playground, drkg wtr, picnic shelters. Boating(l), fishing, waterskiing, hiking. No reservations. **GPS: 34.238038, -93.764121**

STAR OF THE WEST CAMP

2.7 mi E of Newhope on US 70, then SE on access site; along Little Missouri River arm of lake. All year; 14-day limit. 21 sites (8 for tents), $5 during 3/1-10/31 ($2.50 with federal senior pass); free rest of year but reduced amenities. Pit toilets tbls, cfga, drkg wtr. RV limit 50 ft; some pull-through sites. Boating(l), fishing. **GPS: 34.239987, -93.832635**

⓫
LAKE OUACHITA
GPS: 34.56939, -93.19464

This 40,060-acre lake is 13 miles NW of Hot Springs on US 270 and SR 277. It is 67 miles SW of Little Rock. It features 690 mi of shoreline, more than 200 islands -- many available for primitive camping. All reservable campsites are available on a first-come basis between 10/1 and 4/30. The Corps manages 17 campgrounds, with sites ranging from primitive to paved pull-throughs and modern amenities. 20 boat ramps & 10 marinas. Visitors to 10 p.m. ORV prohibited. Visitor center. Day use fees are $3 daily ($30 annually); $4 at beaches, $3 boat ramps; picnicking is free. In addition to typical day use areas, the Corps provides reservable shelters for $50 (call 501-767-2101) at several parks, playgrounds, fish cleaning stations, amphitheaters and even a church arbor. Group camping at Little Fir, Spillway and Denby Point. Reservable campsites are available 5/1-9/30; all sites open without reservations rest of year. For 2015, no extensions of 14-day limits permitted anywhere on the lake. Resource Manager, Lake Ouachita Field Office, 1424 Blakely Dam Road, Royal, AR 71968-9493. (501) 767-2108/2101.

AVANT CAMPGROUND

From Blue Springs at jct with SR 7, 16 mi W

on SR 298; about 3 mi S to Avant on Buckville Rd, then W on Camp Story Rd, continuing on Avant Campground access rd. All year; 14-day limit. Free primitive camping at undesignated sites; no facilities, no drkg wtr.
GPS: 34.636653, -93.383400

BIG FIR RECREATION AREA

From Mt. Ida at jct with US 270, 5.1 mi NE on SR 27; 6.5 mi E on SR 188, then 4.5 mi E on gravel Housey Point Rd; left into campground. On peninsula of lake SE of Little Fir Recreation Area; at Housley Point. All year; 14-day limit. Free by permit. 17 sites without hookups; few level. 2 pit toilets, tbls, cfga, no drkg wtr. 20-ft RV limit. Boating(l), fishing.
GPS: 34.362154, -93.218154

BRADY MOUNTAIN CAMP

13 mi W of Hot Springs on US 270W, 6.1 mi N through Bear on Brady Mountain Rd. 3/1-9/30; 14-day limit. 17 tent sites, $12 & $14 ($6 & $7 with federal senior pass). 57 elec sites, $14 base, $16-$18 at premium locations. 55-ft RV limit. Tbls, flush toilets, cfga, drkg wtr, showers, picnic shelter, fish cleaning station, playground, beach, dump. Interpretive trail, bridle trail, boating(lr). Marina. (501) 760-1146. NRRS (5/1-9/30). **GPS: 34.582121, -93.265166**

BUCKVILLE CAMPGROUND

10 mi NE of Hot Springs on SR 7; W for 18 mi on SR 298; 3.5 mi S through Avant & 3.6 mi on gravel Buckville Rd, following signs; at N end of lake. All year; 14-day limit. 5 free primitive sites. 20-ft RV limit. Pit toilets, tbls, cfga, no drkg wtr. Boating(l), fishing.
GPS: 34.611404, -93.347791

CEDAR FOURCHE CAMP

10 mi NE of Hot Springs; 11 mi W on AR 298 to Lena; 1.1 mi S on gravel Rock Springs Rd; at split with Lena Landing access rd, continue W on Rock Springs Rd; right, then W on Cedar Fourche Rd. All year; 14-day limit. Free primitive camping. No facilities except

showers, toilets. Fishing, boating.
GPS: 34.664520, -93.285044

CRYSTAL SPRINGS CAMP

16.8 mi W of Hot Springs on US 270; 1.5 mi N on Crystal Springs Rd. All year; 14-day limit. 9 tent sites, $10 base, $12 at premium locations during 5/1-9/9 ($5 & $6 with federal senior pass); $8 rest of year but reduced services ($4 with senior pass). 63 elec sites, $18 base, $20 at premium locations during 5/1-9/30 ($9 & $10 with senior pass); some lower fees rest of year but reduced services. 55-ft RV limit; 6 pull-through sites. Tbls, flush toilets, cfga, drkg wtr, showers, dump, picnic shelter, fish cleaning station, change house, playground, beach. Hiking, boating(l), swimming. Marina. Group camping with elec, $80. Overflow camping offered on major holidays. (501) 991-3390. NRRS (5/1-9/30). **GPS: 34.541203, -93.350090**

DENBY POINT CAMPGROUND

8 mi E of Mount Ida on US 270; 0.8 mi N on Denby Rd. All year; 14-day limit. 9 tent sites, $10 base, $12 at premium locations ($5 & $6 with federal senior pass). 58 elec sites, $16 base, $20 at premium locations ($8 & $10 with federal senior pass). Some 50-amp elec. 55-ft RV limit. Tbls, flush toilets, showers, cfga, drkg wtr, dump, fish cleaning station, amphitheater, beach, playground. Boating(l), fishing, swimming, hiking, waterskiing, interpretive trail. Two group camping areas with elec, $55 & $65. Boat rentals nearby. (870) 867-4475. NRRS (5/1-9/8). **GPS: 34.548617, -93.492987**

IRONS FORK

13 mi NE of Mount Ida on SR 27, 8.3 mi E on SR 298; 1.3 mi S on partially paved access rd; at N side of lake. All year; 14-day limit. 45 free primitive sites. Pit toilets, concrete tbls, cfga, drkg wtr, lantern posts. Boating(l), fishing, waterskiing. **GPS: 34.686706, -93.372988**

JOPLIN RECREATION AREA MOUNTAIN HARBOR)

11 mi E of Mt. Ida on US 270; 2.4 mi N

on Mountain Harbor Rd, turning left at campground sign. All year; 14-day limit. Primitive tent sites, $10-$12 ($5 & $6 with federal senior pass); 21 elec tent sites, $10-$16; 36 elec RV/tent sites, $14 base, $16 at premium locations ($7 & $8 with senior pass). 30-ft RV limit, but recommended for small RVs such as fold-outs, truck & van campers without slide-outs (sites unpaved, not level). Tbls, flush toilets, showers, dump, cfga, drkg wtr, fish cleaning station. Bridle trail, boating(l), fishing, swimming. Boat rentals, marina nearby. 870-867-4472. NRRS (5/1-9/8). GPS: 34.574125, -93.441896

LENA LANDING CAMPGROUND

12.4 mi N of Mount Ida on SR 27; right (E) at Story on SR 298 for about 5 mi; 1.2 mi S on Rock Spring Rd; left on Lena Use Area Rd; cross wood bridge, then left into campground; at Fisher Creek arm of lake. All year; 14-day limit. 10 sites without hookups, $8 base, premium sites $14. 35-ft RV limit. Tbls, flush toilets, cfga, drkg wtr, dump, no showers. Boating(l), fishing, waterskiing. GPS: 34.669469, -93.232727

LITTLE FIR CAMPGROUND

From SR 27 just W of Rubie, 3 mi E & 2.2 mi N on SR 188; right at campground sign. All year; 14-day limit. 29 non-elec sites, $12 base, $14 at premium locations during 3/1-10/31 ($6 & $7 with federal senior pass); some sites may be free off-season, but no amenities. 55-ft RV limit. Tbls, flush toilets, cfga, drkg wtr, dump, fish cleaning station. Group camping, $30. Boating(l), fishing, waterskiing. GPS: 34.6627558, -93.472517

RABBIT TAIL CAMPGROUND

From Blue Springs at jct with SR 7, 16 mi W on SR 298; S through Avant on Bucksville Rd; SE on Rabbit Tail Rd to park. All year; 14-day limit. Free primitive camping at undesignated sites. No facilities, no drkg wtr. GPS: 34.637688, -93.333492

STEPHENS PARK

From Mountain Pine, 1 mi W on Blakely Dam Rd past school, below dam. All year; 14-day limit. 9 non-elec sites, $12 base, $14 at premium locations ($6 & $7 with federal senior pass). 35-ft RV limit. Flush showers in-season, concrete tbls, pedestal grills, cfga, lantern posts, fish cleaning station nearby, picnic shelter, playground. Fishing. Boat ramp at Avery Park. GPS: 34.5708, -93.1903

SPILLWAY PARK

Below dam. Group camping area with 6 sites, $30. Tbls, toilets, cfga, drkg wtr, fish cleaning station, shelter. Boating(l), fishing. Call project office for more information. GPS: 34.5667, -93.2186

TOMPKINS BEND CAMP

10 mi E of Mount Ida on US 270; 2.4 mi N on Shangri-La Rd. All year; 14-day limit. 14 tent sites, $10 base, $12 at premium locations ($5 & $6 with federal senior pass). 63 elec sites, $14 base, $18-20 at prime locations (some 50-amp elec); $7-$10 with senior pass. Tbls, flush toilets, cfga, dump, drkg wtr, showers, amphitheater, fish cleaning station. Boating(l), fishing, hiking trails, waterskiing. Marina. Note: Campground to close in Oct 2015 for maintenance of its waste treatment plant. (870) 867-4476. NRRS (5/1-9/30). GPS: 34.568776, -93.469867

TWIN CREEK CAMPGROUND

11 mi E of Mount Ida on US 270; 1 mi N on gravel Twin Creek Rd, following signs. All year; 14-day limit. 15 non-elec sites, $10 base, $14 at premium locations during 3/1-10/31 ($5 & $7 with federal senior pass); some sites free rest of year, but no amenities. 20-ft RV limit. Concrete tbls, flush & pit toilets, cfga, drkg wtr, dump, beach, fishing pier, no showers. Overflow camping offered on major holidays. Boat rentals nearby. GPS: 34.550937, -93.510585

ARKANSAS

WASHITA CAMPGROUND

From Story at jct with SR 298, S on US 27 to town of Washita, then left on Mathews Hill Rd to campground; on Muddy Creek arm of lake at confluence with Ouachita River. All year; 14-day limit. Free primitive camping at undesignated sites. No facilities, no drkg wtr. **GPS: 34.649657, -93.531262**

⑫ MILLWOOD LAKE
GPS: 33.695, -93.9617

This 29,000-acre lake is 9 miles E of Ashdown on SR 32 and 28 miles N of Texarkana on the Little River. For lake level information, call (870) 898-4533/1-888-687-9830. Visitor center, interpretive programs. Again for 2015, none of the Millwood campgrounds is utilizing recreation.gov (the National Recreation Reservation Service) for reservations. Reservations at Beard's Bluff, Cottonshed and White Cliffs Parks can be made by phoning the campground offices. Millwood is quite popular as a bird-watching area. It has 12 recreation areas, 12 boat ramps, eight campgrounds, three picnic shelters and a designated swimming area. Boat ramp fees of $3 daily ($30 annually) are charged. Beard's Lake Trail is a self-guided nature trail and wildlife boardwalk. Project Manager, Millwood Tri Lakes Office, 1528 Highway 32 East, Ashdown, AR 71822. (870) 898-3343.

BEARD'S BLUFF CAMPGROUND

From Ashdown, 13 mi E on SR 32; half mi S on access rd between the road & lake, upstream from dam's E embankment (signs). All year; 14-day limit. Non-elec sites, $10 ($5 with federal senior pass). 25 paved elec/wtr sites (3 with sewer), $13 base, $15 at premium or full-hookup sites during 3/1-10/31 ($6.50 & $7.50 with senior pass); elec/wtr sites $11 rest of year ($5.50 with senior pass); premium or full-hookups $13 off-season ($6.50 with senior pass). Tbls, flush toilets, cfga, dump, drkg wtr, playground, beach, showers. Boating(l),

swimming, fishing. Group camping area available. Picnic shelter & reservable outdoor wedding chapel, $25 (call 870-388-9556 in-season). **GPS: 33.702937, -93.939545**

BEARD'S LAKE CAMPGROUND

9.5 mi E of Ashdown on SR 32; 1.5 mi W on access rd, below the dam. All year; 14-day limit. 3 shoreline tent sites & non-elec RV sites, $9 during 3/1-10/31 ($4.50 with federal senior pass); $8 rest of year ($4 with senior pass). 5 paved wtr/elec sites, $13 during 3/1-10/31 ($6.50 with senior pass); $9 rest of year ($4.50 with federal pass). Tbls, pit toilets, cfga, drkg wtr. Hiking trail with boardwalk, boating(ld). Area inhabited by alligators. Use dump, showers, playground, beach, flush toilets at Beard's Bluff (1-2 mi). **GPS: 33.692778, -93.967102**

COTTONSHED LANDING PARK

From Ashdown, 20 mi E on SR 32; N on SR 355 to Tollette; 8 mi W on CR 234 to Schaal, 2 mi S on Cottonshed Lane. All year; 14-day limit. 43 paved elec/wtr sites, $13 base, $15 at prime locations during 3/1-10/31 ($6.50 & $7.50 with federal senior pass). Sites $11 during Nov-Feb ($5.50 with senior pass). Tbls, toilets, cfga, drkg wtr, dump, fish cleaning station, fishing pier, playground, picnic shelter ($25). Boating(l), fishing, hiking. Reservations, 870-287-7118. **GPS: 33.791805, -93.965244**

PARALOMA LANDING PARK

From Brownstown at jct with SR 317, 4 mi SE through Paraloma on SR 234 to campground on NW shore of lake. 34 paved elec/wtr sites, $13 during 3/1-10/31 ($6.50 with federal senior pass). Reduced fees off-season but fewer amenities. Some pull-through sites. Fish cleaning station, tbls, flush toilets, showers, cfga, drkg wtr, dump, playground. Boating(l), fishing. **GPS: 33.783327, -94.007706**

RIVER RUN EAST CAMP

From Ashdown, 10 mi E on SR 32; S at dam, then immediately turn E & S into campground below the dam on shore of Little River outlet channel. All year; 14-day limit. 8 gravel sites without hookups, $5 ($2.50 with federal senior pass). Pit toilets, cfga. Easy fishing access, boating(l). **GPS: 33.697603, -93.942230**

RIVER RUN WEST CAMP

From Ashdown, 10 mi E on SR 32; S at dam on access rd, at W side of Little River outlet channel below dam. All year; 14-day limit. 4 gravel sites without hookups, $5 ($2.50 with federal senior pass). Pit toilets, cfga. Easy fishing access, boating(l).
GPS: 33.696825, -93.943706

SARATOGA LANDING PARK

18 mi SE of Ashdown on SR 32; 1 mi W on SR 234. All year; 14-day limit. 17 paved elec/wtr sites, $13 ($6.50 with federal senior pass). Flush toilets, showers, playground, tbls, cfga, drkg wtr, picnic shelter, fishing pier. Boating(), fishing. **GPS: 33.732297, -93.922827**

WHITE CLIFFS PARK

10 mi N of Ashdown on SR 71; 5 mi E on SR 27; 6 mi S on gravel SR 317; at E shore of Little River. All year; 14-day limit. 20 paved elec/wtr sites, $13 ($6.50 with federal senior pass). Tbls, flush toilets, showers, cfga, drkg wtr, playground, dump. Boating(l), fishing, hiking. ORV area & hiking trail on adjacent property. Reservations 870-287-4253. **GPS: 33.761560, -94.059089**

⓭
NIMROD LAKE
GPS: 34.9517. -93.06

This 3,550-acre lake is 8.3 miles SE of Ola on SR 7 and 66 miles NW of Little Rock in north-central Arkansas. It is above a dam on the Fourche LaFavre River. Off-road vehicles prohibited. Campground checkout time 1 p.m. Quarry Cove and Carter Cove Campgrounds are on the lake. Sunlight Bay is on Wilson Slough upstream from the lake, and River Road is on the Fourche LaFavre River downstream from the dam. Camping available

all year with reduction of services and facilities off-season. Primitive camping by free permit is allowed in nine designated areas. County Line Campground was been closed in 2014 due to budget cuts and not opened in 2015; check future status with lake office before arrival. Carden Point is the only day use area (fees charged); its facilities include a boat ramp, group shelter, picnicking, playground and beach. Interpretive programs. Day use fees are $3 at boat ramps, $1 per person ($4 vehicle) at swimming areas. The 1.5-mile Forest Hills Trail starts on the S side of the dam; 40 points of interest are explained by signs along its path. Project Office, Nimrod Lake, 3 Highway 7 South, Plainview, AR 72857-9600. (479) 272-4324.

CARTER COVE CAMPGROUND

From Plainview, 3.4 mi SE on SR 60; 1.5 mi SE on CR 229, following signs; 0.5 mi S on CR 233 access rd. All year; 14-day limit. 34 elec/wtr sites, $14 ($7 with federal senior pass). 40-ft RV limit; 1 RV & 1 tent or 2 tents per site. Tbls, flush toilets, cfga, drkg wtr, showers, dump, fish cleaning station, playground, beach, pay phone, picnic shelter ($40). Boating(l), fishing, swimming, hiking. (479) 272-4983. NRRS (5/15-10/25).
GPS: 34.96111, -93.23861

QUARRY COVE CAMPGROUND

8 mi E of Plainview on SR 60; S on access rd; at NE shore of lake. All year; 14-day limit. 31 elec/wtr sites, $14 ($7 with federal senior pass). 40-ft RV limit; 1 RV & 1 tent or 2 RVs per site. Tbls, flush toilets, showers (closed in winter), cfga, drkg wtr, dump, fish cleaning station, amphitheater, pay phone, playground, beach, picnic shelter ($40). Boating(l), fishing, hiking, swimming. NRRS 3/15-10/25. (479) 272-4233. **GPS: 34.959948, -93.164645**

RIVER ROAD PARK

From Ola, 9 mi SE on SR 60; 1 mi SE on SR 7; 0.5 mi S on Nimrod Dam Rd; below dam at N shore of Fourche Lefavre River. Continue

W & NW 1 mi to Project Point loop (formerly Project Point Park). All year; 14-day limit. 15 elec/wtr sites at main River Road Park & 6 elec (no wtr hookups) sites at Project Point. $13 at elec sites, $16 at elec/wtr sites (6.50 & $8 with federal senior pass). 45-ft RV limit 45 ft; 2 pull-through sites. Tbls, flush & pit toilets, dump, cfga, drkg wtr, showers, playground, picnic shelter ($40), pay phone. Boating(l), fishing, hiking, nature trail. (479) 272-4835. NRRS (3/15-10/25). **GPS: 34.950433, -93.157797**

SUNLIGHT BAY CAMPGROUND

0.1 mi W of Plainview on SR 28; 1.5 mi SW on CR 9; 1 mi SE on gravel Sunlight Bay Rd; S on CR 317 to campground; at N shore of Porter Creek. All year; 14-day limit. 29 elec/wtr sites, $14 base, $16 for premium locations ($7 & $8 with federal senior pass). RV limit 45 ft; 1 RV & 1 tent or 2 tents per site. Tbls, showers, flush toilets, cfga, drkg wtr, dump, pay phone, fish cleaning station, playground, picnic shelter ($40). Showers closed in winter. Boating(l), fishing, hiking, (479) 272-4234. NRRS (3/15-10/25). **GPS: 34.954856, -93.30413**

⑭ NORFORK LAKE
GPS: 36.25, -92.24

This 22,000-acre lake is 4 miles NE of Norfork on SR 177 near the Missouri state line and SE of Branson, Missouri. It is 135 miles N of Little Rock and has more than 350 miles of shoreline. Most of the lake's campgrounds are in Arkansas, along with extensive day-use facilities that include boat ramps, hiking shelters, group picnic shelters, designated swimming areas and playgrounds. Jordan Campground was closed in 2013 due to budget cuts and is now operated by a private marina. In addition to the developed campgrounds, free primitive camping is available by permit from the project office. Those areas are Jordan Island, Jordan Cove, Calamity Beach and Curley Point. Day use fees are charged at boat ramps, dump stations and swimming areas.

Concessionaire-operated marinas provide boat and motor rental, fuel and services. Off-road vehicles prohibited. Campground checkout time 3 p.m. Campsites that are free in winter may have reduced amenities. Resource Manager, Norfolk Lake, P. O. Box 2070, Mountain Home, AR 72654-2070. (870) 425-2700. See Missouri listings.

BIDWELL POINT PARK

From Mountain Home at jct with SR 201, 9 mi NE on US 62; 2 mi N across bridge on SR 101; right (E) an access rd to park. 5/1-9/30; 14-day limit. 48 sites. $9 with federal senior pass at wtr/elec 30-amp sites; others pay $18. 50-amp wtr/elec, $20 ($10 with senior pass). 35-ft RV limit. Tbls, flush toilets, cfga, drkg wtr, showers, dump, pay phone, playground, beach, picnic shelter ($50). Boating(l), fishing, swimming, hiking trail. (870) 467-5375. NRRS. **GPS: 36.387528, -92.240664**

CALAMITY BEACH PARK

From Clarkridge about 1 mi N on SR 201; right (E) for 3 mi on CR 37; 2 mi SE on CR 22/24 (Calamity Beach access rd). All year; 14-day limit. Free primitive undesignated sites. Pit toilet, cfga, no drkg wtr. Get camping permit from lake office. Boating(l), fishing. **GPS: 36.478325, -92.258243**

CRANFIELD PARK

From Mountain Home at jct with SR 201, 5.5 mi E on US 62 (signs); 1.6 mi N (left) on CR 34. 4/1-10/31; 14-day limit. Closed off-season. 69 elec sites, $18; $20 at premium locations ($9 & $10 with federal senior pass). 35-ft RV limit; 6 pull-through sites, 2 handicap sites. Tbls, flush toilets, cfga, drkg wtr, showers, dump, playground, beach, amphitheater, change shelter, pay phone, fishing pier, two picnic shelters ($50). Boating(l), fishing, hiking, swimming, canoeing, waterskiing. Marina. (870) 492-4191. NRRS (4/1-10/31). **GPS: 36.406566, -92.321023**

CURLEY POINT PARK

From Elizabeth, 2 mi S on CR 2; 1 mi S on Pine Ridge Rd; 3 mi W on CR 15 (Kerley Point Rd. All year; 14-day limit. Free primitive camping at undesignated sites. No facilities, no drkg wtr. Boating, fishing in Big Creek arm of lake. Get free camping permit from lake office. **GPS: 36.306428, -92.157097**

GAMALIEL PARK

Half mi S of Gamaliel on SR 101; 2 mi SE on CR 42; on Bennetts Bayou section of lake. 4/1-10/31; 14-day limit. 64 elec sites (30 & 50-amp), $18 base, $19 at premium locations ($9 & $9.50 with federal senior pass). 40-ft RV limit; 3 pull-through sites, 3 handicap sites. Tbls, flush toilets, showers, cfga, drkg wtr, dump, beach, playground, pay phone, picnic shelter (40). Interpretive area, nature trail, boating(l), fishing, swimming, waterskiing. Marina. (870) 467-5680. NRRS (4/1-10/31). **GPS: 36.423545, -93.218616**

HENDERSON PARK

From Mountain Home at jct with SR 201, 8.7 mi E on US 62; cross lake bridge; E shore of lake (left, following signs); on a peninsula in central area of lake. 5/1-9/30; 14-day limit. 36 elec sites (30-amp), $18 ($9 with federal senior pass). 30-ft RV limit; 4 pull-through sites. Tbls, flush toilets, cfga, drkg wtr, showers, dump, beach. Boating(lrd), fishing, swimming, waterskiing. Marine dump station, marina. (NRRS). (870) 488-5282. NRRS. **GPS: 36.376463, -92.232928**

JORDAN CAMPGROUND

From Jordan, 2.5 mi N on CR 64. Or, 3 mi E of Norfork Dam on SR 177; 3 mi N on CR 64; on Big Creek at SE end of lake. This campground was closed in 2013 by budget cuts and is now operated by a private marina.

JORDAN COVE PARK

From Jordan, 2.5 mi N on CR 64; just W of Jordan Campground. All year; 14-day limit.

Free primitive camping at undesignated sites. No facilities, no drkg wtr. Get free camping permit from lake office. **GPS: 36.269864, -92.194390**

JORDAN ISLAND

From Jordan, 2.5 mi N on CR 64 to Jordan Marina Campground; launch boat, then N on Lake Norfork to sand-covered Jordan Island (formerly called Sandy Island); in center of Big Creek arm between Hand Cove & Jordan Recreation Area. Free primitive tent camping; no facilities, no drkg wtr. Get free camping permit from lake office. **GPS: 36.272858, -92.198811**

PANTHER BAY PARK

From Mountain Home at jct with SR 201, 8.6 mi E on US 62; 1 mi N on SR 101; right on 1st access rd (signs). 5/1-9/30; 14-day limit. 15 elec sites, $18 ($9 with federal senior pass). Tbls, flush toilets, cfga, drkg wtr, dump, beach, playground, picnic shelter. Boating(l), fishing, swimming, waterskiing. No reservations. Marina, marine dump station. (870) 492-4544. **GPS: 36.374442, -92.254021**

QUARRY COVE PARK
DAM SITE CAMPGROUND

From Norfork, 2.9 mi NE to Salesville on SR 5; 2 mi E on SR 177 (signs). All year; 14-day limit. 68 elec sites (30 & 50-amp), $18 base, $20 at premium locations ($9 & $10 with federal senior pass). RV limit 60 ft; 2 pull-through sites. Group camping, $65. 1 RV & 1 tent or 2 tents per site. Tbls, flush toilets, cfga, showers, dump, drkg wtr, beach, fish cleaning stations, pay phone, playground, picnic shelters ($40 & $50). Boating(l), fishing, swimming, waterskiing. (870) 499-7216. NRRS (3/15-10/25). **GPS: 36.253715, -92.240273**

ROBINSON POINT PARK

From Mountain Home at jct with SR 201, 9 mi E on US 62; 2.5 mi S (right) on CR 279 (signs). 4/1-10/31; 14-day limit. 99 elec sites

30 & 50-amp), $18 base, $20 at premium locations ($9 & $10 with federal senior pass). 40-ft RV limit; 3 pull-through sites, 1 handicap site. Amphitheater, tbls, flush toilets, cfga, showers, dump, playground, tbls, pay phone, beach, picnic shelter ($40). Boating(l), fishing, swimming, waterskiing, hiking. (870) 492-6853. NRRS. **GPS: 36.356196, -92.241511**

⑮ OZARK LAKE
ARKANSAS RIVER
OZARK-JETA TAYLOR
LOCK & DAM 13
GPS: 35.4733, -93.81

This 10,600-acre lake has 173 miles of shoreline and is SW of Ozark, 39 miles E of Ft. Smith. It is part of the McClellan-Kerr Arkansas River Navigation System and extends 36 miles along the river. John Paul Hammerschmidt Lake, with 5,700 acres in Arkansas, is part of the system; it has two park sites and two fishing access areas. Campground checkout time 2 p.m. Alcohol prohibited. In 2013, Citadel Bluff & River Ridge Campgrounds were closed for budget reasons; check current status with park office before arrival. Park Manager, Ozark Lake, 1598 Lock and Dam Road, Ozark, AR 72801. (479) 968-5008.

AUX ARC CAMPGROUND

From Ozark, 1.3 mi S on SR 23; 1 mi E on SR 309; left at Aux Arc access road. All year; 14-day limit. 4 non-elec sites, $10 ($5 with federal senior pass); 57 elec sites (some with 50-amp) $18 base, $20 at premium locations ($9 & $10 with senior pass). RV limit in excess of 65 ft. Tbls, flush toilets, cfga, drkg wtr, dump, showers, playground, 3 picnic shelters with elec ($50). Boating(l), fishing, hiking. (479) 667-1100. NRRS (3/1-10/31).
GPS: 35.471663, -93.819112

CITADEL BLUFF CAMPGROUND

From Cecil, 1.6 mi N on SR 41, then N on park rd to S shore of lake. All year; 14-day limit.

25 primitive sites, $10 ($5 with federal senior pass). Picnic shelter, pit toilets, drkg wtr. 35-ft RV limit. Note: This campground was closed in 2013 due to budget cuts; check current status with lake office before arrival. Boat ramp open; day use fees. **GPS: 35.465337, -93.938062**

CLEAR CREEK PARK

From Kibler, 1 mi E on SR 162, then continue about 6 mi E on Clear Creek Rd, following signs, on Clear Creek Rd; at SE shore of Frog Bayou. All year; 14-day limit. 11 non-elec sites, $10 ($5 with federal senior pass); 25 elec sites, $16 ($8 with senior pass). RV limit in excess of 65 ft; 4 pull-through sites. No reservations. Sites no longer free in winter. Tbls, flush toilets, cfga, showers, dump, drkg wtr, picnic shelter ($50). Day use fees for picnicking, boat ramp, dump station.(479) 632-4882. **GPS: 35.439594, -94.169725**

RIVER RIDGE PARK

3 mi E of Lavaca on AR 255 to AR 96; 9 mi NE, then right 1.5 mi on unpaved Hoover's Ferry Rd. 4/1-9/30; 14-day limit. 18 primitive sites, free. Pit toilets, drkg wtr. Note: This campground was closed in 2013 due to budget issues; check current status with lake office before arrival. **GPS: 35.443761, -94.071103**

SPRINGHILL CAMPGROUND

From Ft. Smith at jct with I-540 exit 3, 7.3 mi S on SR 59 (signs); at S shore of river. All year; 14-day limit. 3 non-elec sites, $10 ($5 with federal senior pass). 15 elec/wtr sites (30-amp), $18; 10 elec sites (50-amp, no wtr hookups, $18; 17 elec/wtr sites (50-amp), $20 (sites $9 & $10 with senior pass). RV limit in excess of 65 ft. Some sites may have reduced fees & limited services in winter. Tbls, flush toilets, dump, showers, cfga, drkg wtr, pay phone, playground. Hiking trails, boating(ld), fishing, biking. Group camping area. 5 picnic shelters ($50). Non-campers pay day use fees for picnicking, boat ramp, dump station. (479) 452-4598. NRRS 3/1-10/31
GPS: 35.341770, -94.296148

16 ARKANSAS RIVER
WILBUR D. MILLS POOL, LOCK N°2 ARKANSAS POST TO PINE BLUFF
GPS: 34.24, -91.96

The Arkansas Post Field Office manages parks on the Arkansas River between Wilbur D. Mills Lock and Dam to the confluence of the Arkansas River, the White River and the Mississippi River. The first village west of the Mississippi was established there in 1686; in 1819, it became capital of the Arkansas Territory. Parks along the river provide boat launching, campgrounds and picnic sites. The area includes the White River National Wildlife Refuge and the Trusten Holder State Wildlife Management Area. Boat ramps are at Big Bayou, Wild Goose Bayou, Moore Bayou, Little Bayou Meto and Jardis Point (which also has picnicking facilities, a basketball court and shore fishing). Private marinas are at Pendleton, Pine Bluff, Little Rock and North Little Rock. Group picnic shelters can be reserved through the National Recreation Reservation Service (NRRS). Arkansas Post, Pine Bluff Project, 35 Wild Goose Lane, Tichnor, AR 72166. 870-548-2291.

MERRISACH LAKE PARK

From Tichnor at jct with SR 44, 8.2 mi S; exit NW near project office (signs); on N shore of Arkansas Post Canal. All year; 14-day limit. 67 total sites. 5 non-elec, $11-$12 ($5.50 & $6 with federal senior pass). 30-amp elec/wtr, $16 base, $18 at premium locations; 50-amp elec/wtr, $19 ($8, $9 & $9.50 with senior pass). RV limit in excess of 65 ft. Tbls, flush toilets, dump, cfga, drkg wtr, showers, picnic shelters ($30 without elec, $40 with elec). Interpretive trail, fishing, boating(l), hiking. 870-548-2291. NRRS. **GPS: 34.030879, -91.262194**

NOTREBES BEND PARK

From Tichnor at jct with SR 44, 8.2 mi S across canal W of project office, then 5.5 mi W; on E side of dam. 3/1-10/31; 14-day limit. 30 elec/wtr sites 20/30/50-amp), $19 ($9.50 with federal senior pass). 50-ft RV limit. Tbls, flush toilets, showers, cfga, drkg wtr, dump. Boating(l), fishing. Non-campers pay $3 at boat ramp. NRRS. Note: During 2015, this park will be closed 8/10-9/30 while crews work at the dam. **GPS: 33.988122, -91.308800**

PENDLETON BEND PARK

7.9 mi S of Gillett on US 165; 1 mi E on SR 212 (signs); on S shore of river. All year; 14-day limit. 31 elec sites: $16 base for 30-amp elec, $17 at premium locations; $19 for 50-amp elec/wtr ($8, $8.50 & $9.50 with federal senior pass). 40-ft RV limit; 2 pull-through sites. Tbls, flush & pit toilets, showers, cfga, drkg wtr, dump, playground, picnic shelter ($40). Boating(l), fishing. Non-campers pay $3 to use boat ramp. (870) 479-3292. NRRS. **GPS: 33.989225, -91.359703**

WILBUR D. MILLS PARK

7.9 mi S of Gillett on US 165; about 5 mi E on SR 212 (signs); on S shore of river about 1 mi downstream from dam. 3/1-10/31; 14-day limit. 21 elec/wtr sites (20/30-amp), $16 ($8 with federal senior pass). 60-ft RV limit. Tbls, flush toilets, cfga, dump, showers, drkg wtr. Boating(l), fishing. Non-campers pay $3 to use boat ramp. NRRS. **GPS: 33.977896, -91.307051**

17 ARKANSAS RIVER
POOL 3, POOL 5 & TERRY LOCK & DAM PINE BLUFF TO LITTLE ROCK
GPS: 34.24, -91.96

Parks along this section of the Arkansas River provide boat ramps, drinking water, picnic sites and campgrounds. The Pine Bluff project includes 125 river miles, part of the McClellan-Kerr Arkansas River Navigation System. Day use parks: Dam Site 5, group shelter; Dam Site 6 West, picnicking; Sheppard Island, picnicking; Ste. Marie, 2 group shelters ($60), $3 day use fee; Dam Site 6 East, boat ramp. Pine Bluff Resident Office, P. O. Box 7835, Pine Bluff, AR 71611. (870) 534-0451.

RISING STAR PARK

From Linwood at jct with US 65, 4.7 mi E on Blankenship Rd, then follow signs; at river by Pool 3 Lock & Dam. 3/1-10/31; 14-day limit. 24 elec/wtr sites (30/50-amp), $19 ($9.50 with federal senior pass). 50-ft RV limit. Tbls, flush toilets, cfga, showers, dump, drkg wtr, playground, picnic shelter ($60). Boating(l), fishing, ball field. NRRS (5/19-9/19).
GPS: 34.16889, -91.73667

TAR CAMP PARK

From Redfield at jct with SR 365/SR 46, 6 mi E on River Rd, following signs (20 mi S of Little Rock on US 65); near Lock & Dam 5 on the river. 3/1-10/31; 14-day limit. 13 non-elec sites, $9 ($4.50 with federal senior pass); 45 elec/wtr sites (30/50-amp), $19 ($9.50 with senior pass). 40-ft RV limit. Tbls, flush & pit toilets, showers, dump, cfga, drkg wtr, playground, 2 picnic shelters ($60). Boating(l), fishing, hiking trails. NRRS 4/1-9/30).
GPS: 34.448326, -92.112594

WILLOW BEACH PARK

From town of Scott (SE of Little Rock) 2 mi N on US 165, then sharp right for 1 mi S on CR 85 along W shore of Willow Beach Lake (an oxbow lake formed when the Arkansas River changed direction); veer right onto secondary Willow Beach Rd, following signs on Blue Heron Pkwy to SW shore of lake & W shore of river. All year; 14-day limit. 21 elec/wtr sites (30/50-amp), $19 ($9.50 with federal senior pass). 40-ft RV limit. Tbls, flush & pit toilets, showers, dump, cfga, drkg wtr, fishing pier,

playground, 2 picnic shelters ($50 no elec, $60 with elec). Boating(l), ball field, hiking, fishing. (501) 961-1332. NRRS (4/1-9/30).
GPS: 34.702124, -92.138219

⑱ ARKANSAS RIVER
TOAD SUCK FERRY & MURRAY L&D LITTLE ROCK TO DARDANELLE
GPS: 34.79, -92.26

Pools formed by Toad Suck Ferry, Murray Lock & Dam and Arthur V. Ormond Lock & Dam stretch upriver 80 miles from Little Rock to Dardanelle, encompassing 19,000 acres of water. Part of the McClellan-Kerr Arkansas River Navigation System. Access roads to numerous parks with drinking water, toilets, boat ramps, picnicking areas and campgrounds. Due to budget cuts in 2013-2015, Old Ferry Landing day use area and boat ramp were closed. In addition, three campgrounds were closed; check with lake office for current status before arrival. Those closed campgrounds are Sequoyah, Cypress Creek and Sweeden Island. Checkout time is 2 p.m. Russellville Project Office, 1598 Lock & Dam Rd, Russellville, AR 72801. 479-968-5008. Toad Suck Ferry, 6298 Hwy 60 W, Conway, AR 72032. (501) 329-2986.

CHEROKEE L&D N°9 PARK

From Morrilton, 0.7 mi S on Cherokee St; 0.7 mi S on Quincy Rd (CR 21), following signs. 3/1-10/31; 14-day limit. 33 elec sites, $18 for 30-amp elec/wtr; $20 for 50-amp elec/wtr. Tbls, flush toilets, showers, cfga, drkg wtr, dump, playground. Ball field, boating(l), fishing. No day use fees. Two picnic shelters available all year (for reservations, office), $50. (501) 354-9155. **GPS: 35.130421, -92.781322**

CYPRESS CREEK PARK

From Houston at jct with SR 216, 2 mi N on SR 113 (15 mi W of Conway), then 2 mi N on CR 70 to S shore of river at Cypress Creek. 3/1-

10/31; 14-day limit. Free. 9 sites, no hookups. 40-ft RV limit. Tbls, toilets, cfga, drkg wtr. Boating(l), fishing. Note: This campground closed in 2013; check current status with lake office before arrival.
GPS: 35.069576, -92.716021

MAUMELLE PARK

From Pinnacle, 2 mi N on SR 300; 4 mi E on Pinnacle Valley Rd to W shore of Arkansas River & mouth of Maumelle River. All year; 14-day limit. 129 elec sites, $22 for 30-amp elec/wtr; $24 for 50-amp elec/wtr; $26 for 50-amp elec/wtr at waterfront sites ($11, $12 & $13 with federal senior pass). RV limit in excess of 65 ft; 3 pull-through sites, 1 handicap site. Tbls, flush toilets, showers, cfga, drkg wtr, dump, playground, 8 picnic shelters ($50). Basketball, boating(ld), fishing, hiking trails. (501) 868-9477. NRRS.
GPS: 34.831551, -92.434405

POINT REMOVE PARK

From Morrilton, 0.7 mi S on Cherokee St; at N shore of river. 3/1-10/31. Free. 16 primitive sites. Tbls, toilets, cfga, drkg wtr. Fishing.
GPS: 35.143863, -92.773533

SEQUOYAH CAMPGROUND

From Morrilton, 4 mi S on SR 9; 2 mi W on River View Rd. 5/1-9/15; 14-day limit. 14 elec sites, $14 ($7 with federal senior pass). Tbls, flush toilets, showers, cfga, dump, drkg wtr, picnic shelter. Boating(l), fishing. Note: This campground was closed in 2013 due to budget cuts; check current status with project office before arrival. **GPS: 35.122787, -92.784777**

TOAD SUCK FERRY PARK

From near Conway at I-40 exit 129, 7 mi W on SR 60 (signs); 0.5 mi S on access road. 5/1-9/15; 14-day limit. 48 elec/wtr sites, $18 for 30-amp elec, $20 for 50-amp ($9 & $10 with federal senior pass). RV limit in excess of 65 ft. Tbls, flush toilets, showers, dump, cfga, drkg wtr, playground, 5 picnic shelters

($50). Boating(l), fishing, basketball, soccer, volleyball. (501) 759-2005. NRRS (3/1-10/31).
GPS: 35.077243, -92.544327

⑲ TABLE ROCK LAKE
GPS: 36.48, -93.30

In north-central Arkansas S of Branson, Missouri, Table Rock is on SR 165 W of US 65. Visitor center with exhibits, auditorium, audiovisual presentations. Due to budget issues, the Corps intended to shift management of four Missouri campgrounds to the Ozarks Rivers Heritage Foundation; however, agreements between the Corps and the foundation were terminated in September 2013. Those campgrounds are Old Highway 86, Mill Creek, Baxter and Campbell Point Campgrounds, all in Missouri. They are still operated by the Corps in 2015. Resource Manager, Upper White River Project Office, 4600 State Road 165 Ste. A, Branson, MO 65616-8976. (417) 344-4101. See Missouri listings.

CRICKET CREEK CAMPGROUND

From Ridgedale, MO, 5.3 mi SW on SR 14 (signs). 4/1-9/15; 14-day limit. 36 elec/wtr sites, $21 ($10.50 with federal senior pass), $147 weekly. RV limit in excess of 65 ft; 4 pull-through sites. Tbls, flush toilets, cfga, drkg wtr, showers, dump, playground, beach. Swimming, volleyball, scuba diving, boating(l), fishing, hiking. Marina. Non-campers pay $4 day use fee for boat ramp, dump station, picnicking, beach, sand volleyball. (870) 426-3331. NRRS. **GPS: 36.483822, -93.291848**

CALIFORNIA

STATE INFORMATION:

CAPITAL: Sacramento
NICKNAME: Golden State
STATEHOOD: 1850 - 31st State
FLOWER: California Poppy
TREE: California Redwood
BIRD: California Valley Quail

STATE TIDBITS:

• The first motion picture theater opened in Los Angeles on April 2, 1902.

• Simi Valley is the home of the Ronald Reagan Presidential Library and Museum.

• San Francisco Bay is considered the world's largest landlocked harbor.

WWW.VISITCALIFORNIA.COM

California Division of Tourism, PO Box 1499, Sacramento, CA 95812-1499. 800-462-2543

CALIFORNIA LAKES

To find campgrounds operated by the U.S. ArmyCorps of Engineers, match the lake's numbers on the preceding map page with the numbered lake entries on the following pages. Campgrounds are listed alphabetically under the appropriate lakes. The following California impoundments have Corps of Engineers campgrounds.

Black Butte Lake. 8 miles W of Orland and I-5, 100 miles NW of Sacramento in north-central California.

Eastman Lake. 25 miles NE of Chowchilla, 55 miles N of Fresno; above Buchanan Dam on the Chowchilla River.

Englebright Lake. 21 miles E of Marysville on SR 20 and 75 miles NE of Sacramento; in the Yuba River Gorge.

Hensley Lake. 17 miles NE of Madera on SR 400 and N of Fresno; above Hidden Dam on Fresno River.

Kaweah Lake. 3 miles NE of Lemoncove on SR 198; SE of Fresno and 21 miles E of Visalia; lake is above Terminus Dam on the Kaweah River.

Lake Mendocino. 2 miles NE of Ukiah on Lake Mendocino Drive, off U.S. 101. It is 1.5 miles E of Calpella off SR 20 and 120 miles N of San Francisco.

Lake Sonoma. 3 miles W of Geyserville from the Canyon Road exit off U.S. 101.

Martis Creek Lake. 6 miles SE of Truckee on SR 267 and 32 miles SW of Reno, Nevada, on I-80.

New Hogan Lake. 30 miles NE of Stockton off SR 26, 1 mile S onHogan Dam Rd.

Pine Flat Lake. 1 mile E of Piedra, 35 miles E of Fresno above Pine Flat Dam on the Kings River.

Stanislaus River Parks. Below Melones Dam on the Stanislaus River, E of San Francisco off SR 99.

Success Lake. 8 miles E of Porterville on SR 190 (in the Sierra Nevada foothills) N of Bakersfield.

❶
BLACK BUTTE LAKE
GPS: 39.8183. -122.3367

This 4,460-acre lake, formed in 1963, has 40 miles of shoreline and is 8 miles W of Orland and I-5, 100 miles NW of Sacramento in north-central California. For dam tours and ranger programs, call for scheduling. Day use fees of $4 are charged ($30 annually) non-campers for recreational facilities. The lake project has three self-guided nature trails, two campgrounds, group camping, dam tours and ranger programs. Summer campfire programs are scheduled at a central amphitheater. Boat ramps are at Buckhorn, Orland Buttes and Eagle Pass Recreation Areas. Grizzly Flat and Burris Creek are undeveloped areas open to equestrians. An 18-hole disc golf course with concrete tee pads is adjacent to Orland Buttes Campground and is open all year. Off-road vehicles and ATVs are prohibited. Park Manager, Black Butte Lake, 19225 Newville Road, Orland, CA 95963-8901. (530) 865-4781.

BUCKHORN CAMPGROUND

From Orland at the Black Butte Lake exit of I-5, 14 mi W on CR 200 (Newville Rd), following signs past dam; 0.5 mi SW of jct with Black Butte Rd; at N end of lake. All year; 14-day limit. 87 non-elec sites. 5 walk-to tent sites, $18 ($9 with federal senior pass). RV/tent sites, $16 base, $20 at premium locations during 4/1-10/31 ($8 & $10 with senior pass); $18 premium sites rest of year ($9 with senior pass). RV limit in excess of 65 ft; most sites okay for 45 ft; 28 pull-through. Tbls, flush toilets, showers, cfga, drkg wtr, dump, beach, playground, picnic shelters, amphitheater, fish cleaning station. Group camping area, $175 by reservation. Swimming, fishing, boating(l), horseback riding, biking, hiking trails, waterskiing, interpretive trail. Non-campers pay $4 day use fee ($30 annually). NRRS (4/1-9/30). **GPS: 39.8121, -122.36684**

ORLAND BUTTES

From Orland at the Black Butte Lake exit of I-5, 6 mi W on CR 200; 3.3 mi SW (left) on CR 206; 0.5 mi W. 4/1-9/30; 14-day limit. 35 non-elec sites, $18 ($9 with federal senior pass). RV limit 35 ft; 18 pull-through. Tbls, flush toilets, cfga, drkg wtr, showers, dump, playground, amphitheater, fish cleaning station, beach. Disc golf, horseback riding, swimming, waterskiing, hiking trails, boating(l), fishing. Limited lake access. Group camping, $100 by reservation. NRRS. **GPS: 39.7722, -122.35265**

❷
EASTMAN LAKE
GPS: 37.2167. -119.9833

This 1,780-acre lake is 25 miles NE of Chowchilla, 55 miles N of Fresno; above Buchanan Dam on the Chowchilla River. Visitor center open daily 9-4 with audiovisual programs, displays. Group tours, ranger programs. Day use fee for non-campers, $4 (annually $30); picnicking, swimming, hiking, volleyball, horseshoe pits, aqua-toy, disc golf; shelters $30. 3 group camping areas & equestrian area by reservation. Park Manager, Eastman Lake, P. O. Box 67, Raymond, CA 93653-0067. (559) 689-3255.

CODORNIZ RECREATION AREA

From Raymond on SR 99, E on 26th Ave; N on Hwy 29 (signs). All year; 14-day limit. 65 sites. 4 tent sites & 42 non-elec RV/tent sites, $20 ($10 with federal senior pass). Elec/wtr sites & full hookup sites, $30 ($15 with federal senior pass). Primitive equestrian sites $20, may be reserved by equestrian groups & non-profit organizations. RV limit in excess of 65 ft; 14 pull-through sites. Tbls, flush toilets, showers, cfga, drkg wtr, dump, playground, beach, picnic shelter, amphitheater, fish cleaning station, Wi-fi. Boating(ld), fishing, biking/hiking/bridle trails, canoeing, disc golf, horseshoe pits, volleyball court, swimming. Visitor center. NRRS. **GPS: 37.207, -119.966**

OTHER CODORNIZ CAMPING:

Wildcat Group Camp, on the E side of the lake. 19 primitive sites (7 pull-through & 3 horse sites) with wtr for overflow, Scouts, non-profit groups & large family equestrian sites, $20 individual sites, $60 groups.

Equestrian Camp for groups of up to 60 people & 30 vehicles, $60. Amphitheater, corral, hitching posts, toilets, dump, drkg wtr, bridle trails access. Individual sites $10.

North Group Camp A for up to 40 people & 15 vehicles, $80. Showers, toilets, drkg wtr, dump, hiking trail access.

North Group Camp B for up to 100 people & 25 vehicles, $90. Showers, toilets, dump, drkg wtr, elec, hiking trail access.

South Group Camp for up to 160 people & 50 vehicles, $100. Showers, toilets, drkg wtr, dump, elec, hiking trail access, playground.

❸ ENGLEBRIGHT LAKE
GPS: 39.24, -121.26

815-acre lake with 24 mi of shoreline 21 miles E of Marysville on SR 20 and 75 mi NE of Sacramento; in the Yuba River gorge. Boat-in camping only. Picnicking at the Narrows Recreation Area. Group tours, ranger programs. Non-campers pay $4 day use fee. Private marina. Park Mgr., Englebright Lake, P. O. Box 6, Smartville, CA 95977-0006. (530) 432-6427.

BOAT IN CAMPING

From Marysville, 21 mi E on SR 20; left on Mooney Flat Rd, then 2.5 mi to Point Defiance Park. Boat-in to 100 primitive shoreline sites. $20 during 5/1-9/30, $4 off-season; 14-day limit. Tbls, fire grates, lantern pole, portable toilets. Showers, coin laundry available, drkg wtr near boat ramps. Boating(ld), fishing, hiking trail, waterskiing, fishing. Non-campers pay $4 day use fee ($30 annually). **GPS: 39.240281, -121.267283**

❹ HENSLEY LAKE
GPS: 37.12, -119.88

This 1,500-acre lake is 17 miles NE of Madera on SR 400 and N of Fresno; above Hidden Dam on Fresno River. Multi-use trails available. Contact office for tours and ranger programs. Non-campers pay $4 day use fee ($30 annually). Buck Ridge day use area provides swimming beach, picnicking, horseshoe pits, wildlife area, picnic shelter ($30). Resource Manager, Hensley Lake, P. O. Box 85, Raymond, CA 93653. (559) 673-5151.

HIDDEN VIEW CAMPGROUND

From Chowchilla at jct with SR 99, follow signs on Avenue 26. All year; 14-day limit. 40 non-elec sites, $20 ($10 with federal senior pass); 15 elec sites, $30 15 ($15 with federal senior pass). RV limit in excess of 65 ft; 17 pull-through, 1 handicap with wtr/elec (call for reservation). Tbls, flush toilets, cfga, drkg wtr, showers, dump, playground, beach. 2 group camping areas no hookups, $100. Self-guided nature trail, biking, hiking trail, fishing, boating(l), swimming, waterskiing. 3-night minimum stay required on holiday weekends. NRRS. **GPS: 37.123011, -119.893241**

❺ KAWEAH LAKE
GPS: 36.44, -119.03

This 1,945-acre lake is 3 miles NE of Lemoncove on SR 198, SE of Fresno and 21 miles E of Visalia; lake above Terminus Dam on the Kaweah River. Visitor center at Lemon Hill Park (559-597-2005). Swimming permitted unless otherwise posted. Non-campers pay $4 day use fee ($30 annually) for showers, dump station, boat ramps, picnicking, swimming areas. Marina concession at Lemon Hill. Contact office for scheduling group tours and ranger programs. Resource Manager, Kaweah Lake, P. O. Box 44270, Lemoncove, CA 93244-4270. (559) 597-2301.

HORSE CREEK CAMPGROUND

From dam just NE of Lemoncove, 3 mi E on SR 198; left side (signs). 10 mi from Sequoia National Park. All year; 14-day limit. 80 non-elec sites, $20 ($10 with federal senior pass). 4 non-elec equestrian sites $20-$25. RV limit 35 ft; 35 pull-through sites, 1 handicap site. Overflow area open on major holidays. During full-pool periods, boat-in tent sites open for $20. Tbls, flush toilets, cfga, drkg wtr, showers, dump, playground, fish cleaning station. Interpretive center, boating(l), fishing, hiking trails, waterskiing. 3-night minimum stay on holiday weekends. Evening programs at amphitheater between MD & LD. Visitor center. (559) 561-3155. NRRS. **GPS: 36.3906, -118.9547**

❻ LAKE MENDOCINO
GPS: 39.1989, -123.1833

Mendocino is 1,822 acres 2 miles NE of Ukiah on Lake Mendocino Dr, off US RT 101. It is 1.5 miles E of Calpella off SR 20 and 120 mi N of San Francisco. Equestrian trail at S end of the lake (off-road vehcles prohibited). Pomo Cultural Center, jointly operated by the Corps and the Coyote Valley Band of Pomos; it is modeled after a traditional Pomo roundhouse, has displays about Pomo hunting, dancing, money and basketry; also outdoor amphitheater; 707-467-4200. Fish hatchery open Dec-Apr. 15 mi of hiking trails. Disc golf courses. Campground checkout time is 11 a.m. 300 campsites. Camping at the Kaweyo Staging Area by permit only. Winter camping at Kyen Campground. Maximum RV lengths determined by narrow access rds with sharp corners, not by site lengths. Park Manager, Lake Mendocino, 1160 Lake Mendocino Drive, Ukiah, CA 95482-9404. (707) 467-4200.

BUSHAY RECREATION AREA

5 mi N of Ukiah on US 101, 2.7 mi E on SR 20; after crossing Russian River bridge, turn left 1 mi; at NE edge of lake. 4/15-9/30; 14-day limit. 133 non-elec sites, $25 base, $30 at premium locations ($12.50 & $15 with federal senior pass). 40-ft RV limit. Tbls, flush toilets, cfga, drkg wtr, coin showers, dump, playground, pay phone, amphitheater with summer weekend programs. Three group camping areas, up to $235. Adjoining day use area has reservable picnic shelter ($40). Boating, fishing, volleyball, biking, waterskiing, hiking trails. Visitor center. 707-467-4200. NRRS. **GPS: 39.23501, -123.16593**

CHEKAKA RECREATION AREA

2 mi N of Ukiah on US 101; N (left) at N. State St; E (right) on Lake Mendocino Dr to top of hill, following signs; at S end of lake near Coyote Valley Dam. All year; 14-day limit. 20 non-elec sites, $20 ($10 with federal senior pass). 42-ft RV limit. Tbls, pit toilets, cfga, drkg wtr, no showers or flush toilets, cfga, drkg wtr, playground, beach. Boating(l), hiking trail, swimming, waterskiing, biking, horseback riding, 18-hol disc golf course. Horse staging aea. Two picnic shelters, $40. 18-hole disc golf course. NRRS (5/1-9/29) **GPS: 39.20306, -123.18639**

MITI PARK

Accessible by boat-in only on E side of dam. 5/1-9/30; 14-day limit. About 15 primitive tent sites, $8. Pit toilets, cfga, no drkg wtr or trash service. Several sites seriously damaged by high lake waters, but replacement sites were built, most close to lake. Swimming, fishing, boating. **GPS: 40.78, -123.22**

❼ LAKE SONOMA
GPS: 38.71, -123.00

This 2,700-acre lake above Warm Springs Dam has 50 miles of shoreline and is 3 miles W of Geyserville from the Canyon Rd exit off US 101. Milt Brandt Visitor Center with exhibits, campfire programs (open Wed-Sun). Group tours & ranger programs scheduled by calling project office. 40 miles of trails for hikers, horseback riders and mountain bikers. Campground checkout time is noon. Steelhead fish hatchery at dam, operated by the state. Boat ramps near dam & at Yorty Creek Recreation Area (car-top launch only). Day use fees charged non-campers. Marina. Beach at Yorty Creek near Cloverdale; park also has picnic shelters, playground, fisherman's trail. Starting in June 2014, reseservations have been required for camping at Liberty Glen Campground. Locked gates are opened only for registered campers. Cash or checks no longer accepted. 2-day advance reservation period no longer required, but campers without reservations are required to pay for sites by phone (877-444-6777) or online via the National Recreation Reservation Service (NRRS) before occupying sites; rangers cannot accept payments. Note: $9 fee charged for reservation. Park Manager, Lake Sonoma, 3333 Skaggs Springs Road, Geyserville, CA 95441-9644. (707) 431-4590.

LIBERTY GLEN CAMPGROUND

From Healdsburg at jct with Dry Creek Rd exit of US 101, 15 mi W on Dry Creek Rd, following signs. All year; 14-day limit. 97 non-elec RV/ tent sites, $15 ($7.50 with federal senior pass). 16 double sites, $32; 7 handicap sites. 46-ft RV limit. Tbls, flush or chemical toilets, showers, cfga, drkg wtr, playground, coin laundry. Dump station closed until further notice. Group camping area, $80. Equestrian area, $80. Amphitheater, chemical vault toilets. Weekend campfire programs, bridle trails, biking, hiking trails, fishing, boating. 707-431-4533. NRRS (4/1-9/30). **GPS: 38.71361, -123.05639**

BOAT-IN OR HIKE-IN SITES

Access by boat or hiking trails from boat ramps or primary public areas around lake but primarily from No Name Flat trailhead. All year; 14-day limit. $10. 15 primitive campgrounds with 109 sites, including 2 group camping areas (Broken Bridge and Island View), both $56. Camps provide chemical vault toilets, tbls, fire rings, lantern

holders. No drkg wtr. Two-day minimum stay on weekends during peak period of 4/1-9/30; 3-day minimum stay on holiday weekends. Toilets, cfga, tbls. Hiking, horseback riding. Register at lake visitor center. NRRS.

8

MARTIS CREEK LAKE
GPS: 39.3267. -120.1117

This 770-acre lake is 6 miles SE of Truckee on SR 267 and 32 miles SW of Reno, Nevada on I-80. Martis Creek Lake was the first "catch and release trophy trout" lake established in the state. Contact office for group tours & ranger programs and also for reservations at handicap sites. Motorized (gas or electric) boats prohibited. Campfire programs in amphitheater July-LD. Wildlife area with 4.3-mi hiking/biking trail; picnicking at Sierra View Recreation Area. Resource Manager, Martis Creek Lake, 11989 Martis Dam Rd, Truckee, CA 96160. 530-587-8623; off-season 530-432-6427.

ALPINE MEADOWS

N side of dam, 4 mi NE of SR 267. 5/15-10/15; 14-day limit. 25 non-elec sites, $18 ($9 with federal senior pass). RV limit 30 ft; 6 pull-through, 2 handicap. Tbls, pit toilets, cfga, drkg wtr. Hiking trail, biking, fishing, boating, canoeing. Amphitheater, phone. **GPS: 39.319857, -120.115521**

9

NEW HOGAN LAKE
GPS: 38.1517. -120.8117

A 4,400-acre lake with 50 miles of shoreline, New Hogan is 30 miles NE of Stockton off SR 26, 1 mil S on Hogan Dam Rd. Pool extends upstream to confluence of the N & S forks of Calaveras River. Nature walks & ranger programs. Picnicking at Fiddleneck Recreation Area ($4 day use fee), Wrinkle Cove & Observation Point. 177 campsites available. 4 boat ramps. Coin showers only at Acorn

Campground. Checkout time 2 p.m. Park Manager, New Hogan Lake, 2713 Hogan Dam Road, Valley Springs, CA 95252-9510. (209) 772-1343.

ACORN CAMPGROUND

From Valley Springs, 0.5 mi S on SR 26; 1 mi S (left) on Hogan Dam Rd (signs); 0.7 mi E on Hogan Parkway. All year; 14-day limit. 128 non-elec sites, $16 on Sun-Thurs & $20 on Fri-Sat during 4/1-9/30; $16 every night during 10/1-3/31 ($8 & $10 with federal senior pass). RV limit in excess of 65 ft; 30 pull-through, 3 handicap sites. Tbls, flush toilets, coin showers, cfga, drkg wtr, beach, dump, fish cleaning stations, amphitheater. Campfire programs, boating(l), fishing, waterskiing, swimming, horseback riding, golf. Non-campers pay $8 for dump station. NRRS (4/1-9/30). **GPS: 38.17626, -120.79972**

COYOTE POINT
GROUP CAMPGROUND

Access through Oak Knoll Campground. 4/1-10/31. Group area $125. Tbls, toilets, cfga, drkg wtr. Combination provided for gate lock for late entry by registered campers. **GPS: 38.181707, -120.792511**

DEER FLAT PARK

Accessible by boat only, on peninsula at E side of the lake. Register at Acorn Campground. 5/1-9/30; 14-day limit. 30 primitive sites & onboard boat camping. All sites $12. Pit toilets, cfga, tbls, no drkg wtr. Boating, canoeing, fishing.

OAK KNOLL CAMPGROUND

From Valley Springs, 0.5 mi E on SR 26; 1.8 mi E on Lime Rd; 1.4 mi S on Petersburg Rd. 4/1-9/30; 14-day limit. 46 primitive sites, $14 ($7 with federal senior pass). RV limit in excess of 65 ft; 8 pull-through sites. Tbls, pit toilets, cfga, drkg wtr, dump. Boating(l), fishing, swimming, waterskiing, horseback riding, canoeing, biking,

hiking. Fish cleaning station & coin showers at Acorn Campground. Amphitheater. NRRS. **GPS: 38.181707, -120.792511**

⑩
PINE FLAT LAKE
GPS: 36.8317, -119.325

This 13,000-acre lake has 67 miles of shoreline above Pine Flat Dam on the Kings River. It is 1 mile E of Piedra, 35 miles E of Fresno. Campground checkout time 2 p.m. Dam tours, ranger programs and group/handicap campsites (for scheduling and reservations, call 559-787-2589). Day use fee $4 for non-campers at Deer Creek, Island, Lakeview and Trimmer Parks. Kirch Flat Campground operated by forest service, Pine Flat Camp by Fresno County. Park Manager, Pine Flat Lake, P. O. Box 117, Piedra, CA 93649-0117.

ISLAND PARK CAMPGROUND

From Piedra, 9.5 mi NE on Trimmer Springs Rd, then S following signs. All year; 14-day limit. 15 tent sites & 54 non-elec RV/tent sites, $20 ($10 with federal senior pass); 25 elec (30-amp, 5 with wtr) sites, $30 ($15 with senior pass). RV limit in excess of 65 ft. Tbls, flush toilets, cfga, drkg wtr, coin showers, dump, fish cleaning station, amphitheater. Boating(ld), fishing, hiking, interpretive trails, swimming. Two group camping areas, each $100. Non-campers pay $4 day use fee ($30 annually). NRRS. **GPS: 36.86465, -119.31573**

TRIMMER RECREATION AREA

From Trimmer, 2 mi E on Trimmer Springs Rd, then follow signs to NW shore of lake. All year; 14-day limit. 10 non-elec sites (5 for tents), $20 ($10 with federal senior pass. 30-ft RV limit. Tbls, flush toilets, cfga, drkg wtr, coin showers. Boating(l), fishing, hiking, swimming. Non-campers pay $4 day use fee ($30 annually). NRRS.
GPS: 36.905525, -119.289336

⑪ STANISLAUS RIVER PARKS
GPS: 37.77, -120.84

Below Melones Dam on Stanislaus River, E of San Francisco off SR 99. From Modesto turn on SR 108/120; 12 miles E of Oakdale, N on Kennedy Rd, then N on Sonora Rd; cross Stanislaus River; Knights Ferry Information Center is on right. Fishing and whitewater rafting & canoeing area. Camping by reservation only with camping permits issued at information center. Nine parks & 3 campgrounds built after completion of New Melones Dam. Termed "environmental camping" by the Corps, access to sites is by boat, foot or bicycle. For reservations (1 to 2 weeks in advance), call (209) 881-3517. Landmark 330-ft historic 1863 covered bridge; information center with, parks video, displays on salmon life, native American culture; historic flour mill. Drinking water only at McHenry Avenue Recreation Area. River open to fishing during 1/1-3/31 and about MD-10/31. Hiking trails, picnickng. Park Manager, Stanislaus River Parks, 17968 Covered Bridge Road, Oakdake, CA 95361-9510.

HORSESHOE ROAD RECREATION AREA

From Knights Ferry, W on Sonoroa & Orange Blossom Roads to Horseshoe Rd. All year; 14-day limit. 16 tent sites, $10; group camping $38. Boat-in, walk-in or bike-in only for individual sites. Tbls, toilets, cfga, no drkg wtr. Hiking, fishing, canoeing. **GPS: 37.81, -120.66**

MC HENRY AVENUE RECREATION AREA

From Modesto, 6 mi N on McHenry Ave across Stanislaus River; 1 mi W on River Rd; left at park sign. 1/1-10/31; 14-day limit. 4 tent sites, $10; group camping $38. Boat-in, walk-in or bike-in only for individual sites. Tbls, toilets, cfga, drkg wtr. Canoeing, fishing, hiking. **GPS: 37.72, -121.11**

VALLEY OAK RECREATION AREA

From Oakdale, 1.5 mi N on SR 120; left on Orange Blossom Rd; 3 mi E on Rodden Rd, then left. All year; 14-day limit. 10 sites, $10; group camping $38. Boat-in, walk-in or bike-in only for individual sites. Tbls, toilets, cfga, no drkg wtr. Hiking, fishing, canoeing. **GPS: 37.78, -120.80**

⑫ SUCCESS LAKE
GPS: 36.0583, -118.9183

This 2,450-acre lake is 8 miles E of Porterville on SR 190 (in theSierra Nevada foothills) N of Bakersfield. Swimming permitted. Off-road vehicles prohibited. Primary day use facilities: Tule Recreation Area -- picnicking, group shelters, playground, boat ramp; Bartlett County Park (just below dam) -- picnicking, group shelters, playgrounds, softball field, fishing ponds, nature trail. Non-campers pay $4 day use fees (or $30 annually). Information, (559) 783/9200. Resource Manager, Success Lake, P. O. Box 1072, Porterville, CA 93258. (559) 784-0215.

TULE CAMPGROUND

From dam near Porterville, 2 mi E on SR 190, then N following signs. All year; 14-day limit. 74 non-elec sites, $20 ($10 with federal senior pass); 29 elec sites, $30 ($15 with senior pass). RV limit 65 ft; 27 pull-through sites, 2 handicap sites. Tbls, flush toilets, cfga, drkg wtr, showers, amphitheater, fish cleaning station, picnic shelter, playground, dump. Golf, boating(l), fishing, hiking, campfire programs on Saturdays MD-LD. 3-day minimum stay required on holiday weekends. NRRS. **GPS: 36.08028, -118.90222**

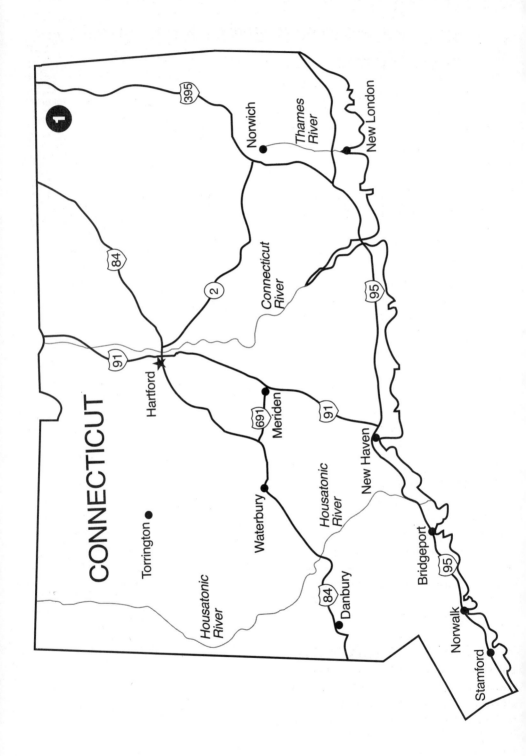

CONNECTICUT

STATE INFORMATION:

CAPITAL: Hartford
NICKNAME: Constitution State
STATEHOOD: 1788 - 5th State
FLOWER: Mountain Laurel
TREE: White Oak
BIRD: Robin

CT

STATE TIDBITS:

• In 1728, the first steel mill operating in America was located in Simsbury.

• America's first trade association was founded in Naugatuck Valley.

• The world's first nuclear powered submarine was built in Groton in 1954.

WWW.CTVISIT.COM

Commission on Culture and Tourism, One Financial Plaza, 755 Main Steet, Hartford, CT 06103. 860-256-8200. Toll-free numbers for travel information: 1-888-CTVisit.

CONNECTICUT LAKES

Connecticut has eight lakes built by the U.S. Army Corps of Engineers, but the Corps operates campgrounds at only one of those.

❶ WEST THOMPSON LAKE
GPS: 41.945, -71.90

This 200-acre lake is NE of Putnam off SR 12 in northeastern Connecticut. It has one Corps-operated campground. Field dog trial area location. Canoe launch at Fabyan Dam. Resource Manager, West Thompson Lake, RFD 1, 449 Reardon Road, North Grosvernordale, CT 06255-9801. (860) 923-2982.

WEST THOMPSON CAMPGROUND

From North Grosvenordale at I-395 exit 99, 1 mi E on SR 200; 2 mi S (right) on SR 193 (signs); cross SR 12 at traffic light; first right 0.5 mi on Reardon Rd; left 0.2 mi on recreation road. 5/20-9/20; 14-day limit. 11 basic sites without hookups, $15 ($7.50 with federal senior pass). 11 elec/wtr sites, $30 ($15 with federal senior pass). 2 lean-to shelters without elec, $20 ($10 with federal senior pass). RV limit 45 ft. 1 handicap site with wtr/elec. Tbls, flush toilets, cfga, drkg wtr, showers, dump, coin laundry, playground, amphitheater. Boating(l), fishing, canoeing, hiking trails, basketball, horseshoe pits, nature programs, free disc golf course. Picnic shelters, $75-$100. No swimming, no waterfront sites. Firewood($). At reserved sites, 2-night minimum stay required on weekends, 3 nights on Holiday weekends. No day use fees. (860) 923-3121. NRRS. **GPS: 41.956052, -71.898898**

FLORIDA

STATE INFORMATION:

CAPITAL: Tallahassee
NICKNAME: Sunshine State
STATEHOOD: 1845 - 27th State
FLOWER: Orange Blossom
TREE: Sabal Palm
BIRD: Mockingbird

FL

STATE TIDBITS:

• Saint Augustine is the oldest European settlement in North America.

• Cape Canaveral is America's launch pad for space flights.

• Key Largo is known as the Dive Capital of the World.

WWW.VISITFLORIDA.COM

VISITFLORIDA.org, Visitor Inquiry, 1-866-972-5280.

FLORIDA IMPOUNDMENTS

The Okeechobee Waterway is the only impoundment within the State of Florida where the U.S. Army Corps of Engineers operates campgrounds. Lake Seminole in partially in Florida, but all Corps camping areas within Georgia.

❶ OKEECHOBEE WATERWAY
GPS: 26.756733, -80.917815

This 154-mile waterway stretches from Ft. Myers on the Gulf of Mexico through 451,000-acre Lake Okeechobee, which is about 30 miles in diameter, exiting at Stuart on the Atlantic Ocean. The waterway project consists of the Caloosahatchee River to the west of the lake and the St. Lucie Canal east of the lake. Five navigation locks and dams are along the waterway: St. Lucie at Stuart, Port Mayaca near Canal Point, Moore Haven at Moore Haven, Ortona near LaBelle and W.P. Franklin near Ft. Myers. Non-campers are charged day use fees of $3-$4 (or $30 annually) at some facilities, including boat ramps (except at Port

Mayaca). In addition to the campgrounds listed here, day use facilities include: W.P. Franklin South -- swimming beach ($4 day use fee), picnicking, 2 shelters ($35), boat ramp ($3), playground, horseshoe pit, sand volleyball court; Ortona North -- picnicking, 2 shelters ($35), boat ramp ($3); St. Lucie North -- fishing pier, picnicking, shelter ($35), nature trail. Twenty-two other recreation areas are managed project-wide by various entities. They include Pahokee City Park, Jaycee Park in Okeechobee, Okeetantie near Buckhead Ridge, Clewiston City Park, Torry Island in Belle Glade, Nubbin Slough, Harney Pond Canal, Henry Creek, Bare Beach (Dyess Ditch Canal) near Lake port, Fisheating Creek, Rardin Park near Belle Glade, South Bay, LaBelle, Phipps County Park near St. Lucie Lock & Dam, Barron Park in LaBelle, Alva, Liberty Point (Uncle Joe's Fish Camp), Indiantown Marina, Buckhead Ridge, Clewiston Marina, Chancy Bay and Moore Haven. Campground checkout time is noon. Lock facility tours scheduled through park rangers. Visitor centers in Alva, 239-694-2582; Stuart, 772-219-4575, and St. Lucie, 772-219-4575. South Florida Operations Office, 525 Ridgelawn Road, Clewiston, FL 33440-5399. 863-983-8101.

ORTONA LOCK & DAM SOUTH

From Labelle, 8 mi E on SR 80; N (left) on Dalton Lane (signs); at the Caloosahatchee River. All year; 14-day limit. 51 elec/wtr sites (30/50-amp), $30 ($15 with federal senior pass). RV limit 40 ft; 4 pull-through sites, 4 handicap sites. Tbls, flush toilets, cfga, drkg wtr, showers, dump, coin laundry, pay phone. Boating(ld), fishing, golf. Picnic shelter with handicap facilities for 2 to 40 people & 15 vehicles. Handicap accessible fishing pier. (863) 675-8400. NRRS. **GPS: 26.787529, -81.308881**

ST. LUCIE SOUTH CAMPGROUND

From Stuart at jct with I-95 exit 101, 0.5 mi W on SR 76; right on Locks Rd, following signs. All year; 14-day limit. 3 tent sites, $20 ($10 with federal senior pass); 8 boat-in elec/wtr tent sites, $30 ($15 with senior pass); 9 elec/wtr RV/tent sites, $30 ($15 with senior pass); 4 sleep-onboard elec/wtr boat sites, $30 ($15 with senior pass). Tbls, flush toilets, cfga, drkg wtr, showers, dump, playground. Boating(ld), fishing, hiking. RV limit 45 ft. Picnic shelter, $35. (772) 287-1382. NRRS. **GPS: 27.109600, -80.285811**

W. P. FRANKLIN NORTH

From E of Fort Myers at jct with I-75 exit 143, about 5 mi E on SR 78; 0.5 mi S on N. Franklin Lock Rd, following signs; at N shore of Caloosahatchee River. All year; 14-day limit. 30 elec/wtr sites (30/50-amp), $30 ($15 with federal senior pass); 8 sleep-onboard boat sites with hookups, $30. Tbls, flush toilets, showers, cfga, drkg wtr, dump, coin laundry, playground, beach. Boating(l), fishing, swimming. Handicap accessible fishing area. RV limit 35 ft; 1 pull-through site, 1 handicap site. Mooring docks closed for repairs about six months starting Oct 2014; check current status before arrival. (239) 694-8770. NRRS. **GPS: 26.724170, -81.692780**

Lake Sidney Lanier

Atlanta

Chattahoochee River

Columbus

Macon

Oconee River

Savannah River

Augusta

Ocmulgee River

Altamaha River

Savannah

Chattahoochee River

Flint River

GEORGIA

GEORGIA

STATE INFORMATION:

CAPITAL: Atlanta
NICKNAME: Peach State
STATEHOOD: 1788 - 4th State
FLOWER: Cherokee Rose
TREE: Southern Live Oak
BIRD: Brown Thrasher

GA

STATE TIDBITS:

• Historic Saint Marys Georgia is the second oldest city in the nation.

• The official state fish is the large-mouth bass.

• Chickamauga National Park is the site of the bloodiest battle in American history.

WWW.EXPLOREGEORGIA.ORG

Dept. of Economic Development, P.O. Box 1776, Atlanta, GA 30301-1776. 404/656-3590 or 800/VISITGA.

GEORGIA LAKES

To find campgrounds operated by the U.S. Army Corps of Engineers, match the lake's numbers on the preceding map page with numbered lake entries on the following pages. Campgrounds are listed alphabetically under the appropriate lakes. The following Georgia impoundments have Corps of Engineers campgrounds.

Allatoona Lake. A 12,000-acre lake with 270 miles of shoreling, Allatoona is 30 miles NW of Atlanta off I-75 and E of Cartersville in NW Georgia on the Etowah -- a tributary of the Cousa River.

Carters Lake. 27 miles N of Cartersville on US 411, N on jct with SR 136 and SW of Ellijay in northwestern Georgia.

Hartwell Lake. 5 miles N of the City of Hartwell on US 29 and SW of Greenville, SC, on the state line.

Lake Seminole. N of Chattahoochee, Florida, in SW Georgia on the state line off US 90.

Lake Sidney Lanier. W of I-985 exit 4, 35 miles NE of Atlanta in north-central Georgia.

J. Strom Thurmond Lake. This 71,100-acre lake is adjacent to Clarks Hill and NW of Augusta on the South Carolina state line (US 221 crosses the top of the dam).

Walter F. George & G.W. Andrews Lakes. Together, the lakes make up 45,000 acres of impoundment on the Chattahoochee River at the Alabama-Georgia state line, adjacent to Ft. Gaines, GA, W of Albany, GA, and N of Dothan, AL. Sometimes referred to as Lake Eufaula.

West Point Lake. Southwest of Atlanta and I-85 on the Alabama/Georgia state line near West Point, Georgia.

❶
ALLATOONA LAKE
GPS: 34.1633, -84.7283

A 12,000-acre lake with 270 miles of shoreline 30 miles NW of Atlanta off I-75, east of Cartersville in NW Georgia. On the Etowah River -- a tributary of the Cousa River. Off-road vehicles prohibited. Visitor center, historic & cultural site, interpretive programs, wildlife viewing. Group picnic shelter fees $50-$175. Restroom facilities available at all day use parks; daily use fees (or $30 annually) charged at most;

$3 at most boat ramps, $4 at beaches. Boat ramps open seasonally depending on lake levels.

DAY USE PARKS: Blockhouse Park -- boat ramp ($3), flush toilets, fishing jetty; Cooper Branch 1 -- free shelter, boat ramp, picnicking, hiking trail, shelter ($50); Galt's Ferry -- boat ramp ($3), fishing jetty, picnic shelter, playground, flush toilets; Knox Bridge -- boat ramp 4/1-9/7; Riverside -- shelters ($75 & $125), boat ramp, playground, picnicking, hiking trail; Stamp Creek - boat ramp; Tanyard Creek -- boat ramp 5/18-9/7. Several non-Corps parks also offer day use facilities and activities. Operations Manager, Allatoona Lake, P. O. Box 487, Cartersville, GA 30120-0487. (678) 721-6700.

CLARK CREEK NORTH CAMP

From Atlanta, N on I-75; from exit 278, 2.3 mi N on Glade Rd (signs), cross lake bridge, then left. 5/15-9/7; 14-day limit. 24 elec/wtr sites (50-amp), $30 ($15 with federal senior pass); 5 pull-through. RV limit 40'. Tbls, flush toilets, cfga, drkg wtr, showers, beach, dump, coin laundry. Fishing, boating(ld), swimming. Non-campers pay boat ramp fee. 2-night stay may be required on weekends. 678-721-6700. NRRS. **GPS: 34.103010, -84.682429**

CLARK CREEK SOUTH

From Atlanta, N on I-75; from exit 278, 2 mi N on Glade Rd (signs), then right before lake bridge. Campground closed in 2011 & not scheduled to reopen. Boat ramp open 5/15-9/7. **GPS: 34.100520, -84.683001**

MCKASKEY CREEK

From Cartersville at I-75 exit 290, 2 mi E (right) on SR 20 (signs); 1.5 mi S on Spur 20; 1.5 mi E on county rd (McKaskey Creek Rd). 3/28-9/7; 14-day limit. 19 tent sites, $20 ($10 with federal senior pass); 32 sites, 50-amp elec/wtr, $26 ($13 with senior pass), $30 at premium locations. RV limit 40'. Tbls, flush toilets, cfga,

drkg wtr, showers, dump, coin laundry, beach, playground. Boating(l), fishing, swimming. NRRS. **GPS: 34.192086, -84.721032**

MCKINNEY CAMPGROUND

From Atlanta, N on I-75 to exit 278; 3 mi E on Glade Rd past Clark Creek to second 4-way stop sign (signs); 1 mi N (left) on King's Camp Rd; left at fork. All year; 14-day limit. 139 elec/wtr sites (50-amp), $26 ($13 with federal senior pass); $30 at 11 premium sites with wood decks (35 pull-through, RV limit 40'). Tbls, flush toilets, cfga, drkg wtr, showers, dump, beach, playground. Boating(l), swimming, fishing, waterskiing. NRRS. **GPS: 34.111756, -84.697369**

OLD HIGHWAY 41 Nº3 CAMP

From Atlanta, N on I-75 to exit 278; 0.5 mi S on Glade Rd; right (SW) on SR 92 (Ackworth Dr) for 1 mi; exit right onto SR 293 (Main St); left at stop sign onto SR 293, following signs to campground just S of I-75. 5/15-9/7; 14-day limit. 50 elec/wtr sites (50-amp), base fee $26 ($13 with federal senior pass); premium locations $34 ($17 with senior pass); 6 double sites $60. RV limit 50'; 4 pull-through. Tbls, flush toilets, cfga, drkg wtr, showers, dump, coin laundry, playground. Basketball, boating(ld), fishing, waterskiing. NRRS. **GPS: 34.087578, -84.703710**

PAYNE CAMPGROUND

From Atlanta, N on I-75 to exit 277; 2 mi E on SR 92; N (left) on Old Alabama Rd to dead end, then 1.5 mi E (right) on Kellogg Creek Rd following signs. 3/29-9/3; 14-day limit. 11 non-elec sites, $20 ($10 federal senior pass); 45 elec/wtr sites (50-amp), $26 base ($13 with federal senior pass), $30 at 2 full-hookup sites; $60 at 3 elec/wtr double sites. RV limit 40'. Tbls, flush toilets, cfga, drkg wtr, showers, dump, beach, playground. Boating(ld), fishing, swimming, waterskiing. NRRS. **GPS: 34.120518, -84.620020**

SWEETWATER CAMPGROUND

S of Canton at jct with SR 5, 5 mi W on SR 20 across Knox Bridge, then 2 mi S. About 3/22-9/7; 14-day limit. During 8/4-8/26, open only Fri & Sat nights; during 8/27-9/7, closed to camping (day use only). 41 non-elec sites, $20 ($10 with federal senior pass); 105 elec/wtr sites (50-amp), $26 ($13 with senior pass); $30 at 1 full-hookup site ($15 with senior pass); $60 at 1 double site; 23 pull-through. 9-site group camping w/picnic shelter, 50-amp elec/wtr $250. RV limit in excess of 65'. Tbls, flush toilets, cfga, drkg wtr, showers, dump, playground, beach, coin laundry. Boating(l), fishing, swimming. NRRS.
GPS: 34.19444, -84.57889

UPPER STAMP CREEK CAMP

From Cartersville at I-75 exit 290, 4 mi E on SR 20; 1.3 mi S on Wilderness Rd (signs); dirt road to left. 5/15-9/7; open only Fri-Sun nights. 2 non-elec sites, $20 ($10 with federal senior pass); 18 elec/wtr sites (50-amp), $26 base ($13 with senior pass), $30 at premium locations ($15 with senior pass). RV limit 30'. Tbls, showers, flush toilets, cfga, drkg wtr, dump, beach. Boating(ld), fishing, swimming. NRRS. **GPS: 34.203016, -84.677349**

VICTORIA CAMPGROUND

From I-75 exit 290 at Cartersville, 12 mi E on SR 20; right on Butterworth Rd; at 4-way stop sign, turn right, follow signs. About 3/29-10/6; 14-day limit. 73 elec/wtr sites (all 50-amp), $26 ($13 with federal senior pass); $30 for 2 full hookups ($15 with senior pass). Numerous pull-through. RV limit 65'. Tbls, flush toilets, cfga, drkg wtr, showers, dump, coin laundry, beach. Boating(ld), fishing, swimming. NRRS.
GPS: 34.150965, -84.617933

2
CARTERS LAKE
GPS: 34.6133. -84.685

A 3,200-acre lake 27 miles N of Cartersville on US 411, N of jct. with SR 136 and SW of Ellijay in NW Georgia. 62-mile shoreline. Visitor center. Most boat ramps open all year. Day use facilities: Damsite Park -- boat ramp, picnicking, group shelter $30; Northbank Park -- picnicking, group shelters $30 & $50, playground, interpretive trail; Reregulation Dam -- picnicking, group shelter $50, interpretive trail. $4 day use fee charged at most areas ($30 annually). Site Manager, Carter Lake, P. O. Box 96, Oakman, GA 30732-0096. (706) 334-2248.

BOAT IN CAMPGROUND

From dam boat launch, E to peninsula near dam via boat or hike 2 mi to sites on the Amadahy Trail from Woodring Branch Campground access rd. All year; 14-day limit. 12 free primitive tent sites. Pit toilets, cfga, tbls, tent pads, no drkg wtr. Boating(l), fishing, hiking.

DOLL MOUNTAIN CAMP

From jct with US 411 about 1 mi N of Oakman, 5.5 mi E on SR 136; 3.2 mi E on SR 382, then NW on Doll Mountain access rd (across rd from fire station); on peninsula at S side of lake. CAUTION: Steep downhill grade to campground. About 4/1-10/30; 14-day limit. 26 tent sites, $18 ($9 with federal senior pass); 39 elec/wtr sites, $22 base ($11 with senior pass), $24 at premium locations ($12 with senior pass); 4 full-hookup sites, $28 ($14 with senior pass). RV limit 40 ft; 5 pull-through. Picnic shelter, amphitheater, tbls, flush toilets, cfga, drkg wtr, dump, playground, coin laundry, pay phone. Boating(d), fishing, hiking, basketball, canoeing. Night-time emergency exit provided. (706) 276-4413. NRRS.
GPS: 34.603718, -84.6613760

HARRIS BRANCH CAMP

From jct with US 411 about 1 mi N of Oakman, 5.5 mi E on SR 136; 1 mi E on SR 382, then N about 3 mi on Harris Branch Rd; at S side of lake. 10 non-elec sites $18. About 5/1-9/1; 14-day limit. Tbls, flush toilets, cfga, drkg wtr, showers, coin laundry, playground, beach, pay phone. Hiking trail, swimming, fishing. Group camping area $60 (call 706-276-4545 for reservations). **GPS: 34.602250, -84.622715**

RIDGEWAY CAMPGROUND

From jct with US 411 just S of Ramhurst, about 8 mi E on US 76; right (S) on Dotson Rd (becoming Ridgeway Rd) about 2.5 mi to campground at N shore of lake's Coosawattee River arm. All year; 14-day limit. 18 primitive sites, $10 (self-register). Tbls, pit toilets, cfga, drkg wtr (hand pump). Hiking & mountain biking trails, boating(l), fishing. **GPS: 34.649962 -84.600155**

WOODRING CAMPGROUND

From Ellijay, 11 mi W on US 76, then 3.5 mi S on Woodring Branch Rd, following signs; at N side of lake. About 4/1-10/30; 14-day limit. 12 non-elec sites in separate primitive camping area, $10 ($5 with federal senior pass). Main campground, 11 tent sites, $18 ($9 with federal senior pass); 31 elec/wtr sites, $22 base ($11 with senior pass). RV limit 40 ft. Picnic shelter, amphitheater, tbls, flush toilets, cfga, drkg wtr, showers, coin laundry, dump, playground, pay phone. Canoeing, fishing, hiking, boating(ld). (706) 276-6050. NRRS. **GPS: 34.623674, -84.639702**

❸
HARTWELL LAKE
GPS: 34.46, -82.19

A 56,000 acre lake with 962 miles of shoreline, Hartwell is 5 miles N of the City of Hartwell on US 29 and SW of Greenville, SC on state line. It borders Georgia and South Carolina on the Savannah, Tugaloo and Seneca Rivers and was created by Hartwell Dam on the Savannah about seven miles below the confluence of the other two rivers. It extends 49 miles up the Tugaloo and 45 miles up the Seneca; its shoreline is 962 miles. Guided tours of dam and power plant available. Visitor center provides maps, displays and information about the lake. Nearby Big Oaks Recreation Area has picnic tables, group shelter, playground, courtesy dock, boat ramp. Hartwell Dam Walking Trail follows the shoreline to the dam. Campground checkout time is 2 p.m. Alcohol prohibited. Off-road vehicles, golf carts and motorized scooters also prohibited.

The Corps operates 8 campgrounds and 15 major day use areas on Hartwell. $4 day use fees are charged, $3 at most boat ramps (or $30 annually). Picnic shelters now must be reserved through the National Recreation Reservation Service (NRRS) either online or by phone. In addition to developed day use facilities listed below, the Corps manages 29 access areas with boat ramps.

Georgia day use facilities: Big Oaks -- ramp, toilets, picnicking, shelter ($80), drinking water, playground, dock, paved walking trail; Elrod Ferry -- boat ramp, toilets, picnicking, shelters ($60 & $90), drinking water, beach, playground, dock, volleyball court; Georgia River -- toilets, picnicking, fishing piers; Glenn Ferry -- boat ramp, dock; Long Point -- boat ramp, picnicking, shelters $30 and $40 but closed in 2013, playground, dock (all facilities closed in 2014); Mary Ann Branch -- dock, boat ramp, toilets; Poplar Spring -- boat ramp, picnicking, dock shelter $40 (no beach or playground); Spring Branch -- boat ramp, dock.

Stephens County Park, with boat ramp, picnicking, dock is now being operated by the county. Long Point Park (boat ramp, shelter & playground) and Milltown Campground are now operated by Hart County after being closed by the Corps for financial reasons.

Mullins Ford, Fair Play and Lawrence Bridge Campgrounds were leased by the Corps to Oconee County in South Carolina for operation and maintenance. They are operating as county parks in 2015. One of two camping loops at Weldon Robb Park was closed in 2014; the entire park open in 2015 during 5/1-9/9; Hattons Ford boat ramp &

picnic area there open all year. See SC section for day use areas there. Project Manager, Hartwell Lake and Powerplant, 5625 Anderson Hwy, Hartwell, Ga. 30643-5259. (706) 856-0300/(888) 893-0678. See SC listings.

GEORGIA RIVER RECREATION AREA

From Hartwell, 6.5 mi N on US 29 (between Hartwell and Anderson, SC); on Savannah River just below dam. 5/1-9/8; 14-day limit. 15 primitive sites, $6 ($3 with federal senior pass). Some sites may be open & free off-season. Small RVs welcome, but sites most suitable for folding trailers, pickup campers & tents. Register at lake visitor center on Hwy 29. Fishing piers, central wtr spigot, tbls, flush toilets, cfga. Dump nearby. Fishing, picnicking. 35 acres.
GPS: 34.35449, -82.82095

PAYNES CREEK CAMPGROUND

From Hartwell, 10 mi N on SR 51 following signs; on Tugaloo arm of lake. 5/1-9/8; 14-day limit. 44 elec/wtr sites (50-amp), $24 base, $26 at premium locations ($12 & $13 with federal senior pass); double sites $52. 60-ft RV limit. 37 sites at waterfront. Tbls, flush toilets, cfga, drkg wtr, dump, beach, playground, showers. Boating(ld), fishing, 7.2-mi hiking/biking trail. NRRS. **GPS: 34.473183, -82.972333**

WATSADLERS CAMPGROUND

From Hartwell, 5.5 mi N on US 29, following signs; near Hartwell Dam, overlooking lake. All year; 14-day limit. 51 elec/wtr sites (50-amp), $26 ($13 with federal senior pass). double sites $52. RV limit 50'. 49 sites are lakefront; 17 pull-through. All sites open 4/1-11/30; 21 sites open in winter. Tbls, flush toilets, cfga, drkg wtr, showers, dump, playground, pay phone. Boating(ld), fishing. NRRS. **GPS: 34.341815, -82.842311**

❹
LAKE SEMINOLE
JIM WOODRUFF LOCK & DAM
GPS: 30.711131. -84.847172

This 37,500-acre lake with 376 miles of shoreline is N of Chattahoochee, Florida, in SW Georgia on the state line off US 90. Campground checkout time 3 p.m. Alcohol prohibited. Picnicking at visitor center. Group picnic shelters, $30 (229-662-2001 for reservations). Day use facilities: Chattahoochee Park -- boat ramp, picnicking, group shelter, playground, drinking water, toilets, fishing pier; Cypress Pond -- boat ramp, picnicking, pit toilets; Desser Landing -- boat ramp, picnicking, pit toilets; Fairchilds Park -- boat ramp, picnicking, pit toilets, fishing pier; Rays Lake -- boat ramp, group shelter, drinking water, toilets, fishing pier; Reynoldsville Landing -- boat ramp, pit toilets; Lower Pool/Dam area -- toilets, fishing pier. $3 boat launch fee charged at Chattahoochee, Hales Landing and Rays Lake. Resource Site Manager, Lake Seminole, P. O. Box 96, Chattahoochee, FL 32324-0096. (229) 662-2001.

EASTBANK CAMPGROUND

From Chattahoochee, Florida, at jct with US 90, 1.5 mi N on Bolivar St (Booster Club Rd); left Jim Woodruff Powerhouse Rd, then right on East Bank Rd about 0.5 mi; near Jim Woodruff Dam. All year; 14-day limit. 2 tent sites, $14 ($7 with federal senior pass); 63 elec/wtr sites (50-amp), $20 ($10 with senior pass); double sites $44. RV limit in excess of 65'. Tbls, flush toilets, showers, cfga, drkg wtr, beach, playground, shelter, fish cleaning station, coin laundry, pay phone. Horseshoe pits, boating(ld), biking, hiking, swimming, volleyball, nature trail. (229) 622-9273. NRRS. **GPS: 30.716928, -84.851277**

FACEVILLE LANDING CAMP

From Bainbridge, 14 mi S on SR 97, then N on Faceville Landing Rd; between Bainbridge and Chattahoochee, FL. All year; 14-day limit. 7 primitive sites, 4 for tents, $8. RV limit 40'. Picnic shelter, pit toilets, cfga, fishing pier, no drkg wtr. Fishing, boating(ld). Maintained by Florida Game and Fresh Water Commission. **GPS: 30.786853, -84.665558**

HALES LANDING CAMPGROUND

SW of Bainbridge on GA 253; S on county's Ten Mile Still Rd, following signs, then S. All year; 14-day limit. 25 elec/wtr sites (50-amp), $18 ($9 with federal senior pass). Picnic shelter, tbls, flush toilets, showers, cfga, drkg wtr, beach. Boating(ld), fishing. 1 handicap site. **GPS: 30.847453, -84.661138**

RIVER JUNCTION CAMP

4 mi N of Chattahoochee, Florida, across state line on SR 386, follow signs. All year; 14-day limit. 11 elec/wtr sites (50-amp), $18 ($9 with federal senior pass). Group primitive camping. RV limit 40'. Tbls, flush toilets, showers, cfga, drkg wtr, beach, dump. Boating(ld), fishing, swimming. **GPS: 30.749355, -84.839596**

❺
LAKE SIDNEY LANIER
GPS: 32.9347, -84.3589

A 38,000 acre lake with 690 miles of shoreline, located W of I-985 exit 4, 35 miles NE of Atlanta in north-central Georgia. Alcoholic beverages prohibited. Campground checkout time 3 p.m. Chestnut Ridge and Shoal Creek Campgrounds were leased to Lake Lanier Islands Resort and no longer operate as part of the Corps parks system. Shady Grove Campground is operated by Forsyth County. Van Pugh South day use park was converted into a campground in 2010 and is still managed as a Corps campground. Primitive campsites are $13; tent sites without hookups, $22; sites with 30-amp water/electric, $30; sites with 50-amp electric/water, $32.

Vehicle day use fees $3 or $4 (or $30 annually) are charged at primary boat ramps,

beaches and day use parks. Group picnic shelters, available by reservation (770-945-9531), are $50, $75 & $90 daily. The lake complex provides 3.8-mile Laurel Ridge Hiking Trail near Buford Dam and 1-mile Little Ridge Hiking Trail at Little Ridge Park.

Other day use facilities include Lower East Pool -- fishing pier; Upper Overlook -- shelter, playground; Lower Overlook -- picnicking, hiking; Buford Dam Park -- beach, shelter, playground; Van Pugh North -- boat ramp, shelter, playground, beach; Balus Creek -- boat ramp; Mountain View -- boat ramp, picnicking; Lula Park -- boat ramp, hiking trails; Little River -- boat ramp, picnicking; Thompson Bridge -- boat ramp; Thompson Creek -- boat ramp, shelter, hiking; Sardis Creek -- boat ramp, picnicking; Simpon Park -- boat ramp; Robinson -- boat ramp, picnicking; Little Hall -- beach, boat ramp, shelter, playground, hiking; Nix Bridge -- boat ramp, picnicking; Keith's Bridge -- boat ramp, beach, picnicking, playground, hiking trail; Long Hollow -- boat ramp, beach, picnicking, playground; Vann's Tavern -- boat ramp, shelter, hiking; Two Mile -- boat ramp, picnicking; Six Mile Creek -- boat ramp, hiking; Tidwell -- boat ramp; Lanier -- boat ramp, beach, shelter, hiking; West Bank -- boat ramp, shelter, playground, beach, fitness trail.

Several parks around the lake are operated by other government agencies, including city, county and state park systems. The lake's project headquarters includes a visitor center, interpretive programs, picnicking. Lanier Project Manager, Lake Sidney Lanier, P. O. Box 567, Buford, GA 30515-0567. (770) 945-9531.

BALD RIDGE CREEK CAMP

From Cumming, N on SR 400 to exit 16; right on Pilgrim Mill Rd; right on Sinclair Shoals Rd; left on Bald Ridge Rd. 4/1-9.8; 14-day limit. 82 elec/wtr sites (30/50-amp), $30 for 30-amp sites ($15 with federal senior pass), $32 for 50-amp ($16 with senior pass). RV limit in excess of 65 ft; 9 pull-through sites. Tbls, flush toilets, cfga, drkg wtr, showers, dump, beach, playground, coin laundry. Swimming, boating(l), fishing, hiking. (770) 889-1591. NRRS. **GPS: 34.210046, -84.087403**

BOLDING MILL CAMPGROUND

From Cumming, N on SR 400 to exit 17, then NE on SR 306 about 7 mi; continue E on SR 53 (Dawsonville Hwy); left on Old Sardis Rd, then left on Chestatee Rd to campground. 4/11-9/30; 14-day limit. 9 tent sites, $18 ($9 with federal senior pass); 88 elec/wtr sites, $30 with 30-amp elec ($15 with senior pass), $32 with 50-amp ($16 with senior pass). RV limit in excess of 65'. Tbls, flush toilets, cfga, drkg wtr, showers, dump, beach, playground, coin laundry. Boating(ld), fishing, swimming, hiking. (770) 534-6960. NRRS. **GPS: 34.33793, -83.95114**

DUCKETT MILL CAMPGROUND

From Cumming N on SR 400 to exit 17; right on Hwy 306; right on Hwy 53; right on Duckett Mill Rd. 4/1-9/30; 14-day limit. 14 tent sites, $18 ($9 with federal senior pass); 95 wtr/elec sites, $30 for 30-amp, $32 for 50-amp ($15 & $16 with senior pass). Tbls, flush toilets, cfga, drkg wtr, showers, dump, beach, coin laundry. Boating(l), swimming, fishing. (770) 532-9802. NRRS. **GPS: 34.305380, -83.933487**

OLD FEDERAL CAMPGROUND

From I-985N exit 8, left on SR 347 (Friendship Rd); right on McEver Rd; left on Jim Crow Rd (signs). 4/1-9/30; 14-day limit. 7 walk-to primitive tent sites, $18 ($9 with federal senior pass); 12 non-elec tent sites, $22 ($11 with senior pass); 58 elec/wtr sites, $30 for 30-amp elec, $32 for 50-amp elec ($15 & $16 with senior pass). Tbls, flush toilets, cfga, drkg wtr, showers, coin laundry, dump, beach. Boating(l), fishing, swimming. (770) 967-6757. NRRS. **GPS: 34.22222, -83.94944**

SAWNEE CAMPGROUND

From Cumming at jct with SR 400N exit 14, E (left) on Hwy 20; left on Sanders Rd; at lst stop sign, 3.5 mi right on Buford Dam Rd; on left. Typically open 4/1-9/30, but open all winter in 2014-15; 14-day limit. 11 non-elec tent sites, $18 ($9 with federal senior pass); 5 elec tent sites, $30 ($15 with senior pass); 43 elec/wtr sites, $30 for 30-amp elec, $32 for 50-amp elec ($15 & $16 with senior pass). RV limit 40'. Tbls, flush toilets, cfga, drkg wtr, showers, playground, beach, dump, coin laundry. Boating(l), fishing, swimming. (770) 887-0592. NRRS. **GPS: 34.17667, -84.07528**

TOTO CREEK CAMPGROUND

From Cumming, N on SR 400; right on SR 136 (Price Rd); right at stop sign; left on park rd before crossing bridge. About 4/1-9/15; 14-day limit (boat ramp open all year). 10 primitive sites, $22 ($11 with federal senior pass). Campground may be turned into county park. **GPS: 34.394561, -84.984283**

VAN PUGH SOUTH CAMP

From I-985 exit 8, left on Hwy 347/Friendship Rd; right on McEver Rd; left on Gaines Ferry Rd, follow signs. About 4/1-9/8; 14-day limit. 18 non-elec sites, $22 ($11 with federal senior pass); 37 elec/wtr sites, $30 for 30-amp, $32 for 50-amp ($15 & $16 with senior pass). Tbls, flush toilets, showers, cfga, drkg wtr, coin laundry. Boating(l), fishing. 770-967-6375. NRRS. **GPS: 34.182856, -83.987603**

6

J. STROM THURMOND LAKE
GPS: 33.69, -82.35

A 71,100-acre lake with 1,200 miles of shoreline adjacent to Clarks Hill and NW of Augusta on the SC state line (US 221 crosses top of dam). The lake extends 39.4 miles up the Savannah River, 29 miles up the Little river and 6.5 miles up the Broad River -- all in Georgia -- as well as 17 miles up the Little River in South Carolina. Exhibits on display daily in visitor center at 510 Clarks Hill Hwy, Clarks Hill, SC (864-333-1147); tours of dam just S of visitor center. Campground checkout time 2 p.m. Alcoholic beverages prohibited. $4 day use fees charged, $3 boat ramps. In addition to developed day use areas, the Corps manages 29 access areas with boat ramps.

Georgia day use facilities: Amity (park open 5/1-9/1, boat ramp all year) -- toilets, drinking water, picnicking, 3 shelters ($10 & $75), 7 beaches, playgrounds, baseball field, dock, fishing pier; Gill Point -- boat ramp open, but day use closed in 2014 (check current status before arrival); Lake Springs -- partial closure (check current status before arrival); Deer Run & boat ramp open all year) -- dock, fish cleaning station, fishing pier, toilets, 4 shelters ($75 & $125), 13 beaches, volleyball courts, horseshoe pits, biking/hiking trails; West Dam (park open 5/1-9/1, boat ramp all year) -- entry to 9-mile Bartram Trail, toilets, 2 playgrounds, shelter $125, 10 small shelters $10, 7 beaches; Chamberlain Ferry -- boat ramp; Double Branches -- boat ramp; Leathersville - boat ramp; Keg Creek -- boat ramp, dock; Murray Creek -- boat ramp; Morrahs -- boat ramp, dock; Calouse Falls -- boat ramp. See SC section for day use in that state.

Management of five Thurmond campgrounds was scheduled to be turned over to the non-profit Lake Thurmond Campgrounds agency for five years, but in 2013 that agreement was terminated because the Corps learned it did not have authority to make it. The agreement included Petersburg, Ridge Road, Raysville and Winfield Campgrounds in Georgia and Modoc Campground in South Carolina. The Corps announced plans to close Raysville, Broad River, Clay Hill and Hesters Ferry Campgrounds in Georgia, as well as Leroys Ferry and Mt. Carmel Campgrounds in South Carolina.

Leroys Ferry and Mt. Carmel were closed in 2014, but in early 2015, the Corps was negotiating with McCormick County in South Carolina for lease of the two campgrounds.

Raysville in Georgia was closed in 2014 but was leased to McDuffie County for operation during 2015. Lincoln County, Georgia, agreed to 5-year leases and is now managing the Broad River, Clay Hill and Hesters Ferry Campgrounds.

To check current status of any parks, contact the lake's resource manager, J. Strom Thurmond Lake, Route 1, Box 12, Clarks Hill, SC 29821-9701. (864) 333-1100/(800) 533-3478. See SC listing.

BIG HART CAMPGROUND

From Thomson, 3 mi N on US 78 past jct with SR 43; 4 mi E (right) on Russell Landing Rd (signs); at confluence of Big Creek & Hart Creek on W end of lake. About 4/1-9/30; 14-day limit. 31 elec/wtr sites (30/50-amp), $24 base, $26 at premium locations ($12 & $13 with federal senior pass). RV limit 60'. 7-site 50-amp elec/wtr group camping area with picnic shelter & showers, $182. Group picnic shelter, $75. Tbls, flush toilets, cfga, drkg wtr, showers, dump, playground, beach, fish cleaning stations, pay phone. Boating(ld), fishing, fishing pier, swimming. (706) 595-8613. NRRS. **GPS: 33.61458, -82.50875**

BUSSEY POINT CAMPGROUND

From Lincolnton, S on SR 47 to SR 220 NE; exit S at Kenna on gravel rd; at entrance to Bussey Point Wilderness Recreation Area, a peninsula on the lake. All year; 14-day limit. 14 primitive equestrian sites plus 6 hike/bike/ride/boat-in sites along equestrian trail, $6 self-registration. Pit toilets, tbls, cfga, drkg wtr. 12.5-mi trail for hiking, biking, horseback riding. Picnic shelter. No reservations. Note: This campground is scheduled for $25,000 in improvements, primarily for equestrian camping. **GPS: 33.703900, -82.26000**

PETERSBURG CAMPGROUND

From Pollards Corner, 2 mi NE on US 221, then E on Petersburg Rd to lakeshore. All year at 27 sites; sites 28-93 open about 3/1-11/30; 14-day limit. 8 non-elec sites, $18 ($9 with federal senior pass); 85 elec/wtr sites (most 50-amp), $24 ($12 with senior pass), $26 for 50-amp elec/wtr ($13 with senior pass). RV limit 45'; 54 pull-through. Tbls, pit & flush toilets, cfga, drkg wtr, dump, playground, showers, beach, coin laundry, fish cleaning stations, picnic shelters($), pay phone. Boating(ld), fishing dock, hiking trail, swimming. (706) 541-9464. NRRS. **GPS: 33.661595, -82.259338**

RIDGE ROAD CAMPGROUND

From Highway 221 at Pollards Corner, 4 mi W on SR 47 toward Lincolnton, then 4 mi E on Ridge Rd to lake. 4/1-9/30; 14-day limit. 6 non-elec sites, $18 ($9 with federal senior pass); 63 elec/wtr 50-amp sites, $24 ($12 with senior pass); double sites up to $52. RV limit 50'; 27 pull-through sites. Flush toilets, tbls, drkg wtr, showers, dump, beach, playground, fish cleaning stations, pay phone. Boating(ld), fishing, hiking, waterskiing. (706) 541-0282. NRRS. **GPS: 33.677412, -82.263707**

WINFIELD CAMPGROUND

From Hwy 221 at Pollards Corner, 4 mi W on Hwy 150; 5 mi N on Winfield Rd; on Little River section of lake near Mistletoe State Park. 4/1-9/30; 14-day limit. 80 elec/wtr sites (50-amp), $26 ($13 with federal senior pass). RV limit 65'; 35 pull-through sites. Tbls, flush toilets, cfga, drkg wtr, dump, playground, beach, pay phone. Boating(l), fishing, swimming, waterskiing. (706) 541-0147. NRRS. **GPS: 33.647975, -82.415164**

⑦ WALTER F. GEORGE AND GEORGE W. ANDREWS LAKES
GPS: 31.6267, -85.0633

Together, these lakes make up 45,000 acres of impoundment on the Chattahoochee River at the Alabama-Georgia state line, adjacent to Ft. Gaines, GA, W of Albany, GA, and N of Dothan, AL. Sometimes referred to as Lake Eufaula, the lakes extend 85 miles and have 640 miles of shoreline. Eight county and municipal parks are on the lakes. Campground checkout time 3 p.m. Off-road vehicles prohibited. For picnic shelter reservations, call 229-768-2516. Georgia day use facilities at Rood Creek (boat ramp, picnicking, drinking water) and the resource site office (drinking water, fishing pier). See Alabama section for other facilities. Day use fees charged for beaches, boat launches. Visitor center, historic & cultural site, interpretive programs. Resource Site Manager, Walter F. George Lake, route. 1, Box 176, Ft. Gaines, GA 31751-9722. (229) 768-2516. See AL listings.

COTTON HILL CAMPGROUND

From Ft. Gaines, 7 mi N on SR 39, then W following signs. All year; 14-day limit. 10 tent sites, $20 ($10 with federal senior pass); 91 full-hookup sites, $24 ($12 with senior pass). RV limit 40'; 10 pull-through sites. Tbls, flush toilets, cfga, drkg wtr, showers, dump, picnic shelter, fish cleaning stations, 2 playgrounds, pay phones, beach. Boating(ld), fishing, swimming, hiking, waterskiing. (229) 768-3061. NRRS. **GPS: 31.675462, -85.060240**

ROOD CREEK CAMPGROUND

From Georgetown at jct with US 27, 9.5 mi N on SR 39, across Rood Creek about 1 mi, then left (SW) on Rood Creek Landing Rd. 3/1-10/31; 14-day limit. Free primitive, undesignated sites. Fire rings, lantern posts, pit toilets, drkg wtr. Boat landing(ld), fishing. **GPS: 32.025042, -85.037237**

⑧ WEST POINT LAKE
GPS: 32.9183, -85.1883

This 25,900-acre lake is 35 miles along the Chattahoochee River, located SW of Atlanta and I-85 on the Alabama/Georgia state lone near West Point, Georgia. It has 525 miles of shoreline. Four county and municipal parks are on the lake in addition to six Corps-operated campgrounds. Power house visitor facility and dam tours, interpretive programs. Restrooms at launch areas 3/7. Half Moon Park picnic area closed permanently by shrinking budget.

Day use facilities: Anderson Park -- picnicking, group shelter, playground; Clark Park -- boat ramp, picnicking; Eagle View Park -- picnicking, group shelter ($125), toilets, playground, drinking water; East Cook Recreation Area -- boat ramp, picnicking, group shelter ($100), ball field, basketball court, tennis court, horseshoe pits, playground, beach ($4), hiking/nature trail; Georgia Park -- boat ramp; Hardley Creek Park -- picnicking, group shelter ($125), playground, walking trail, 2 fishing piers, pond, toilets, ball field, horseshoe pits, basketball court, tennis court; Horace King Park -- boat ramp, picnicking, group shelter ($75); Long Cane Park -- boat ramp, picnicking, group shelter, hiking/nature trail; McGee Bridge Park, boat ramp, picnicking, 2 group shelters ($125); Rocky Point Recreation Area -- boat ramp, picnicking, group shelter, playground, beach, hiking/nature trail, handicap trail, horseshoe pits, drinking water, toilets, fishing pier; Sunny Point Park -- boat ramp, picnicking, group shelter, trails; Veasey Creek Park -- boat ramp, group shelter ($75), toilets, drinking water; Whitewater Park -- boat ramp; Yellowjacket Recreation Area -- boat ramp, picnicking, playground, beach ($4), group shelter ($75). Resource Manager, West Point Lake, 500 Resource Managers Drive, West Point, GA 31833-9517. (706) 645-2937.

AMITY CAMPGROUND

From Lanett in Alabama, 7 mi N on CR 212; 0.5 mi E on CR 393, then N following signs to campground in Georgia at W shore of West Point Lake. Open Thurs-Sun during 4/23-9/9, plus MD & LD; 14-day limit. 3 tent sites, $16 ($8 with federal senior pass); 93 elec/wtr sites, but sites 1-22 closed; $24 base, $28 at premium locations ($12 & $14 with senior pass). Tbls, flush toilets, cfga, drkg wtr, showers, coin laundry, dump, playground, amphitheater. Interpretive trails, boating(l), fishing, waterskiing, basketball, tennis, hiking. (334) 499-2404. NRRS during 4/23-9/6. **GPS: 32.978910, -85.2205154**

HOLIDAY CAMPGROUND

From LaGrange, 7 mi W on SR 109, following signs; 2.3 mi S on Thompson Rd. About 2/22-9/29; 14-day limit. 37 tent sites & 6 non-elec RV/tent sites, $16 ($8 with federal senior pass); 92 elec/wtr sites, $24 ($12 with senior pass). Three group camping areas (primitive sites 113-143 closed for 2015) -- one with 10 primitive tent sites, $16; one with 8 elec RV/tent sites, $24, and the third with 14 RV sites & 5 tent sites, $160-$170. RV limit 65'. Tbls, flush toilets, showers, cfga, drkg wtr, dump, beach, playground, coin laundry. Boating(l), fishing, ball fields, basketball, tennis, swimming, waterskiing, hiking. (706) 884-6818. NRRS. **GPS: 33.015429, -85.188932**

INDIAN SPRINGS GROUP CAMP

From La Grange, 8 mi W on SR 109 (Roanoke Rd); N side near Rock Mills Rd. Contact the host at Whitetail campground at (706) 884-8972 for status. All year; 14-day limit. Four group tent camping areas, $50-$110. Tbls, flush toilets, cfga, drkg wtr, beach. Swimming, fishing, boating. NOTE: Campground was closed in 2010, still closed in 2015. **GPS: 33.040139, -85.180065**

RINGER ACCESS CAMPGROUND

From LaGrange, 8.7 mi N on US 27, then W
on Ringer Access Rd. All year; 14-day limit. 37
free primitive sites. 20-ft RV limit. Toilets, cfga,
no drkg wtr. Nature trail, boating(l), fishing.
Note: This campground was closed in 2013 by
budget cuts, still closed in 2015; check current
status with lake office before arriving.
GPS: 33.151125, -85.046928

R. SHAEFER HEARD CAMP

From West Point, 4 mi N on US 29 to dam
road; left at signs; on S shore of lake. Open
3/16-10/25; 14-day limit. 117 elec/wtr sites,
$24 ($12 with federal senior pass); 10 sites
with decks, 7 pull-through. RV limit in
excess of 65 ft. Tbls, flush toilets, cfga, drkg
wtr, showers, dump, coin laundry, beach,
amphitheater. Boating(l), fishing, hiking trails,
swimming, waterskiing, tennis. 706-645-2404.
NRRS. **GPS: 32.928616, -85.161080**

WHITETAIL RIDGE CAMP

From LaGrange, 7 mi W on SR 109; 0.8 mi S
on Thompson Rd; on left. 3/6-11/29; 14-day
limit. 58 elec/wtr sites, $24 ($12 with federal
senior pass); 4 pull-through. Double sites $48.
RV limit in excess of 65'. Tbls, flush toilets,
cfga, drkg wtr, dump, coin laundry, beach,
showers. Boating(l), fishing, hiking trails,
swimming, waterskiing. (706) 884-8972.
NRRS. **GPS: 33.021583, -85.183203**

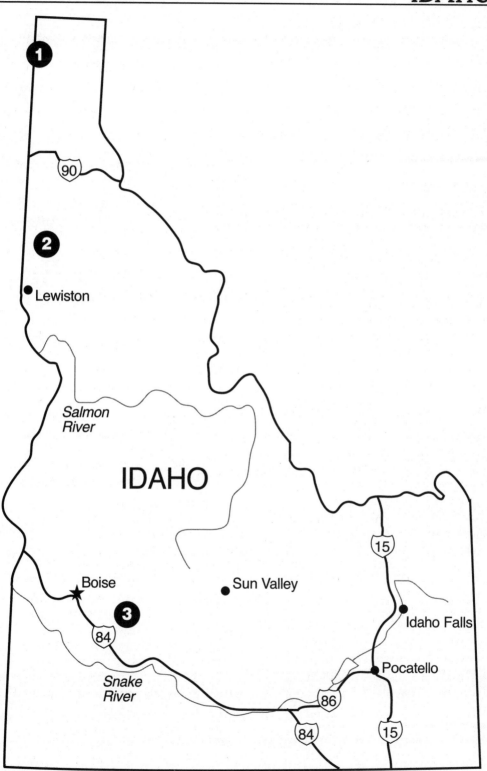

IDAHO

STATE INFORMATION:

CAPITAL: Boise
NICKNAME: Gem State
STATEHOOD: 1890 - 43rd State
FLOWER: Mock Orange
TREE: Western White Pine
BIRD: Mountain Bluebird

STATE TIDBITS:

• Hell's Canyon is the deepest gorge in America.

• Downey's first mercantile store, the W. A. Hyde Co., was built in 1894.

• Anderson Dam is known for its blue-ribbon fly-fishing.

WWW.VISITIDAHO.ORG

Idaho Division of Tourism Development, 700 West State St, PO Box 83720, Boise, ID 83720-0093; 208-334-0093; 800/VISIT-ID.

IDAHO LAKES

To find campgrounds operated by the U.S. Army Corps of Engineers, match the lake's numbers on the preceding map page with numbered lake entries on the following pages. Campgrounds are listed alphabetically under the appropriate lakes. The following Idaho impoundments have Corps of Engineers campgrounds.

Lake Pend Oreille, Albeni Falls Dam. In the Panhandle of NW Idaho across from Newport, Washington, and S of US 2, 4 miles W of Priest River. It is one of the largest and deepest natural lakes in the wetern U.S.

Dworshak Reservoir. A 54-mile lake located 5 miles NE of Orofino on SR 7, E of Lewiston and N of US 12 in northwestern Idaho on the North Fork of the Clearwater River. Its fish hatchery is the largest steelhead trout hatchery in the world.

Lucky Peak Lake. A Located about 10 miles SE of Boise, this lake is in the foothills of souhtwestern Idaho on the Boise River.

❶
ALBENI FALLS DAM LAKE PEND OREILLE
GPS: 48.25, -116.54

Located in Panhandle of NW Idaho across from Newport, Washington, and S of US 2, 4 miles W of Priest River. 140-plus campsites in four campgrounds. Fee charged for second vehicle overnight. No unlicensed vehicles permitted. 25-cent fee for showers. Checkout time 2 p.m. Visitor center (2 miles E of the Washington border on US 2) -- historic & cultural site, interpretive programs, dam tours, picnics; open daily (208-437-4617).

Other recreation areas: Johnson Creek Recreation, leased to State of Idaho for free primitive camping (3-day limit) & boat launch (pit toilet, no drkg wtr); Clark Creek Driftyard, licensed to state with boat ramp, portable toilet, free 3-day primitive camping, no drkg wtr; Vista Recreation Area, visitor center, movie theater, picnicking, amphitheater, restrooms; Morton Slough Access Area, leased to state for boat ramp (pit toilets, no drinking water); Trestle Creek Recreation Area, picnicking, swimming, boat ramp, pit toilet. For recorded campground status, call (208) 437-5517. Resource Manager, Albeni Falls Project, 2576 E Highway 2, Oldtown, ID 83822-9243. (208) 437-3133.

IDAHO

ALBENI COVE CAMPGROUND

From Newport, SE on SR 41; 3 mi E (left) on Fourth St (part gravel); stay on the dirt road, veering left at the forks; directly across from dam. Rough access, not suitable for large RVs. 5/9-9/13; 14-day limit. 5 walk-to tent sites & 10 gravel non-elec RV/tent sites, $20 ($10 with senior pass). Sites up to 40 ft. Tbls, flush toilets, cfga, drkg wtr, coin showers, coin laundry, pay phone, beach, no dump. Canoeing, birdwatching, interpretive programs, boating(ld), fishing, swimming, waterskiing, kayaking. Firewood($). Visitor center. NRRS. **GPS: 48.175974, -116.999878**

PRIEST RIVER RECREATION AREA

From Priest River at jct with SR 57, 1 mi E on US 2; turn right; at confluence of Priest & Pend Oreille Rivers. 5/9-9/13; 14-day limit. 20 non-elec RV sites (8 pull-through), $20 ($10 with federal senior pass); 5 bike-in tent sites, $5 ($2.50 with senior pass). 60-ft RV limit. Tbls, flush toilets, coin showers, cfga, drkg wtr, dump, shelter ($50), amphitheater, beach, playground, dishwashing sinks. Picnicking open to non-campers (no day use fee). Boating(l), fishing, swimming, ball field, weekend campfire programs. Also known as Mudhole Campground. 208-437-3133. NRRS. **GPS: 48.178650, -116.890132**

RILEY CREEK RECREATION AREA

From Priest River Park, 9 mi E on US 2 to LaClede; 1 mi S on Riley Creek Rd. 5/9-9/27; 14-day limit. 67 gravel sites with elec/wtr, $25 ($12.50 with federal senior pass). 40-ft RV limit. Tbls, flush toilets, cfga, drkg wtr, coin showers, coin laundry, beach, playground, dump, amphitheater, dishwashing sinks, pay phone. Biking, boating(ld), hiking, horseshoe pits, sand volleyball, hiking trail, swimming, waterskiing, birdwatching, weekend campfire programs, canoeing. No day use fees. Two picnic shelters, $50 (call 208-437-3133). NRRS. **GPS: 48.159874, -116.770838**

SPRINGY POINT RECREATION AREA

From Sandpoint at jct with US 2, S on US 95 across long bridge; 3 mi W on Lakeshore Dr, N of rd. 5/9-9/27; 14-day limit. 37 gravel non-elec sites, including 1 walk-in tent site & 7 pull-through RV sites, $20 ($10 with federal senior pass). Coin showers, pay phone, tbls, flush toilets, cfga, drkg wtr, showers, dump, beach, dishwashing sinks. Boating(ld), fishing, swimming, weekend campfire programs. NRRS. **GPS: 48.235715, -116.586635**

②

DWORSHAK RESERVOIR
GPS: 46.51. -116.2961

A 54-mile lake located 5 miles NE of Orofino on SR 7 E of Lewiston & N of US 12 in NW Idaho. The dam and reservoir were completed on the North Fork of the Clearwater River in 1973. Noted for Kokanee salmon, rainbow trout and smallmouth bass. Guided group tours, audio-visual programs, displays, visitor center, fish hatchery.

Day use facilities include Big Eddy Recreation Area -- boat ramp, marina, picnicking, group shelter, playground, beach, hiking trail, fish cleaning station; Bruce's Eddy Recreation Area -- boat ramp, flush toilets, hiking trails, pay phone; Dam Viewpoint -- picnicking, flush toilets, shelters; Merrys Bay -- picnicking, hiking trails, toilets; Cold Springs Trail -- hiking. For reservoir information call 1-800-321-3198. Resource Manager, P. O. Box 48, Ahsahka, ID 83520-0048. (208) 476-1255/1261/ 1-800-321-3198.

CANYON CREEK CAMPGROUND

From Orofino, 11 mi NE off Elk River, Wells Bench & Eureka Ridge Rds, following signs. Steep, winding gravel rd. 17 free primitive RV/tent sites. 22-ft RV limit. Open 4/1 through fall, weather permitting; 14-day limit. Pit toilets, tbls, cfga, no drkg wtr or trash service. Boating(ld), fishing, hiking trail. **GPS: 46.553563, -116.236103**

COLD SPRINGS
GROUP CAMPGROUND

On S shore of lake across from Dent Acres boat ramp. Boat-in or hike-in access only (on W end of Cold Springs Trail). Free primitive tent camping area. Open 4/1 through fall, weather permitting; 14-day limit. Fire pits, cfga, tbls, pit toilets, no drkg wtr. Boating, hiking. **GPS: 46.613838, -116.222563**

DAM VIEW CAMPGROUND

From Orofino, 5 mi W on SR 7 to Dworshak entrance, follow signs 2 mi; turn on Big Eddy Rd. Open 4/1-11/30; 14-day limit. Free primitive sites. Chemical toilet, fire pits, tbls, drkg wtr. **GPS: 46.516070, -116.505153**

DENT ACRES CAMPGROUND

From Orofino, 20 mi NE on Elk River Rd via Wells Bench Rd (signs). 4/1-10/15; 14-day limit. 49 pull-through elec/wtr sites (50-amp), $18 during peak season of 5/20-9/7 ($9 with federal senior pass); $10 during 4/1-5/19 & 9/8-12/15 ($5 with senior pass). RV limit 35 ft. Tbls, flush toilets, cfga, drkg wtr, showers, dump, playground, beach, fish cleaning station, marine dump station, picnic shelter($25). Boating(ld), fishing, swimming, hiking trails. 208-476-9029. NRRS during 5/20-9/7. **GPS: 46.625922, -116.218143**

DENT ACRES
GROUP CAMPGROUND

From Orofino, 18 mi NE on Elk River Rd via Wells Bench Rd (2 mi from Dent Acres campground). MD-LD. 3-acre tent camping area for up to 200 people and 48 vehicles, $50; limited RV elec hookups at shelter. Pit toilets, tbls, cfga, drkg wtr. Hiking trails. Picnic shelter with elec. NRRS.

GRANDAD CREEK
RECREATION AREA

From Orofino, W on Grangemont Rd to jct with SR 11; left on SR 11 for 7.5 mi; at Headquarters, left (N) about 9 mi on FR 249, then left on Grandad Bridge Rd for 16 mi to site. 10 free primitive sites. Pit toilets, tbls, cfga, no drkg wtr. Open spring through fall, subject to weather conditions. Boating(ld), fishing.

LITTLE MEADOW CREEK

From Orofino, W on Grangemont Rd to jct with SR 11; left on SR 11 for 7.5 mi; at Headquarters, left (N) about 1.5 mi, then left on Silver Creek Rd for 20 mi to site. 6 free primitive sites. Tbls, cfga, pit toilet, no drkg wtr. Spring through fall, weather permitting. Boating, fishing.

MINI CAMPS CAMPGROUNDS

Accessible by boat-in or hiking trail, marked by signs, at various locations around the lake. Group camping with maps available. 121 free primitive tent sites at 72 locations. Open spring through fall. Pit toilets, tbls, cfga, no drkg wtr. Hiking, fishing, boating.

❸
LUCKY PEAK LAKE
GPS: 43.529074, -116.050129

About 10 miles SE of Boise, most of this lake is within Boise National Forest. Camping is available at boat-in areas and at Macks Creek Park. Day use sites include Lucky Peak Dam Recreation Area -- boat ramp ($3), picnicking, group shelter, playground, disc golf; Mores Creek -- picnicking; Robie Creek -- picnicking, playground, boat ramp, swimming area. Resource Manager, 9723 East Hwy 21, Boise, ID 83716; 208-343-0671.

BOAT-IN CAMPING

Working jointly with Ada County Parks & Recreation, which provides dock spaces, the Corps provides more than 80 free primitive boat-in tent camping/picnic sites. Tbls, cfga, shelters, no drkg wtr or trash service. All year; 3-day limit.

MACKS CREEK PARK

From Boise, 18 mi SE on SR 21; 4.5 mi E
on Arrowrock Dam Rd; at Boise River arm
of Lucky Peak Lake. 15 free primitive sites,
$10 for reserved sites ($20 double sites).
Open Easter weekend trough Thanksgiving
weekend; 3-day limit. 45-ft RV limit. Tbls, pit
toilets, cfga, drkg wtr, beach, amphitheater.
Boating(ld), fishing, swimming. NRRS 5/15-
9/15. **GPS: 43.610280, -115.938060**

Rockford

94

39

90

Chicago

88

80

4

74

Peoria

57

ILLINOIS

Bloomington

Champaign

Illinois
River

Springfield

72

36

55

3

Kaskaskia
River

70

1

East
St. Louis

Wabash
River

2

5

64

Ohio
River

57

STATE INFORMATION:

CAPITAL: Springfield
NICKNAME: Prairie State
STATEHOOD: 1818 - 21st State
FLOWER: Purple Violet
TREE: White Oak
BIRD: Cardinal

IL

STATE TIDBITS:

• The world's first Skyscraper was built in Chicago, 1885.

• Des Plaines is home to the first McDonald's.

• Dixon is the boyhood home of President Ronald Reagan.

WWW.ENJOYILLINOIS.COM

Toll-free number for travel information:
1-800-406-6418

ILLINOIS LAKES

To find campgrounds operated by the U.S. Army Corps of Engineers, match the lake's numbers on the preceding map page with numbered lake entries on the following pages. Campgrounds are listed alphabetically under the appropriate lakes. The following Illinois impoundments have Corps of Engineers campgrounds.

Carlyle Lake. This 26,000-acre lake is 50 miles E of St. Louis and N of Carlyle on US 50.

Kaskaskia Lock & Dam 7. Built for flood control of the Kaskaskia River, the lock and dam are about three-fourths mile N of the confluence of the Kaskaskia and Mississippi Rivers. Its pool extends 36 miles upstream to Fayetteville.

Lake Shelbyville. An 11,100-acre lake NE of Shelbyville, 31 miles S of Decatur and SW of I-57 from Matoon.

Mississippi River Public Use Areas.
Mississippi River Visitor Center is N of SR 92 between I-74 and US 67 on Rock Island Arsenal, an island just N of Rodman Avenue near Government Bridge. There, information is available about the river's campgrounds and recreation areas.

Rend Lake. An 18,900-acre lake located N of Benton on SR 14 W of I-57 in south-central Illinois.

❶
CARLYLE LAKE
GPS: 37.7167, -89.0183

A 26,000-acre lake 50 miles E of St. Louis and N of Carlyle on US 50. Dam East Lakeview parking lot has a handicap fishing pier. All comfort stations, buildings and camping areas provide handicap facilities. Dam tours, seaplane usage, visitor center, interpretive programs, historic & cultural sites. Campground checkout time 4 p.m.

Swimming at four beaches: Dam West, Keyesport, Coles Creek and McNair. Boat ramp fees are $3 (or $30 annually) at Keyesport, Dam West, Coles Creek, Boulder & Dam East; other ramps are free. 13 picnic shelters are $30 with reservation, free if not reserved. Visitor center open daily during 5/30-9/5, weekends in April, May & Sept; exhibits, aquarium. Keyesport Recreation Area equipped with picnic shelter, boat ramp, fishing pier, fish cleaning station, playground, beach, multi-use trails. Bike trail map available at lake office or visitor center.

For daily lake information, call (618) 594-4637. Project Manager, Carlyle Lake, 801 Lake Rd., Carlyle, IL 62231-9703. (618) 594-2484/5253.

BOULDER RECREATION AREA

From Carlyle, 8 mi E on US 50; 5 mi N on Boulder-Ferrin Rd (CR 3); 1 mi E on CR 1850N, becoming Boulder Marina Rd; at E shore of lake. About 4/15-10/15; 14-day limit. 84 sites with elec, $16 base ($8 with federal senior pass); full hookups $24 ($12 with federal senior pass); double sites $32 ($16 with federal senior pass). RV limit in excess of 65 ft. Tbls, flush toilets, cfga, drkg wtr, showers, dump, coin laundry, playground, amphitheater, picnic shelter, fish cleaning stations. Boating(l), fishing, swimming. Boat rentals nearby. (618) 594-5253. NRRS. **GPS: 38.694847, -89.235892**

COLES CREEK RECREATION AREA

From Carlyle, 8 mi E on US 50; 3.5 mi N (sign) on Boulder Rd; look for signs & turn left on CR 1700N following it around the curve; at E shore of lake. 5/1-9/30; 14-day limit. 119 sites with elec, $16 ($8 with federal senior pass); full hookups $24 ($12 with federal senior pass); double sites $32 ($16 with federal senior pass); 2 group camping areas, $150 & $250. Tbls, flush toilets, cfga, drkg wtr, dump, showers, playground, beach, coin laundry, fish cleaning station, amphitheater. Picnic shelter $30 reserved. RV limit in excess of 65'. Boating(ld), fishing, swimming, basketball, waterskiing. 618) 226-3211. NRRS. **GPS: 38.656996, -89.260451**

DAM EAST SPILLWAY RECREATION AREA

1 mi N of Carlyle below dam on E side of river. All year; 14-day limit. $14 at elec sites ($7 with federal senior pass). Flush toilets, tbls, cfga, drkg wtr, picnic shelter. Boating, fishing, waterskiing. No reservations. **GPS: 38.617742, -89.353604**

DAM WEST RECREATION AREA

From Carlyle, 1 mi N on CR 1800E; 0.5 mi E on William Rd, then N on Lake Rd & right into campground; at S shore of lake. 4/1-10/30; 14-day limit. 109 sites with elec, $18 at 30-amp elec sites, $20 at 50-amp elec; $22 at 50-amp elec/wtr premium sites; $26 full hookups ($9, $10, $11 & $13 with federal senior pass). Double sites $36 ($52 with full hookups). RV limit in excess of 65 ft. Tbls, flush toilets, cfga, drkg wtr, showers, dump, coin laundry, beach, playground, fish cleaning station, amphitheater, pay phone, picnic shelters $30 reserved. Boating, fishing, hiking trail, swimming, tennis, basketball, volleyball, waterskiing. Boat rentals nearby. 618-594-4410. NRRS. **GPS: 38.631112, -89.360325**

LOTUS GROUP CAMPGROUND

Within the Coles Creek Recreation Area at E shore of lake. 5/1-9/30; 14-day limit. Group camping area for up to 80 people & 25 vehicles with 10 mini shelters, 4 bunk beds in each, and a sheltered dining area that seats 30 people, $75-$125. Tbls, flush toilets, cfga, drkg wtr, showers, dump, fish cleaning station, beach. Boating(l), fishing, swimming, waterskiing. Reservations required. NRRS. Info, 618-594-5253.

MCNAIR CAMPGROUND

2 mi W of Carlyle on US 50 to Dam East entrance rd, then 1 mi N to campground. 5/1-10/31; 14-day limit. 44 sites, $14 at non-elec sites if space not reserved by groups, $18 for elec sites ($5 & $8 with federal senior pass). Also 4 group camping areas with elec & picnic shelters, $50-$175. Tbls, flush toilets, cfga, drkg wtr, showers, dump, playground, beach, fish cleaning station. Hiking, boating(ld), fishing, swimming, waterskiing. When not reserved, single sites are available. NRRS. **GPS: 38.630615, -89.29248**

❷
KASKASKIA JERRY F. COSTELLO LOCK & DAM
KASKASKIA RIVER PROJECT
GPS: 37.59011, -8956817

Built for flood control of the Kaskaskia River, the lock and dam are about 3/4 mile N of the confluence of the Kaskaskia & the Mississippi Rivers. Its pool extends 36 miles upstream to Fayetteville. The Corps operates Kaskaskia Dam Lock & Dam Recreation Area SE of Modoc. Campsites also are available at the state's Kaskaskia River Fish & Wildlife Area and at the Kaskaskia River Marina & Campground in New Athens (no information available). The Lock & Dam Recreation Area has two boat ramps -- one on the Kaskaskia River, one on the Mississippi. Public ramps also are in Fayetteville, New Athens, Baldwin and Evansville. A day use area at the dam's upper ramp provides toilets, tables and a picnic shelter ($30, or free if not reserved). A visitor center is open daily; free tours provided. For information, contact project rangers at 618-284-7160.

KASKASKIA LOCK & DAM RECREATION AREA

About 4 mi S of Modoc on CR 7 (Bluff Rd), then 2.4 mi S on Lock & Dam Rd; E onto campground on river's W shore (about 0.5 mi N of confluence of Kaskaskia River with Mississippi River). $10 at 15 elec 30/50-amp sites. All year; 14-day limit. Tbls, toilets, cfga, drkg wtr. Boating(l), hiking, fishing. Group shelter, $30 or free if not reserved.
GPS: 37.980769, -89.944972

❸
LAKE SHELBYVILLE
GPS: 39.41, -88.7767

An 11,100-acre lake NE of Shelbyville, 31 miles S of Decatur and SW of I-57 from Matoon. Visitor center at Dam East Recreation Area) has interpretive audiovisual programs and exhibits, covered observation platform, outdoor classroom, butterfly house and garden. Dam tours on weekends from Memorial Day weekend through Labor Day; they start at the visitor center at 3 p.m. Saturday and 11 a.m. Sunday. Equestrian trail nearby. Checkout time 4 p.m. Unreserved picnic shelters are free. $3 boat launch fees (or $30 annually) at eight ramps. Campfire programs May-August. Weekend nature hikes at Coon Creek Trail. Swimming beaches $4 per vehicle, $1 person. Non-Corps camping at Eagle Creek State Park, Wolf Creek State Park & Sullivan Marina.

Day use facilities: Camp Campbell Environmental Study Area -- group picnic shelter, multi-use trails; Dam East Park -- picnicking, shelter ($30), playground; Dam West Park -- boat ramp, picnic shelter ($30), playground, beach, trails, fish cleaning station; Eagle Cove Road -- hiking trail; Lithia Springs Chautauqua -- picnicking; Okaw Bluff -- hiking trail; Spillway Area -- picnic shelter ($30), playground; Whitley Creek Park -- boat ramp, picnicking, fish cleaning station; Dam West Beach -- shelter ($30), beach; Wilborn Creek -- beach. Operations Manager, Lake Shelbyville, RR #4, Box 128B, Shelbyville, IL 62565-9804. (217) 774-3951/3313.

COON CREEK RECREATION AREA

From Shelbyville, 4.5 mi N on SR 128; 0.9 mi E on CR 1750N; left (N) for 0.35 mi on CR 1900E, then right (E) for 1.75 mi on CR 2075E; right (S) for 1.7 mi to campground. S; 0.2 mi W on CR 1900; 1.7 mi S on CR 2075; on W side of lake. About 4/7-10/12; 14-day limit. $18 at 12 tent sites with elec & 30 or 50-amp elec RV sites ($9 with federal senior pass); $24 at 8 full-hookup 50-amp sites; 13 double sites $48. 197 elec sites; RV limit in excess of 65 ft; 30 pull-through. 1 RV & 3-4 tents per site; 2 RVs & 6-8 tents at double sites. Tbls, flush toilets, cfga, drkg wtr, showers, dump, coin laundry, beach, playground, fish cleaning station, amphitheater, phone. Boating(ld), fishing, hiking trails, swimming, volleyball, horseshoe pits, nature trail, basketball. Non-campers $3 for boat ramp. (217) 774-3951. NRRS. Note: Reservation service considers campground full when its site allotment is gone, but first-come sites may be available. **GPS: 39.453211, -88.757944**

F.W. "BO" WOOD CAMPGROUND

From Sullivan, 2.6 mi S on SR 32; 0.5 mi W at sign. About 4/6-10/25, with sites 114-141 open into December, weather permitting; 14-day limit. 4 elec tent sites & 50-amp elec RV sites $18 ($9 with federal senior pass); $20 at 50-amp elec/wtr sites ($10 with senior pass); $24 for 38 full-hookup 50-amp sites ($12 with senior pass); double sites $40. 138 elec sites; RV limit in excess of 65'. 1 RV & 3-4 tents per site; 2 RVs & 6-8 tents at double sites. Tbls, flush toilets, cfga, drkg wtr, showers, dump, coin laundry, playground, picnic shelter ($30), amphitheater, fish cleaning station, pay phone. Non-campers pay $3 for boat ramp. NRRS. Note: Reservation service considers campground full when its site allotment is gone, but first-come sites may be available. **GPS: 39.553477, -88.612043**

LITHIA SPRINGS CAMPGROUND

From Shelbyville, 3.2 mi E on SR 16; 2.1 mi N on CR 2200E; 1.4 mi W on CR 1500N; on E side of lake. About 4/15-10/25; 14-day limit. 30-amp & 50-amp elec sites, $18 ($9 with federal senior pass); $24 at 8 full-hookup 50-amp sites ($12 with senior pass); 6 double sites $36. 112 elec sites; RV limit in excess of 65 ft; 4 pull-through. 1 RV & 3-4 tents per site; 2 RVs & 6-8 tents at double sites. Tbls, flush toilets, cfga, drkg wtr, dump, coin laundry, showers, playground, beach, picnic shelter ($30), amphitheater, fish cleaning station, pay phone. Boating(ld), fishing, swimming, horseshoe pits. Non-campers pay $3 for boat ramp. NRRS. Note: Reservation service considers campground full when its site allotment is gone, but first-come sites may be available. **GPS: 39.434478, -88.762525**

LONE POINT CAMPGROUND

From Shelbyville, 4.5 mi N on SR 128; right (E) for 0.9 mi on CR 1750N; left for 0.35 mi on CR 1900E; right on CR 1785N for 2.5 mi; right on CR 2150E for 0.7 mi; left on CR 1725N for 0.25 mi; right on CR 2175E for 0.5 mi to campground (E of Coon Creek Rd); at lake's W shore. About 5/15-LD; 14-day limit. $16 at 7 tent sites & 30-amp or 50-amp elec RV/tent sites; $24 for 50-amp full hookups ($9 & $12 with federal senior pass); $32 at double sites. 4 group camping ares, including Wallleye Camp, 10 elec RV sites, and Mayapple Camp, 8 elec RV sites), $80-$160. 78 elec sites; RV limit in excess of 65 ft. 1 RV & 3-4 tents per site. Tbls, flush toilets, cfga, drkg wtr, dump, showers, playground, fish cleaning station, amphitheater, picnic shelter ($30), phone. Boating(ld), fishing, hiking (11-mi backpack trail), golf, volleyball. Non-campers pay $3 for boat ramp. NRRS. Note: Reservation service considers campground full when its site allotment is gone, but first-come sites may be available. **GPS: 39.453211, -88.757944**

OKAW BLUFF GROUP CAMPGROUND

From Sullivan, 4.7 mi S on SR 32. About 5/15-LD; 14-day limit. 2 group camping areas, $140. Tbls, flush toilets, showers, drkg wtr. 2 houses for up to 34 persons, $130; bunk beds, no linens; kitchen with utensils, showers, ice machine; picnic tables; outdoor grills; interior fireplace. Recreation facilities, meeting room($). Basketball, hiking trails, volleyball. For information and reservations ($30 fee), call 217-774-3122.

OPOSSUM CREEK RECREATION AREA

From Shelbyville, 3.4 mi N on SR 128; 0.9 mi E on CR 1650N; 0.5 mi S on CR 1880E; 1.2 mi E on CR 1600N. About 5/15-LD; 14-day limit. $16 at tent sites & at 30-amp & 50-amp elec RV/tent sites ($8 with federal senior pass); $20 at 50-amp elec/wtr sites ($10 with senior pass); $24 at 12 new 50-amp full-hookup sites ($12 with senior pass). 80 sites, most with elec; RV limit in excess of 65 ft. Tbls, flush toilets, cfga, drkg wtr, showers, dump, playground, fish cleaning station, phone, fishing pier. Boating(ld), fishing. NRRS. Note: Reservation service considers campground full when its site allotment is gone, but first-come sites may be available. NRRS. **GPS: 39.446086, -88.773437**

WILBORN CREEK GROUP CAMPGROUND

From Sullivan at jct with SR 121, 3.5 mi W on CR 5; 2.5 mi S on CR 16; 0.75 mi W on CR 18, then left into park; at N end of lake. About MD-LD; 14-day limit. Small group camping area for up to 80 people, about 10 RVs & 25 tents. No elec. $120. Tbls, flush toilets, cfga, drkg wtr, playground, fish cleaning station, nearby beach. 2-night minimum stay on weekends, 3 nights on holiday weekends. Campers use showers at Bo Wood Campground (8 mi). Non-campers pay $3 for boat ramp, $1 per person for swimming beach. 217-774-3951, ext 3. Reservations required. **GPS: 39.572558, -88.705673**

MISSISSIPPI RIVER
PUBLIC USE AREAS
GPS: 44.95, -93.10

Mississippi River Visitor Center is N of SR 92 between I-74 and US 67 on the Rock Island Arsenal, an island just N of Rodman Ave near Government Bridge. Observation area for locking operations, exhibits, theater with seasonal hours, instructional programs. At campgrounds, free sites during winter may have reduced amenities. Illinois day use areas include: Big Slough Recreation area -- boat ramp ($3), fishing, picnicking; Cattail Slough Recreation Area, boat ramp ($3), fishing; Canton Chute Recreation Area -- pit toilets, boat ramp; Lock & Dam 21 -- boat & wildlife observation deck, picnicking, toilets, tours of lock. For info, contact park rangers. No's 1-3, L&D #11, Dubuque, IA 52001, (563) 582-0881. No's 4-10, P. O. Box 398, Thomson, IL 61285, (815) 259-3628. No's 12-17, L&D #16, 1611-2nd

Ave., Muscatine, IA 52761, (563) 263-7913. No's 18-23, L&D #21, Quincy, IL 62301, (217) 228-0890. Visitor center, PO Box 2004, Rock Island, IL 61204-2004 (309) 794-5338. See IA, MO, WI listings.

ANDALUSIA SLOUGH RECREATION AREA

From Andalusia, across river S of Davenport, IA, 2 mi W on SR 92; along the river. All year; 14-day limit. Road-style primitive camping, $6 during 5/15-10/15 ($3 with federal senior pass); free rest of year. Self-registration. 16 sites, some pull-through. Tbls, pit toilets, cfga, drkg wtr, picnic shelter. Boating(ld), fishing. 563-263-7913. **GPS: 41.438295, -90.769891**

BEAR CREEK RECREATION AREA

From Quincy, 12 mi N on SR 96 to Marcelline; 1.5 mi W on Bolton Rd; 3 mi W across levee. All year; 14-day limit. 40 free primitive sites. Tbls, pit toilets, cfga, picnic shelter. Boating(l), fishing. 563-263-7913.
GPS: 40.112052, -91.481918

BLANCHARD ISLAND RECREATION AREA

From Muscatine at the Iowa bridge, 1.5 mi E on SR 92; 4 mi S; 4 mi S, then second right past Copperas Creek Bridge; off the river's main channel. All year; 14-day limit. 34 primitive sites. $8 during 5/15-10/15 ($4 with federal senior pass); free rest of year, but no amenities. Tbls, pit toilets, cfga, drkg wtr. Boating(l), fishing. Volunteer host. 6.5 acres. **GPS: 41.347193, -91.056372**

BLANDING LANDING RECREATION AREA

From Galena at jct with US 20, S on county rd to Blanding, then W. About 5/1-10/25; 14-day limit. 7 non-elec sites, $10 ($5 with federal senior pass); 30 elec sites, $20 ($10 with senior pass). Free primitive camping off-season, no amenities or wtr service. Tbls, flush toilets,

cfga, drkg wtr (no wtr hookups), showers, playground, dump, picnic shelter ($25), amphitheater, pay phone. Boating(l), fishing, hiking, kayaking, canoeing, biking. RV limit 50'. 815-591-2326. NRRS reservations now available in-season ($9).
GPS: 42.285832, -90.402538

FISHERMAN'S CORNER RECREATION AREA

From Hampton, 1 mi N on SR 84 or from I-80, 1 mi S on SR 84; near Lock & Dam 14. About 5/1-10/25; 14-day limit. 5 tent sites, $10 ($5 with federal senior pass); 51 RV/tent sites with 20/30/50-amp elec, $20 ($10 with senior pass). RV limit in excess of 65'. Tbls, flush toilets, cfga, drkg wtr, showers, playground, dump, amphitheater. Boating(l), fishing, biking,, interpretive programs, horseshoe pits. Good view of river barges, lock & dam. (309) 496-2720. NRRS. **GPS: 41.569939, -90.389505**

JOHN HAY RECREATION AREA

On Hwy 106 near East Hannibal. All year; 14-day limit. 8 free primitive sites. Pit toilet, cfga, tbls, picnic shelter, no drkg wtr. Boating(l), fishing.

LOCK 8 DAM №13 RECREATION AREA

From Fulton, 2 mi N on SR 84; W on Lock Rd (signs). All year; 14-day limit. 6 free primitive sites, $3 day use fee for boat ramp during 5/1-11/30 ($1.50 with federal senior pass); free rest of year; $30 annual pass. Tbls, toilets, cfga, picnic shelter, drkg wtr, observation deck overlooking lock chamber. Boating(l), fishing, biking. **GPS: 41.896508, -90.154860**

PARK-N-FISH RECREATION AREA

From Hull, about 3 mi W, just off SR 106 on Illinois side of Lock & Dam 22; off Hwy 106 on paved rd. All year; 14-day limit. 6 free primitive sites. Tbls, pit toilets, cfga, picnic shelter, drkg wtr. Boating, fishing.

THOMSON CAUSEWAY RECREATION AREA

On W edge of Thomson, 4-5 blocks W on Main St; S on Lewis Ave, following signs; on island in river's backwater. During about 4/12-10/27, $10 at 5 tent sites, $20 at 131 50-amp elec sites ($5 & $10 with federal senior pass); free primitive camping off-season. All year; 14-day limit. 4 pull-through sites. RV limit in excess of 65'. Tbls, flush toilets, showers, cfga, drkg wtr, dump, playground,2 picnic shelters($20, amphitheater. Boating (l), fishing, biking, hiking. New & renovated shower facilities, sewer line added, dump station renovated in 2011. (815) 259-3628. NRRS.
GPS: 41.948858, -90.116397

❺ REND LAKE
GPS: 38.0383, -88.97

An 18,900-acre lake located N of Benton on SR 14 W of I-57 in S-central Illinois. Checkout time 4 p.m, Visitor center offers exhibits, interpretive programs, live snake display daily MD-10/22 & weekends rest of year. Boat rentals nearby.

Day use areas: Dam West Area -- boat ramp($), picnicking, shelter, playground, trails; North Marcum -- boat ramp, picnicking, shelter ($25), playground, pay phone, beach, hiking trail; Spillway -- picnicking, playground, toilets, phone. New visitor center features exhibits, aquarium, snake display, demonstration wetland garden, demonstration wildlife garden, demonstration bee hives, picnicking, shelter, playground, interpretive trails. Project Manager, Rend Lake, 12220 Rend City Rd., Benton, IL 62812-9803. (618) 724-2493.

DALE MILLER YOUTH GROUP AREA

From I-57 exit 71, 2.5 mi W on SR 14; 2.5 mi N on Rend City Rd; E (right) on Rend Lake Dam Rd; N (left) on Trail Head Lane. 5/15-10/30. Group camping for up to 200 people and 50 vehicles, $75-$150. 5 cabins with bunk beds

(sleep 8); RV & tent sites available. Tbls, flush toilets, cfga, drkg wtr, dump, coin laundry, amphitheater, picnic shelters, playground, beach, showers. Boating(ld), fishing, hiking trail, basketball, ball fields, swimming, tennis. Boat rentals nearby. ORV prohibited w/o prior approval. NRRS. 618-724-2493.
GPS: 38.03528, -88.9425

GUN CREEK RECREATION AREA

From Benton, 6 mi N on I-57 to exit 77; 0.2 mi W on SR 154, then S. About 3/15-11/30; 14-day limit. 99 elec sites, $16 base; some full hookups, $24 ($8 & $12 with federal senior pass). 65-ft RV limit. 1 RV & 3-4 tents per site. Tbls, flush toilets, cfga, drkg wtr, showers, coin laundry, playground, dump, picnic shelter $25, amphitheater. Boating(ld), fishing, hiking trail, biking, interactive programs. (618) 724-2493. NRRS. **GPS: 38.079565, -88.930609**

NORTH SANDUSKY RECREATION AREA

From Benton, 6 mi N on I-57 to exit 77; 6 mi W on SR 154; S on Rend City Rd to stop sign, then continue S following signs; at Sandusky Cove. About 3/25-11/1; 14-day limit. 118 elec sites, $16 base ($8 with federal senior pass); full hookups $24 ($12 with federal senior pass). Shagbark group camping area with elec, $100. 65-ft RV limit; 1 RV & 3-4 tents per site. Tbls, flush toilets, cfga, drkg wtr, dump, coin laundry, beach, playground, store. Boating(ld), fishing, swimming, hiking trails, biking trail. 3 large picnic shelters with tbls, cfga, drkg wtr ($25). (618) 724-2493. NRRS.
GPS: 38.067403, -88.995931

SOUTH MARCUM RECREATION AREA

From Benton, 1 mi N on Hwy 37; 2 mi W to end of Main Dam. About 3/25-10/1; 14-day limit. 14 walk-to tent sites, $12 ($6 with federal senior pass); 146 elec/wtr RV sites, $16 base ($8 with senior pass), $24 at 6 full hookups ($12 with senior pass). RV limit in excess

of 65'. 1 RV & 3-4 tents per site. Tbls, flush toilets, cfga, drkg wtr, dump, coin laundry, playground, picnic shelter ($25), amphitheater. Boating(ld), fishing, hiking/biking trails, basketball, swimming. Boat rentals, horseback riding nearby. (618) 724-2493. NRRS.
GPS: 38.034775, -88.935399

SOUTH SANDUSKY RECREATION AREA

2.5 mi W of Benton on SR 14; N on CR 900; 2.5 mi E; N on CR 850E following signs. About 3/25-11/1; 14-day limit. 8 walk-to tent sites, $12 ($6 with federal senior pass); 119 elec sites (no wtr hookups), $16 ($8 with senior pass); full hookups $24 ($12 with senior pass). 1 RV & 3-4 tents per site. Tbls, flush toilets, cfga, drkg wtr, dump, coin laundry, playground, beach, picnic shelter $25, amphitheater. Boating(ld), fishing, swimming, hiking/biking trails. Boat rentals, horseback riding nearby. RV limit 65'. (618) 724-2493. NRRS.
GPS: 38.058229, -89.008205

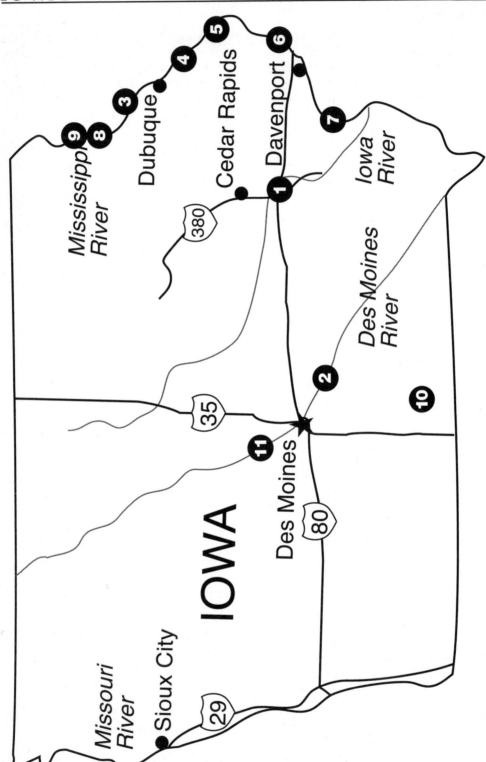

IOWA

STATE INFORMATION:

CAPITAL: Des Moines
NICKNAME: Hawkeye State
STATEHOOD: 1846 - 29th State
FLOWER: Wild Prairie Rose
TREE: Bur Oak
BIRD: Eastern Goldfinch

STATE TIDBITS:

• Iowa's longest and highest bridge crosses Lake Red Rock.

• Iowa is the only state name that starts with two vowels.

• Crystal Lake is home to a statue of the world's largest bullhead fish.

WWW.TRAVELIOWA.COM

Iowa Division of Tourism, Department of Economic Development, 200 E. Grand Ave., Des Moines, IA 50309. 515/725-3084 or 800-472-6035.

IOWA LAKES

To find campgrounds operated by the U.S. Army Corps of Engineers, match the lake's numbers on the preceding map page with numbered lake entries on the following pages. Campgrounds are listed alphabetically under the appropriate lakes. The following Iowa impoundments have Corps of Engineers campgrounds.

Coralville Lake. A 5,430-acre lake 3 miles N of Coralville/Iowa City on the Iowa River. Off exit 244 of I-80, 55 miles W of Davenport.

Lake Red Rock. A 15,00-acre lake 4 miles SW of Pella off SR 163. SE of Des Moines in southwestern Iowa.

Lock & Dam 11, Mississippi River. Located on the river just N of Dubuque, it is the first of a series of locks extending between the point where Iowa, Wisconsin and Illinois join borders and more than 11 southerly pools.

Lock & Dam 12, Mississippi River. Located on the river near Bellevue, Iowa, the pool extends upriver 26.3 miles to Lock & Dam 11 just N of Dubuque.

Lock & Dam 13, Mississippi River. Pool 13 is 2.5 miles upsgream from the North Clinton bridge S of Fulton, Illinois (N of Camanche, IA). It extends 34.2 river miles upstream to Bellevue, IA.

Lock & Dam 14, Mississippi River. Pool 14 extends 29.2 miles upstream from the dam just downstream from LeClaire, IA, and from near Hampton, IL, to Lock & Dam 13 near Clinton, IA.

Lock & Dam 16, Mississippi River. From Muscatine, IA, Pool 16 extends 25.7 miles upstream to Rock Island, IL, at the I-280 bridge.

Lock & Dam 17, Mississippi River. The dam is 3 miles upstream from the mouth of the Iowa River and New Boston, IL. The pond extends 20.1 miles upriver to Muscatine, IA.

Lock & Dam 18, Mississippi River. The dam for Pool 18 is a half mile upstream from the mouth of Henderson Creek, 6.3 river miles from MacArthur Hwy US 34 bridge. It extends upstream 26.6 river miles from Gladstone, IL, to New Boston, IL.

Rathbun Lake. An 11,000-acre reservoir 7 miles N of Centerville off SR 85, 85 miles SE of Des Moines in southeastern Iowa near the Missouri state line.

Saylorville Lake. A 5,950-acre lake N of Des Moines and Johnston on the Des Moines River.

❶ CORALVILLE LAKE
GPS: 41.723772, -91.522174

A 5,430-acre lake 3 miles N of Coralville/ Iowa City on the Iowa River. Off exit 244 of I-80, 55 miles W of Davenport. Visitor center with displays on history & natural resources of lake area; includes replica eagle's nest, fossils, 12-minute movie about flood of 1993. Campground checkout time 5 p.m. Off-road vehicles prohibited.

Day use areas: Curtis Bridge -- boat ramp; Mehaffey Bridge -- boar ramp($3); Squire Point -- hiking; Turkey Creek Recreation Area -- picnic shelter, playground, hiking, disc golf; Sugar Bottoms Day Use Area -- disc golf, mountain biking trails; Sandy Beach Day Use Area -- boat ramp($3). Park Manager, Coralville Lake, 2850 Prairie du Chien Rd., NE, Iowa City, IA 52240-7820. (319) 338-3543.

Dam Complex: This complex comprises Cottonwood, Linder Point, Tailwater East and West, and West Overlook campgrounds. Full hookups with 50-amp electric are available at Linder Point and Tailwater West. Electric sites are at Linder Point, Tailwater East and West Overlook. Primitive tent sites are available at Cottonwood, Tailwater East and Tailwater West. Visitor center, disc golf course at Turkey Creek, Devonian Fossil Gorge, interpretive trail. Several sites are reservable. 319-338-3543, ext. 6300. NRRS.

COTTONWOOD CAMPGROUND

On W side of spillway. 4/15-10/14; 14-day limit. 15 walk-in tent sites. $14 ($7 with federal senior pass). Tbls, flush & pit toilets, cfga, drkg wtr, showers, beach. Boating(l), fishing, swimming, waterskiing, disc golf. NRRS. Campground: 515-276-4656. **GPS: 41.722775, -91.534719**

LINDER POINT CAMPGROUND

On W side of dam, N of access rd. 4/15-10/14; 14-day limit. 26 sites (9 with 50-amp elec, 9 full hookups), some walk-in sites. Walk-in tent sites, $14 ($7 with federal senior pass); non-elec sites, $16 ($8 with senior pass); 30-amp elec sites, $20 ($10 with senior pass); full hookups, $26 ($13 with senior pass). RV limit in excess of 65'. Tbls, flush & pit toilets, cfga, drkg wtr, showers, dump, beach. Hiking, fishing, boating(l), swimming, waterskiing. **GPS: 41.724461 -91.543214**

SANDY BEACH CAMPGROUND

From Solon, 2 mi NW on SR 382; 0.7 mi N on CR W6E; 3 mi W & S on CR W4F to park; at N shore of lake. 5/1-9/30; 14-day limit. 60 sites. 8 primitive walk-to tent sites, $14 ($7 with federal senior pass); 48 elec sites, $20 ($10 with senior pass); 2 full hookup sites, $24 ($12 with senior pass). RV limit in excess of 65'. Tbls, flush & pit toilets, showers, cfga, drkg wtr, dump, pay phone, beach, playground, shelter. Horseshoe pits, boating(l), fishing, swimming, disc golf, waterskiing. Campground: 319-338-3543, ext 6300. NRRS. **GPS: 41.814114, -91.598436**

SUGAR BOTTOM CAMPGROUND

From North Liberty at jct with SR 965, 2.6 mi NE on CR F28 (Mehaffey Bridge Rd); cross Mehaffey bridge, then 1.3 mi S (right) on access rd; at east-central shore of lake. 5/1-9/30; 14-day limit. 17 walk-to tent sites, $14 ($7 with federal senior pass); 224 elec sites, including 13 full hookups, 33 pull-through. Base 30-amp elec rate $20; 50-amp elec, $22; 50-amp elec/ wtr, $24; 50-amp full hookups $26 (rates $10, $11, $12 & $13 with senior pass). RV limit in excess of 65'. Amphitheater, tbls, flush toilets, cfga, drkg wtr, showers, dump, playground, beach. Boating(l), fishing, horseshoe pits, 18-

hold disc golf course, mountain bike trails, horseback riding, hiking trails, swimming, waterskiing. Four group camping areas, $72-$200. Campground: 319-338-543, ext 6300. NRRS. **GPS: 41.755683, -91.55917**

TAILWATER EAST CAMP

2 mi N of Iowa City on SR W66; E at Coralville Lake sign; follow signs across Coralville Dam, then turn right; below dam on E side of outlet. 4/15-10/15; 14-day limit. 28 sites, 22 with electric (5 with 50-amp) & 5 walk-to tent sites. 1 pull-through RV site. Walk-to tent sites $14 ($7 with federal senior pass; non-elec RV/tent sites $16 ($8 with senior pass); 30-amp elec sites $20 ($10 with senior pass); 50-amp elec $22 ($11 with senior pass). RV limit in excess of 65'. Tbls, flush & pit toilets, cfga, drkg wtr, fish cleaning station, beach, dump, playground. Boating(l), fishing, swimming, waterskiing. Disc golf at Turkey Creek. **GPS: 41.720897, -91.527817**

TAILWATER WEST CAMP

Follow directions to Tailwater East; below dam on W side of the outlet. 4/15-10/15; 14-day limit. 30 sites (5 walk-in tent sites). Walk-to tent sites $14 ($7 with federal senior pass); 30-amp elec $20 ($10 with senior pass); 50-amp elec/wtr $24 ($12 with senior pass); full hookups $26 ($13 with senior pass). Picnic shelter, fish cleaning station, tbls, flush & pit toilets, cfga, drkg wtr, showers, dump, beach. Boating(l), fishing, swimming, waterskiing. Disc golf at Turkey Creek. **GPS: 41.722472, -91.529536**

WEST OVERLOOK CAMP

On W side of dam, N of dam access rd. 4/15-10/15. 89 elec sites (1 handicap site, 1 pull-through), $20 ($10 with federal senior pass); premium elec sites $22 ($11 with senior pass). Picnic shelter, fish cleaning station, tbls, flush & pit toilets, cfga, showers, drkg wtr, beach, dump. Boating(l), swimming, fishing, waterskiing. Disc golf at Turkey Creek. **GPS: 41.726325, -91.535167**

② LAKE RED ROCK
GPS: 41.3708, -92.9794

A 15,000-acre lake 4 miles SW of Pella off SR 163, SE of Des Moines in southwestern Iowa. It is the state's largest lake. Visitor center features interpretive programs, campfire programs, paved 13-mile hiking/biking trail. Checkout time 4 p.m. Day use areas: Fifield Recreation Area -- picnic shelter ($30), playground, bike trail; North Tailwater -- shelter ($30), playground (closed until 2018 due to hydro-power project); South Overlook -- boat ramp, shelter ($30); South Tailwater -- shelter ($30), fish cleaning station, bike trail access. Cordova County Park at lake's N side features nature trail, butterfly garden, picnicking, observation tower, boat ramp. Camping & boat ramps at Roberts Creek County Park and at Elk Rock State Park (see Guide to Free & Low-Cost Campgrounds). For Corps camping/lake information, recording, call (641) 828-7522. Operations Manager, Lake Red Rock, 1105 Highway T-15, Knoxville, IA 50138-9522. (641) 828-7522/628-8690.

HICKORY RIDGE
WILDERNESS CAMPGROUND

From boat ramps at Whitebreast Campground or Elk Rock East Park, S about 1.8 to 3.2 mi by boat, canoe or kayak to 200-acre primitive tent area (or hike 0.25 mi to site from Jersey Dr parking lot). Free. All year; 14-day limit. 8 tent sites. Portable toilets, campfire areas, shelter, no trash service or drkg wtr. Boating, fishing, hiking. No reservations. Future plans include wtr hydrant. **GPS: 41.359787, -93.034544**

HOWELL STATION
RECREATION AREA

From SR 163 at Pella, half mi W on SR 28; 5 mi SW on CR T-15; E on Idaho; S on 198th Place, then S following signs. On shore of Des Moines River. 4/15-10/19; 14-day limit. $20 at 143 elec sites ($10 with federal senior pass). RV limit in excess of 65 ft. Fish cleaning station, tbls, flush toilets, cfga, drkg wtr, showers, dump, playground. Boating(l), fishing, hiking trail, biking trail. Amphitheater with weekend programs during MD-LD. Non-campers pay $3 for boat launch. NRRS. Campground: 641-838-7522. **GPS: 41.365259, -92.969404**

IVAN'S RECREATION AREA

Below dam, SW side of the outlet on Des Moines River. From Knoxville, about 7 mi NE on CR T15; 0.5 mi E on Jewell Dr, then veer left on 198th Pl to park, on left. $16 at 21 elec sites ($8 with federal senior pass). 4/23-9/28; 14-day limit. Tbls, flush toilets, cfga, drkg wtr, showers, fish cleaning station. Access to biking/hiking trail. No fee booth; ranger collects fees. No reservations. **GPS: 41.359668, -92.973097**

NORTH OVERLOOK RECREATION AREA

From jct with SR 163 at Pella, 0.5 mi W on SR 28; 3 mi SW on CR T-15; at N side of dam off CR T-15. About 4/25-9/30; 14-day limit. $18 at 54 elec sites ($9 with federal senior pass); $10 at 8 tent sites ($5 with senior pass). RV limit in excess of 65 ft. Tbls, flush toilets, cfga, drkg wtr, dump, showers, playground, beach. Boating(l), fishing, swimming. Hiking/biking trail access. Amphitheater with weekend programs MD-LD. Non-campers pay $1 ($4 per vehicle) for swimming beach. Picnic area closed until 2018. Campground: 641-828-7522. NRRS. **GPS: 41.377598, -92.970825**

WALLASHUCK CAMPGROUND

From Pella, 4 mi W on CR G-28; 2 mi S on 190th Ave; at N shore of lake. About 4/25-9/30; 14-day limit. $18 at 83 elec sites ($9 with federal senior pass). 23 sites have 50-amp service. RV limit in excess of 65'. Tbls, flush toilets, cfga, playground, dump, drkg wtr, showers, beach, fish cleaning station. Swimming, boating(l), fishing, access to hiking/biking trail. Amphitheater offers campfire programs MD-

LD. Campground: 641-838-7522. NRRS. **GPS: 41.400514, -92.992240**

WHITEBREAST CAMPGROUND

From Knoxville, 8 mi NE on CR T15; 2 mi N on CR S-71; at S side of lake. About 4/25-9/30; 14-day limit. $18 at 109 elec sites ($9 with federal senior pass). 60-ft RV limit. Group camping areas with elec $126-216. Picnic shelter ($30), amphitheater, fish cleaning station, tbls, flush toilets, cfga, drkg wtr, dump, playground, beach. Fishing, boating(l), swimming. Non-campers pay $1 at swimming beach ($4 vehicle). Campground: 641-838-7522. NRRS. **GPS: 41.384666, -93.026712**

LOCK & DAM 11 MISSISSIPPI RIVER
GPS: 42.540279, -90.644294

Located on the river just N of Dubuque, Iowa. This is the first of a series of locks extending between the point where Iowa, Wisconsin and Illinois join borders and more than 11 southerly pools. Near this lock, the Corps operates a popular recreation area in Wisconsin, but none in Iowa. Project Manager, Pools 11-22, PO Box 534, Pleasant Valley, IA 52767. 309-794-4522.

GRANT RIVER RECREATION AREA

From Dubuque, IA, E across river into Wisconsin, then N on US 61; 2 mi W on SR 133, following signs 2 mi S of Potosi, then left (E) on River Lane Rd; right (S) on Park Lane to campground on N shore of Mississippi River. Fees 5/1-10/24 (free primitive camping off-season); 14-day limit. 10 tent sites, $10 ($5 with federal senior pass); 63 elec 50-amp elec sites, $20 ($10 with senior pass); premium 50-amp elec, $18 ($9 with senior pass). No wtr hookups. 55-ft RV limit. Tbls, flush toilets, campfire grill areas, drkg wtr, showers, playground, dump, picnic shelter ($25), amphitheater. Boating(l), fishing.

Campground: 608-736-2140, 1-800-645-0248. NRRS. **GPS: 42.651061, -90.700432**

❹
LOCK & DAM 12
MISSISSIPPI RIVER
GPS: 42.2728, -90.42111

Located on the river near Bellevue, Iowa, this pool extends upriver 26.3 miles to Lock & Dam 11 just N of Dubuque. Dam is 3 blocks N of Hwys 62 & 52, just off Franklin St. in Bellevue. The Corps operates only one campground at this pool -- Pleasant Creek Recreation Area -- but camping also is available at a state park, two county parks and a Dubuque city park (see Guide to Free and Low-Cost Campgrounds). The pool is within the Upper Mississippi River National Wildlife and Fish Refuge. For information, contact park rangers at 1611 2nd Ave, Muscatine, IA 52761. 563-582-0881.

PLEASANT CREEK
RECREATION AREA

3.5 mi S of Bellevue on US 52, following signs for L&D 12; on river's main channel. All year; 14-day limit. 55 primitive sites, $8 during 5/15-10/15 ($4 with federal senior pass), free rest of year but no services. Pit toilets, cfga, drkg wtr, dump. Boating(l), fishing Boat ramp $3 or $30 annually. Self registration. 32 acres. **GPS: 42.2216345, 90.382939**

❺
LOCK & DAM 13
MISSISSIPPI RIVER
GPS: 41.894444, -90.15667

Pool 13 is 2.5 miles upstream from the North Clinton bridge S of Fulton, Illinois (N of Camanche, IA). It extends 34.2 river miles upstream to Bellevue, IA. Access on Lock Rd. just off Hwy 84. Visitors can view barges & boats locking through the widest pool of the river. Free primitive camping is available near the observation deck at Fulton;

a $3 daily fee ($30 annually) is charged for boat launching. The Corps also operates a full-service campground on the W edge of Thomson, IL. In Iowa, the lock's only Corps park is Bulger's Hollow near Clinton, but Jackson County's South Sabula Lakes Park is nearby and quite popular (see Guide to Free and Low-Cost Campgrounds). Cattail Slough Recreation Area S of Fulton is a day-use facility with boat ramp ($3 daily) and pit toilets. For information, contact park rangers at 1611 2nd Ave, Muscatine, IA 52761; 563-263-7913.

BULGER'S HOLLOW
RECREATION AREA

From Clinton, 3 mi N on US 67; 1 mi E on 170th St; at widest point on the river. All year; 14-day limit. $4 during 5/15-10/15 ($2 with federal senior pass); some sites free rest of year, but no services; 14-day limit. 17 non-elec RV sites, 9 tent sites. Pit toilets, picnic shelter($25), cfga, drkg wtr, dump, playground. Boating(l), fishing, horseshoe pits. Volunteer host. Ranger office: 815-259-3628. **GPS: 41.93457, -90.181641**

❻
LOCK & DAM 14
MISSISSIPPI RIVER
GPS: 41.57444, -90.40306

Pool 14 extends 29.2 miles upstream from the dam just downstream from LeClaire, IA, and from near Hampton, IL, to Lock & Dam 13 near Clinton, IA. The dam is 2.1 river miles downstream from the I-80 bridge and is accessed off Hwy 67. Middle portion of the pool contains several islands, side channels and backwaters. The Wapsipinicon River empties into Pool 14. Smith Island Recreation Area provides hiking trails, picnicking and fishing facilities, but no camping. The Corps does not operate campgrounds at this pool, but Clinton County's Rock Creek Marina offers camping (see Guide to Free and Low-Cost Campgrounds). Contact park rangers at 1611 2nd Ave, Muscatine, IA 52761.

IOWA

7
LOCK & DAM 16
MISSISSIPPI RIVER
GPS: 41.4253889. -90.01278

From Muscatine, IA, Pool 16 extends 25.7 miles upstream to Rock Island, IL at the I-280 bridge. The dam is 1.3 miles upstream from the Muscatine bridge (Illinois SR 92); access (with picnicking) is via 102nd Ave W on the Illinois side of river. The Corps operates two Iowa campgrounds (and one in Illinois) at Pool 16, and camping also is available at Scott County's Buffalo Shores Park and Fairport State Recreation Area. Nearby camping is at Wildcat Den State Park, Scott County's West Lake Park and Muscatine County's Saulsbury Bridge Recreation Area (see Guide to Free and Low-Cost Campgrounds). For information, contact park rangers at 1611 2nd Ave, Muscatine, IA 52761. 563-262-7913. See Illinois section.

CLARKS FERRY RECREATION AREA

From Muscatine, 15 mi E on SR 22 (W 2nd St), following signs; along main river channel. 5/12-10/15; 14-day limit (day use only off-season). $20 at 45 concrete 50-amp elec sites ($10 with federal senior pass). Tbls, flush toilets, cfga, drkg wtr, showers, dump, playground, picnic shelter ($25), amphitheater. Boating(l), fishing, volleyball, horseshoe pits. Non-campers pay $3 for boat ramp (or $30 annually). 11 acres. (563) 381-4043.
GPS: 41.458239, -90.809501

SHADY CREEK RECREATION AREA

From Muscatine, 10 mi E on SR 22 following signs. 5/1-10/25; 14-day limit (11 sites free off-season but no services). $20 at 53 concrete sites with 50-amp elec ($10 with federal senior pass). RV limit in excess of 65'. Tbls, flush toilets, showers, cfga, drkg wtr, dump, playground, picnic shelter $25, amphitheater. Horseshoe pits, boating(ld), fishing, hiking. 16-acre park. (563) 262-8090. NRRS.
GPS: 41.446788, -90.877157

8
LOCK & DAM 17
MISSISSIPPI RIVER
GPS: 41.19139. -91.05556

The dam is 3 miles upstream from the mouth of the Iowa River and New Boston, IL. Pond 17 extends 20.1 miles up-river to Muscatine, IA. The Corps operates two campgrounds on this pond as well as Ferry Landing Recreation Area (on Pond 18) at the Iowa River. A boat ramp and picnic area is at Kilpec Landing Recreation Area (once a Corps campground). Louisa County offers camping at two parks (see Guide to Free and Low-Cost Campgrounds). One is on the shore of Lake Odessa, which was once part of the Mississippi River's main channel; it is owned by the Corps and managed jointly with the U.S. Fish & Wildlife Service and the Iowa Department of Natural Resources. Contact park rangers at 1611 2nd Ave, Muscatine, IA 52761. See Illinois section.

BLANCHARD ISLAND
RECREATION AREA

From Muscatine bridge in Illinois, 1.5 mi E on Illinois SR 92; 4 mi S, then second right past Copperas Creek bridge; off the river's main channel in Illinois. $8 during 5/15-10/15 ($4 with federal senior pass); free rest of year but no amenities. 34 primitive sites on 6.5 acres. Tbls, pit toilets, cfga, drkg wtr. Boating(l), fishing. Volunteer host.
GPS: 41.347193, -91.056372

9
LOCK & DAM 18
MISSISSIPPI RIVER
GPS: 40.88224722. -91.0239

The dam for Pool 18 is one-half mile upstream from the mouth of Henderson Creek, 6.3 river miles from MacArthur Hwy US 34 bridge. It extends upstream 26.6 river miles from Gladstone, IL, to New Boston, IL. The only Corps campground on the pool is on the Iowa side just below the mouth of the Iowa River.

Another campground is operated in Iowa by Des Moines County (see Guide to Free and Low-Cost Campgrounds). Contact park rangers at Corps of Engineers, Quincy, IL 61204. 217-228-0890.

FERRY LANDING RECREATION AREA

From N edge of Oakville, 6 mi E & N on CR X71 to levee (follow signs); at mouth of Iowa River. Free. All year; 14-day limit. 22 primitive sites. Pit toilets, tbls, cfga, dump, no drkg wtr. Boating(l), fishing. Ranger office, 563-263-7913. **GPS: 41.162176, -91.014196**

⑩ RATHBUN LAKE
GPS: 40.8283, -92.8767

An 11,000-acre lake 7 miles N of Centerville off SR 5, 85 miles SE of Des Moines in southeastern Iowa near the Missouri state line. A fish hatchery is below the dam. The area around the lake has more than 700 campsites, most operated by the Corps (see Guide to Free and Low-Cost Campgrounds for other listings). Outlet Area Park is equipped with a boat ramp, picnic area with shelter, playground and interpretive trail. For information call (641) 647-2464. Resource Manager, Rathbun Lake, 20112 Highway J-5-T, Centerville, IA 52544-8308.

BRIDGEVIEW CAMPGROUND

From SR 5 at Moravia, 10.4 mi W on SR 142; 1.2 mi S; N of bridge at NW shore of lake. 5/1-9/30; 14-day limit. $12 for 11 non-elec sites ($6 with federal senior pass); $16 at 30-amp elec sites, $18 for 50-amp ($8 & $9 with senior pass), $32 at 7 double sites. 95 elec sites; RV limit in excess of 65'; 6 pull-through. Tbls, fish cleaning station, flush toilets, cfga, drkg wtr, showers, playground, dump. Boating(l), fishing. Picnic shelter for up to 24 people and 12 vehicles, $25. All-terrain vehicle park nearby. Campground: 614-724-3062. NRRS. **GPS: 40.876409, -93.030038**

BUCK CREEK CAMPGROUND

From SR 5 at Moravia, 2 mi W on SR 142; 3 mi S on CR J5T; E end of lake. $16 for 30-amp elec sites, $18 for 50-amp ($8 & $9 with federal senior pass). 42 elec sites; RV limit in excess of 65 ft; 10 pull-through sites. 5/8-9/30; 14-day limit. Picnic shelter, fish cleaning station, tbls, flush toilets, cfga, drkg wtr, showers, dump, playground, beach. Swimming, boating(ld), fishing. 641-724-3206. NRRS. **GPS: 40.844439, -92.871176**

ISLAND VIEW CAMPGROUND

1.8 mi N of Mystic on CR T-14; 2.6 mi E on CR J5T; half mi N; at SE shore of lake. 5/1-9/30; 14-day limit. 186 elec sites. $16 at 30-amp sites ($8 with federal senior pass), $32 at double sites ($16 with senior pass); $18 at 50-amp premium sites ($9 with senior pass). RV limit in excess of 65'. Group camping area, $125 Sun-Thurs, $200 Fri & Sat; 12 elec sites, picnic shelter, showers. Tbls, flush toilets, cfga, drkg wtr, fish cleaning station, dump, playground, beach, showers. Swimming, boating(ld), fishing, basketball, ball fields, biking. Picnic shelters, $25-$50. 641-647-2079. NRRS. **GPS: 40.833984, -92.917428**

PRAIRIE RIDGE CAMPGROUND

From SR 5 at Moravia, 4 mi W on SR 142; 3 mi S; on N side of lake. 5/15-9/15; 14-day limit. 54 elec sites (50-amp), $18 ($9 with federal senior pass). RV limit in excess of 65'. Group camping area, $50 Sunday-Thursday, $100 on Friday and Saturday. Tbls, flush toilets, cfga, drkg wtr, showers, dump, playground, fish cleaning station. Picnic shelter, $25. 641-724-3103. NRRS. **GPS: 40.858746, -92.887452**

ROLLING COVE CAMPGROUND

1.8 mi N of Mystic on CR T-14; 2.7 mi W on CR J5T; 4 mi N on CR 160th Rd to campground on S shore of lake;. 5/1-9/15; 14-day limit. Formerly $12, now free. 31 non-elec sites; RV limit in excess of 65'. Tbls, toilets, cfga, drkg

wtr, dump, fish cleaning station. Boating(ld), fishing. No reservations. 641-647-2464.
GPS: 40.849304, -92.98305

⑪ SAYLORVILLE LAKE
GPS: 41.7036. -93.6811

A 5,950-acre lake N of Des Moines & Johnston on the Des Moines River. Exit 131 off I-35/80 on Merle Hay Rd, then N on NW Beaver Dr. Visitor center (515) 964-0672. All campsites are now reservable at the Bob Shetler, Cherry Glen and Prairie Flowers Campgrounds. Neal Smith Trail runs 23.7 mi from Big Creek Beach to Des Moines. Campgrounds are closed off-season.

Day use fees are $3 ($30 annually) at Sandpiper, Lakeview & Cherry Glen boat ramps; $4 at Oak Grove & Sandpiper swimming beaches. Day use areas: Cottonwood -- picnicking, playground, trails, 9 picnic shelters ($); Lakeview -- boat ramp, picnicking; Oak Grove -- beach, picnic shelters ($), playground, multi- use trails; Sandpiper -- boat ramp, picnic shelter($), playground, beach, hiking trail; Walnut Ridge -- picnic shelter($), playground, hiking trail. For lake information/ recording, call (515) 276-0433. Park Manager, Saylorville Lake, 5600 NW 78th Ave, Johnston, IA 50131. (515) 276-4656/270-6173.

ACORN VALLEY PARK

From dam near Johnston, 1 mi W on NW 78th Ave; 2.5 mi NW on Beaver Dr, then E. About MD-LD; 14-day limit. 69 primitive walk-to tent sites, $14 ($7 with federal senior pass); 29 elec sites $18 base ($9 with senior pass); premium elec sites $20 ($10 with senior pass). RV limit 65'. Tbls, flush toilets, cfga, drkg wtr, showers, playground, dump, picnic shelter with elec, $50. Interpretive programs, visitor center, shooting range, boating(l), fishing, hiking trail, volleyball, ball fields, waterskiing. (515) 276-0429. NRRS.
GPS: 41.737288, -93.721533

BOB SHETLER RECREATION AREA

From I-35/80 N of Des Moines, exit 131 onto Johnson/Saylorville Rd., then 2.8 mi N on Merle Hay Rd through Johnston; from 4-way stop sign, 1 mi NW (left) on Beaver Dr; at large concrete water storage tank on right, turn right for 0.8 mi NW on 78th Ave; right at T-intersection for 0.4 mi; at Tailwater area below dam. 5/1-9/30; 14-day limit. 67 elec sites (8 pull-through), $18 base ($9 with federal senior pass), $22 at premium sites ($11 with senior pass). RV limit in excess of 65'. Tbls, flush toilets, cfga, drkg wtr, dump, showers, playground, fish cleaning stations, 2 picnic shelters $50. Biking trail, hiking, ball field, volleyball, boating(l), fishing, waterskiing. (515) 276-0873. NRRS.
GPS: 41.700041, -93.688788

CHERRY GLEN CAMPGROUND

From I-35/80 exit 90 N of Des Moines, 2.4 mi on Hwy 160 to its end; continue N 4.1 mi on Hwy 415; at campground sign, left turn lane, then 0.6 mi on NW 94th Ave. 4/15-10/15; 14-day limit. 125 elec sites with 50-amp, $20 base ($10 with federal senior pass), $24 at premium locations ($12 with senior pass). RV limit in excess of 65'. Tbls, flush toilets, cfga, drkg wtr, dump, showers, playground, picnic shelter $50, fish cleaning station. Boating(l), fishing, volleyball, biking trail, hiking, ball field, waterskiing, nature programs, bike rentals nearby. (515) 964-8792. NRRS.
GPS: 41.731347, -93.680549

PRAIRIE FLOWER RECREATION AREA

From I-35 exit 90 N of Des Moines, 2.4 mi on Hwy 160 to its end; continue 5.6 mi on Hwy 415N; at campground sign, turn left, then 0.2 mi on NW Lake Dr. 5/1-10/15; 14-day limit. 158 elec sites (69 with 50-amp), $18 ($9 with federal senior pass); premium elec sites, $20 ($10 with senior pass); full hookups & 50-amp elec, $24 ($12 with senior pass). RV limit in excess of 65'. Tbls, flush toilets, cfga, drkg wtr, dump, showers, playgrounds, beach. Hiking/

biking trail, swimming, volleyball, bike rentals
nearby. Ten group camping areas, $72-$280.
(515) 984-6925. NRRS.
GPS: 41.745669, -93.688123

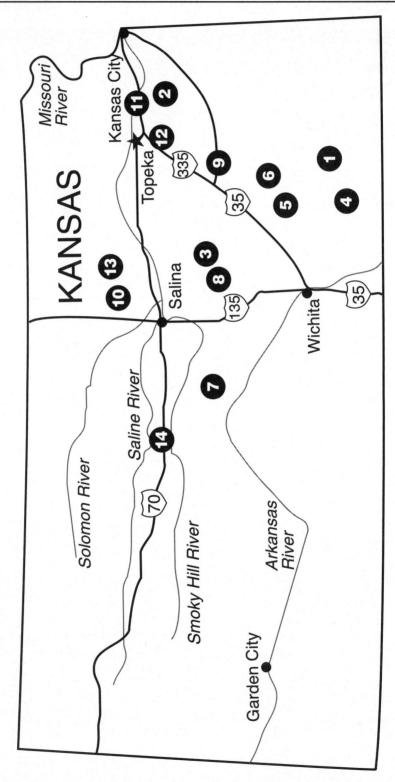

KANSAS

State Information:

CAPITAL: Topeka
NICKNAME: Sunflower State
STATEHOOD: 1861 - 34th State
FLOWER: Sunflower
TREE: Eastern Cottonwood
BIRD: Western Meadowlark

State Tidbits:

• Sumner County is known as The Wheat Capital of the World.

• The fast-food chain of Pizza Hut opened its first store in Wichita.

• Smith County is the geographical center of the 48 contiguous states.

WWW.TRAVELKS.COM

Dept. of Commerce, Travel and Tourism Division, 1000 S.W. Jackson St., Suite 100, Topeka, KS. 785-296-2009.

KANSAS LAKES

To find campgrounds operated by the U.S. Army Corps of Engineers, match the lake's numbers on the preceding map page with numbered lake entries on the following pages. Campgrounds are listed alphabetically under the appropriate lakes. The following Kansas impoundments have Corps of Engineers campgrounds.

Big Hill Lake. A 1,240-acre lake 4.5 miles E of Cherryvale on CR 5000 and 11 miles SW of Parsons and US 400, 160 miles SW of Kansas City in southeastern Kansas.

Clinton Lake. A 7,000-acre lake with 85 miles of shoreline located one mile SW of Lawrence, W of US 59, and 45 miles W of Kansas City. It is on the Rock Creek, Elk Creek and Wakarusa Rivers.

Countil Grove Lake. A 3,310-acre lake 1.5 mile NW of Council Grove off US 56 and SR 177, 101 miles SW of Kansas City. It is near the headwaters of the Neosho River.

Elk City Lake. A 4,122-acre lake 5 miles NW of Independence and US 160, 127 miles E of Wichita in southern Kansas.

Fall River Lake. A 2,450-acre lake 5 miles NW of the town of Fall River off US 400, 70 miles E of Wichita. Fall River is a tributary of the Verdigris River.

John Redmond Dam and Reservor. A 9,400-acre lake 6 miles N and W of Burlington off US 75, 110 miles SW of Kansas City.

Kanapolis Lake. A 3,400-acre lake with 41 miles of shorelne located 31 miles SW of Salina off Hwy 141, 85 miles NW of Wichita.

Marion Reservoir. A 6,200-acre lake 3 miles NW of Marion off US 56, 46 miles NE of Wichita.

Melvern Lake. A 6,900-acre lake on the Marais des Cygnes River with 101 miles of shoreline on the eastern edge of the state's Finthills prairie region. It is 3.5 miles W of Melvern on SR 31 and W of US 75, N of I-35 and 39 miles S of Topeka.

Milford Lake. A 15,700-acre lake 5 miles NW of Junction City/I-70 on Hwy K-57, W of US 77 and 65 miles W of Topeka.

Perry Lake. An 11,150-acre lake 3 miles NW of Perry off US 24, 15 miles NE of Topeka at the Delaware River.

Pomona Lake. A 4,000-acre lake 17 miles W of Ottawa on SR 268/68; 1 mile N on Pomona Dam Rd, 35 miles S of Topeka.

Tuttle Creek Lake. A 12,570-acre lake 5 miles N of Manhattan on US 24 and SR 13; 55 miles W of Topeka.

Wilson Lake. A 9,000-acre lake 7 miles S of Lucas on SR 232, 135 miles NW of Wichita on the Saline River.

❶
BIG HILL LAKE
GPS: 37.2683, -95.47

A 1,240-acre lake 4.5 mi E of Cherryvale on CR 5000 and 11 miles SW of Parsons and US 400, 160 mi SW of Kansas City in SE Kansas. Includes 17-miles Big Hill Lake Horse Trail through varied terrain with 3 equestrian trailheads. Day use areas: Downstream Point -- picnic shelter $30, water trail; Highway 160 Horse Trail -- boat ramp, trails; Overlook Park -- picnic shelter $30, playground, interpretive trail, fishing dock. Non-campers pay $3 day use fees at boat ramps and $4 per vehicle at beaches and other facilities. Horse trail features tethering areas and three parking areas that may be used for overnight camping by riders. 1-mi Ruth Nixon Memorial Hiking Trail. Lake Manager, Big Hill Lake, P. O. Box 426, Cherryvale, KS 67335-0426. (620) 336-2741.

CHERRYVALE CAMPGROUND

From Olive St on W side of Cherryvale, 4.5 mi E on CR 5000 (becoming 1900 Rd); 2 mi N on Cherryvale Pkwy, following signs; NW of dam at W shore. During about 4/1-11/1, 9 elec sites (30/50-amp), $17 ($8.50 with federal senior pass); 11 full hookups $20 ($22 at 2 premium sites ($10 & $11 with senior pass). Elec sites $15, full hookups $18 off-season with reduced

services, no showers. 14-day limit. RV limit in excess of 65'. Tbls, flush toilets, cfga, drkg wtr, showers, dump, playground, beach. Group camping with elec & picnic shelter, $148 in-season, $138 off-season. Boating(ld), fishing, hiking, ball fields, horseback riding, swimming. Non-campers pay $3 for boat ramp, $1 per person for swimming beach, $4 showers, $4 dump. NRRS. **GPS: 37.26944, -95.45833**

MOUND VALLEY CAMPGROUND

From Olive St on W side of Cherryvale, 5 mi E on CR 5000 (becoming 1900 Rd); N on Mound Valley Pkwy, following signs; NE of dam at SE shore. About 4/1-11/1; 14-day limit (closed in winter). 8 non-elec sites, $12 ($6 with federal senior pass); 74 elec sites, $16 & $17 base or $18 & $19 premium location (30-amp); $17, $18 & $20 base for 50-amp; $20 for 2 full hookups (50-amp). RV limit in excess of 65'. Tbls, flush toilets, cfga, drkg wtr, showers, dump, beach. Non-elec group camping areas, $40-$90. Boating(ld), fishing, swimming, hiking, horseback riding. Non-campers pay $3 for boat ramp, $1 for swimming beach, $4 dump, $4 showers. Change house at beach. (620) 328-2050. NRRS. **GPS: 37.26944, -95.45833**

TIMBER HILL CAMPGROUND

From Olive St on W side of Cherryvale, 5.5 mi E on CR 5000 (becoming 1900 Rd); 3 mi N on Elk Rd; W on gravel Timber Rd, following signs; at E shore of lake. About 4/1-11/1; 14-day limit. 20 non-elec sites, some pull-through, $10; 40-ft RV limit. Sites free off-season but no amenities. Drkg wtr, pit toilets, cfga, tbls, dump. Boating(ld), fishing pier, fishing, horseback riding. Non-campers pay $3 for boat ramp, $4 dump.
GPS: 37.2963, -95.4462

❷
CLINTON LAKE
GPS: 38.9233, -95.33

A 7,000-acre lake with 85 miles of shoreline located 1 mile SW of Lawrence, W of US 59

& 45 miles W of Kansas City. It is on the Rock Creek, Elk Creek and Wakarusa Rivers. Visitor center on NW side of dam features displays. Day use fees are charged for picnic shelter reservations, boat ramps & swimming beaches. During winter of 2014-15, all campgrounds were closed except Woodridge, offering primitive tent camping only; drinking water available.

Besides the camping areas listed here, the project's Overlook Park day use area at the N end of the dam provides picnicking with two reservable shelters, a lake overlook area, playground, hiking trailhead and restrooms. Day use hiking, picnicking all year, with wtr available but shut off at Bloomington East/West Parks. Lawrence's Outlook City Park below the dam also has shelters as well as a sports complex, golf course, model aircraft field and a off-leash dog area. Additional facilities are at the nearby Clinton State Park. Resource Manager, Clinton Lake, 872 N. 1402 Rd., Lawrence, KS 66049-9176. (785) 843-7665.

BLOOMINGTON EAST PARK

From Lawrence, 4 mi W on Highway 40 (6th St); 5 mi W (left) on CR 442 to Stull; 6 mi S (left) on CR 458; 4 mi NE (left) on CR 6 through Clinton, then follow signs. Between the Rock Creek & Wakarusa River arms of the lake. It contains Ash, Cedar Ridge, Elm, Hickory/Walnut and Oak Campgrounds. It also features Bloomington Beach picnic shelters, a swimming beach, horseshoe pits, sand volleyball courts, 3 boat ramps and playgrounds (non-campers pay day use fees). Clinton Lake Museum has historical exhibits.

Ash Group Campground in Bloomington East Park near Hickory/Walnut Campgrounds. 5/1-9/30; 14-day limit. Grassy, undesignated-site group camping area, primarily for tent groups, $50. Also open to small RVs such as pop–ups & pickup campers on the gravel circle drive. No hookups. Picnic shelter, fish cleaning station, horseshoe pits. Pit toilets; shower

at Hickory/Walnut Campground. NRRS (through Hickory/Walnut Campground). **GPS: 38.9125, -95.3744**

Cedar Ridge Campground in Bloomington East Park. 5/1-9/30; 14-day limit. 101 elec/wtr sites (61 pull-through & 13 offering 50-amp service), $18 base for 20/30-amp ($9 with federal senior pass), $20 for 50-amp. RV limit in excess of 65'. Tbls, flush toilets, beach, fish cleaning station, playground. Biking trail, volleyball, swimming, horseshoe pits. Access to shower, coin laundry facilities, amphitheater. Sat evening programs. NRRS. **GPS: 38.91278, -95.37472**

Elm Group Campground in Bloomington East Park near Hickory/Walnut campgrounds. 5/1-9/30; 14-day limit. Grassy, undesignated-site group camping area, $50. Primarily for group tent camping, but small RVs such as folding trailers & pickup campers okay on gravel circle drive. Pit toilets, drkg wtr, cfga, access to showers, picnic shelter, volleyball court. Pick up gate keys at the Walnut Creek Campground. NRRS.

Hickory Campground in Bloomington East Park. 5/1-9/30; 14-day limit. 47 non-elec sites, $12 ($6 with federal senior pass); 50 elec sites, $16 base ($8 with senior pass), $18 for elec/wtr ($9 with senior pass), $22 for 50-amp elec/wtr. Tbls, flush toilets, cfga, drkg wtr, showers, dump, beach, playground; access to laundry facilities, amphitheater, fish cleaning station. Swimming, boating(l), fishing, hiking, Sat evening programs. NRRS.

Walnut Campground in Bloomington East Park. 5/1-9/30; 14-day limit. 50 non-elec sites, $12 ($6 with federal senior pass); 40 elec sites, $16 ($8 with senior pass); 10 elec/wtr sites $18 ($9 with senior pass); 50-amp full hookups $22 ($11 with senior pass). Tbls, flush toilets, cfga, drkg wtr, beach, playground; access to shower, laundry facilities, amphitheater, fish cleaning station, dump. Sat evening programs, swimming, boating(l), fishing. 22 non-elec sites at Oak Loop, $10 ($5 with senior pass); loop has 1 pit toilet, 2 wtr hydrants; campers must drive 1 mi to shower/laundry facility. NRRS. **GPS: 38.9125, -95.37444**

BLOOMINGTON WEST GROUP CAMPGROUND

From Lawrence, 4 mi W on Hwy 40 (6th St); 5 mi W (left) on CR 442 to Stull; 6 mi S (left) on CR 458; 4 mi NE (left) on CR 6: 0.5 mi E (right) on CR 1200N, then first gravel rd on left (near N corner of Clinton). Group camping area with sites, $125. 4/1-10/15. 20 non-elec sites, 4 with wtr/elec; up to 150 people. Sheltered dining area with elec & lights, playground , shower bldg, ball field, basketball. Access to flush toilets, showers, drkg wtr, coin laundry, beach. Boating(l), canoeing, courtesy dock, waterskiing, horseshoe pits. NRRS. **GPS: 38.92833, -95.39028**

ROCKHAVEN PARK

From just SW of Clinton, 2 mi SW on CR 6; 3 mi E on CR 458; 0.8 mi N on gravel CR 700E. 4/1-11/30; 14-day limit. 48 sites. At non-elec sites, $8 for self-registration, $10 if ranger collects ($4 & $5 with federal senior pass); at elec sites, $12 self-registration, $14 if ranger collects ($6 & $7 with senior pass). No reservations. Elec sites 1-5 & 22-50 only for equestrian campers; only campground on the lake providing mule or horse camping. Flush & pit toilets, plus pit toilet just outside campground for non-campers. New showers, picnic shelter, corrals. Day use parking area for non-campers. NRRS during 4/1-9/30. **GPS: 38.890137, -95.365234**

WOODRIDGE PARK

From Stull, 3.4 mi S on CR 458; 1 mi E on CR 2; 0.4 mi N on gravel CR 350E. All year; 14-day limit (park gate closed 11/1-3/15, so campers must hike in). Free primitive tent camping in small clearings along 4.5-mi trail or in mowed

area near park's entrance. Fire rings, all year drkg wtr, pit toilets, cfga. **GPS: 38.93431, -95.42531**

❸
COUNCIL GROVE LAKE
GPS: 38.698372, -96.50116

A 3,310 acre lake 1.5 miles NW of Council Grove off US 56 and SR 177, 101 miles SW of Kansas City. It is near the headwaters of the Neosho River. All-terrain vehicle area below the dam. Checkout time 4 p.m. Swimming permitted unless otherwise posted. Day use facilities include ORV trail at Outlet Park, hiking trails at Woodridge Park. All campsites have concrete slabs with picnic tables, utility table and grill or fire ring. Most have sun shelters over the tables as well as water hookups. Group camping areas are $80-$200 per night. The only designated swimming area is at Richey Cove Park. Three picnic shelters are $20 or $30. Some campsites free during winter with reduced amenities; wtr/elec service off 11/1-3/31, but hydrants provided at Neosho Park and the lake office. 50-amp electrical upgrades made at Canning Creek, Santa Fe Trail and Richey Cove Campgrounds. Non-campers pay $3 day use fees at the lake's eight Corps-operated boat ramps, $4 at other facilities and $1 per person at the swimming beach. Pioneer Nature Trail is just west of the lake office. The state's Council Grove Wildlife Area has two ramps. Lake Manager, Council Grove Lake, 945 Lake Rd., Council Grove, KS 66846-9322. (620) 767-5195.

CANNING CREEK COVE CAMP

From SR 177 at Council Grove, 0.1 mi W on US 56; 1.4 mi NW on Mission St (becoming Lake Rd) to spillway, then 2 mi NW on Lake Rd & N on park access rd. All year; 14-day limit. 4 non-elec sites, $12 during 4/1-10/31 ($6 with federal senior pass), free off-season. Elec sites, $17 base, $22 for 50-amp elec at premium locations ($8.50 & $11 with senior pass). RV limit in excess of 65'. Picnic shelters $20. Tbls, flush toilets, cfga, drkg wtr, showers, dump, playground, shelters. Hiking trails, fishing, boating(ld), horseshoe pits. Non-campers pay day use fee for boat ramp, picnicking, dump. Three group camping areas (2 with full hookups at 16 & 20 sites), $80-$200 (2-night minimum stay). (620) 767-6745. NRRS during 4/14-9/30. **GPS: 38.41539, -96.32237**

CUSTER PARK

From Council Grove at jct with US 56, 3.5 mi N on SR 55/177, then W to park. 3/1-11/30; 14-day limit. 10 small sites without hookups, most suitable for tent camping, $8 ($4 with federal senior pass). Pit toilets, tbls, drkg wtr, cfga. Non-campers pay day use fee for boat ramp. Self-registration. **GPS: 38.709499, -96.503098**

KANZA VIEW CAMPGROUND

2 mi N of Council Grove on SR 177; qtr mi W on dam rd; at E end of dam. All year; 14-day limit. 5 primitive sites, $8 ($4 with federal senior pass) during 4/1-11/1; some sites free rest of year, but get wtr from Neosho campground & office area. Pit toilets, cfga, drkg wtr (no hookups). Free picnic shelter, no boat ramp. Most suitable for tent camping.

KIT CARSON COVE CAMP

From Council Grove at jct with US 56, 2 mi N on SR 177/57, then W. All year; 14-day limit. 1 site without hookups, $10 ($4 with federal senior pass); 14 elec/wtr sites (30-amp), $17; 1 full hookup site $19. 3/1-10/31. In winter, some sites free without services (after 11/1, no wtr except at Neosho campground and near project office). Tbls, flush toilets, cfga, drkg wtr, showers. Boating(l), hiking, fishing. Non-campers pay day use fee at boat ramp. **GPS: 38.695313, 96.4956052**

MARINA COVE CAMPGROUND

From SR 177 at Council Grove, 0.1 mi W on US 56; 1.4 mi NW on Mission St (becoming Lake Rd) to spillway, then 1.5 mi W on Lake Rd; on right. All year; 14-day limit. During 4/1-10/31, 1 primitive site $8 ($4 with federal senior pass), 3 elec sites (30-amp), $12 ($6 with senior pass). Off-season, some sites free without services (after 11/1, no wtr except at Neosho campground and near project office). Tbls, pit toilets, cfga, drkg wtr (no wtr hookups), fish cleaning station. Boating(l), fishing. Private marina with elec/wtr sites. Non-campers pay day use fee for boat ramp. **GPS: 38.680401 -96.50203**

NEOSHO CAMPGROUND

From SR 177 at Council Grove, 0.1 mi W on US 56; 1.4 mi NW on Mission St (becoming Lake Rd) to spillway, then 0.3 mi W; on right. All year; 14-day limit. 7 elec sites, $13 during 4/1-10/31 ($6.50 with federal senior pass), $18 at 1 full-hookup site. Off-season, some sites free without elec. Pit toilets, tbls, cfga drkg wtr from campground hydrant. Boating(ld), fishing. Non-campers pay day use fee for boat ramp. **GPS: 38.68042, -96.517822**

RICHEY COVE CAMPGROUND

From Council Grove at jct with US 56, 2.8 mi N on SR 57/177, W side. All year; 14-day limit. 11 sites, $17 during 4/1-10/31 ($8.50 with federal senior pass; 21 elec/wtr sites, $18 during 4/1-10/31 ($9 with senior pass); full hookups $25 ($12.50 with senior pass). Wtr/elec off during 11/1-3/31; some sites free. Tbls, flush & pit toilets, cfga, drkg wtr, showers, dump, playground, beach wi-fi. Hiking trails, fishing, boating(ld), swimming, horseshoe pits. RV limit in excess of 65 ft. Group camping area, $100 with 2-night minimum stay. 620-767-5195. NRRS during 4/15-9/30. **GPS: 38.42050, -96.32237**

SANTA FE CAMPGROUND

From SR 177 at Council Grove, 0.1 mi W on US 56; 1.4 mi NW on Mission St (becoming Lake Rd) to spillway, then 2 mi W on Lake Rd; right on access rd. All year; 14-day limit. During 3/1-10/31, 2 non-hookup sites $11-

$12 ($5.50-$6 with federal senior pass); 5 elec sites (no wtr hookup), $15 ($7.50 with senior pass); 28 elec/wtr sites, $18 base, $22 full hookups ($9 & $11 with senior pass). No wtr service after 11/1. Tbls, flush & pit toilets, cfga, drkg wtr, dump, playground. Boating(ld), fishing, waterskiing, hiking trails, horseshoe pits. Group camping area, $140 with a 2-night minimum stay. Non-campers pay day use fee for boat ramp. (620) 767-7125. NRRS during 4/15-9/30. **GPS: 38.40897, -96.31489**

❹
ELK CITY LAKE
GPS: 37.2817, -96.7833

A 4,122-acre lake 5 miles NW of Independence and US 160, 127 miles E of Wichita in southern Kansas. Six scenic hiking trails, including Eagle Rock Mountain Bike Trail, two nature trails and a multi-purpose, all-weather trail. The Corps manages two campgrounds. Elk City State Park contains a boat ramp, beach, campground, playgrounds and hiking trails. Lake Manager, P. O. Box 426, Cherryvale, KS 67335-0426. (620) 336-2741.

CARD CREEK RECREATION AREA

From Elk City at jct with SR 39, 7 mi S then E on US 160; 1.3 mi N on 2500 Rd; W then N on 4600 rd; 1.7 mi W on 4800 Rd. All year; 14-day limit. 7 primitive tent sites, $10 ($5 with federal senior pass), free during 11/1-3/31; 7 RV sites with 50-amp elec, some pull-through, $16 ($8 with senior pass), free during 11/1-3/31 no utilities & reduced services. Tbls, flush toilets, cfga, drkg wtr, dump ($4 non-campers), playground, picnic shelter $30. Hiking, boating(ld), fishing.
GPS: 37.25708, -95.848145

OUTLET CHANNEL RECREATION AREA

From US 75 in Independence, about 3 mi W on Taylor Rd (becoming CR 4675); half mi N on CR 3525; 2 mi W on CR 4800; N on Table Mound Rd, then veer left at "Y" onto 3300

Rd; NW on 3300 Rd; W on dam rd to W side of spillway, then NE (right) on access rd to campground. All year; 14-day limit. 4 non-elec sites, $12 ($6 with federal senior pass) during 3/26-11/1; free rest of year, but no wtr. 15 elec sites (30-amp), $16 ($8 with senior pass) during 3/26-11/1; free rest of yr, but no elec or wtr. Tbls, flush & pit toilets, cfga, drkg wtr, picnic shelter $30, playground, dump, showers. Fishing, boating. Non-campers pay $4 showers & dump. **GPS: 37.280377, -95.782517**

❺
FALL RIVER LAKE
GPS: 37.64667, -96.07

A 2,450-acre lake 4 miles NW of the town of Fall River off US 400, 70 miles E of Wichita. Fall River is a tributary of the Verdigris River. Lake pool stretches upstream about 15 miles. All-terrain vehicles, golf carts must be street legal with tags and lights. Visitor center. Swimming beach at Whitehall Bay, on NE side of lake. Lake Manager, Fall River Lake, Rt.. 1, Box 243E, Fall River, KS 67047-9738. (620) 658-4445.

DAMSITE RECREATION AREA

From W of Fall River on US 400, N at milemarker 344 on Z50 Rd for 0.9 mi; right (E), then NE 2.4 mi on Cummins Rd; right (S) on access rd into park. All year; 14-day limit. 12 non-elec sites, $13 ($6.50 with federal senior pass) during 4/1-10/31; 8 elec 30-amp sites, $17 during 4/1-10/31 ($8.50 with senior pass). Sites $12 off-season with wtr but no showers & reduced amenities. 13 premium 50-amp elec sites, $19 during 4/1-10/31 ($9.50 with senior pass). 1 wtr/elec handicap site, $21 ($11.50 with senior or disabled pass). RV limit in excess of 65'. Tbls, flush & pit toilets, cfga, drkg wtr, showers, dump, playground, beach, free picnic shelter, coin laundry. Nature trails, interpretive programs, canoeing, jet skiing, swimming, boating(l). Group camping area, $84. NRRS during 4/1-10/30.
GPS: 37.64493, -96.06927

ROCK RIDGE NORTH RECREATION AREA

From W of Fall River on US 400, at milemarker 344, 0.9 mi N on Z50 rd; at "Y," continue straight on Twp Rd 534 about 1 mi into Fall River State Park area; left (W) on Twp Rd 50B, and follow its curves N & E to Rock Ridge Park at W lakeshore on Casner Creek. 4/1-10/31; 14-day limit. 19 non-elec sites, $9 ($4.50 with federal senior pass); 23 elec sites, $13 ($6.50 with senior pass); 2 wtr/elec sites, $16 ($8 with senior pass). Off-season, some sites open with elec for $10 ($5 with senior pass). Tbls, toilets, cfga, drkg wtr, dump. Hiking, boating(l), fishing. **GPS: 37.662217, -96.106124**

WHITEHALL BAY CAMP

From W of Fall River on US 400, N at milemarker 344 on Z50 Rd for 0.9 mi; right (E), then 2.4 mi NE on Cummins Rd; at "Y," veer left on CR 20 across dam, then left (N) 0.8 mi; left (W) 0.7 mi; right (N) 1.7 mi to low water crossing, then N 0.1 mi, W 0.4 mi & left (S) for 1.1 mi to park. 4/1-10/31; 14-day limit. 1 site without hookups, $13 ($6.50 with federal senior pass); 14 elec sites, no wtr hookup, $17 ($8.50 with senior pass); 11 elec/wtr sites, $19 or $21 with 50-amp elec ($9.50 & $10.50 with senior pass). Some winters, some sites open & free but no utilities or services. RV limit in excess of 65 ft. Tbls, flush toilets, cfga, drkg wtr, showers, beach, coin laundry, picnic shelters. Boating(l), fishing, canoeing, waterskiing, hiking, jet skiing, swimming. Group camping areas with elec, $50-$84. NRRS. **GPS: 37.66717, -96.06268**

6

JOHN REDMOND DAM & RESERVOIR
GPS: 38.2417, -95.755

A 9,400-acre lake 6 miles N and W of Burlington off US 75, 110 miles SW of Kansas City. Off-road vehicle area at Otter Creek provides 240 acres for dirt bikes and all-terrain vehicles. 20-mile Hickory Creek Trail is currently being renovated for improved mountain biking, hiking and horseback riding. Hartford Recreation Area has a boat ramp and fish cleaning station. The U.S. Fish & Wildlife Service leases 18,500 of Corps property as part of the Flint Hills National Wildlife Refuge's migratory waterfowl program; hiking and interpretive trails are available. Picnicking at Overlook Park, boat ramp at Strawn Park. Lake Manager, John Redmond Dam, 1565 Embankment Rd. SW, Burlington, KS 66839-8911. (620) 364-8613.

DAMSITE AREA CAMPGROUND

3 mi N of Burlington on US 75; 0.5 mi W on 16th Rd, then 0.5 mi SW on Embankment Rd; right (W) on JRR Rd into campground; at W shore of lake. 4/1-10/31; 14-day limit. 4 non-elec sites, $10 ($5 with federal senior pass); 22 elec/wtr sites, some pull-through, $15 ($7.50 with senior pass). Tbls, flush toilets, cfga, drkg wtr, showers, dump, beach, playground, 3 picnic shelters $10. 3 group camping areas with elec, $30-$80. Nature trail, horseshoe pits, Hickory Creek trail, boating(ld), fishing, hiking, swimming, horseback riding, biking. No day use fees. Reservations 5/1-9/30, 620-364-8613; some sites usually free earlier & later. **GPS: 38.249253, -95.754604**

HARTFORD RECREATION AREA

From CR 130 at Hartford, 0.5 mi E on gravel Rd, following signs; NW of lake at Neosho River. Campsites removed; now lake access point. **GPS: 38.269926, -95.856991**

RIVERSIDE E. CAMPGROUND

From Burlington, 3 mi N on US 75; 0.5 mi W on 16th Rd, then 0.5 mi SW on Embankment Rd; left (E & S) on JRR Rd, following signs; at E shore of Neosho River below dam. 4/1-10/31; 14-day limit, 28 days with written permission. 53 elec/wtr sites with elec/wtr, $15 ($7.50 with federal senior pass); 6 pull-through. RV limit in excess of 65 ft. Tbls, pit toilets, cfga, drkg wtr, showers, dump, two picnic shelters $10. Interpretive trail (ticks are a problem), 11-mi multi-use (mountain biking, hiking, horseback) Hickory Creek Trail, fishing. No day use fees. 168 acres. 620-364-8613. NRRS during 4/1-9/30. **GPS: 38.240944, -95.751257**

RIVERSIDE W. CAMPGROUND

From Burlington, 3 mi N on US 75; 0.5 mi W on 16th Rd; left (S) about 1 mi, across dam, then left & right on JRR Rd into campground; at W bank of Neosho River below dam. 4/1-10/31; 14-day limit. 6 non-elec sites, $10 ($5 with federal senior pass). 47 elec sites (21 also with wtr, and 50-amp elec recently added to 13 sites), $15 ($7.50 with senior pass). Tbls, pit toilets, cfga, drkg wtr, dump, playground, picnic shelter $10. Universal access ramp to fishing dock. RV limit in excess of 65 ft. Boating(l), fishing, basketball. No day use fees. NRRS during 4/1-9/30. **GPS: 38.236461, -95.788789**

❼ KANOPOLIS LAKE
GPS: 38.6217, -97.97

A 3,400-acre lake with 41 miles of shoreline located 31 miles SW of Salina off Highway 141, 85 miles NW of Wichita. Historical & cultural site, visitor center. Camping is available at four Corps facilities and at two state parks. Day use includes hiking trails, an ATV riding area, boat ramps, picnic areas and playgrounds. Operations Manager, Kanopolis Lake, 105 Riverside Drive, Marquette, KS 67464-7464. (785) 546-2294.

BOLDT BLUFF PUBLIC USE AREA

From Marquette, about 6 mi W on SR 4; 1 mi N on SR 141; about 5 mi W on Avenue T; 3 mi N on gravel 25th Rd, then 2 mi E on Avenue Q; at east-central shore of lake. All year; 14-day limit. Free primitive camping area, no designated sites. Toilets, cfga, no drkg wtr. Boating(l), fishing. **GPS: 38.633779, -98.005956**

RIVERSIDE CAMPGROUND

From Marquette, about 6 mi W on SR 4; 3 mi N on SR 141; 0.5 mi E on Riverside Dr, following signs; at SE end of dam on Smoky Hill River. 5/1-9/30; 14-day limit. During 5/1-9/30, $12 at 12 primitive sites, $16 at elec sites, $18 for elec/wtr ($6, $8 & $9 with federal senior pass). Off-season, primitive sites free, 16 elec sites $6 ($3 with senior pass). RV limit in excess of 65'. Tbls, flush & pit toilets, cfga, drkg wtr, showers, dump, playground, beach, fish. Boating(l), fishing, basketball, swimming. NRRS. **GPS: 38.59972, -97.93333**

VENANGO CAMPGROUND

From Marquette, about 6 mi W on SR 4; 5 mi N on SR 141; on left, at NW end of dam. All year; 14-day limit. During 5/1-9/30, $12 at 72 primitive sites, $16 at 83 elec sites ($18 at 32 with elec/wtr); seniors pay $6, $8 & $9 with federal senior pass. Off-season, primitive sites free, no elec or wtr service. 85 total sites; RV limit in excess of 65 ft. Primitive group camping area with shelter house, $60. 1 tbl, flush & pit toilets, cfga, drkg wtr, showers, beach, playground, dump, four picnic shelters ($20). ATV trail, nature trail, boating(l), fishing, swimming, waterskiing, hiking. NRRS. **GPS: 38.632411, -97.983128**

YANKEE RUN POINT

From Marquette, about 6 mi W on SR 4; 1 mi N on SR 141; about 5 mi W on gravel Avenue T; 3 mi N on gravel 25th Rd; 1 mi E on Avenue Q; 1 mi N on gravel 25th Rd; at E shore of lake. All year; 14-day limit. Free primitive camping at undesignated sites. Pit toilet, cfga, no drkg wtr. Boating(l), trails. **GPS: 38.6430636, -98.0169947**

❽ MARION RESERVOIR
GPS: 38.3683, -97.0833

A 6,200-acre lake 3 miles NW of Marion off US 56, 46 miles NE of Wichita, Marion features

171 campsites at four parks. Unregistered vehicles, all-terrain vehicles, golf carts prohibited. 1-mile Willow Walk Nature Trail at Cottonwood Point. Non-campers pay day use fee for campground boat ramps, but undeveloped ramps at Durham Cove & Broken Ridge are free. Campgrounds open in fall until water is turned off about 11/15. Cottonwood Point Campground was expanded & renovated in 2011-2012. Lake Manager, Marion Reservoir, 2105 Pawnee Rd., Marion, KS 66861-9740. (620) 382-2101.

COTTONWOOD POINT CAMP

From Marion, 3 mi W on US 56; about 3.5 mi N on Quail Creek Rd; 2 mi W on 220th St; at E shore of lake. 3/15-11/15; 14-day limit. 53 elec sites (30-amp), $18 ($9 with federal senior pass); 41 elec/wtr sites (50-amp), $21 ($10.50 with senior pass); 7 pull-through. Closed off-season. 50-ft RV limit. Tbls, flush toilets, cfga, drkg wtr, showers, dump, beach, playground, 2 picnic shelters $20. Boating(ld), fishing, hiking, swimming. Two group camping areas with elec, 10 sites for $80, 14 sites for $100. No NRRS service. Note: During early 2015, expansion plans called for this campground to have 36 full-hookup sites priced at $23 ($11.50 with senior pass).
GPS: 38.391237, -97.086396

FRENCH CREEK COVE PUBLIC USE AREA

3 mi E of Hillsboro on US 56; 3 mi N on Limestone Rd; at S shore of lake's French Creek cove. 3/15-11/15; 14-day limit. 20 elec sites, $12 ($6 with federal senior pass). No off-season camping. Tbls, toilets, cfga, drkg wtr. Boating(ld), fishing. Non-campers pay day use fee for boat ramp, picnicking.
GPS: 38.86948, -97.149063

HILLSBORO COVE CAMP

From Marion, about 7 mi W on US 56; qtr mi N on Nighthawk Rd, then E on access rd to park; at SW shore of lake. 3/15-11/15; 14-

day limit. 20 elec sites 20/30-amp, $17 base ($8.50 with federal senior pass); 30 elec/wtr sites 20/30/50-amp, $19 base ($9.50 with senior pass). 1 RV & 2 tents or 3 tents per site. No camping off-season. 50-ft RV limit; 8 pull-through sites. Tbls, flush & pit toilets, cfga, drkg wtr, showers, dump, pay phone, playground, beach. Group camping area, $80. Boating(ld), fishing, swimming, hiking. NRRS during 4/10-10/15.
GPS: 38.362556, -97.104560

MARION COVE CAMPGROUND

From Marion, 3 mi W on US 56; 2 mi N on Quail Creek Rd; 2 mi W on 210th St; right on park access rd; at SE shore of lake. All year; 14-day limit. Free (formerly $8). 2 RV sites, 4 tent sites. All year; 14-day limit. Tbls, pit toilets, cfga, drkg wtr. Boating(l), fishing. No day use fees. GPS: 38.382542, -97.076064

9

MELVERN LAKE
GPS: 38.515, -95.705

A 6,900-acre lake on the Marais des Cygnes River with 101 miles of shoreline on eastern edge of the state's Flinthills prairie region. It is 3.5 miles W of Melvern on SR 31 and W of US 75, N of I-35 and 39 miles S of Topeka. Historic and cultural site, visitor center with interpretive programs, displays, exhibits. Group tours provided upon request. The Corps operates five parks & charges day use fees for boat launching ($3 or $30 annually), beach use ($4 per vehicle or $30 annually) and shelter reservations ($20 & $40). All campgrounds are open and free during the winter, but no facilities or utilities are available. Eisenhower State Park is on the N shore of the lake; it offers camping, hiking, mountain biking, boat launching and outdoor games. Project Office, Melvern Lake, 31051 Melvern Parkway, Melvern, KS 66510-9759. (785) 549-3318.

ARROW ROCK PARK

From Melvern, 3 mi W on SR 31 (Melvern Rd); 3 mi S on US 75 to Olivet exit; 1.5 mi W on CR 276; 1 mi N on S. Fairlawn Rd; 1 mi W on Arrow Rock Pkwy; at S shore of lake. All year; 14-day limit. 24 non-elec sites, $12 during 5/1-9/30 ($6 with federal senior pass), free rest of year; 19 elec/wtr sites (30-amp), $18 ($9 with senior pass). 43 total sites (5 pull-through); RV limit in excess of 65'. Fish cleaning station, tbls, flush toilets, cfga, drkg wtr, showers, playground, dump, coin laundry. Boating(ld), fishing. NRRS during 5/1-9/30. **GPS: 38.490749, -95.75924**

COEUR D'ALENE PARK

From Melvern, 3 mi W on SR 31 (Melvern Rd) to just past jct with US 75; 2 mi S on Melvern Lake Pkwy; 1 mi NW on Coeur D'Alene Pkwy access rd; at SE corner of lake. All year; 14-day limit. 22 non-elec sites, $12 during 5/1-9/30 ($6 with federal senior pass), free rest of year; 33 elec (30-amp) sites, $17 during 5/1-9/30 ($8.50 with senior pass); 1 handicap site with 50-amp elec/wtr/sewer, $20. 56 total sites; RV limit 50'. Tbls, flush toilets, cfga, drkg wtr, playgrounds, 2 picnic shelters ($20), fish cleaning station, dump, beach, coin laundry, showers. Horseshoe pits, 2 nature trails, boating(ld), fishing, hiking, swimming. NRRS during 5/1-9/30. **GPS: 38.497501, -95.718126**

OUTLET PARK

From Melvern, 3 mi W on SR 31 (Melvern Rd) to just past jct with US 75; 0.3 mi W on Melvern Lake Pkwy; 0.3 mi W on Cutoff Rd; 0.5 mi N on River Pond Pkwy, below dam. All year; 14-day limit. During 4/1-10/31, 61 elec 30-amp sites, $17 ($8.50 with federal senior pass); 89 full-hookup 50-amp sites, $22 ($11 with senior pass). Some sites free off-season, but no utilities. 150 total sites; RV limit in excess of 65'. Tbls, flush toilets, cfga, drkg wtr, dump, showers, coin laundry, 2 playgrounds, beach, amphitheater, fish cleaning station,

change house at beach, pay phones. Boating(ld), fishing, swimming, 3-mi hiking/biking trail, 2 sand volleyball courts. 90-acre fishing pond (elec mtrs), historic suspension bridge. Youth camping, $25. Group pavilion with grill/smoker, restrooms, sink, ceiling fan, serving tbl. NRRS during 4/1-10/31. **GPS: 38.513453, -95.706228**

SUN DANCE PARK

From just N of Lebo at I-35/US 50, 4.5 mi N on Fauna Rd NW (becoming S. Hoch Rd); right on W. 325th St into park just S of Arvonia; at SW shore of lake. All year; 14-day limit. 25 free primitive gravel sites. Tbls, toilets, cfga, no drkg wtr. Boating(l), fishing, horseback riding. No day use fee for picnicking, shelter or boat ramp. **GPS: 38.477648, -95.851313**

TURKEY POINT PARK

From Melvern, 3 mi W on SR 31 (Melvern Rd); 2.5 mi N on US 75; about 5 mi W on SR 278 (past Eisenhower State Park); at "Y" jct with 293rd St, veer right (S) for 1 mi on SR 278 (S. Indian Hills Rd), then continue S on Indian Hills; follow Turkey Point Pkway 0.5 mi into campground at N shore of lake. All year; 14-day limit. During 5/1-9/30, $12 at 13 non-elec sites ($6 with federal senior pass), free off-season; 15 elec/wtr sites (30-amp), $18 ($9 with senior pass). 48 total sites; 3 pull-through; 65-ft RV limit. Tbls, flush toilets, cfga, drkg wtr, showers, coin laundry, playground, fish cleaning station. Fishing, boating(ld), horseshoe pits, volleyball. Lake View group camping area & shelter with elec & grills; restrooms, playground; 12 sites with wtr/elec 50-amp, $160. Group camping with elec, $160. Turkey Point primitive group camping area with 3 large camping pads & shelter with wtr, elec, grill, $40. NRRS during 5/1-9/30. **GPS: 38.499281, -95.789773**

⑩ MILFORD LAKE
GPS: 39.0833, -96.895

A 15,700-acre lake 5 miles NW of Junction City/I-70 on Hwy K-57 W of US 77, 65 miles W of Topeka. Project office/information center has displays and exhibits along with a 24-hour accessible brochure information area. 11 free picnic shelters can be reserved for $25. Non-campers day use fees: $1 per person or $4 per vehicle at swimming beaches; $3 at boat ramps; $2 dump station (or $30 annually). Day use areas: School Creek ORV Areas -- an off-road vehicle area for vehicles less than 50 inches wide only; East Rolling Hills Park -- boat ramp, picnic shelter, playground, beach, interpretive trail; North Overlook Park -- picnic shelter, playground; Outlet Park -- boat ramp, picnic shelter, playground, beach, bridle trails. Free campsites during winter (at School Creek & Timber Creek Parks) may have reduced amenities. Some free sites available all year at West Rolling Hills Park. Other Milford camping includes Clay County Park, Flagstop RV Park, Milford State Park, Thunderbird Marina. Milford Nature Center and Fish Hatchery is below dam. Project Manager, Milford Lake, 5203 North Highway K/57, Junction City, KS 66441. (785) 238-5714.

CURTIS CREEK PARK

2 mi NW of Junction City on SR 57 (N. Jackson St); W on SR 244 until it curves N, becoming Trail Rd; about 3 mi N on Trail Rd; at "Y," veer right on 3500 Ave about 1 mi to park access rd. 4/15-9/30; 14-day limit. 8 tent sites & 20 RV sites without hookups, $12 ($6 with federal senior pass); 48 elec sites (30-amp), $16, $18 for elec/wtr ($8 & $9 with senior pass). RV limit in excess of 65'. Tbls, flush & pit toilets, cfga, drkg wtr, dump, playground, showers, pay phone, fishing pier. Boating(ld), fishing. Non-campers pay $3 for boat ramp, dump. 785-238-2474. NRRS. **GPS: 39.09278, -96.955**

FARNUM CREEK PARK

From Milford at Houston Rd, about 2 mi S on US 77 across bridge, then left on access rd, following signs; pass Acorns Resort entry, then left into park; at S shore of bay, east-central part of lake. 4/15-9/30; 14-day limit. 23 non-elec sites, $12 ($6 with federal senior pass); 36 elec sites -- $18 for 30-amp elec/wtr, $19 for 50-amp elec/wtr ($9 & $9.50 with senior pass); 5 pull-through sites; 60-ft RV limit. Tbls, flush & pit toilets, cfga, drkg wtr, dump, playground, showers, fish cleaning station. Boating(ld), fishing. Non-campers pay $3 for dump station, boat ramp. 785-463-5791. NRRS 4/15-9/30. **GPS: 39.15125, -96.90245**

SCHOOL CREEK PARK

From just W of Wakefield at jct with SR 82, about 5 mi S, then 4 mi E on SR 837; 1.9 mi E on Luttman Rd to ORV entrance into park; at W shore of lake. All year; 14-day limit. 56 sites, 12 primitive. During 4/15-9/30, $8 ($4 with federal senior pass); off-season, some sites are free. RV limit 30'. Tbls, pit toilets, cfga, drkg wtr, playground. Boating(l), fishing, ORV riding area on 300 acres. **GPS: 39.14770, -96.94135**

TIMBER CREEK PARK

From Wakefield, 1 mi E across lake bridge on SR 82, then S into park; at NE shore of lake. All year; 14-day limit. 36 sites, $8 during 4/15-9/30 ($4 with federal senior pass). Some sites free off-season. Tbls, pit toilets, cfga, drkg wtr, playground. Nature trail, boating(l), fishing. **GPS: 39.21333, -96.97388**

WEST ROLLING HILLS CAMP

2 mi NW of Junction City on SR 57 (N. Jackson St); about 4 mi W on SR 244; N on W. Rolling Hill Rd, following signs to campground; at lake's SE shore. All year; 14-day limit. During 4/15-9/30, 12 tent sites & 6 non-elec RV sites, $12 ($6 with federal senior pass); 38 elec/wtr sites, $18 for 30-amp, $19 for 50-amp ($9 & $9.50 with senior pass). 3 pull-through sites;

RV limit in excess of 65'. Some free primitive campsites also available all year (locations in Milford Lake brochure). Tbls, flush & pit toilets, cfga, drkg wtr, dump, playground, beach, fish cleaning stations, pay phone. Boating(ld), fishing, swimming, hiking, ORV activities. Marina. Non-campers pay $3 for boat ramp, dump, picnicking. NRRS.
GPS: 39.0748, -96.92319

⑪ PERRY LAKE
GPS: 39.1117, -95.425

An 11,150-acre lake 3 miles NW of Perry off US 24, 15 miles NE of Topeka; at Delaware River. Unregistered vehicles, offroad vehicles, motorcycles, golf carts prohibited. 29-mile Perry Lake National Recreation Trail follows eastern shoreline; other trails include the 140-acre Perry Lake ATV & Motorcycle Trail, 2.5-mile Thunder Ridge Trail at Slough Creek Park, the 1.75-mile Delaware Marsh Trail and two trailheads of the 25-mile Perry Lake Equestrian Trail. Visitor center. Day use facilities: Outlet Park -- picnicking, ORV trail, multi-use trail; Perry Park -- boat ramp, beach; Thompsonville Park -- picnicking. Non-campers pay $3 fees at boat ramps, $1 per person or $4 vehicle at the beach. Picnic shelters that may be reserved are at the beach ($20), Dedication Point ($20), Old Town Park ($20) and Rock Creek Park ($30). Project Manager, Perry Lake, 10419 Perry Park Drive, Perry, KS 66073-9717. (785) 597-5144.

LONGVIEW PARK

From Oskaloosa, 5.5 mi W on SR 92; 2.1 mi S on Ferguson Rd; 1.5 mi W on 86th St; 1 mi S on Hamilton Rd into park; at E shore of lake. 5/1-9/30; 14-day limit. 6 walk-to tent sites & 13 RV/tent sites without hookups, $12 ($6 with federal senior pass); 26 elec sites, $16 ($8 with senior pass). No off-season camping. Group walk-to tent camping area, $30. RV limit in excess of 65'. 316 acres. Tbls, flush toilets, cfga, drkg wtr, showers, dump, playground.

Boating(ld), fishing, Perry Hiking Trail, 18-hole disc golf course. NRRS.
GPS: 39.189359, -95.440679

OLD TOWN PARK

From Oskaloosa, 6 mi W on SR 92; on the S side before the bridge (signs); at E side of lake. 5/1-9/30; 14-day limit (no off-season camping). 43 non-elec sites, $12 ($6 with federal senior pass); 33 elec/wtr sites ($8.50 with senior pass). Tbls, flush toilets, cfga, drkg wtr, showers, dump, playground, picnic shelter ($20). Boating(ld), fishing, hiking, biking. RV limit in excess of 65'. NRRS. **GPS: 39.226187, -95.441043**

ROCK CREEK PARK

From Perry, about 6 mi W on US 24; 3 mi N on SR 237; E on Rock Creek Park Rd, following signs; at W side of lake. 5/1-9/30; 14-day limit. 20 walk-to tent sites & 56 RV/tent sites without hookups, $12; 30-amp elec sites (no wtr hookup) $16, 30-amp elec/wtr $17; 50-amp elec/wtr $18 ($6, $8, $8.50 & $9 with federal senior pass). RV limit in excess of 65'. 2 tents or 1 RV & 1 tent per site. Tbls, flush toilets, cfga, drkg wtr, showers, dump, playground, fish cleaning station, picnic shelter ($30). Boating(d), fishing, horseback riding trails, biking. 658 acres. NRRS 5/1-9/30. **GPS: 39.120680, -95.451343**

SLOUGH CREEK PARK

From Perry at jct with Hwy 24, 7 mi N on Ferguson Rd (CR 1029), crossing bridge over Slough Creek arm of lake; 1 mi S on Slough Creek Rd; on peninsula at NE shore. 4/15-10/15; 14-day limit. 18 walk-to tent sites & 120 sites without hookups, $12 ($6 with federal senior pass); 127 elec sites -- 30-amp elec (no wtr hookup) $16, 30-amp elec/wtr $17; 50-amp elec/wtr $18 ($8, $8.50 & $9 with senior pass). 15 pull-through sites, RV limit in excess of 65 ft. Two group camping areas, $30. Tbls, flush toilets, cfga, drkg wtr, dump, playground, fish cleaning stations. Boating(ld), fishing, biking, hiking (2.5-mi interpretive trail & 30-

mi Perry Hiking Trail). 833 acres. NRRS.
GPS: 39.135354, -95.428362

⑫ POMONA LAKE
GPS: 38.6517, -95.5567

A 4,000-acre lake 17 mi W of Ottawa on SR 268/68; 1 mile N on Pomona Dam Rd. 35 miles S of Topeka. The dam releases water into 110-Mile Creek, which flows into the Marais de Cygnes, Osage and Missouri Rivers. Visitor center. Besides Corps facilities, camping is provided by Pomona State Park. Day use facilities include accessible fishing docks at Michigan Valley Park; boat ramp, picnicking facilities and playground at Management Park, and nature trails at Outlet Area & 110-Mile Parks. Project Manager, Pomona Lake, 5260 Pomona Dam Rd., Vassar, KS 66543-9743. (785) 453-2201.

CARBOLYN PARK

From Lyndon, 4.5 mi N on US 75; E on E. 217th St before Dragoon Creek bridge (signs), then right on access rd; at W side of lake on Dragoon Creek arm (former Carbolyn State Park). 5/1-9/30; 14-day limit. 3 primitive sites, $12 ($6 with federal senior pass); 26 elec sites, $16 ($8 with senior pass). 55-ft RV limit. Tbls, flush toilets, cfga, drkg wtr, dump, playground, picnic shelter. NRRS. **GPS: 38.675125, 95.67684**

CEDAR PARK

From Michigan Valley, 2 mi W on E 213th St; 1 mi N on S. Shawnee Heights Rd; 3 mi W on E. 205th St across Valley Brook bridge, then about 1 mi farther to access rd on left; at NE side of lake on Plummer Creek arm. Or, 1 mi N of Michigan Valley on S. Michigan Rd, then W on 205th St to park. All year; 14-day limit. 8 free primitive sites. Tbls, pit toilets, cfga, no drkg wtr. Rock boat ramp.
GPS: 38.693382, -95.609207

MICHIGAN VALLEY PARK

From Michigan Valley, 1 mi S on S. Stubbs Rd; 1 mi W on E. 221st St; S on access rd; at NE side of dam. 5/1-9/30; 14-day limit. 38 primitive sites $14 ($7 with federal senior pass); 57 wtr/elec sites -- $18 base for 30-amp, $20 for 8 prime pull-through 50-amp elec sites, $22 for 9 full hookups ($9, $10 & $11 with senior pass). RV limit in excess of 65 ft. Tbls, flush & pit toilets, cfga, drkg wtr, dump, playground, beach, amphitheater. Boating(l), fishing, swimming, basketball, ball field, accessible fishing pier. Group primitive camping area with beach, playground, $40. Three picnic shelters, $30, $40 & $60. Marina. NRRS. **GPS: 38.659292, -95.550027**

OUTLET AREA PARK

From Michigan Valley, 2 mi S on S. Stubbs Rd; 1.5 mi W on gravel E. 229th St, then left (SW) on access rd; below dam along S shore of 110 Mile Creek at S side of lake. All year; 14-day limit. During 4/1-10/31, $16 base at 36 elec/wtr sites, $18 for premium locations ($8 & $9 with federal senior pass). Off-season, $10 for elec sites ($5 with senior pass), but no wtr services. Tbls, flush & pit toilets, cfga, drkg wtr, dump, playground, picnic shelters ($30), amphitheater. Interpretive nature trail, boating(l), fishing, hiking. NRRS (4/1-10/31). **GPS: 38.643272, -95.560176**

WOLF CREEK PARK

From Michigan Valley, about 3 mi W on E. 213th St, then SW on Pomona Dam Rd to park; on W side of lake's Wolf Creek arm. 4/1-9/15; 14-day limit. 43 primitive sites, $14 ($7 with federal senior pass); 44 elec sites, $18 ($9 with senior pass). 65-ft RV limit. Tbls, flush & pit toilets, cfga, drkg wtr, dump, playground. 18-hole disc golf, boating(l), fishing, ball field. Group camping area $150 with 23 elec/wtr sites, shelter. NRRS. **GPS: 38.677571, -95.567837**

110 MILE PARK

From Michigan Valley, 1 mi N on S. Michigan Rd; about 2.5 mi W on E. 205th St; 1 mi S on Lake Rd; 1 mi E on E. 209th St; 2 mi S on S. Paulen Rd; about 1 mi S into park, following signs. On tip of peninsula between lake's 110-Mile Creek & Wolf Creek arms. All year; 14-day limit. Free. 25 primitive sites. No wtr during 10/1-4/30. Group equestrian camping area may be reserved through lake office. Short walking trail & 33-mi trail for hikers, bikers, horse riders. **GPS: 38.670401, -95.579166**

⑬ TUTTLE CREEK LAKE
GPS: 39.2567, -96.59

A 12,570-acre lake 5 miles N of Manhattan on US 24 and SR 13, 55 miles W of Topeka. Campsites that are free sites during winter may have reduced amenities. The state of Kansas also operates campgrounds around the lake as part of Tuttle Creek State Park -- Randolph Park on the NE side; River Pond Park below the dam; Spillway Park on E side of lake; Fancy Creek Park on NW end of lake, and Rocky Ford Campground on S side of lake. County-operated Carnahan Creek Park on the E side offers free random camping. Corps day use areas include Observation Point -- shelter, interpretive trail; ORV Area -- picnicking, off-road vehicle trails; Outlet Park -- picnicking, fish cleaning station, shelters, playground, interpretive trail; Spillway Cycle Area -- picnicking, off-road vehicle trails, multi-purpose trail. Project Manager, Tuttle Creek Lake, 5020 Tuttle Creek Blvd, Manhattan, KS 66502-8812. (785) 539-8511.

STOCKDALE PARK

From Riley, about 4 mi E on US 24 about 2 mi W of jct with US 77; 1.5 mi N on CR 895; 2.5 mi E on Stockdale Park rd; at W shore of lake at Mill Creek arm. 188 acres. All year; 14-day limit. 12 elec/wtr sites (30/50-amp), $18 during 4/15-10/31 ($9 with federal senior pass). During 11/1-4/14, some sites free with reduced amenities and no utilities. RV limit in excess of 65 ft. Flush toilets, tbls, cfga, drkg wtr, dump, picnic shelter. Boating(l), fishing. 188 acres. No day use fees. NRRS during 4/15-9/30. **GPS: 39.305231, -96.653380**

TUTTLE CREEK COVE PARK

From Manhattan at the Kansas River, about 8 mi N on US 24; right (N) on SR 13, then immediately left (NW) on Tuttle Cove Rd for 3 mi into park; at SW corner of lake. 252 acres. $12 at 17 non-elec sites; $18 at 39 elec/wtr sites ($6 & $9 with federal senior pass). 4/15-10/31; 14-day limit. Some sites open & free off-season (11-1/4/14), but no utilities. Tbls, Picnic shelter. NRRS (4/15-10/31). Tbls, flush toilets, showers, cfga, drkg wtr, dump, beach, playground. Boating(ld), fishing, swimming. Day use fees, $3 boat ramp, $4 beach (per vehicle). **GPS: 39.279674, -96.631751**

⑭ WILSON LAKE
GPS: 36.9683, -98.495

A 9,000-acre lake 7 miles S of Lucas on SR 232, 135 miles NW of Wichita on the Saline River. Offroad vehicles prohibited. Campsites that are free or have lower fees off-season may have reduced amenities. State of Kansas operates Wilson & Otoe State Park campgrounds (marina at Wilson SP). Visitor center. Day use fees charged to non-campers ($3 daily or $30 annually at boat ramps); no fees at swimming beaches. Resource Manager, Wilson Lake, 4860 Outlet Boulevard, Sylvan Grove, KS 67481. (785) 658-2551.

LUCAS PARK

From Lucas, about 6 mi S on SR 232; just before curve, right (S) on 203 St for 2 mi to park; on N side of lake. All year; 14-day limit. During 5/15-9/15, 28 non-elec RV/tent sites, $12 during ($6 with federal senior pass); 54 elec sites (no wtr), $18 ($9 with senior pass); 16 elec/wtr sites, $20 ($10 with senior pass). During off-season, basic sites are free, elec sites $10 ($5 with senior pass). No wtr hookups or showers & reduced amenities off-season; pit toilets. RV limit in excess of 65 ft. 1 RV & 2 tent or 2 tents per sites ($12 for additional tent). Fishing pier, tbls, flush & pit toilets, cfga, drkg wtr, dump, playground, beach. Group camping area with 20 sites (15 elec, 8 with 50-amp), $150-$225; area includes playground, large fire ring, grill, shelter, sand volleyball, tbls, restroom. Volleyball courts, visitor center, 3-mile loop trail, boating(l), fishing, swimming, horseshoes. NRRS during 4/15-9/30. **GPS: 38.949597, -98.519704**

MINOOKA PARK

From Dorrance at I-70 exit 199, 7 mi N on Dorrance Rd (200th Rd), following signs; on S side of lake. All year; 14-day limit. During 5/1-9/30, 28 non-elec sites $12 ($6 with federal senior pass); 66 elec sites $18 ($9 senior pass); 52 elec/wtr sites $20 ($10 with senior pass). During off-season, basic sites are free, elec sites $10 ($5 with senior pass); no wtr hookups or showers & reduced amenities off-season; pit toilets. RV limit in excess of 65 ft. Tbls, flush & pit toilets, tbls, cfga, drkg wtr, showers, dump, playground, beach, fish cleaning station, visitor center, amphitheater, picnic shelter $20. Group camping area with 12 back-in RV sites (6 with elec, 6 with elec/wtr), $200; typically 55 ft sites up to 120 ft; area includes playground, large fire ring, grill, shelter, restrooms. Sand volleyball courts, boating(l), fishing, swimming. NRRS during 4/15-9/30. **GPS: 38.939518, -98.571782**

SYLVAN PARK

From Lucas, 7 mi S on SR 232, then over dam; left on Outlet Rd; below the dam on N side of spillway; at W shore of Saline River. All year; 14-day limit. During 5/1-9/30, 4 non-elec sites $12 ($6 with federal senior pass); 24 elec/wtr sites $20 ($10 with senior pass). During off-season, basic sites are free, elec sites $10 ($5 with senior pass); no wtr hookups or showers & reduced amenities off-season; pit toilets. RV limit in excess of 65 ft. 1 RV & 1 tent or 2 tents per site (additional tent $12). Tbls, flush & pit toilets, cfga, drkg wtr, visitor center, showers, dump, playgrounds, beach, picnic shelters $20. Group camping area with 8 elec/wtr RV sites (1 pull-through), typically 75 ft, $125; area includes large fire ring, group shelter, sand volleyball,

horseshoe pit, tbls, flush toilets, showers. Horseshoe pits, volleyball court, boating(l), fishing, hiking, skiing. NRRS during 5/1-9/30. **GPS: 38.972264, -98.495028**

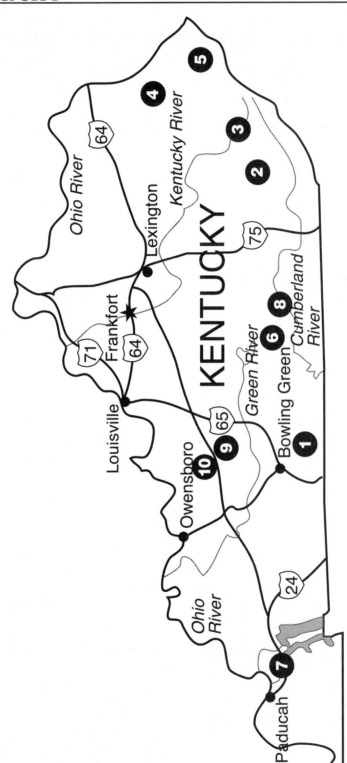

KENTUCKY

STATE INFORMATION:

CAPITAL: Frankfort
NICKNAME: Bluegrass State
STATEHOOD: 1792 - 15th State
FLOWER: Goldenrod
TREE: Tulip
BIRD: Cardinal

STATE TIDBITS:

• Fleming County is recognized as the Covered Bridge Capital of Kentucky.

• Cumberland is the only waterfall in the world to regularly display a Moonbow.

• Shelby County is recognized as the Saddlebred Capital of Kentucky.

WWW.KENTUCKYTOURISM.COM

Kentucky Dept of Tourism, 500 Mero St, Frankfort, KY 40601; 502-564-4930.

KENTUCKY LAKES

To find campgrounds operated by the U.S. Army Corps of Engineers, match the lake's numbers on the preceding map page with numbered lake entries on the following pages. Campgrounds are listed alphabetically under the appropriate lakes. The following Kentucky impoundments have Corps of Engineers campgrounds.

Barren River Lake. A 10,000-acre lake 20 miles E of Bowling Green and 1.5 miles SW of Finney on SR 252 or SR 1533.

Buckhorn Lake. A 1,230-acre lake 28 miles W of Hazard and N of Daniel Boone National Forest on SR 28, 0.5 miles from Buckhorn in southeastern Kentucky. It is on the Middle Fork of the Kentucky River.

Carr Creek Lake. A 710-acre lake 16 miles S of Hazard on SR 15, then 1 mile N on SR 1089 in southeastern Kentucky. The dam is 8.8 miles above the mouth of Carr Creek -- a tributary of the North Fork of Kentucky River.

Dewey Lake. A 1,100-acre lake 10 miles S of Van Lear on SR 302/3 in eastern Kentucky, SW of Huntington, West Virginia.

Fishtrap Lake. A 1,131-acre lake 16 miles S of Hazard on SR 15, then 1 mile N on SR 1089 in southeastern Kentucky near the Virginia/West Virginia state line.

Green River Lake. An 8,210-acre lake 9 miles S of Campbellsville on SR 55, 95 miles S of Louisville.

Lake Barkley. A 57,920-acre lake SE of I-24/US 62 near Gilbertsville, E of Paducah and S into Tennessee. It is the westernmost lake in a series of dam projects along the Cumberland River and its tributaries.

Lake Cumberland. A 50,000-acre lake S of Lexington near the Tennessee state line and S of the Cumberland Parkway. Wolf Creek Dam is on US 127, 4.2 miles S of the junction of SR 55/US 127.

Nolin River Lake. A 5,795-acre lake 2 miles N of Mammoth Cave National Park on SR 13/52. It is 15 miles N of Brownsville on SR 259, 22 miles S of Leitchfield on SR 259.

Rough River Lake. A 5,100-acre lake 1.4 miles N of Falls of Rough post office on SR 79, 51 miles N of Bowling Green.

Louisville District - All fee campgrounds may charge a visitor fee. Nashville District - Fees may be higher on weekends. A visitors fee may be charged.

❶

BARREN RIVER LAKE
GPS: 36.8967, -86.125

A 10,000-acre lake 20 miles E of Bowling Green and 1.5 miles SW of Finney on SR 252 or SR 1533. Alcohol and offroad vehicles prohibited. Campground checkout time 5 p.m. Camping also at Barren River State Park and Walnut Creek Campground. Visitor center. Day use facilities include: Browns Ford Park -- boat ramp; Overlook Park -- picnicking; Port Oliver Recreation Area -- boat ramp, picnicking, shelter, playground; Quarry Road Park -- fishing pier, picnicking, shelter, playground beach, hiking trail. $50 reservation fee for shelters, otherwise free. $4 day use fee at Quarry Road beach; Beaver Beach free; campers only at Bailey's Point & The Narrows beaches. Non-campers pay $3 at boat ramps ($4 for Quarry Road). Non-corps ramps free. All campgrounds closed off-season except primitive sites & pit toilets at Tailwater Park. Project Manager, Barren River Lake, 11088 Finney Rd., Glasgow, KY 42141-9642. (270) 646-2055.

BAILEY'S POINT CAMPGROUND

From Cedar Springs at jct with US 231/31E, 2 mi N on SR 252; 1.5 mi E on CR 517 (signs). About 4/15-10/25; 14-day limit. 53 non-elec sites, $17 ($8.50 with federal senior pass), $18 wtr hookup ($9 with senior pass). 150 elec/wtr sites, $23 ($11.50 with senior pass). 215 total sites; RV limit in excess of 65 ft. Tbls, flush & pit toilets, cfga, drkg wtr, dump, showers, 2 playgrounds, coin laundry, beach, amphitheater. Sand volleyball, basketball, boating(l), fishing, interpretive trail, horseshoe pits, swimming, waterskiing. C.E. Rager Nature Trail, Robert Foster Hiking Trail. Site of pre-Civil War homestead. 3-night minimum

stay on holiday weekends. (270) 622-6959. NRRS. **GPS: 36.889873, -86.096307**

BEAVER CREEK CAMPGROUND

5 mi S of Glasgow on US 31E (Scottsville Rd); 3 mi W on SR 252 following signs; left on Beaver Creek Boat Ramp Rd to lake; at jct of Skaggs Creek & Beaver Creek. About 4/15-10/25; 14-day limit. 12 primitive sites on hill above lake, $12. Pit toilet, cfga, drkg wtr, tbls. Boating(l), swimming, fishing; no-ski zone. **GPS: 36.928699, -86.029127**

TAILWATER CAMPGROUND

2 mi S of Glasgow on US 31E (Scottsville Rd); W on SR 252 to park below the dam. From jct of SRs 252/1533, N to entrance rd at S end of dam; follow signs. About 5/1-9/15; 14-day limit. 48 elec/wtr sites, $19 ($9.50 with federal senior pass). Off-season, some primitive sites free with reduced services & no utilities, pit toilets. RV limit in excess of 65'. Tbls, flush & pit toilets, cfga, drkg wtr, dump, showers, beach, playground, amphitheater. Boating(l), fishing, hiking, horseshoes, ball field, swimming. Group primitive tent camping area, $50. Picnic shelter ($50 reservation fee). Amphitheater, horseshoe pits. 3-night minimum stay on holiday weekends. (270) 622-7732. NRRS during 5/1-9/20. **GPS: 36.89444, -86.13306**

THE NARROWS CAMPGROUND

From Lucas, 1.7 mi W on The Narrows Rd, following signs. About 5/1-9/20; 14-day limit. 92 elec/wtr sites, $23 ($11.50 with federal senior pass). RV limit in excess of 65'. Tbls, flush toilets, cfga, drkg wtr, showers, dump, beach, playground, amphitheater, coin laundry, picnic shelter with elec ($50). Boating(l), fishing, interpretive trail, horseshoes, volleyball, hiking. Marina, boat rentals nearby. 3-night minimum stay on holiday weekends. (270) 646-3094. NRRS. **GPS: 36.90417, -86.07083**

❷ BUCKHORN LAKE
GPS: 37.34. -83.4717

A 1,230-acre lake 28 miles W of Hazard and N of Daniel Boone National Forest on SR 28, 0.5 mile from Buckhorn in southeastern Kentucky. On Middle Fork of the Kentucky River. Alcohol prohibited by local law. Historic & cultural site. Day use facilities: Buckhorn Lake Dam -- boat ramp, fishing pier, trails; Confluence Recreation Area -- boat ramp, picnicking, picnic shelter with water/electric $30, playground; Leatherwood Recreation Area -- boat ramp, shelter $30, playground, fishing pier; Tailwater Recreation Area -- picnicking, playground, shelter ($60). Stillhouse Branch Nature Trail 2.5 mi when completed. No swimming beaches. Resource Manager, Buckhorn Lake, 804 Buckhorn Dam Rd, Buckhorn, KY 41721. (606) 398-7251.

BUCKHORN BOAT-IN CAMPS

Accessible by boat only, near the emergency spillway, dock provided; within rowing distance of dam & boat ramp. 5/1-9/7; 14-day limit 15 primitive shoreline tent sites, $12 ($6 with federal senior pass). 3-night minimum stay required on holiday weekends. Pit toilets, trash stations, drkg wtr, security lighting, lantern posts, sand paths, playground, tbls, drkg wtr. Swimming, boating, waterskiing, fishing No reservations. Register at Buckhorn Campground.

BUCKHORN CAMPGROUND

From jct with SR 28 just S of Buckhorn, 0.5 mi S on Hwy 1387, following signs, then right (E) on access rd; at W side of Stilling Basin below dam, adjacent to Tailwater Recreation Area at Middle Fork of Kentucky River. 5/1-9/30; 14-day limit. 4 walk-in tent sites & 18 primitive & overflow sites, $12 ($6 with federal senior pass); 31 elec/wtr sites (optional CATV) $22 ($11 with senior pass), $30 at double sites. 50-ft RV limit. Tbls, flush toilets, cfga, drkg

wtr, dump, pay phone, playground, beach, coin laundry. 2 horseshoe pits, boating(ld), fishing, hiking, swimming, interpretive trails. 3-night minimum stay on holiday weekends. (606) 398-7220. NRRS. **GPS: 37.348702, -83.476296**

TRACE BRANCH CAMPGROUND

6 mi N of Hyden on SR 257; E across Dry Hill Bridge near Confluence, then 6 mi N on Grassy Branch Rd (CR 1055) to Confluence boat dock & 2 mi S to campground on Mosely Bend Rd; at E shore of Middle Fork Kentucky River. 5/1-9/30; 14-day limit. 13 paved primitive sites (8 along shoreline), $12 ($6 with federal senior pass); 15 elec/wtr sites, $22 ($11 with senior pass). 50-ft RV limit. Tbls, flush toilets, cfga, drkg wtr, dump, showers, beach, playground, shelters. Horseshoe pits, volleyball net, swimming, ball field, boating(ld), fishing. 3-night minimum stay on holiday weekends. 606-672-3670. NRRS. **GPS: 37.258579, -83.377511**

❸ CARR CREEK LAKE
GPS: 37.2233. -83.0567

A 710-acre lake 16 miles S of Hazard on SR 15, then 1 mile N on SR 1089 in SE Kentucky. The dam is 8.8 miles above the mouth of Carr Fork -- a tributary of the North Fork of Kentucky River. Checkout time 4 p.m. Visitor center, nature trail, interpretive programs, 8 picnic areas with shelters. 6-mile Sugar Branch hiking trail begins at dam. $3 day use fees are charged non-campers at the Corps marina & Littcarr boat ramps. Other day use facilities include a fishing shelter at Dogwood shelter; boat ramp, picnicking and playground at Carrfork Marina; showers, boat ramp, picnicking, playground at Damsite Park. Resource Manager, Carr Creek Lake, 843 Sassafras Creek Rd, Sassafras, KY 41759-8806. (606) 642-3308.

LITTCARR CAMPGROUND

From Hazard, about 20 mi E on SR 15, past entry to Carr Creek State Park, then 2.4 mi NE on SR 160; on NE side lake, E of SR 160 on access rd. About 4/1-10/1; 14-day limit. 32 elec/wtr sites, $22 ($11 with federal senior pass); 14 full-hookup sites, $28 ($14 with senior pass). 50-ft RV limit; 1 RV & 1 tent or 2 tents per site. Tbls, flush toilets, cfga, drkg wtr, dump, showers, coin laundry, beach, playground, pay phone, shelters. Horseshoe pits, boating(l), fishing, swimming, waterskiing. Marina, store. 3-night minimum stay on holiday weekends. Non-campers pay $3 vehicle day use fee. (606) 642-3052. NRRS.
GPS: 37.237831, -82.948766

❹ DEWEY LAKE
GPS: 37.7367, -82.73

A 1,100-acre lake 10 miles S of Van Lear on SR 302/3 in eastern Kentucky SW of Huntington, W Virginia. Lake extends 18.8 miles upstream from dam. Day use facilities at Damsite Park -- picnic shelter, playground, hiking trail; Picnic Hollow -- picnic shelter, playground, hiking trail For lake information, call (606) 886-6398. Modern campsites at nearby Jenny Wiley State Park. No designated swimming areas. Off-road vehicles prohibited. Resource Manager, Dewey Lake, HC 70, Box 540, Van Lear, KY 41265. (606) 886-6709/789-4521.

SHORELINE CAMPGROUND I

From East Point at US 23, 3 mi E on SR 3 (merging with SR 321); right on SR 302 to dam. Accessible by foot (from top of dam or Picnic Hollow parking lots) or by boat (boat rentals nearby). Campground relocated near dam. 5/20-LD; 14-day limit. $10. 10 primitive tent sites; drkg wtr now available; portable toilets; access to playground; fire rings, lantern post. 15 other more primitive boat-in sites at Shoreline #2.

❺ FISHTRAP LAKE
GPS: 37.7367, -82.73

A 1,131-acre lake 16 mi S of Hazard on SR 15, then 1 mi N on SR 1089 in SE Kentucky near the Virginia/West Virginia state lines. The dam is 8.8 mi above the mouth of Carr Fork -- a tributary of the North Fork of Kentucky River; it is on the Levisa Fork of Big Sandy River. The lake is 16.5 miles long. Checkout time 4 p.m. Visitor center, nature trail, interpretive programs, 8 picnic areas. 6-mi Sugar Branch hiking trail begins at dam. $3 use fees are charged non-campers at Grapevine Park and the marina boat ramps. Free launching at Lick Creek Park. Resource Manager, Carr Creek Lake, 2204 Fishtrap Rd, Shelbiana, KY 41562. (606) 437-7496.

GRAPEVINE CAMPGROUND

From Pikeville, 9.5 mi E on US 119; 16 mi S on SR 194 (Grapevine Rd); right on access rd into park; at Grapevine Creek arm of lake. MD-LD; 14-day limit. 18 primitive sites, $12 ($6 with federal senior pass); 10 elec/wtr sites, $20 ($10 with senior pass). Tbls, flush toilets, cfga, drkg wtr, showers, dump, playground. Fishing, boating(l). Three picnic shelters ($50 reservations fee). No campsite reservations. (606) 835-4564. **GPS: 37.43229, -82.35802**

❻ GREEN RIVER LAKE
GPS: 37.245, -85.3417

An 8,210-acre lake 9 miles S of Campbellsville on SR 55, 95 miles S of Louisville. Alcohol prohibited by local law. Off-road vehicles prohibited. Outside the campgrounds, day use facilities include Dam Area -- picnic shelter, playground, boat ramp, fishing pier, hiking trail; Tailwater -- boat ramp, picnic shelter, playground. Visitor center with historic & cultural site, interpretive programs, theater, picnic area, hiking trail. Holmes Bend, Pikes Ridge & Smith Ridge Parks closed to camping off-season. 4 of 10 boat ramps managed by Corps ($3 for non-campers). Five picnic shelters ($50 reservations). 2 Corps beaches, 50 mi of multi-use trails. Park Manager, Green River Lake, 544 Lake Rd., Campbellsville, KY 42718-9705. (270) 465-4463.

HOLMES BEND CAMPGROUND

From Columbia at exit 49 of Louie B. Nunn Pkwy, 1.2 mi N on SR 55S; 1 mi NE on SR 55; 3.8 mi N on SR 551, becoming Holmes Bend Rd; at W shore of lake. About 4/15-10/30; 14-day limit. 23 primitive sites, $17 ($8.50 with federal senior pass); 101 elec sites (41 have wtr hookups), $23 ($11.50 with senior pass). Picnic shelter ($50). RV limit in excess of 65 ft. Tbls, flush toilets, cfga, drkg wtr, dump, showers, playground, beach, coin laundry, amphitheater, picnic shelter. Interpretive trail, hiking trail, boating(ld), fishing, swimming, hiking. Boat rentals nearby. 3-night minimum stay on holiday weekends. (270) 384-4623. NRRS. **GPS: 37.212012, -85.264301**

PIKES RIDGE CAMPGROUND

From Knifley, 4.8 mi NW on SR 76 (7 mi SE of US 68 at Campbellsville); about 5 mi SW on Pikes Ridge Rd, following signs; at E shore of lake. About 4/15-9/30; 14-day limit. 40 primitive sites, $15 ($7.50 with federal senior pass); 19 elec/wtr sites, $21 ($10.50 with senior pass). Tbls, pit toilets, cfga, drkg wtr, dump, playground, beach. RV limit in excess of 65 ft. Picnic shelter, $50. Boating(l), fishing, swimming, hiking, horseback riding, interpretive trails. 3-night minimum stay on holiday weekends. (270) 465-6488. NRRS. **GPS: 37.284749, -85.292959**

SMITH RIDGE CAMPGROUND

From Campbellsville, 1 mi E on Hwy 70; 3 mi S on SR 372; W (right) on County Park Rd (signs). About 5/15-9/15; 14-day limit. 18 non-elec sites, $17 ($8.50 with federal senior pass); 62 elec sites, $23 ($11.50 with senior pass). RV limit in excess of 65 ft. Tbls, flush

toilets, cfga, drkg wtr, showers, dump, beach, playground. Nature trail, boating(l), fishing, hiking, swimming. 3-night minimum stay on holiday weekends. (270) 789-2743. NRRS. **GPS: 37.286459, -85.296366**

WILSON CREEK CAMPGROUND

From Campbellsville, 4 mi E on SR 70; 7 mi E on SR 76; on right. All year; 4-day limit. 5 free primitive tent sites. Pit toilet, cfga, no drkg wtr

❼
LAKE BARKLEY
GPS: 37.0217, -88.22

A 57,920-acre lake SE of I-24/US 62 near Gilbertsville, E of Paducah and S into Tennessee. It is the westernmost lake in a series of dam projects along the Cumberland River and its tributaries. It has 1,004 miles of shoreline. Campground checkout time 3 p.m. Visitor center with display on early lifestyles and river usage, interpretive programs. Historic & cultural site. Non-campers pay $3 day use fees for boat ramps, beaches, picnicking. Reservation fees of $35-$55 are charged for picnic shelters.

Day use facilities: Blue Creek -- boat ramp; Boyds Landing -- boat ramp, picnicking; Buzzard Rock -- boat ramp; Cadiz Rec. Area -- boat ramp, picnicking, picnic shelter ($35), playground; Calhoun Hill -- boat ramp; Coleman Bridge -- boat ramp; Tailwater Left Bank -- boat ramp, picnicking, hiking trail; Tailwater Right Bank -- boat ramp, picnicking; Devils Elbow -- boat ramp; Old Eddyville -- boat ramp, picnicking; Old Kuttawa -- boat ramp, picnicking, shelters ($35 & $55), playground, beach, hiking trails; Rivers End -- boat ramp; Rockcastle -- boat ramp, picnicking, shelter, beach; Saline Creek -- boat ramp; Tobacco Port -- boat ramp; Linton Park -- boat ramp, shelter ($35), playground, beach; Dyers Creek -- boat ram, shelter ($35), playground, picnicking. The 170,000-acre Land Between the Lakes National Recreation Area is managed by the U.S. Forest Service. Resource Manager, Lake Barkley, Box 218, Highway 62, Grand Rivers, KY 42045-0218. (270) 362-4236. See Tennessee listings for Bumpus Mills Campground.

CANAL CAMPGROUND

From Paducah, E on I-24 to exit 31 jct with "The Trace" (at Land Between the Lakes); 3 mi S on The Trace (SR 453), then E to lake, following signs on access rd. About 3/25-10/30; 14-day limit. 112 elec/wtr sites, $16 base; extra fees for 50-amp & premium locations; $29 full hookups ($8.50 & $14.50 with senior pass); tent sites $16. RV limit in excess of 65 ft. Tbls, flush toilets, cfga, drkg wtr, showers, coin laundry, amphitheater, playground, beach, dump. Fishing, swimming, boating(ld). Group camping area with shelter, $192. 3-night minimum stay on holiday weekends. (270) 362-4840. NRRS. **GPS: 36.993985, -88.215934**

EUREKA CAMPGROUND

From just N of Grand Rivers on US 62/641, S on Hwy 810, then W on Hwy 1271; near spillway on E side of dam. About 4/25-LD; 14-day limit. 26 elec/wtr sites (50-amp), $15 base, $23 for premium locations ($7.50 & $11.50 with federal senior pass). RV limit in excess of 65'; 3 pull-through. Tbls, flush toilets, cfga, drkg wtr, dump, showers, playground, beach, coin laundry, pay phone. 5-mi hiking/biking trail, fishing, swimming, boating(l). Group shelter with elec, $35. (270) 388-9459. NRRS. **GPS: 37.024442, -88.200222**

HURRICANE CREEK CAMP

From Cadiz, 7.5 mi N on SR 139; 6.5 mi W on SR 276; 0.3 mi N on SR 274, then W on access rd following signs, on left. About 4/25-10/30; 14-day limit. 6 walk-to tent sites, $10 & $12 ($5 & $6 with federal senior pass); 51 elec/wtr sites, $16 base for 30-amp, $22 for 50-amp and premium locations ($8 & $11 with senior pass). 11 pull-through sites. RV limit in excess of 65

ft. Tbls, flush toilets, cfga, drkg wtr, showers, dump, coin laundry, beach, playground. Boating(ld), fishing, swimming. (270) 522-8821. NRRS. **GPS: 36.920049, -87.978328**

⑧
LAKE CUMBERLAND
WOLF CREEK DAM
GPS: 36.8717. -85.145

A 50,000-acre lake S of Lexington near the Tennessee state line and S of the Cumberland Parkway. Wolf Creek Dam is on US 127, 4.2 miles S of the jct. of SR 55/US 127. It is 101 miles long and has 1,255 miles of shoreline. Visitor center with exhibits. Historic & cultural site, interpretive programs. $3 day use fees charged non-campers at Waitsboro, Cumberland Point Halcomb's Landing, Kendall & Fall Creek Recreation Areas. Day use facilities: Halcomb Landing -- boat ramp; Lakeview Park -- boat ramp; Mill Springs Mills-- picnicking, shelters ($35), old mill, interpretive trail; Seventy-Six Falls Park -- picnicking, shelter (no reservations), multi-use trails. Primitive shoreline tent camping free at 53 designated camping areas; carry-out trash, bury waste; no toilets; 14-day limit. Resource Manager, Lake Cumberland, 855 Boat Dock Rd., Somerset, KY 42501-0450. (606) 679-6337/6338.

CUMBERLAND POINT RECREATION AREA

From Nancy, 0.2 mi E on SR 80; 1 mi S on SR 235; 8 mi SE on SR 761; on peninsula off main channel at mouth of Faubush Creek. 30 acres. About 5/15-9/15; 14-day limit. 30 elec/wtr sites, $22 ($11 with federal senior pass). RV limit in excess of 65 ft. Tbls, flush toilets, cfga, drkg wtr, dump, showers, coin laundry, playground, amphitheater, beach, group shelter $50. Boating(ld), horseshoe pits, fishing, swimming, waterskiing. 606-871-7886. NRRS. **GPS: 36.966143, -84.840835**

FALL CREEK RECREATION AREA

From Monticello, 0.4 mi NW on SR 92; 1.5 mi NE on SR 90; 6 mi N on SR 1275, then NW on access rd. About 5/1-9/15; 14-day limit. Newly renovated facilities & sites. 10 elec/wtr sites, $20 ($10 with federal senior pass). Tbls, flush toilets, cfga, drkg wtr, showers, dump, playground, picnic shelter $35. (606) 348-6042. NRRS 3/1-10/31. **GPS: 36.927104, -84.845064**

FISHING CREEK RECREATION AREA

From Somerset at jct with US 27, 5.5 mi W on SR 80; exit prior to lake bridge, then 2 mi N on Hwy 1248, following signs. About 5/1-9/30; 14-day limit. 20 tent sites with elec, $20 ($10 with federal senior pass); 26 wtr/elec RV/tent sites, $25 ($12.50 with senior pass). RV limit in excess of 65 ft. Tbls, flush toilets, cfga, drkg wtr, showers, dump, new playground, beach, coin laundry. Boating(l), fishing, swimming, waterskiing. Boat ramp closed by low lake wtr in early 2015; check current status before arrival. (606) 679-5174. NRRS. **GPS: 37.071617, -84.687968**

KENDALL CAMPGROUND

From Jamestown, 10 mi S on US 127; right on Kendall Rd before crossing dam, following signs. About 4/1-11/1; 14-day limit. 115 elec/wtr sites, $28 ($14 with federal senior pass). RV limit in excess of 65 ft. Tbls, flush toilets, cfga, drkg wtr, showers, dump, 2 playgrounds, fish cleaning stations, picnic shelter $50, coin laundry. Horseshoe pits, hiking trail, biking, boating(ld), fishing. (270) 343-4660. NRRS. **GPS: 36.872576, -85.146824**

WAITSBORO CAMPGROUND

From Somerset, 5 mi S on US 27, then W (right) on Waitsboro Rd, following signs; steep, curvy hill to park. About 5/1-LD; 14-day limit. 3 basic tent sites, $15 ($7.50 with federal senior pass); 1 tent site with elec & 22 elec RV/tent sites, $20 base, $25 for premium locations ($10 & $12.50 with senior pass). RV limit in excess of 65 ft. Tbls, flush toilets, cfga, drkg

wtr, showers, playground, dump, coin laundry, two shelters $25. Boating(ld), fishing, hiking, waterskiing. (606) 561-5513. NRRS. **GPS: 37.0036095, -84.6230324**

❾ NOLIN RIVER LAKE
GPS: 37.30246, -86.261902

A 5,795-acre lake 2 miles N of Mammoth Cave National Park on SR 13/52. It is 15 miles N of Brownsville on SR 259, 22 miles S on Leitchfield on SR 259. Much of the river is within the boundary of Mammoth Cave National Park. Alcohol prohibited by local law. Camping also available at Nolin Lake State Park. Day use facilities: Iberia Park -- boat ramp, picnic shelter, beach; Tailwater Park -- boat ramp, picnic shelter, playground; Vanmeter Park -- boat ramp. Non-campers pay $3 fee at 5 boat ramps; Tailwater ramp free. $50 reservation fee for picnic shelters. Campers only at Dog Creek beach. Park Manager, Nolin Lake, 2150 Nolin Dam Rd., P. O. Box 339, Bee Springs, KY 42207-0289. (270) 286-4511.

DOG CREEK CAMPGROUND

8 mi N of Brownsville on SR 259; 5 mi N on SR 1015, following signs. About 5/15-LD; 14-day limit. 20 non-elec sites, $15 base, $19 at premium locations ($7.50 & $9.50 with federal senior pass); 50 elec/wtr sites, $22 ($11 with senior pass). RV limit in excess of 65 ft. Tbls, flush toilets, cfga, drkg wtr, dump, showers, playground, beach, picnic shelter. Boating(ld), fishing, swimming, hiking, watchable wildlife area. Beach open only to campers. (270) 524-5454. NRRS. **GPS: 37.318931, -86.131096**

MOUTARDIER CAMPGROUND

From Leitchfield, 16 mi S on SR 259; 2 mi SE on SR 2067 (Moutardier Rd). Open about 5/1-10/15; 14-day limit. 86 non-elec sites, $15 base, $19 at premium locations ($7.50 & $9.50 with federal senior pass); 81 wtr/elec sites, $21 base, $24 at premium locations ($10.50 & $12 with senior pass). RV limit in excess of 65 ft. Tbls, flush toilets, cfga, drkg wtr, showers, beach, dump, picnic shelter, fish cleaning station. Boating(ld), fishing, horseshoe pits, hiking trails. Boat rentals nearby. (270) 286-4230. NRRS. **GPS: 37.316263, -86.232364**

WAX CAMPGROUND

From Munfordville, 20 mi W on SR 88. About 5/15-LD; 14-day limit. 24 non-elec sites, $15 base, $19 at premium locations ($7.50 & $9.50 with federal senior pass); 86 elec/wtr sites, $22 base, $24 at premium locations ($11 & $12 with senior pass). 7 pull-through sites; RV limit in excess of 65 ft. Tbls, flush toilets, cfga, drkg wtr, showers, beach, dump, picnic shelter, fish cleaning station. Boating(ld), fishing, hiking trails, swimming. Boat rentals nearby. (270) 242-7578. NRRS.
GPS: 37.344521, -86.130486

⑩
ROUGH RIVER LAKE
GPS: 37.589207, -86.510468

A 5,100-acre lake 1.4 miles N of Falls of Rough post office on SR 79, 51 miles N of Bowling Green. Alcohol prohibited by local law. Off-road vehicles prohibited. Campground checkout time 4:30 p.m. Horse trails nearby. Sites open during winter may have reduced amenities. A large number are lakeside sites. Visitor center with picnic area, interpretive trail. Non-campers pay $3 boat ramp fees except at Everleigh ramp. Free swimming at North Fork beach; campers only at Axtel beach. Reservation fee $50 for North Fork & Tailwater group shelters. Park Manager, Rough River Lake, 14500 Falls of Rough Rd., Falls of Rough, KY 40119-9801. (270) 257-2061.

AXTEL CAMPGROUND

From Harned, 9 mi S on SR 259; 0.5 mi W on SR 79, on left. About 4/1-10/31; 14-day limit. 61 non-elec sites $17; 92 elec/wtr sites $22 base, $24 at premium locations ($8.50, $11 & $12 with federal senior pass). 45-ft RV limit. Tbls, flush toilets, dump, showers, cfga, drkg wtr, playground, picnic shelter, beach. Boating(ld), swimming, fishing. Boat rentals nearby. Non-campers pay $3 boat ramp fee. (270) 257-2584. NRRS.
GPS: 37.620684, -86.454177

CAVE CREEK CAMPGROUND

From the dam, 2.9 mi S on SR 79; 0.8 mi E on SR 736. About 5/15-LD; 14-day limit. 5 tent sites & 23 non-elec RV/tent sites, $17; 36 elec/wtr sties, $22 ($8.50 & $11 with federal senior pass). 40-ft RV limit. Tbls, flush & pit toilets, cfga, drkg wtr, showers, playground, dump, fishing pier. Boating(ld), fishing, hiking. Non-campers pay $3 for boat ramp. (270) 879-4304. NRRS. **GPS: 37.572999, -86.493867**

LAUREL BRANCH CAMP

From Roff, 3 mi S on SR 259; 1 mi W on SR 110, following signs. About 3/1-10/30; 14-day limit. 13 non-elec sites, $17; 48 elec/wtr sites, $22 ($8.50 & $11 with federal senior pass). 40-ft RV limit. Off-season, some sites may be open at reduced rates. Tbls, pit toilets, cfga, drkg wtr, playground, beach, dump, no showers. Boating(ld), fishing, hiking, swimming. Non-campers pay $3 for boat ramp. (270) 257-8839. NRRS during 5/1-11/1.
GPS: 37.607859, -86.453326

NORTH FORK CAMPGROUND

1.5 mi S of Roff on SR 259. About 5/1-9/15; 14-day limit. 56 non-elec sites, $17; 48 elec/wtr sites $22 ($8.50 & $11 with federal senior pass). 60-ft RV limit. Tbls, flush toilets, cfga, drkg wtr, showers, dump, beach, playground, fishing pier, picnic shelter ($50). Swimming, boating(ld), fishing, waterskiing. Non-campers pay $3 for boat ramp. (270) 257-8139. NRRS during 5/5-9/11. **GPS: 37.62972, -86.43667**

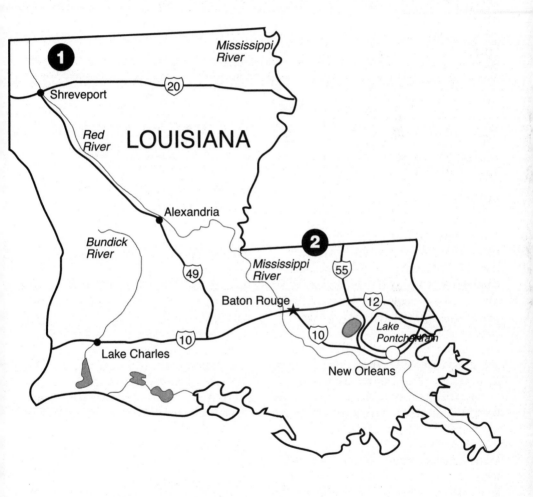

LOUISIANA

STATE INFORMATION:

CAPITAL: Baton Rouge
NICKNAME: Pelican State
STATEHOOD: 1812 - 18th State
FLOWER: Magnolia
TREE: Bald Cypress
BIRD: Brown Pelican

LA

STATE TIDBITS:

• The town of Jean Lafitte was once a hideaway for pirates.

• Baton Rouge hosted the 1983 Special Olympics International Summer Games.

• bayou: \BUY-you\ n. a French name for slow-moving "river."

WWW.LOUISIANATRAVEL.COM

Office of Tourism, Dept of Culture, Recreation and Tourism, PO Box 94291, Baton Rouge, LA 70804-9291. 504-342-8119. 1-800-99-GUMBO.

LOUISIANA LAKES

To find campgrounds operated by the U.S. Army Corps of Engineers, match the lake's numbers on the preceding map page with numbered lake entries on the following pages. Campgrounds are listed alphabetically under the appropriate lakes. The following Louisiana impoundments have Corps of Engineers campgrounds.

Bayou Bodcau Reservoir. Bayou Bodcau is a dry reservoir without a permanent pool. It is 20 miles NE of Shreveport and I-20, 18 miles N on SR 157, the site of major waterfowl and upland game management areas.

Ouachita Black River Project. A 337-mile-long waterway through southern Arkansas and Louisiana, consisting of four locks and dams.

❶ BAYOU BODCAU RESERVOIR
GPS: 32.705, -93.5133

Bayou Bodcau is a dry reservoir without a permanent pool. It is 20 miles NE of Shreveport and I-20, 18 miles N on SR 157. Site of major waterfowl and upland game management area. Cabin of an original settler used for public classroom study. Biking, hiking, horseback riding, interpretive programs, picnicking and wildlife viewing on 33,500 acres. A $4 day use fee is charged ($30 annually). Picnic shelter at Tom Merrill Recreation Area may be reserved for a fee. Basic campsites include a picnic table, lantern post, fire ring, trash can and grill. The 7-mi Durden Hills Nature Trail is open for biking and hiking. Project Manager, Bayou Bodcau Office, 1700 Bodcau Dam Rd, Haughton LA 71035. (318) 949-1804.

BODCAU ROAD PRIMITIVE CAMPING AREA

From Sarepta, 2 mi E on SR 2; turn right (S) for 2 mi on CR 529, then 2 mi E on improved gravel Bodcau Rd through wooded area to bayou. All year; 14-day limit. Free primitive undesigned sites. No facilities, no drkg wtr. Boat ramp for hand launching, fishing.
GPS: 32.8709, -93.4767

CORNER OF THE OLD FIELD

About 3 mi S of Sarepta on US 371 to just W of Cotton Valley; 3 mi W on SR 160; S on Young Rd, then E through wooded area on improved gravel rd to Old Field Rd. All year; 14-day limit. Free primitive camping at undesignated sites on rock parking lot. No facilities, no drkg wtr. Boating(l), fishing. **GPS: 32.7877, -93.4746**

CROW LAKE RECREATION AREA

1 mi S of Sarepta on US 371; 2 mi W on Park Rd 238 (becoming Crow Lake Rd) to camping area. All year; 14-day limit. 2 free primitive sites, no facilities, no drkg wtr. Rock boat ramp, fishing. **GPS: 32.8824, -93.4609**

DELLA FIELD PRIMITIVE AREA

2 mi W of Springhill on SR 157; about 2 mi S on Timothy Church Rd; turn right (W) on improved gravel rd for about 1 mi, then left (SW) on access rd for about 1 mi to bayou. All year; 14-day limit. Free primitive undesignated sites. No facilities, no drkg wtr. Boat ramp for hand launching, fishing. **GPS: 32.9876, -95.5209**

HIGHWAY 157 PRIMITIVE AREA

From Springhill, about 4 mi W on SR 157. Free primitive camping on rock parking lot. No facilities, no drkg wtr. All year; 14-day limit. Gravel boat ramp, fishing. **GPS: 33.0188, -93.5214**

HIGHWAY 160 PRIMITIVE AREA

From Sarepta, about 3 mi S on US 371 to just W of Cotton Valley; 2 mi W on SR 160 to bridge, then S on gravel rd to site. All year; 14-day limit. Free primitive camping at undesignated sites. No facilities, no drkg wtr. Concrete boat ramp, fishing. **GPS: 32.8138, -93.4309**

HIGHWAY 2 PRIMITIVE CAMPING AREA

From Sarepta, about 5 mi E on SR 2. All year; 14-day limit. Free primitive camping at undesignated sites. No facilities, no drkg wtr. Concrete boat ramp, fishing. **GPS: 32.9049, -93.4829**

HORSE CAMPGROUND

From Bellevue, about 4 mi N on Bodcau Dam Rd; at N end of dam near the spillway. All year; 14-day limit. Large groups should call for a permit and information. More than 50 mi of horse trails available. Free primitive camping.

IVAN LAKE RECREATION AREA

About 3 mi S of Sarepta on US 371 to just W of Cotton Valley; about 5 mi E on SR 160; right (N) for 1 mi on Ivan Lake Rd (NE of Bellevue). Overlooks 520-acre Ivan Lake. All year; 14-day limit. Free. 4 primitive sites. Pit toilets, fire rings, no drkg wtr. Boat ramp nearby, fishing. **GPS: 32.8317, -93.4931**

PARDEE CALLOWAY PRIMITIVE AREA

About 3 mi S of Sarepta on US 371 to Cotton Valley; 3 mi SW on Adkins Rd (AKA Bellevue Rd); right (W) on improved gravel Pardee Rd. All year; 14-day limit. Free primitive camping at undesignated sites. No facilities, no drkg wtr. Rock boat ramp, fishing. **GPS: 32.7726, -93.4622**

RAINEY WELLS RECREATION AREA

2 mi W of Springhill on SR 157; about 5 mi S on Timothy Church Rd; on N shore of Bodcau Bayou Reservoir. All year; 14-day limit. 2 free primitive sites. No facilities, no drkg wtr. Rock boat ramp, fishing. **GPS: 32.9588, -93.5193**

TOM MERRILL RECREATION AREA

From Bellevue, 2 mi NE on Bodcau Dam Rd, following signs. All year; 14-day limit. 20 elec/wtr sites, $12 ($6 with federal senior pass); non-elec sites, $6 ($3 with senior pass). 2 pull-through sites. Tbls, flush toilets, cfga, drkg wtr, showers, dump. Boating(l), fishing. Durden Hill Trail starts at campground and extends

6 mi for hikers & mountain bikers. Picnic shelter, $35. **GPS: 32.705779, -93.51692**

SOUTH ABUTMENT EAST RECREATION AREA

From Bellevue, 2 mi N on Bodcau Dam Rd; just past Bodcau lookout tower near SE shore of Bodcau Bayou Reservoir; on upstream side of the dam. All year; 14-day limit. 12 primitive sites, $6. Toilet, cfga, no drkg wtr. Boating(l), fishing. **GPS: 32.7022, -93.5079**

TEAGUE LAKE PRIMITIVE CAMPING AREA

From Springhill, about 4.5 mi S on SR 157, past Highway 157 Primitive Area; right (N) on Oglee Rd about 2 mi, then 2 mi N on improved gravel Teague Lake Rd to bayou. All year; 14-day limit. Free primitive camping pad. No facilities, no drkg wtr. Gravel boat ramp, fishing. **GPS: 33.0188, -93.5214**

WENK'S LANDING

From Sarepta, about 1 mi S on US 371; left (W) for half mi on Wenk's Landing Rd, following signs. All year; 14-day limit. Free primitive camping in designated areas only. Toilets, cfga, no drkg wtr. Boating(l), fishing. **GPS: 32.5206, -93.2655**

❷

OUACHITA BLACK RIVER PROJECT
GPS: 32.466382, -92.11555

The Ouachita Black River Navigation Project is a 337-mile-long waterway through southern Arkansas and Louisiana and consists of 4 locks and dams. Several recreation areas are along the waterway, including the two listed here that offer primitive camping areas. Day use fees are charged: $3 at boat ramps, $1 per person at beaches ($30 annually).

FINCH BAYOU RECREATION AREA

From Haile, 4 mi E on Hooker Hole Rd (PR 2204E); N on River Rd (PR 2293); within the Upper Ouachita National Wildlife Refuge at the Ouachita River. All year; 14-day limit. Free primitive sites in designated area. 8 picnic sites, pit toilet, cfga, drkg wtr. Boating(l), fishing, hiking.

FT. NECESSITY RECREATION AREA

From Columbia, about 7 mi E on SR 4; along Boeuf River. All year; 14-day limit. Free primitive sites in designated areas. 10 picnic sites, pit toilet, cfga, no drkg wtr. Boating(l), fishing, hiking.

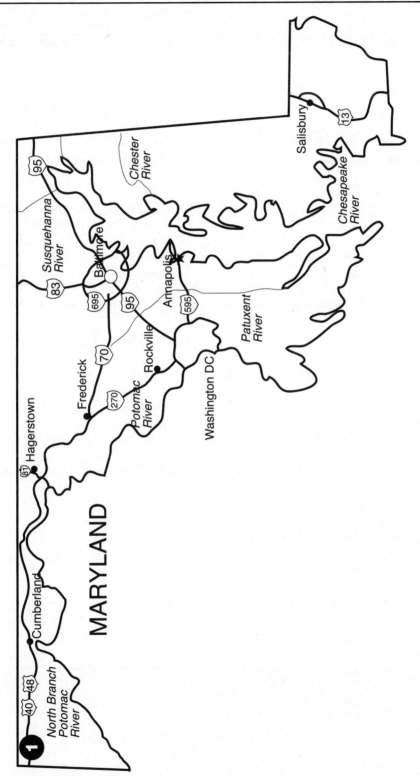

MARYLAND

STATE INFORMATION:

CAPITAL: Annapolis
NICKNAME: Old Line State
STATEHOOD: 1788 - 7th State
FLOWER: Black-Eyed Susan
TREE: White Oak
BIRD: Baltimore Oriole

STATE TIDBITS:

• Maryland was first to enact Workmen's compensation laws in 1902.

• Babe Ruth, the Sultan of Swat, was born in Baltimore.

• King Williams School opened in 1696. It was the first school in the United States.

WWW.VISITMARYLAND.ORG

Office of Tourism Development, 401 East Pratt St, 14th Floor, Baltimore, MD 21202. 866-639-3526 or 866-MDWELCOME.

MARYLAND LAKES

To find campgrounds operated by the U.S. Army Corps of Engineers, match the lake's number on the preceding map page with the numbered lake entry on this page; the only campground is listed under it. The Pittsburgh District does not permit alcoholic beverages at any project.

❶

YOUGHIOGHENY RIVER LAKE
GPS: 39.7983, -79.3683

A 2,840-acre, 16-mile-long lake S of Confluence off SR 281 and N of US 40 in SW Pennsylvania, spanning the Mason-Dixon Line between Pennsylvania and Maryland. Trout stockings from April through September. Visitor center, interpretive programs, picnicking, wildlife viewing. The Youghiogheny River Hiking-Biking Trail South runs from Confluence to Ohiopyle State Park and extends into the Outflow Campground. Non-campers pay $3 daily at boat ramps ($30 annually). User fees also charged non-campers at swimming beaches.

Resource Manager, Youghiogheny River Lake, 497 Flanigan Road, Confluence, PA 15424-1932. (814) 395-3242/3166. See Pennsylvania listings for Outflow & Tub Run Campgrounds.

MILL RUN RECREATION AREA

From Friendsville, 3.7 mi NE on SR 53; 1 mi W on Mill Run Rd. All year; 14-day limit. 30 sites, no hookups. $15 self-registration ($7.50 with federal senior pass) during 5/1-LD; 8 sites free for self-contained RVs rest of year but no amenities. Tbls, flush toilets, cfga, drkg wtr, dump, coin laundry, beach, playground. Boating(l), fishing, swimming, waterskiing. **GPS: 39.71586, -79.384933**

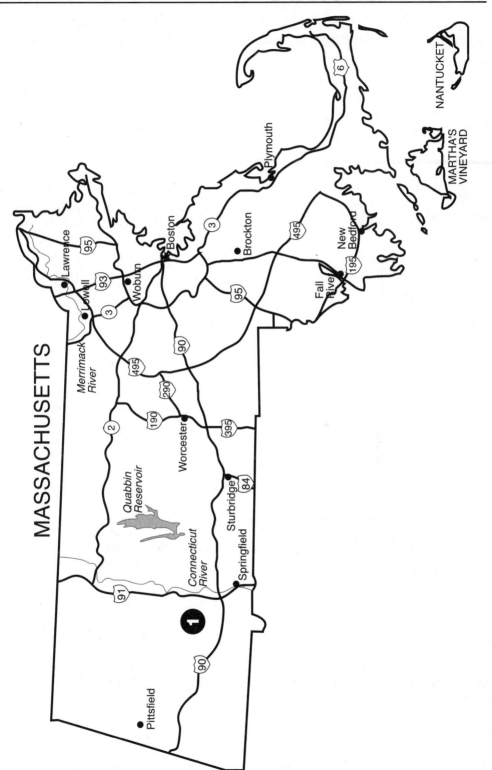

MASSACHUSETTS

Lawrence
95
Lowell
93
Woburn
3
Merrimack River
Boston
95
3
Brockton
495
New Bedford
195
Fall River
90
495
290
190
Worcester
2
395
Quabbin Reservoir
Sturbridge
84
Springfield
Connecticut River
91
90
Pittsfield

Plymouth
6
NANTUCKET
MARTHA'S VINEYARD

1

MASSACHUSETTS

STATE INFORMATION:

CAPITAL: Boston
NICKNAME: Bay State
STATEHOOD: 1788 - 6th State
FLOWER: Mayflower
TREE: American Elm
BIRD: Chickadee

MA

STATE TIDBITS:

• Boston built the first subway system in the United States in 1897.

• The state dessert of Massachusetts is Boston cream pie.

• Glaciers formed the islands of Nantucket and Martha's Vineyard during the ice age.

WWW.MASSVACATION.COM

Massachusetts Office of Travel and Tourism, 10 Park Plaza, Suite 4510, Boston, MA 02116; 800-227-MASS or 617-973-8500. E-mail: Vacationinfo@state.ma.us

MASSACHUSETTS LAKES

To find campgrounds operated by the U.S. Army Corps of Engineers, match the lake's number on the preceding map page with the numbered lake entry on this page; the only campground is listed under it.

❶

KNIGHTVILLE DAM
GPS: 42.261811, -72.876434

Four miles S of Chesterfield and SR 143 in west-central Massachusetts. Picnicking, group picnic shelter, hiking, mountain biking, horseback riding. 2,430 acres. The only campground operated by the Corps of Engineers is a group facility. Knightville Dam, RR 1, Box 285, Huntington, MA 01050-9942. (413) 667-3430/(508) 249-2547.

INDIAN HOLLOW
GROUP CAMPGROUND

From Chesterfield, 4 mi SE on SR 143; access on South St. 5/20-9/12; 14-day limit Two group camping areas: GN1 for up to 100 peo-

ple & 31 vehicles, $85; GS1 for up to 100 people & 41 vehicles, $90. Amphitheater. Picnic shelter $50. By reservation only. NRRS. **GPS: 42.34194, -72.84944**

Upper Red Lake

Lower Red Lake

MINNESOTA

Winnibigoshish Lake

Leech Lake

Moorhead

Mississippi River

Duluth

Mille Lacs Lake

94

35

St. Croix River

Minneapolis

St. Paul

Minnesota River

Mississippi River

35

90

MINNESOTA

STATE INFORMATION:

CAPITAL: Saint Paul
NICKNAME: North Star State
STATEHOOD: 1858 - 32nd State
FLOWER: Pink & White Lady Slipper
TREE: Red Pine
BIRD: Common Loon

MN

STATE TIDBITS:

• Minnesota has 90,000 miles of shoreline, more than CA, FL and HI combined.

• In 1919 a Minneapolis factory turned out the nations first armored cars.

• The Mall of America in Bloomington is the size of 78 football fields.

WWW.EXPLOREMINNESOTA.COM

Toll-free number for travel information:
1-888-TOURISM.

Travel Information Center, Minnesota Office of Tourism, 121 7th Place East, Metro Square, Suite 100, St. Paul, MN 55101. 651-296-5029.

MINNESOTA LAKES

To find campgrounds operated by the U.S. Army Corps of Engineers, match the lake's numbers on the preceding map page with numbered lake entries on the following pages. Campgrounds are listed alphabetically under the appropriate lakes. The following Minnesota impoundments have Corps of Engineers campgrounds.

Cross Lake/Pine River Dam. Cross Lake is about 22 miles N of Brainerd on Crow Wing CR 3.

Gull Lake. North of Brainerd off SR 371, Gull Lake is 115 miles SW of Duluty, 130 miles N of Minneapolis.

Lake Winnibigoshish. A 67,000-acre lake, Big Winnie, as it's called, is NW of Deer River and N of US 2, off SR 46, 102 miles northwest of Duluth.

Leech Lake. A 126,000-acre lake E of Walker on SR 371, Leech is 35 miles W of Grand Rapids, 120 miles W of Duluth and 30 miles W of Deer River.

Pokegama Lake. A 16,000-acre lake W of Grand Rapids off US 2 and 169, 82 miles NW of Duluth.

Sandy Lake. A 9,400-acre lake off SR 65 N of McGregor, Sandy Lake (also known as Big Sandy) is 60 miles W of Duluth and 1.2 miles above the junction of the Sandy and Mississippi Rivers.

❶
CROSS LAKE
PINE RIVER DAM
MISSISSIPPI RIVER
GPS: 46.671502, -94.110957

Cross Lake is about 22 miles N of Brainerd on Crow wing CR 3. The recreation area offers camping, day use facilities, a boat ramp and interpretive programs. Day use parks provide picnicking, boat launch, swimming and picnic shelter. Cross Lake is 13,660 acres with 119 miles of shoreline. Campground checkout time noon. Off-road vehicles prohibited. Resource Manager, Cross Lake, 35507 CR 66, Box 36, Cross Lake, MN 56422-0036. (218) 692-2025.

CROSSLAKE CAMPGROUND

From Crosby at jct with SR 210, 12 mi N on SR 6; 6 mi W on CR 11; NE on CR 3. 4/1-10/31; 14-day limit. 6 tent sites & 30 non-elec RV/tent sites, $20 ($10 with federal senior pass) during 5/1-9/30; sites $10 during 4/1-4/30 & 10/1-10/31 ($5 with senior pass). 73 elec sites, $26 during 5/1-9/30 ($13 with senior pass) but $13 during 4/1-4/30 & 10/1-10/31 ($6.50 with senior pass). Tbls, flush toilets, cfga, drkg wtr, dump, fish cleaning station, picnic shelter ($40), playground, beach, coin laundry, pay phone, fishing pier. Boating(l), swimming, biking. NRRS during 5/1-9/16.
GPS: 46.670820, -94.111290

②
GULL LAKE
MISSISSIPPI RIVER
GPS: 46.413541, -94.35462

N of Brainerd off SR 371, Gull Lake is 115 mi SW of Duluth, 130 mi N of Minneapolis. Burial mound display. Campground checkout time noon. Off-road vehicles prohibited. Government Point Park has a public boat ramp, picnic area, beach, trails. Resource Manager, Gull Lake, 10867 E Gull Lake Drive, Brainerd, MN 56401-9413. (218) 829-3334.

GULL LAKE RECREATION AREA

From Brainerd, 10 mi NW on SR 371; W on CR 125 to dam; on Gull River at outlet of lake. All year; 14-day limit. 37 elec sites, $26 during 5/1-9/30 ($13 with federal senior pass); $13 during 10/1-4/30 ($6.50 with federal senior pass). Tbls, flush & pit toilets, cfga, drkg wtr, dump, fish cleaning station, pay phone, playground, beach, visitor center. Showers open 5/1-10/1; wtr available 4/15-11/1. Group picnic shelter with elec for up to 40 people & 10 vehicles, $40. Boating(ld), fishing, interpretive trail, swimming, hiking, interpretive trails. NRRS (5/1-9/30).
GPS: 46.41083, -94.35139

③
LAKE WINNIBIGOSHISH
MISSISSIPPI RIVER
GPS: 47.253718, -93.584633

A 67,000 acre lake, Big Winnie, as it's called, is NW of Deer River & N of US 2, off SR 46, 102 miles NW of Duluth. Off-road vehicles prohibited. The Corps operates one campground -- Winnie Dam Campground -- and has day use facilities for boat launching, picnicking, playground and trails. Two campgrounds operated by the National Forest Service provide inexpensive campsites (see Guide to Free & Low-Cost Campgrounds). Campground checkout time noon. Resource Manager, Lake Winnibigoshish, 34385 Highway 2, Grand Rapids, MN 55744-9663. (218) 326-6128.

WINNIE DAM CAMPGROUND

From Deer River, 1 mi NW on US 2; 12 mi N (right) on SR 46; 2 mi W (left) on CR 9 (signs). 5/1-10/31; 14-day limit. 22 elec sites, $18 & $20 ($9 & $10 with federal senior pass). RV limit in excess of 65 ft. Tbls, pit toilets, cfga, drkg wtr, dump, playground, pay phone, picnic shelter, fish cleaning station. Boating(l), fishing. NRRS during 5/1-9/15. **GPS: 47.429960, -94.049706**

④
LEECH LAKE (SP)
GPS: 47.26, -94.20

A 126,000-acre lake E of Walker on SR 371, Leech is 35 miles W of Grand Rapids, 120 miles W of Duluth and 30 miles SW of Deer River. It has 316 miles of shoreline and is within the Chippewa National Forest. The only Corps of Engineers facility with camping is Leech Lake Recreation Area. Interpretive programs, snowmobile trail. Campground checkout time noon. Off-road vehicles prohibited. Chippewa National Forest's only campground at the lake is Stony Point (see Guide to Free & Low-Cost Campgrounds).

Resource Manager, Leech Lake, P. O. Box 111, Federal Dam, MN 56641-0111. (218) 654-3145.

LEECH LAKE CAMPGROUND

From Cass Lake at jct with US 2, 8 mi S on Hwy 8; on SW side of dam. 5/1-10/31; 14-day limit. 4 walk-to tent sites, $12 ($6 with federal senior pass); 73 elec sites, $24 ($12 with senior pass). RV limit in excess of 65 ft; 3 pull-through. Tbls, flush toilets, cfga, drkg wtr, showers, coin laundry, playground, dump, group shelter $35, fish cleaning station, pay phone. Boating(l), fishing, horseshoe pits, interpretive programs, nature trails, badminton, basketball, shuffleboard, hiking. (218) 654-3145. NRRS during 5/1-9/30. **GPS: 47.245853, -94.223428**

❺
POKEGAMA LAKE
MISSISSIPPI RIVER
HEADWATERS
GPS: 47.25, -93.58

A 16,000-acre lake W of Grand Rapids off US 2 and 169, 82 miles NW of Duluth. On Mississippi River, 3 miles upstream from Grand Rapids. Campground checkout time noon. Off-road vehicles prohibited. Resource Manager, Pokegama Lake, 34385 Highway 2, Grand Rapids, MN 55744-9663. (218) 326-6128.

POKEGAMA DAM
RECREATION AREA

From Grand Rapids, 2 mi W on US 2; S (left, following signs) of road. 4/1-10/31; 14-day limit. 2 tent sites, $14 ($70 with federal senior pass); 19 elec RV sites, $26 ($13 with federal senior pass). RV limit in excess of 65 ft. Tbls, flush & pit toilets, cfga, drkg wtr, dump, fish cleaning station, playground, pay phone. Picnic shelter for up to 50 people & 50 vehicles, $40. Boating(l), fishing. NRRS during 5/1-9/15. **GPS: 47.250674, -93.586049**

❻
SANDY LAKE
MISSISSIPPI RIVER
GPS: 46.7883, -98.3283

A 9,400-acre lake off SR 65 N of McGregor, Sandy Lake (also known as Big Sandy) is 60 miles W of Duluth and 1.2 miles above the junction of the Sandy and Mississippi Rivers. Interpretive facility and programs. An old lock house has been turned into interpretive display. Sandy Lake Recreation Area is on the canoe route that linked Lake Superior with the Mississippi River during the fur trading period. Campground checkout time noon. Off-road vehicles prohibited. Resource Manager, Big Sandy Lake, 22205 531st Lane, McGregor, MN 55760-0192. (218) 426-3482.

SANDY LAKE RECREATION AREA

From McGregor, 13 mi N on SR 65 to town of Libby, then follow signs E to outlet of Sandy Lake. 4/1-10/31; 14-day limit. $24 at 49 elec sites ($12 with federal senior pass); double sites $48 ($24 with senior pass). 8 walk-to tent sites $16 ($8 with senior pass). RV limit in excess of 65 ft; 8 pull-through sites. Some sites may have lower fees during April & October. Tbls, flush & pit toilets, showers, cfga, drkg wtr, dump, playground, beach, pay phone, fish cleaning stations, fishing pier, coin laundry. Two group camping areas, $60. Picnic shelters with elec, $25-$35. Horseshoe pits, boating(ld), fishing, hiking, badminton, basketball, swimming, educational programs, interpretive trails, volleyball. Museum, visitor center. NRRS during 5/1-9/30. **GPS: 46.787643, -93.320910**

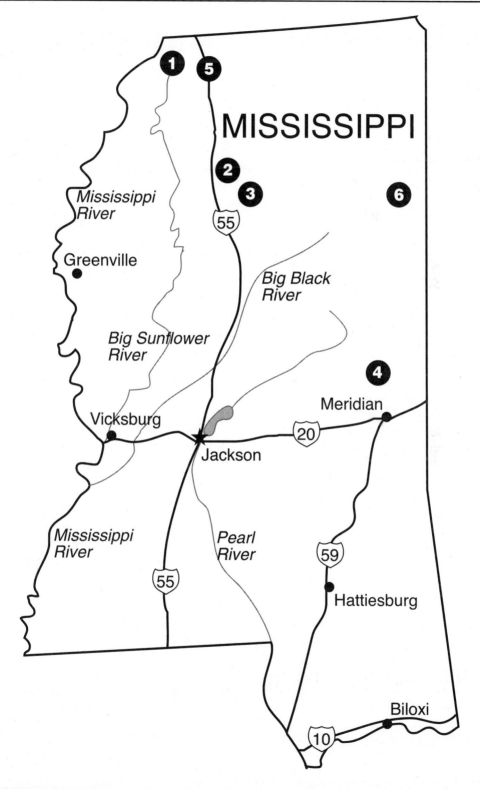

MISSISSIPPI

Mississippi
River

Greenville

Big Black
River

Big Sunflower
River

Meridian

Vicksburg

Jackson

Mississippi
River

Pearl
River

Hattiesburg

Biloxi

MISSISSIPPI

STATE INFORMATION:

CAPITAL: Jackson
NICKNAME: Magnolia State
STATEHOOD: 1817 - 20th State
FLOWER: Magnolia
TREE: Southern Magnolia
BIRD: Mockingbird

MS

STATE TIDBITS:

• Elvis Presley was born in Tupelo, on January 8, 1935.

• The first football player on a Wheaties box was Walter Payton of Columbia.

• Belzoni is called the Catfish Capital of the World.

WWW.VISITMISSISSIPPI.ORG

Tourism Division, Mississippi Development Authority, P.O. Box 849, Jackson, MS 39205; 1-866-SEE-MISS. 601/359-3297.

MISSISSIPPI LAKES

To find campgrounds operated by the U.S. Army Corps of Engineers, match the lake's numbers on the preceding map page with numbered lake entries on the following pages. Campgrounds are listed alphabetically under the appropriate lakes. The following Mississippi impoundments have Corps of Engineers campgrounds.

Arkabutla Lake. This 12,730-acre lake is N of Arkabutla on SR 301, 30 mi S of Memphis, Tennessee.

Enid Lake. This 15,560-acre lake is 26 miles N of Grenada and 1.7 mile E of Enid off I-55 exit 233 on SR 233.

Grenada Lake. A 35,820-acre lake with 148 miles of shoreline, Grenada is 2 miles NE of the town of Grenada, off I-55 exit 206, then E on SR 8. It is 99 miles S of Memphis, Tennessee.

Okatibbee Lake. A 4,144-acre lake with 28 miles of shoreline, it is 10 miles N of I-20/I-59

and NW of Meridian off SR 19, 20 miles W of the Alabama state line.

Sardis Lake. A 32,100-acre lake NE of Batesville and I-55 exit 246 on SR 35, 9 miles SE of Sardis and 50 miles S of Memphis, Tennessee.

Tennessee-Tombigbee Waterway. The waterway is a navigable link between the lower Tennessee Valley and the Gulf of Mexico. It stretches 234 miles from Demopolis, Alabama, to Pickwick Lake in the NE corner of Mississippi. The Mississippi section of the waterway includes the following impoundments:

Aberdeen Lake -- Just NE of Aberdeen
Columbus Lake -- Near Columbus
Bay Springs Lake -- Near Tisomingo
Fulton Pool -- At the City of Fulton

❶ ARKABUTLA LAKE
GPS: 34.7567, -90.1233

This 12,730-acre lake is N of Arkabutla on SR 301, 30 miles S of Memphis, TN. Visitors to 10 p.m. Campground checkout time 4 p.m. Sites that are free during winter may have reduced amenities. Non-campers pay $3 at boat ramps except Coldwater Point ($30 annual permit). Day use facilities: Bayou Point Park -- boat ramp, picnicking, group shelter, playground, biking trail; Coldwater Point Park -- boat ramp, picnicking; Highway 51 Landing -- boat ramp, picnicking; Plantation Point -- boat ramp, picnicking; Sunfish Bay -- multi-use trails. Visitor center. Although all campgrounds have 14-day camping limits, an additional 14-day extension is available at Hermando Point, Dub Patton & South Abutment campgrounds during 3/1-10/31. Resource Mgr. Arkabutla Lake Field Office, 3905 Arkabutla Dam Road, Coldwater, MS 38618-9737. (662) 562-6261.

DUB PATTON RECREATION AREA

From Coldwater, 7 mi W on Arkabutla Rd; 5 mi N on Arkabutla Dam Rd, then across dam; on N side (signs). All year; 14-day limit. 8 tent sites with elec & 51 elec RV/tent sites, $18 base, $20 at premium locations during 3/1-10/31 ($9 & $10 with federal senior pass); $16 base, $18 at premium locations during 11/1-2/28 ($8 & $9 with senior pass). 50-ft RV limit. Tbls, flush toilets, cfga, drkg wtr, dump, amphitheater, playground, two picnic shelters with elec $30. Boating(l), fishing, hiking, nature trails. NRRS during 3/1-10/31.
GPS: 34.77444, -90.11472

HERNANDO POINT CAMPGROUND

From Coldwater, 5 mi N on US 51; about 5 mi W on Wheeler Rd; follow signs into campground. On N shore of lake. All year; 14-day limit. 83 elec/wtr sites, $18 base, $20 at premium locations during 3/1-10/31 ($9 & $10 with federal senior pass); $16 base, $18 at premium locations during 11/1-2/28 ($8 & $9 with senior pass). RV limit in excess of 65 ft. Tbls, flush toilets, cfga, drkg wtr, dump, playground, beach, amphitheater picnic shelter with elec $30. Boating(l), fishing, swimming. 662-562-6261. NRRS. **GPS: 34.732602, -90.069314**

KELLEY'S CROSSING CAMP

From Coldwater, 6.5 mi W on Arkabutla Rd; 3 mi N on Kelley Crossing Rd, following signs. All year; 14-day limit. 24 primitive sites, $5

during 5/1-9/30 ($2.50 with federal senior pass); free rest of year. 20-ft RV limit. Pit toilets, cfga, drkg wtr, tbls. Boating(l), fishing.
GPS: 34.729190, -90.107991

SOUTH OUTLET CHANNEL

From Coldwater, 7 mi W on Arkabutla Rd; 4.5 mi N on Arkabutla Dam Rd; W below dam following signs. All year; 14-day limit. 22 primitive sites, $6 during 5/1-9/30 ($3 with federal senior pass); free rest of year. 20-ft RV limit. Pit toilets, tbls, cfga, drkg wtr, playground, picnic shelter ($30). Boating(l), fishing, hiking.
GPS: 34.758856, -90.128467

PLEASANT HILL CAMPGROUND

From Hernando, 5 mi W on SR 304; 5 mi S on Fogg Rd; right on access rd, following signs. All year; 14-day limit. 10 primitive sites, $5 during 5/1-9/30 ($2.50 with federal senior pass); free rest of year. 20-ft RV limit. Pit toilets, cfga, tbls, drkg wtr, showers, beach, playground. Swimming, fishing, boating.
GPS: 34.778525, -90.101257

SOUTH ABUTMENT RECREATION AREA

From Coldwater, 7 mi W on Arkabutla Rd; 5 mi N on Arkabutla Dam Rd; just S of dam, following signs. All year; 14-day limit. 80 elec sites, $18 base, $20 at premium locations during 3/1-10/31 ($9 & $10 with federal senior pass); $16 base, $18 at premium locations during 11/1-2/28 ($8 & $9 with senior pass). 60-ft RV limit. Tbls, flush toilets, cfga, drkg wtr, dump, playground, beach. Group camping area with 2 sites, $50; picnic shelter with elec, $30. NRRS. 662-562-6261. **GPS: 34.747030, -90.126477**

❷
ENID LAKE
GPS: 34.1583, -89.8217

This 15,560-acre lake is 26 miles N of Grenada and 1.7 miles E of Enid off I-55 exit 233 on SR 233. At the Yocona River, it is part of the Yazoo Headwaters Project, designed to help protect the Mississippi Delta from flooding. Visitors center, 15 day use areas. Picnic shelters ($50 reservation fee) at McCurdy Point, Hickory Ridge, Wallace Creek, Outlet Channel, Riverview, Persimmon Hill, Chickasaw Hill, Water Valley Landing and Ford's Well. Non-campers pay $3 at boat ramps & $1 per person ($4 vehicle) at beaches. 7 parks have playgrounds. Six trails, including 9-mi Plum Point hiking/equestrian trail and 20-mi Spyglass Hill multi-use trail (which also features historical buildings. Besides Corps-managed facilities, camping also is available at George Payne Cossar State Park. Visitor center, interpretive programs. Resource Manager, Enid Lake, 931 County Road 36, Enid, MS 38927. (662) 563-4571.

BYNUM CREEK LANDING

From Water Valley at jct with SR 7, 8.3 mi NW on SR 315; 2.8 mi SW on Pope Water Valley Rd; 2.4 mi SE on all-weather Cliff Finch Rd; at NE shore of lake. All year; 14-day limit. 5 primitive sites, free. 20-ft RV limit. Pit toilets, cfga, drkg wtr, tbls, beach. Boating(l), fishing, swimming. **GPS: 34.177841, -89.735234**

CHICKASAW HILL CAMP

From Pope, 8.8 mi SE, then 1.6 mi SW; on N side of lake. All year; 14-day limit. 7 tent sites & 45 RV/tent sites with elec/wtr, $15 during 3/1-10/31; $10 during 11/1-2/28 ($7.50 & $5 with federal senior pass). 65-ft RV limit. Tbls, flush toilets, cfga, drkg wtr, amphitheater, showers, beach, playground, dump, picnic shelter $30. Boating(l), swimming, fishing, bridle trails, OHV trails, hiking. NRRS. (662) 563-4571. **GPS: 34.165227, -89.824519**

FORD'S WELL RECREATION AREA

From I-55 exit 227 S of Enid, E on SR 32 to CR 557, then N to campground. All year; 14-day limit. 18 sites with elec/wtr, $14 for campers using the 17-mi Spyglass Equestrian Trail ($7 with federal senior pass). Tbls, toilets, cfga, drkg wtr, picnic shelter. Campground features

hitching rails, horse wash station & overlook with hitching rails; joint effort involving Corps, state parks department & a private equestrian club. **GPS: 34.136922, -89.797397**

LONG BRANCH CAMPGROUND

From I-55 exit 227 S of Enid, 3.8 mi NE on SR 32; 1.9 mi N on CR 26. All year; 14-day limit. 14 primitive sites, $6. 20-ft RV limit. Pit toilets, tbls, cfga, drkg wtr, beach. Swimming, boating(l), fishing. No reservations. **GPS: 34.126362, -89.842511**

PERSIMMON HILL CAMP

From I-55 exit 233, 1 mi E on CR 36 to dam; cross dam, turn NE on CR 34; at S end of dam (signs). All year; 14-day limit. 72 elec sites, $18 during 3/1-10/31 ($9 with federal senior pass); $12 during 11/1-2/28 ($6 with senior pass). 65-ft RV limit; 2 pull-through sites. Tbls, flush toilets, cfga, drkg wtr, showers, dump, playground, beach, picnic shelters $50. Boating(l), fishing, swimming, hiking, equestrian trails. 662-563-4571. NRRS during 3/1-10/31. **GPS: 34.133996, -89.903843**

PLUM POINT CAMPGROUND

From Pope, 5.3 mi SE on Pope Water Valley Rd; 3.7 mi SE on all-weather Plum Point Rd. All year; 14-day limit. 10 primitive sites, $6 ($3 with federal senior pass). 20-ft RV limit. Pit toilets, cfga, drkg wtr, tbls, beach, playground. Horseback riding, waterskiing, boating(l), fishing. No reservations. **GPS: 34.160764, -89.8555509**

WALLACE CREEK CAMP

From I-55 exit 233, 2.5 mi E on CR 36 to the dam; across the spillway on W side of the dam (signs). All year; 14-day limit. 101 elec/wtr sites, $16 base, $18 at premium locations during 3/1-10/31 ($8 & $9 with federal senior pass); $10 base, $12 at premium locations during 11/1-2/28 ($5 & $6 with senior pass). 65-ft RV limit; 7 pull-through sites. Picnic shelter, $50. At reserved sites, 2-night minimum stay required on weekends, 3 nights on holiday weekends. Hiking trail, interpretive trail, amphitheater, fish cleaning station, phone, ORV trail. NRRS during 3/1-10/31. **GPS: 34.160398, -89.891950**

WATER VALLEY LANDING

From Water Valley at jct with SR 315, 2 mi S on SR 7; 5.3 mi W on SR 32; 3.2 mi NW on CR 553; on S side of lake. 3/1-10/1; 14-day limit. 26 elec/wtr sites, $15 ($7.50 with federal senior pass). 60-ft RV limit. Tbls, flush toilets, cfga, drkg wtr, showers, playground, beach, picnic shelter $50. Boating(l), fishing, hiking, swimming, horseback riding, OHV trails. 662-563-4571. NRRS. **GPS: 34.144239, -89.765913**

❸
GRENADA LAKE
GPS: 33.8083, -89.7717

A 35,820-acre lake with 148 miles of shoreline, Grenada is 2 miles NE of Grenada, off I-55 exit 206, then E on SR 8. It is 99 miles S of Memphis, TN, on the Yalobusha & Skuna Rivers. Visitor center with displays, interpretive programs & exhibits. Sports complex area below dam. Campsites that are free sites during winter may have reduced amenities. Non-campers pay $3 at boat ramps & $1 per person fee at beaches. Trails include a one-mi fitness trail (at Dam Area Central Park) with 18 exercise stations; 2-mi Lost Bluff hiking trail to a Civil War-era earthen fort; 1.5-mi Haserway Wetland Management Nature Trail along Toe Rd, and Old River Run Nature Trail. Picnic shelter reservations are $50 & $100.

Other day use facilities: Cape Retreat -- picnicking, beach; Choctaw Landing -- boat ramp, picnicking; Dam Area Central -- picnicking, 2 group shelters, playground, interpretive trail, fitness trail, ball fields, tennis courts, basketball court; Lost Bluff -- hiking trail; Lower Torrance --boat ramp; Piney Woods -- boat ramp, multi-use trail; South Abutment A -- boat ramp, picnicking, group shelter, playground, interpretive trail; South Graysport -- boat ramp; Upper Yalobusha -- boat ramp,

picnicking; Willow Run -- picnicking, beach; Wolf Creek - boat ramp; Young's Landing -- boat ramp. Resource Manager, Grenada Lake Field Office, 2202 Scenic Loop 333, Grenada, MS 38901. (662) 226-5911.

BRYANT CAMPGROUND

From I-55 exit 55 N at Grenada, NE on SR 7, then SE on CR 74 to campground. All year; 14-day limit. 6 sites. Elec/wtr sites, $12; wtr sites, $6 ($6 & $3 with federal senior pass). Pit toilet, tbls, cfga, drkg wtr. Boating(l), fishing, waterskiing. **GPS: 33.923291, -89.704673**

CHOCTAW CAMPGROUND

From Gore Springs at SR 8, N on Graysport Crossing Rd across lake bridge, past North Graysport Campground; N (left) on Gums Crossing Rd; S (left) on Rounsville Church Rd; at "Y," veer right on Choctaw Landing Rd, following signs. All year; 14-day limit. 5 free primitive sites. Pit toilet, cfga, no drkg wtr. Boating, fishing. **GPS: 33.828127, -89.647193**

GUMS CROSSING CAMP

From Gore Springs at SR 8, N on Graysport Crossing Rd across lake bridge, past North Graysport Campground, then N on CR 221 (Gums Crossing Rd) to river. All year; 14-day limit. 14 free primitive sites. Pit toilet, no drkg wtr, cfga, boating, fishing. **GPS: 33.904314, -89.627087**

NORTH ABUTMENT CAMP

From I-55 exit 55 N of Grenada, 5 mi NE on SR 7, then S on SR 333 past the primitive campground; at N end of dam. All year; 14-day limit. 88 elec/wtr sites (50-amp), $20 ($10 with federal senior pass). 40-ft RV limit; 4 pull-through sites. Tbls, flush toilets, cfga, drkg wtr, showers, playground, dump, amphitheater, fish cleaning station, picnic shelter $50. Boating, fishing, hiking, swimming, archery, ball fields, waterskiing. 662-226-5911. NRRS. **GPS: 33.84694, -89.77444**

NORTH GRAYSPORT CAMP

From Gore Springs at jct with SR 8, 5.8 mi N on Graysport Crossing Rd, across bridge, then right at first rd (Old Hwy 8), left into campground; on NE side of lake between rivers. All year; 14-day limit. 50 elec/wtr sites, $14 ($7 with federal senior pass). 55-ft RV limit. Tbls, flush toilets, cfga, drkg wtr, showers, dump, playground, amphitheater. Boating(l), fishing. (662) 226-5911. NRRS. **GPS: 33.834827, -89.603881**

OLD FORT CAMPGROUND

From Grenada, 2 mi NE on Scenic Loop Rd (Old Hwy 8); right (E) on access rd, following signs to W shore of Gibbs Creek S of dam & just S of FFA Camp Rd. All year; 14-day limit. 21 primitive sites, $6 ($3 with federal senior pass). 20-ft RV limit. Pit toilets, tbls, cfga, drkg wtr, picnic shelter $50. Hiking, boating(l), fishing. No reservations. **GPS: 33.794275, -89.760253**

SKUNA-TURKEY CREEK CAMP

From Coffeeville, 4.5 mi SE on SR 330; 2.1 mi S on CR 221(Elam S Rd); 3.8 mi SW on CR 229; W on CR 202 to NE shore of lake. All year; 14-day limit. 6 free primitive sites. 20-ft RV limit. Pit toilets, tbls, cfga, drkg wtr. Boating(l), fishing. **GPS: 33.877471, -89.689078**

❹ OKATIBBEE LAKE
GPS: 34.307144. -88.681641

A 4,144-acre lake with 28 miles of shoreline 10 miles N of I-20/I-59 and NW of Meridian off SR 19, 20 miles W of the Alabama state line. Visitor center. Day use facilities: Collinsville Park -- boat ramp, picnicking, group shelter, playground, beach; East Bank Park -- picnicking, group shelter, trails; Pine Springs Park -- boat ramp, picnicking, group shelter, playground, beach, interpretive trail; Tailrace Area -- picnicking, hiking trail West Bank Park -- boat ramp, picnicking, group shelter, playground, beach, fitness trail. Non-campers pay day use fees: $4 per vehicle at beaches, $3 at boat ramps. Okatibbee Water Park campground is operated by the Pat Harrison Waterway District; federal senior passes accepted. Project Manager, Okatibbee Lake,8490 Okatibbee Dam Rd, Collinsville, MS 39325. (601) 626-8431.

GIN CREEK CAMPGROUND

From Collinsville at jct with SR 19, 2.8 mi NE on CR 17 (W. Lauderdale School Rd) past "T"; 1 mi E on Martin-Center Hill/Causeway Rd; on right. All year; 14-day limit. 7 primitive sites, $8 ($4 with federal senior pass). Tbls, toilets, cfga, drkg wtr. Boating(l), fishing. **GPS: 32.521369, -88.808622**

TWILTLEY BRANCH CAMP

From Collinsville at jct with SR 19, 1 mi E on CR 17; exit 1.7 mi E on Hamrick Rd W, then S on Hamrick Rd W, following signs. All year; 14-day limit. 12 RV/tent sites no hookups, $12 ($6 with federal senior pass); 50 elec/wtr sites, $18 base, $20 at premium locations ($9 & $10 with senior pass). RV limit in excess of 65 ft; 4 pull-through. Tbls, flush toilets, cfga, drkg wtr, dump, pay phone, playground, beach, coin laundry, showers, picnic shelter. Boating(l), hiking, swimming, fishing. 3 group camping areas, $50-$60. (601) 626-8068. NRRS. **GPS: 32.495572, -88.809088**

❺ SARDIS LAKE
GPS: 34.25245. -89.661

A 32,100-acre lake NE of Batesville and I-55 exit 246 on SR 35, 9 miles SE of Sardis and 50 miles S of Memphis, Tennessee. Campground checkout time 2 p.m. Campsites that are free during winter may have reduced amenities. Visitor center, interpretive programs. Non-campers pay $3 day use fees at boat ramps, $1 at beaches. Picnic shelter reservations $50-$100.

Day use facilities: Big Acres -- shelter, playground; Coles Point -- boat ramp; Coontown Crossing -- boat ramp, picnicking; Cypress Point -- picnicking, group shelter, playground, beach; Engineers Point -- boat ramp, picnicking, group shelter; Lespedeza Point -- boat ramp; Paradise Point -- shelter, playground, beach; Sandstone -- picnicking, fitness & interpretive trail; Teckville -- boat ramp, picnicking; Weir -- boat ramp; Wyatt Crossing -- boat ramp. Project Manager, Sardis Lake Field Office, 29949 Hwy. 315, Sardis, MS ·38666-3066. (662) 563-4531.

BEACH POINT CAMPGROUND

From Sardis at jct with I-55 exit, 8 mi E on SR 315. All year; 14-day limit. 14 primitive sites, $8 during 4/1-9/30 ($4 with federal senior pass), free during 10/1-3/31. 20-ft RV limit. Flush & pit toilets, cfga, drkg wtr, playground. Boating(l), fishing, waterskiing.
GPS: 34.42079, -89.810838

CLEAR CREEK CAMPGROUND

From Oxford at jct with SR 7, 10.5 mi NW on SR 314, then 2 mi SW on CR 100. All year; 14-day limit. 52 sites with wtr/elec, $18 ($9 with federal senior pass). RV limit 65 ft. Tbls, flush toilets, cfga, drkg wtr, showers, dump, playground, beach, picnic shelter $30. Boating(l), ORV activities, swimming, fishing, waterskiing, 13-mi mountain biking trail. 205-384-4792. NRRS during 4/1-9/30.
GPS: 34.427766, -89.695537

GRAHAM LAKE CAMPGROUND

From Abbeville, 2 mi N on CR 201, then qtr mi N on SR 7; right (E) for 2 mi on CR 244; left (N) on CR 297 to Little Tallahatchie River. All year; 14-day limit. Free primitive sites, 6 picnic sites. Pit toilets, tbls, cfga no drkg wtr. Boating(l), fishing.
GPS: 34.533748, -89.457421

HAYES CROSSING CAMP

From Como, about 6 mi E on SR 310; 2 mi S on Fredonia Rd; 4 mi E on Simon Chapel Rd; 2 mi S on Farris Fonville Rd; 1 mi S on Hayes Crossing Rd to lake. All year; 14-day limit. Free primitive sites, 5 picnic sites. Pit toilet, cfga, tbls, no drkg wtr. Boating, fishing.
GPS: 34.455642, 89.763807

HURRICANE LANDING CAMP

From Abbeville, 3.6 mi W on CR 214, becoming CR 108 (Hurricane Landing Rd); at south-central shore of lake. All year; 14-day limit. 19 primitive sites, $18. ($9 with federal senior pass). RV limit 20'. Flush & pit toilets. No reservations. **GPS: 34.493577, -89.584279**

LOWER LAKE CAMPGROUND

From Sardis, 3 mi SE on SR 315, across dam, following signs. All year; 14-day limit. Free primitive sites. Tbls, pit toilets, cfga, drkg wtr, playground, beach. Boating(l), swimming, fishing. 250 picnic sites.
GPS: 34.401439, -89.792483

OAK GROVE CAMPGROUND

From Batesville, 11 mi NE on SR 35; below the dam on Lower Lake. All year; 14-day limit. 82 elec/wtr sites, $18 ($9 with federal senior pass). 40-ft RV limit. Tbls, flush toilets, cfga, drkg wtr, amphitheater, picnic shelter. Boating(l), fishing, hiking. No reservations.
GPS: 34.406220, -89.798019

PATS BLUFF CAMPGROUND

From Batesville at I-55 exit 243A, 9 mi on Hwy 6, then N on county rd; watch for signs. 4/1-9/30; 14-day limit. 14 primitive sites, $8 ($4 with federal senior pass). 20-ft RV limit. Tbls, toilets, cfga, drkg wtr, playground, picnic shelter $30. Boating(l), fishing, waterskiing. Note: In 2015, the campground was still closed for renovations and site upgrades with wtr & elec; check current status with lake office before visiting. (662) 563-4531.
GPS: 34.420919, -89.732127

SLEEPY BEND CAMPGROUND

From Batesville, N on I-55 to exit 246, E on SR 35 to Lower Lake below John Kyle State Park. All year; 14-day limit. 50 primitive sites, $8 during 4/1-9/30 ($4 with federal senior pass); free 10/1-3/31. 20-ft RV limit. Flush & pit toilets, cfga, drkg wtr. Fishing, boating. **GPS: 34.410593, -89.813018**

❻
TENNESSEE-TOMBIGBEE WATERWAY
GPS: 33.52, -88.51

The Tennessee-Tombigbee Waterway is a navigable link between the lower Tennessee Valley and the Gulf of Mexico. Stretching 234 miles from Demopolis, Alabama, to Pickwick Lake in the NE corner of Mississippi, this man-make channel has a series of ten locks and dams forming ten pools. Fishing piers are available. Off-road vehicles prohibited. Jamie L. Whitten Historical Center, Fulton, MS (662) 862-5414 and the Bay Springs Resource & Visitor Center, Bay Springs Lake, near Dennis, MS (662) 423-1287, open daily except during winter months and on some federal holidays. Interpretive exhibits, artifacts, 120-seat auditorium with audiovisual equipment, group tours, (662) 862-5414. Campground checkout time 3 p.m. Registered campers may use any of the day use areas on the waterway without paying fees charged to non-campers. Contact Resource Manager, Waterway Management Center, 3606 W Plymouth Road, Columbus, MS 39701. (662) 327-2142. See entries in Alabama.

BLUE BLUFF CAMPGROUND

From Aberdeen at jct with Commerce St (US 145), N on Meridian through town, cross railroad tracks and bridge (becoming Coontail Rd), then 1st right & left onto Bluff Rd, following signs; S end of Aberdeen Lake at river. All year; 14-day limit. 92 elec/wtr sites ($50-amp), $20 base, $22 for full hookups & waterfront sites ($10 & $11 with federal senior pass). RV limit in excess of 65 ft. Tbls, flush toilets, cfga, drkg wtr, dump, showers, pay phone, coin laundry, playground, beach, information center, amphitheater, fish cleaning station, picnic shelter. Boating(ld), fishing, swimming, hiking trails, interpretive programs, guided interpretive walks, multi-use court, wildlife viewing, waterskiing. (662) 369-2832. NRRS during 3/1-10/31. **GPS: 33.846269, -88.536077**

DEWAYNE HAYES RECREATION AREA

From Columbus, 4 mi N on US 45; 1.5 mi W on SR 373; 2 mi SW on Stinson Creek Rd; 0.5 mi left on Barton Ferry Rd, then SW on access rd; at E shore of Columbus Lake near Stinson Creek. All year; 14-day limit. 10 walk-to tent sites, $14 ($7 with federal senior pass); 100 RV/tent sites with elec/wtr, $20 base, $22 at premium locations ($10 & $11 with senior pass); 25 full hookups, $24 ($12 with senior pass). RV limit in excess of 65 ft. Flush toilets, tbls, cfga, drkg wtr, showers, fish cleaning station, picnic shelter, information center, pay phone, playground, coin laundry. Interactive water sprayground, interpretive programs, interpretive trail, guided interpretive walks, game courts, boating(ld), fishing, hiking, waterskiing. (662) 434-6939. NRRS during 3/1-10/31. **GPS: 33.603052, -88.469864**

PINEY GROVE CAMPGROUND

From Tishomingo, 1 mi N on SR 25; about 6 mi W on SR 30 past town of Burton; left (SE) for 3 mi on CR 3501; right (E) on CR 3550, following signs; at W shore of Bay Springs Lake. All year; 14-day limit. 141 elec/wtr sites, $22 base, $24 at premium locations ($11 & $12 with federal senior pass). Tbls, flush toilets, cfga, drkg wtr, showers, playground, beach, coin laundry, dump, fish cleaning stations, amphitheater. Also RV limit in excess of 65 ft; 6 pull-through. 10 primitive tent sites with boat-in access are free (no drkg wtr, but tbls, pads & cfga).

Interpretive trail, boating(ld), fishing, hiking, swimming, basketball, waterskiing. (662) 423-1287. NRRS during 3/1-9/25.
GPS: 34.568453, -88.327541

TOWN CREEK CAMPGROUND

From Columbus at jct with US 45N, W on SR 50; 1 mi W of Tenn-Tom Bridge on SR 50; 1.5 mi N; right on J. Witherspoon Rd following signs; on Columbus Lake. Ordinarily open all year, but closed 10/1-2/21 during winter of 2014-2015; 14-day limit. 10 walk-to tent sites, $14 ($7 with federal senior pass); 100 wtr/elec RV/tent sites, $20 base, $22 at premium locations ($10 & $11 with senior pass). RV limit in excess of 65 ft. Tbls, flush toilets, cfga, drkg wtr, dump, showers, beach, playground, coin laundry, fish cleaning station, pay phone. Boating(ld), fishing, bike trail, interpretive programs, guided interpretive walks, basketball, waterskiing, hiking, multi-use court. Visitor center. (662)494-4885. NRRS during 3/1-9/15.
GPS: 33.612761, -88.495603

WHITTEN CAMPGROUND

Adjacent to the City of Fulton at Fulton Pool. From jct with US 78, about 0.5 mi N on N. Cummings St; left 0.1 mi on Vo Tech Rd, then right on North Access Rd & left into access rd (within Jamie L. Whitten Historical Center Park). All year; 14-day limit. 60 elec/wtr sites, $20 base, $22 at premium locations ($10 & $11 with federal senior pass). RV limit in excess of 65'; 3 pull-through sites. Tbls, flush toilets, cfga, drkg wtr, showers, dump, playground, beach, coin laundry, pay phone, picnic shelters, amphitheater. Interpretive trail, nature trails, game courts, swimming, boating(ld), fishing, hiking, swimming. (662) 862-5414 or 862-7070. NRRS.
GPS: 34.291416, -88.417679

MISSOURI

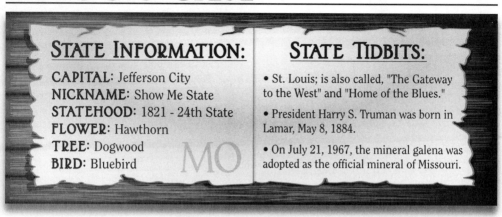

STATE INFORMATION:

CAPITAL: Jefferson City
NICKNAME: Show Me State
STATEHOOD: 1821 - 24th State
FLOWER: Hawthorn
TREE: Dogwood
BIRD: Bluebird

STATE TIDBITS:

• St. Louis; is also called, "The Gateway to the West" and "Home of the Blues."

• President Harry S. Truman was born in Lamar, May 8, 1884.

• On July 21, 1967, the mineral galena was adopted as the official mineral of Missouri.

WWW.VISITMO.COM

Missouri Division of Tourism, PO Box 1055, Jefferson City, MO 65102.For travel information by mail: 800-519-2100.

MISSOURI LAKES

To find campgrounds operated by the U.S. Army Corps of Engineers, match the lake's numbers on the preceding map page with numbered lake entries on the following pages. Campgrounds are listed alphabetically under the appropriate lakes. The following Missouri impoundments have Corps of Engineers campgrounds.

Bull Shoals Lake. This 45,440-acre lake is 15 miles west of Mountain Home, Arkansas, on SR 178 and southeast of Branson near the Missouri state line.

Clearwater Lake. A 1,600-acre lake 5 miles southwest of Piedmont on CR HH off SR 34, east of Springfield and northwest of Mark Twain National Forest in southeastern Missouri.

Harry S Truman Lake. This 55,600-acre lake is near Warsaw on US 65, 94 miles southeast of Kansas City.

Mark Twain Lake. This 18,600-acre lake is 14 miles southeast of Monroe City on CR J, 120 miles northwest of St. Louis.

Lock & Dam 20, Mississippi River. Pool 20 extends from river mile 343.2 upstream to Keokuk, Iowa. The dam is off Old Highway 61 about 0.5 mile north of Henderson Avenue in Canton, Missouri, on Lock and Dam Road.

Norfork Lake. Located four miles northeast of Norfork, Arkansas, on Arkansas SR 177 near the Missouri state line, 135 miles north of Little Rock.

Pomme De Terre Lake. This 7,900-acre lake with 113 miles of shoreline is 3 miles south of Hermitage on SR 254, 140 miles southeast of Kansas City.

Stockton Lake. This 24,900-acre lake has 298 miles of shorelne. It is at the east side of Stockton on SR 32, 136 miles southeast of Kansas City.

Table Rock Lake. A 43,100-acre lake 7 miles southwest of Branson on SR 165, west of US 65.

Wappapello Lake. This 8,400-acre lake is 16 miles northeast of Poplar Bluff and north of US 60, east of US 67 on CR T, 150 miles south of St. Louis.

❶ BULL SHOALS LAKE
GPS: 36.3633, -92.5433

This 45,440-acre lake is 15 miles W of Mountain Home, Arkansas, on SR 178 and SE of Branson near the Missouri state line. Off-road vehicles prohibited. Campground checkout time 3 p.m. Campsites that are free off-season may have reduced amenities. The Corps operates three developed campgrounds in Missouri and six in Arkansas. A former Corps facility, Pontiac Campground, is now privately operated by Pontiac Cove Marina, and federal senior passes are not honored. Day use fees at swimming areas. Resource Manager, Bull Shoals Lake, 324 W. 7th St., Mountain Home, AR 72653. (870) 425-2700. See AR listings.

BEAVER CREEK CAMPGROUND

6.6 mi E of Forsyth on US 160 (2.5 mi S of Kissee Mills) on CR O. 4/1-10/31; 14-day limit. $18 base at 33 elec sites, $19 for premium 50-amp service ($9 & $9.50 with federal senior pass). 40-ft RV limit. Tbls, flush toilets, showers, cfga, drkg wtr, dump, playground, beach, coin laundry, group picnic shelter ($42). Boating(l), swimming, waterskiing, fishing. Non-campers pay day use fee at boat ramp. 417-546-3708. NRRS during 5/17-9/13. **GPS: 36.639714, -93.045777**

RIVER RUN CAMPGROUND

From Forsyth, E on SR 60 across bridge, then S following sign, then W; at upper end of lake. 4/1-9/15; 14-day limit. 32 elec sites, $18 ($9 with federal senior pass); $20 at 10 premium 50-amp sites ($10 with senior pass). 40-ft RV limit. Tbls, flush & pit toilets, cfga, drkg wtr, showers, dump, playground, coin laundry. Boating(l), waterskiing, biking, fishing. (417) 546-3646). No reservations. **GPS: 36.679932, -93.10174**

THEODOSIA PARK

From Isabella (sign), 3 mi W on US 160, across bridge, then S (left). Also 1 mi E of Theodosia on Hwy 160. 5/1-9/15; 14-day limit. 2 sites without hookups, $14 ($7 with federal senior pass); 31 elec sites, $18 base, $19 with 50-amp service ($9 & $9.50 with senior pass). 45-ft RV limit. Tbls, flush toilets, showers, cfga, drkg wtr, dump, beach, playground, coin laundry, pay phone, store, picnic shelter ($40). Ball field, boating(l), swimming, fishing. (870) 273-4626. NRRS. **GPS: 36.575232, -92.652844**

YOCUM CREEK

From town of Cedarcreek (about 8 mi NW of Protem), 2 mi S on SR M, then 1 mi W on Yocum Creek Rd to lake. Free primitive, undesignated sites; no facilities. Boating(l), fishing. **GPS: 36.531114, -93.045541**

❷ CLEARWATER LAKE
GPS: 37.367, 90.7717

A 1,600-acre lake 5 miles SW of Piedmont on CR HH off SR 34, E of Springfield and NW of Mark Twain National Forest in southeastern Missouri. Non-campers charged day use fees for dump stations. Campsites that are free off-season may have reduced amenities. The lake has no Corps-managed boat docks, but swimming areas are available at four Corps parks ($4 pr vehicle daily fees), an the lake has eight developed boat launches. The 3.5-mi Black River hiking & biking trail winds along the Black River below Clearwater Dam. $3 day use fees are charged at the Webb Creek, Bluff View and Piedmont boat ramps. Besides the Corps campgrounds, nearby overnight facilities include Funk Memorial State Forest & Wildlife Area near Annapolis and Clearwater Lake State Wildlife Management Area near Piedmont (see Guide to Free Campgrounds). Free primitive, undeveloped camping by permit available at various places around the lake, including at Overlook Park. Visitor center, interpretive programs. Operations Manager, Clearwater Lake, RR 3, Box 3559D, Piedmont, MO 63957-9559. (573) 233-7777.

BLUFF VIEW CAMPGROUND

From Piedmont at jct with SR 34, 0.9 mi N on SR 49; 6.9 mi W on CR AA. All year; 14-day limit. 7 non-elec sites, $14 ($7 with federal senior pass) during 5/15-9/15; free rest of year, but no services. 41 elec sites (20 wtr hookups), $16 base & $20 for 50-amp elec/wtr ($8 & $10 with federal senior pass) during 5/15-9/15; free rest of year, but no utilities. RV limit in excess of 65 ft. Tbls, flush toilets, showers, dump, cfga, drkg wtr, beach, playground, pay phone, picnic shelter ($40-$50). Canoeing, interpretive trail, boating(lr), hiking, swimming. Marina. NRRS during 5/15-9/15. **GPS: 37.183151, -90.787175**

CLEARWATER DAM

From Piedmont, about 9 mi SW on SR HH to dam, then S on access rds to both shores of Black River below dam. Free primitive, undeveloped sites with permit from Corps project office. Tbls, pit toilet, grill area, no drkg wtr. Fishing, boating. Dam. **GPS: 37.131300, -90.769837**

FUNK BRANCH WILDERNESS CAMPING SITE

From Annapolis, half mi W on SR K; 3 mi SW on CR 149, then S on CR 446 to site; along Funk Branch of Black River within Clearwater Lake project. Free primitive camping with Corps permit at undesignated sites. No amenities. Fishing, boating. **GPS: 37.292833, -90.768700**

HIGHWAY K CAMPGROUND

From Annapolis, 5 mi SW on CR K; campsites both before & after bridge, following signs; above lake on Bear Branch of Black River. 5/15-9/15; 14-day limit. 21 non-elec sites, $14 ($7 with federal senior pass) during 4/1-10/31; some sites usually free rest of year but limited amenities. 45 elec sites (some wtr hookups), $16 base & $20 for 50-amp elec/wtr ($8 & $10 with senior pass) during 5/15-9/15. Some sites typically free off-season without utilities,

but off-season camping eliminated in 2013-2014 due to budget cuts; check current status before off-season arrival. 60-ft RV limit; 2 pull-through; 1 RV & 1 tent or 2 tents per site. Tbls, flush & pit toilets, cfga, drkg wtr, showers, dump, playground, beach, pay phone, picnic shelter ($50). Canoeing, fishing, swimming. NRRS. **GPS: 37.324232, -90.768587**

PIEDMONT PARK

From SR 49 at Piedmont, half mi S on SR 34; 5.6 mi SW on CR HH; 1.5 mi NE on Lake Rd; on ridge above lake. All year; 14-day limit. 8 non-elec sites, $14 ($7 with federal senior pass) during 4/15-9/30; some sites free rest of year but limited amenities. 69 elec sites (some wtr hookups), $16 base & $20 for 50-amp elec/wtr ($8 & $10 with federal senior pass) during 4/15-9/30; some sites free rest of year, but no utilities. RV limit in excess of 65 ft; 7 pull-through sites; 1 RV & 1 tent or 2 tents per site. Tbls, flush toilets, cfga, showers, drkg wtr, pay phone, dump, playground, beach, 2 picnic shelters ($50). Group camping area with elec for up to 40 people & 10 vehicles, $50. Canoeing, boating(l), swimming, fishing. Marina. NRRS. **GPS: 37.1425, -90.77028**

RIVER ROAD CAMPGROUND

1.4 mi S of Piedmont on SR 34; 5.6 mi SW on CR HH; below dam on shore of Black River. All year; 14-day limit. 4 non-elec sites, $14 ($7 with federal senior pass) during 3/15-10/31; some sites free rest of year, but limited amenities. 87 elec sites (some wtr hookups), $16 base & $20 for 50-amp elec ($8 & $10 with senior pass) during 3/15-10/31; some sites free rest of year but no utilities. RV limit in excess of 65 ft; 11 pull-through sites; 1 RV & 1 tent or 2 tents per site. Tbls, flush toilets, showers, dump, beach, playground, pay phone, 3 picnic shelters ($50). Interpretive trail, hiking trail, canoeing, boating(l), fishing, swimming, waterskiing. NRRS. **GPS: 37.133866, -90.767423**

THURMAN POINT PUBLIC USE AREA

From Piedmont, about 5 mi W on SR HH, across Clearwater Dam, then 3 mi N on CR RA; on W shore of lake. Free undeveloped camping. Pit toilet, no drkg wtr. Boating(l), fishing. **GPS: 37.1465, -90.79567**

WEBB CREEK CAMPGROUND

From Ellington, 2.6 mi SE on SR 21; 10.3 mi SE on CR H. All year; 14-day limit. 10 non-elec sites, $14 during 5/15-9/15 ($7 with federal senior pass); some sites free rest of year, but limited amenities. 25 elec sites (no wtr hookups, some pull-through), $16 during 5/15-9/15 ($8 with senior pass); some sites free rest of year, but no utilities. Tbls, flush toilets, showers, cfga, drkg wtr, pay phone, beach, playground, picnic shelter. Boating(l), fishing, swimming. Overflow camping, store. No reservations. **GPS: 37.149525, -90.810049**

❸
HARRY S. TRUMAN LAKE
GPS: 38.2548, -93.4080

This 55,600-acre lake is near Warsaw on US 65, 94 miles SE of Kansas City. Visitor center open 3/1-10/31 with exhibit area, theater, interpretive programs about the Osage River Valley, fossils, artifacts; view bald eagles & turkey vultures from observation deck; nature trail features historic buildings (660-438-2216). Campground checkout time 6 p.m. Corps day use facilities: Bledsoe Ferry -- boat ramp, picnicking, group shelter; Cooper Creek -- boat ramp; Crowes Crossing -- boat ramp; Fairfield -- boat ramp; Sac River -- boat ramp. Facilities not managed by the Corps include Harry S Truman State Park; Osceola Campground (City of Osceola); Sterett Creek Park -- campground, boat ramp, marina, restaurant, playground (concession). Resource Manager, Harry S Truman Lake, Rt.. 2, Box 29A, Warsaw, MO 65355-9603. (660) 438-7317.

BERRY BEND PARK

From Warsaw, 4.4 mi W on SR 7; 3 mi W on CR Z; 1.8 mi S on Berry Bend Rd; on Osage arm of lake, a peninsula in bend of river; equestrian camp on the N. All year; 14-day limit. 77 non-elec sites, $14 during 4/15-10/15 ($7 with federal senior pass); $8 rest of year but reduced amenities ($4 with senior pass). 114 elec sites, $18 during 4/15-10/15 ($9 with federal senior pass); $8 rest of year but reduced amenities. No wtr or elec off-season. RV limit in excess of 65 ft; 4 pull-through sites. Tbls, flush & pit toilets, showers, dump, cfga, drkg wtr, playground, beach, picnic shelter, amphitheater, change house, coin laundry. Horseshoe pits, fishing, swimming, boating(l), hiking. (660) 438-3872. NRRS. **GPS: 38.194701, -93.513361**

BERRY BEND EQUESTRIAN PARK

From Warsaw, 4.4 mi W on SR 7; 3 mi W on CR Z; 1.8 mi S on Berry Bend Rd; on Osage arm of lake, N of Berry Bend Park. Limited to horse campers. All year; 14-day limit. 65 non-elec sites, $12 base & $14 at premium locations during 4/15-10/15 ($6 & $7 with federal senior pass). Some non-elec sites $8 during 10/16-4/14, but reduced amenities. 24 elec sites, $16 base & $18 at premium locations during 4/15-10/15 ($8 & $9 with senior pass). RV limit in excess of 65 ft. Tbls, flush & pit toilets, showers, dump, cfga, drkg wtr, coin laundry, playground, corrals, overhead tie posts, all-season wtr hydrants, 2 picnic shelters with elec ($25). Hiking/bridle trails, swimming, boating(l), fishing. Call for special rules on horses (660) 438-3912. Note: Loop A sites and equestrian overflow sites may be closed except as needed on holiday weekends. NRRS. **GPS: 38.209279, -93.506076**

BUCKSAW PARK

From Clinton, 7.8 mi E on SR 7; 3.3 mi S on CR U (signs); left on SE 803 for 3 mi; on Grand River arm of lake. All year; 14-day limit. 29 non-elec sites, $14 during 4/15-10/15

($7 with federal senior pass); $8 rest of year but reduced amenities. 140 elec sites, some with 50-amp elec/wtr, $18 base & $22 for 50-amp sites during 4/15-10/15 ($9 & $11 with federal senior pass); rest of year, $8 & $22 but reduced amenities ($4 & $11 with senior pass). RV limit in excess of 65 ft. Amphitheater, fish cleaning station, change house, tbls, flush & pit toilets, showers, drkg wtr, cfga, coin laundry, playground, beach. Boating(l), fishing, swimming. Boat rentals nearby. (660) 447-3402. NRRS (4/15-10/15). **GPS: 38.261826, -93.604862**

LONG SHOAL PARK

From Warsaw, 4.4 mi W on SR 7 (signs); on Grand River arm of lake. All year; 14-day limit. 12 non-elec sites, $14 during 4/15-10/15 ($7 with federal senior pass); $8 rest of year but reduced amenities ($4 with senior pass). 95 elec sites, $18 for 30-amp & $22 for 50-amp during 4/15-10/15 ($9 with senior pass); $8 rest of year but no utilities ($4 with senior pass). RV limit in excess of 65 ft; 3 pull-through sites. Tbls, flush & pit toilets, showers, dump, cfga, drkg wtr, playground, change house, beach, coin laundry, picnic shelter ($20). Boating(ld), fishing, swimming. Boat rentals nearby. (660) 438-2342. NRRS (4/15-10/15). **GPS: 38.270263, -93.471304**

OSAGE BLUFF CAMPGROUND

From Warsaw at jct with SR 7, 3 mi S on US 65; 3 mi SW on SR 83, then 1 mi W on SR 295 following signs; at confluence of Osage & Pomme De Terre Rivers. All year; 14-day limit. 27 non-elec sites, $14 during 4/15-10/15 ($7 with federal senior pass); $8 rest of year but reduced amenities ($4 with senior pass). 41 elec sites, $18 during 4/15-10/15 ($9 with senior pass); $8 rest of year but no utilities ($4 with senior pass). RV limit in excess of 65 ft. Tbls, flush & pit toilets, cfga, drkg wtr, showers, dump, playground, coin laundry. Boating(ld), fishing. Boat rentals nearby. NRRS (4/15-10/15). **GPS: 38.184557, -93.377835**

SPARROWFOOT PARK

From Clinton, 6 mi S on SR 13; 1.5 mi E on SE 450 Rd, then S on access rd following signs; near confluence of Grand River & Deepwater Creek. 18 non-elec sites, $12 base, $14 at premium locations during 4/15-10/15 ($6 & $7 with federal senior pass); $8 rest of year but reduced amenities ($4 with federal senior pass). 93 elec sites, $16 base & $18 at premium locations during 4/15-10/15 ($8 & $9 with senior pass); $8 rest of year but no utilities ($4 with senior pass). RV limit in excess of 65 ft; 3 pull-through sites. Tbls, flush & pit toilets, cfga, drkg wtr, showers, dump, coin laundry, playground, beach, change house, 3 picnic shelters ($20). Horseshoe pits, boating(l), fishing, swimming. NRRS (4/15-10/15). 660-885-7546. **GPS: 38.293878, -93.733860**

TALLEY BEND PARK

17 mi S of Clinton on Hwy 13; 5 mi E on CR C (about 7 mi E of Lowry City); cross bridge over Osage arm of lake, then right (S) 0.5 mi on access rd. 3 primitive sites, $12 & $14 during 4/15-9/30 ($6 & $7 with federal senior pass); $8 rest of year but no utilities ($4 with senior pass). 45 elec sites, $18 during 4/15-9/30 ($9 with senior pass); $8 rest of year but no utilities ($4 with senior pass). RV limit in excess of 65 ft; 8 pull-through sites. Tbls, flush & pit toilets, cfga, showers, dump, drkg wtr, playground, coin laundry. Boating(l), fishing. Note: In 2013, Loop B sites were closed, and the number of other sites was reduced dramatically for budget cuts. 417-644-2024. NRRS (4/15-9/30). **GPS: 38.130270, -93.616176**

THIBAUT POINT PARK

From Warsaw, 4.3 mi N on US 65; 2.8 mi W on CR T; 1 mi S on gravel CR 218; at confluence of Little Tebo & Sterett Creeks. All year; 14-day limit. 5 non-elec sites, $14 during 4/15-10/15 ($7 with federal senior pass); $8 rest of year but no utilities ($4 with senior pass). 26 elec sites, $18 & $20 during 4/15-10/15 ($9 & $10 with senior pass); $8 rest of year but no utilities. RV limit in excess of 65 ft. 4 concrete sites for disabled, equipped with accessible grills, tbls, lantern holders (2 without elec); they are available to other campers if campground is full. Tbls, flush & pit toilets, cfga, drkg wtr, showers, dump, coin laundry, playground, beach, change house, 2 picnic shelters with elec ($25). Horseshoe pits, boating(l), swimming, fishing. Group camping, $50 tent area, $80 non-elec, $100 with elec. (660) 428-2767. NRRS (4/15-10/15). **GPS: 38.301481, -93.392909**

WINDSOR CROSSING PARK

From Clinton, E on SR 7 to Rt PP (3.5 mi N of Tightwad); follow signs 4 mi N; at Tebo Creek arm of lake. All year; 14-day limit. 46 non-elec sites, $10 during 4/15-9/30 ($5 with federal senior pass); $6 rest of year but reduced amenities ($3 with senior pass). RV limit in excess of 65 ft; 6 pull-through sites; 3 handicap sites with accessible grills, tbls, lantern holders. Tbls, pit toilets, cfga, drkg wtr, beach. Boating(ld), swimming, fishing. (660) 477-9275. NRRS (4/15-9/30). **GPS: 38.363599, -93.542587**

4

MARK TWAIN LAKE
CLARENCE CANNON DAM
GPS: 39.525, -91.6433

This 18,600-acre lake is 14 miles SE of Monroe City on CR J, 120 miles NW of St. Louis. Campground checkout time 4 p.m. The M.W. Boudreaux Recreation Area Visitor Center (opened in 2010) offers self-guided tours of hydroelectric power plant on weekends from May through August, exhibits and special events throughout summer (closed 12/14-1/5); outdoor theater, viewing deck, accessible trail. David C. Berti shooting range is under three covered shelters which are handicap accessible. For lake information, 24 hours, recorded, call (573) 735-2619. Mark Twain Birth Place State Historical Site at lake.

Corps-operated day use facilities: Bluff View Recreation Area -- boat ramp, picnicking, group shelter, playground; Elk Fork Park -- boat ramp; HF 10 Park -- playground, biking/hiking trails; HF 13 Park -- hiking, interpretive trails; HF 16 Park -- biking/hiking trails; Highway 24 Park -- boat ramp; Hoot Owl Hollow -- boat ramp, picnicking; John F. Spalding Recreation Area -- boat ramp, picnicking, group shelter, playground, beach, hiking/biking & interpretive trails; Middle Ford Park -- boat ramp; North Fork Recreation Area -- boat ramp; Robert Allen Recreation Area -- boat ramp, picnicking; Rt BB HF 60 Park -- boat ramp; Rt FF HF 11 Park -- boat ramp; Rt N HF 11 Park -- boat ramp, biking/hiking trails; South Fork Recreation Area -- boat ramp, picnicking; Spillway Recreation Area -- boat ramp, picnicking, playground, nature trail. Day use fees $3 at boat ramps, $1 per person at beaches; annual day use passes $30. Picnic shelters $30. Operations Manager, Mark Twain Lake, 20642 Highway J, Monroe City, MO 63456-9359. (573) 735-4097.

FRANK RUSSELL CAMPGROUND

From Monroe City at jct with US 36, 4 mi E on US 24/36; 9 mi S on Rt J; 1 mi N of dam. 5/1-10/15; 14-day limit (4 equestrian sites 4/1-11/1). 65 elec sites, $18 ($9 with federal senior pass). RV limit in excess of 65 ft. Tbls, flush toilets, amphitheater, showers, cfga, drkg wtr, dump, playground, horse corral with stalls. Hiking/bridle/mountain biking trails (access to 32-mi Joanna Trail). 573-735-4097. NRRS. **GPS: 39.535201, -91.651039**

INDIAN CREEK CAMPGROUND

From Monroe City, 6 mi SW on US 24; 1.7 mi S on Rt. HH; about 5.5 mi SE on CR 581. 4/1-11/24 14-day limit. $8 at 12 non-elec RV/tent sites & hike-in tent sites ($4 with federal senior pass). 4/5-11/23; 14-day limit. 215 elec sites, $18 base, $24 full hookups, some with 50-amp elec ($9 & $12 with federal senior pass). RV limit in excess of 65 ft. 37-site group camping area. Tbls, flush toilets, showers, cfga, drkg wtr, beach, playground, dump, pay phone, fish cleaning stations, amphitheater, pay phone, 2 picnic shelters ($30). Boating(l), swimming, fishing, biking, hiking trails, interpretive trails. 573-735-4097. NRRS. **GPS: 39.535094, -91.732600**

JOHN C. "JACK" BRISCOE GROUP CAMPGROUND

From the dam, S side, 0.5 mi on CR J. Six group camping areas, GRP1 & GRP4 for up to 32 people and 4 vehicles are $64 and GRP2, GRP5 & GRP6 for up to 24 people and 3 vehicles are $45, a picnic shelter for up to 125 people and 10 vehicles is $30. 4/20-9/24. Visitor center, horseshoe pits. 20 sites, $18 each; minimum of 3 sites required. Tbls, flush toilets, showers, cfga, drkg wtr, picnic shelters, playground. Check in at the Frank Russell Recreation Area. 60-ft RV limit. 573-735-4097. 4/20-9/10. NRRS. **GPS: 39.51889, -91.64583**

RAY BEHRENS RECREATION AREA

From Perry at jct SR 154, 6.6 mi N on CR J, N side. About 4/5-11/25; 14-day limit. 112 elec/wtr sites, $18 base, $24 full hookups ($9 & $12 with federal senior pass). 60-ft RV limit in excess of 65 ft. Tbls, flush toilets, cfga, drkg wtr, dump, showers, playground, fish cleaning stations, amphitheater, picnic shelter ($30). Basketball, boating(l), fishing, interpretive trails, biking. 573-735-4097. NRRS (4/15-10/24). **GPS: 39.508470, -91.665845**

⑤
LOCK & DAM 20
MISSISSIPPI RIVER
GPS: 40.14385833, -91.514625

Pool 20 extends from river mile 343.2 upstream to Keokuk, IA. The dam is off Old Hwy 61 about 0.5 miles N of Henderson Ave in Canton, MO, on Lock and Dam Rd. For information, contact park ranger, RR #4, L&D #21, Quincy, IL 62301, (217) 228-0890. See Illinois, Iowa & Wisconsin listings.

FENWAY LANDING CAMP

From Canton, 4.5 mi N on US 61, then E on CR 454; camping area is across the levee. All year; 14-day limit. 15 free sites. Tbls, toilets, cfga, drkg wtr. Boating(l), fishing. **GPS: 40.136604, -91.515298**

⑥
NORFORK LAKE
GPS: 36.45, -92.59

Located 4 miles northeast of Norfork, Arkansas, on Arkansas SR 177 near the Missouri state line, 135 miles N of Little Rock. Norfork Lake has more than 350 miles of shoreline. Most of the lake's campgrounds are in Arkansas, along with extensive day use facilities that include boat ramps, hiking trails, group picnic shelters, designated swimming area and playgrounds. In addition to the developed campgrounds, free primitive camping is available by permit from the project office; those primitive areas are Jordan Island, Jordan Cove Calamity, Beach and Curley Point. Jordan Campground was closed in 2013 due to budget cuts. Concessionaire-operated marinas provide boat and motor rental, fuel and services. Resource Manager, Norfork Lake, 324 W. 7th St, Mountain Home, AR 72653. (870) 425-2700. See Arkansas listing.

TECUMSEH CAMPGROUND

11 mi E of Gainesville on US 160 at Tecumseh on W shore of White River. 5/1-9/30; 14-day limit. 7 non-elec sites, $11 ($5.50 with federal senior pass). Pit toilet, tbls, cfga, drkg wtr. Boating(l), fishing. 10 acres. **GPS: 36.589473, -92.290140**

UDALL CAMPGROUND

9 mi W of Bakersfield on CR O (1.5 mi W of Udall); 0.7 mi on access road. 5/1-9/15; 14-day limit. 7 sites, no hookups, $11 ($5.50 with federal senior pass). Pit toilets, tbls, cfga, drkg wtr, dump. Boating(l), fishing. Marina. Non-campers pay boat ramp fee. **GPS: 36.544297, -92.286725**

⑦ POMME DE TERRE LAKE
GPS: 37.9017, -93.32

This 7,790-acre lake with 113 miles of shoreline is 3 miles S of Hermitage on SR 254, 140 miles SE of Kansas City. The lake has 10 campgrounds, six managed by the Corps. Hickory Ridge & Highway 83 Parks are managed by a concessionaire, and the State of Missouri has two campgrounds within Pomme de Terre State Park. Corps campsites that are free off-season may have reduced amenities. Reservation fee of $20 for picnic shelters. Trails include 3.1-mile Healthy Active Community Running Trail for bikers & hikers, at Outlet Park, and Pomme de Terre Multipurpose Trail (primarily an equestrian trail) at Boliver Landing. Day use fees charged for facilities. Resource Manager, Pomme de Terre Lake, Rt. 2, Box 2160, Hermitage, MO 65668-9509. (417) 745-6411.

DAMSITE CAMPGROUND

From Hermitage, 3 mi SE on SR 254, then half mi W at Carson's Corner. All year; 14-day limit. 9 tent sites, $12 ($6 with federal senior pass). 22 non-elec RV/tent sites, $12 base, $14 at premium locations ($6 & $7 with senior pass). 80 elec sites, $20 base, $22 with elec/wtr ($10 & $12 with senior pass). Sites free off-season 10/1-4/15, but no utilities & reduced amenities. 40-ft RV limit. Tbls, flush & pit toilets, cfga, showers, drkg wtr, dump, playground, coin laundry, amphitheater, 2 picnic shelters with elec ($20). Boating(l), fishing. (417) 745-2244. NRRS (4/1-9/30). GPS: 37.903557, -93.308237

LIGHTFOOT LANDING CAMP

9 mi S of Wheatland on SR 83 (2.3 mi S of Elkton); 3.4 mi E on CR RB. All year; 14-day limit. 1 tent site & 6 non-elec RV/tent sites, $12 base, $14 at premium locations ($6 & $7 with federal senior pass) during 4/15-10/1; free

rest of year but reduced amenities. 29 elec/wtr sites, $20 ($10 with senior pass). RV limit in excess of 65 ft; 6 pull-through sites. Tbls, flush toilets, showers, dump, cfga, drkg wtr, playground, picnic shelter, heated fishing pier. Three group camping areas without elec for up to 50 people 16 vehicles ($30). Boating(ld), fishing, horseshoe pits. Boat rentals nearby. (417) 282-6890. NRRS (4/16-9/30). GPS: 37.832073, -93.363597

NEMO LANDING PARK

3 mi SE of Hermitage on SR 254; 1 mi W from Carson's Corner before bridge at Lindley Creek. All year; 14-day limit. $12 base at 64 non-elec RV/tent sites during 4/16-10/15; $14 at premium locations ($6 & $7 with federal senior pass); some sites free during off-season, but no wtr or services. 41 elec sites (no wtr hookups), $16 base, $18 at premium locations with 30-amp elec; $20 at premium locations with 50-amp elec & at 12 elec/wtr sites ($8, $9 & $10 with federal senior pass). 60-ft RV limit. Tbls, flush & pit toilets, cfga, drkg wtr, showers, dump, coin laundry, amphitheater, playground, beach, picnic shelter. Boating(ld), horseshoe pits, fishing, swimming. Boat rentals nearby. (417) 993-5529. NRRS (4/16-9/30). GPS: 37.862039, -93.273121

OUTLET PARK CAMPGROUND

From Hermitage, 3 mi SE on SR 254; 2 mi W from Carson's Corner; below dam on W side of outlet. All year; 14-day limit. 7 non-elec RV/tent sites, $12 ($6 with federal senior pass); 14 elec/wtr sites, $20 ($10 with senior pass). During 10/16-/15, some sites without hookups are free, but no wtr or elec. 50-ft RV limit; 10 pull-through sites. Group camping area with elec, $30. Tbls, flush toilets, showers, cfga, drkg wtr, playground, picnic shelter with elec, fish cleaning station. Boating(l), horseshoe pits, ball field, canoeing, fishing, multi-purpose court, ball field. (417) 745-2290. NRRS (4/16-9/30). GPS: 37.904425, -93.323729

PITTSBURG LANDING PARK

From Pittsburg at jct with CR J, 1 mi S on SR 64; 3 mi E on CR RA; on Lindley Creek arm of lake. All year; 14-day limit. 40 free, undesignated primitive sites. Picnic shelter, 2 pit toilets, tbls, cfga, drkg wtr, playground. Boating(ld), fishing. 173 acres.
GPS: 37.836949, -93.261612

WHEATLAND PARK

From Wheatland at jct with US 54, 4.2 mi S on SR 83; 2 mi E on SR 254; 1 mi S on SR 205. 15 non-elec sites, $12 base during 4/16-10/15, $14 at premium locations ($6 & $7 with federal senior pass); free off-season but no wtr, elec or dump. 26 elec sites, $16 base, $20 at premium locations ($8 & $10 with senior pass). 41 elec/wtr sites, $20 ($10 with senior pass). 35-ft RV limit; 8 pull-through sites. Tbls, showers, dump, flush & pit toilets, cfga, drkg wtr, beach, playground, coin laundry, picnic shelter ($20). Boating(ld), swimming, fishing. (417) 282-5267. NRRS (4/16-9/30).
GPS: 37.878144, -93.373811

⑧
STOCKTON LAKE
GPS: 37.6917, -93.7583

This 24,900-acre lake has 298 mi of shoreline. It is on the E side of Stockton on SR 32, 136 mi SE of Kansas City. Campsites that are free off season may have reduced amenities. Non-Corps camping facilities include Mutton Creek Marina, Orleans Trail Marina and Stockton State Park. Boat ramps are at Greenfield and Masters Park; Overlook Park, Old Mill Park and the Stockton Power Plant have fishing piers. Visitor center Operations Manager, Stockton Lake, 16435 E Stockton Lake Drive, Stockton, MO 65785-9471. (417) 276-3113.

CEDAR RIDGE CAMPGROUND

From Stockton, 2 mi N on SR 245 & SR RA from jct with SR 215; 340-acre park on Little Sac arm of lake. All year; 14-day limit. 33 non-elec sites, $12 base, $14 at premium locations during 4/16-9/30 ($6 & $7 with federal senior pass); sites $5 during 3/15-4/15 & 10/1-11/30; free rest of year but no flush toilets or showers. 21 elec sites, $14 base, $18 at premium locations & $20 with 50-amp service during 4/16-9/30 ($7, $9 & $10 with senior pass); elec sites are $9 during 3/15-4/15 & 10/1-11/30 ($4.50 with senior pass); some sites free rest of year, but no utilities. 60-ft RV limit. Tbls, flush & pit toilets, cfga, showers, drkg wtr, dump, beach, picnic shelter, pay phone. Sailing, scuba diving, swimming, boating(ld), fishing. (417) 995-2045. NRRS (4/15-9/30).
GPS: 37.575769, -93.681198

CRABTREE COVE PARK

From Stockton at jct with SR 39, 3.5 mi E on SR 32, then SW; 168-acre park on NW corner of lake. All year; 14-day limit. 32 non-elec sites, $12 base, $14 at premium locations during 4/16-9/30 ($6 & $7 with federal senior pass); sites $5 during 3/15-4/15 & 10/1-11/30; free rest of year, but no wtr amenities. 32 elec sites, $16 base, $18 at premium locations during 4/16-9/30 ($8 & $9 with federal senior pass); elec sites $9 during 3/15-4/15 & 10/1-11/30 ($4.50 with senior pass); some sites free rest of year, but no wtr or elec amenities. 50-ft RV limit; 3 pull-through; 2 handicap without elec, 1 handicap with elec. Tbls, flush & pit toilets, showers, cfga, drkg wtr, dump, playground, picnic shelter. Boating(l), handicap accessible fishing area, basketball, hiking. NRRS (4/16-9/30). **GPS: 37.666259, -93.753934**

HAWKER POINT CAMPGROUND

From Stockton at jct with SR 32, 6.2 mi S on SR 39; 5.2 mi E on CR H; 518-acre park at N end of Big Sac arm of lake. All year; 14-day limit. 32 non-elec sites, $12 base, $14 at premium locations during 4/15-9/30 ($6 & $7 with federal senior pass); sites $5 during 3/15-4/15 & 10/1-11/30; free rest of year, but reduced services & no wtr available. 30 elec sites, $16 base, $18 at premium locations during 4/15-9/30 ($8 & $9 with senior pass); sites $9 during 3/15-4/15 & 10/1-11/30 ($4.50

with senior pass); some sites free rest of year, but no utilities. 60-ft RV limit; 1 RV & 1 tent or 2 tents per site. Tbls, flush & pit toilets, showers, dump, cfga, drkg wtr, playground. Boating(l), fishing, bridle trails. Non-campers pay $3 boat ramp fee 3/1-11/30. (417) 276-7266. NRRS (4/16-9/30).
GPS: 37.604933, -93.783483

MASTERS CAMPGROUND

10 mi SE of Stockton on Hwy 32; 3.5 mi S on CR RA, then W; 836-acre park on Little Sac arm of lake. All year; 14-day limit. 66 non-elec sites, $10 base, $14 at premium locations during 5/15-9/15 ($5 & $7 with federal senior pass); sites $5 during 3/15-4/15 & 10/1-11/30; free rest of year, but no wtr services & reduced amenities. 60-ft RV limit; 8 overflow sites; 1 RV & 1 tent or 2 tents per site. Tbls, pit toilets, cfga, drkg wtr, dump, beach, playground, fishing pier. Boating(ld), swimming, fishing. (417) 276-6847. NRRS during 5/15-9/15.
GPS: 37.598363, -93.682308

ORLEANS TRAIL PARK

From SE edge of Stockton, 0.5 mi E on CR RB; 0.5 mi right on Blake St; 959-acre park on NW shore of lake. All year at N campground; 14-day limit. 68 non-elec sites, $12 during 5/9-9/15 ($6 with federal senior pass); free rest of year, but no wtr services & reduced amenities. 18 elec 30/50-amp sites, $18 base; $20 at premium locations. 50-ft RV limit; 4 pull-through sites. 5 sites at equestrian trailhead. Group camping area with 12 elec sites, $85-$110. Tbls, flush & pit toilets, cfga, showers, dump, drkg wtr, beach, picnic shelters ($30-$35). Boating(ld), fishing, swimming, bridle trails, hiking. (417) 276-6948. NRRS (5/9-9/15). **GPS: 37.674514, -93.785058**

RUARK BLUFF EAST PARK

12 mi S of Stockton on Hwy 39; 4 mi E on CR 6; 1 mi S on CR H; turn right on park access rd & follow signs; on Big Sac arm of lake at confluence with Sac River. 87 non-elec sites, $12 base, $14 at premium locations during

4/16-9/30 ($6 & $7 with federal senior pass); sites $5 during 3/15-4/15 & 10/1-11/30; free rest of year, but no wtr services & reduced amenities. 28 elec sites, $16 base, $18 at premium locations during 4/16-9/30 ($8 & $9 with federal senior pass); sites $9 during 3/15-4/15 & 10/1-11/30 ($4.50 with senior pass); some sites free rest of year, but no utilities & reduced amenities. RV limit in excess of 65 ft; 4 pull-through sites; 1 RV & 1 tent or 2 tents per site. Tbls, flush & pit toilets, showers, dump, cfga, playground, beach, drkg wtr, fishing pier. Boating(ld), swimming, fishing. Non-campers pay $3 boat ramp fee. (417) 637-5303. NRRS (4/16-9/30).
GPS: 37.520185, -93.800143

RUARK BLUFF WEST PARK

12 mi S of Stockton on Hwy 39; 4 mi E on CR 6; 1 mi S on CR H; left on park access rd & follow signs; before bridge; on Sons Creek arm of lake. 4/16-9/30; 14-day limit. About 40 non-elec sites, $12 base, $14 at premium locations ($6 & $7 with federal senior pass). 46 elec sites, $16 base, $18 at premium locations ($8 & $9 with federal senior pass). 50-ft RV limit; 1 RV & 1 tent or 2 tents per site. Tbls, flush & pit toilets, dump, cfga, drkg wtr, showers, beach, playground, fishing pier. Group camping area with 11 elec sites, $85 Mon-Thursday, $110 Fri-Sun & on holidays. Boating(ld), fishing, swimming. Non-campers pay $3 boat ramp fee 3/1-11/30. (417) 637-5279. NRRS during 4/16-9/30. **GPS: 37.521751, -93.814048**

⑨

TABLE ROCK LAKE
GPS: 36.595, 93.3083

A 43,100-acre lake 7 miles SW of Branson on SR 165, W of US 65. The Dewey Short Visitor Center (at S end of dam) has exhibits, auditorium audiovisual presentations, nature trail, overlook, dam tours and picnicking. Off-road vehicles prohibited. 13 modern Corps of Engineers campgrounds are adjacent to the lake. Campground checkout time 3 p.m.

Campsites that are free off-season may have reduced amenities. Non-Corps camping areas include Big Bay Recreation Area (Mark Twain National Forest) and Table Rock State Park. Boat ramps are available at Big Indian, Coombs Ferry, Joe Bald and Kings River Parks. Day use fees, $4-$5. A swimming beach, flush toilets, showers, playground and boat ramp are available at Moonshine Beach, at N end of dam. Due to budget issues, the Corps intended to shift management of four Missouri campgrounds to the Ozark Rivers Heritage Foundation; however, agreements between the Corps and the foundation were terminated in September 2013. Those campgrounds are Old Highway 86, Mill Creek, Baxter and Campbell Point Campgrounds. Resource Manager, Upper White River Project Office, 4600 State Road 165 Ste. A, Branson, MO 65616-8976. (417) 334-4101. See Arkansas listings.

AUNTS CREEK PARK

2 mi N of Kimberling City on SR 13; 2.7 mi W on SR OO & CR 00-9, following signs; on James River arm of lake. 5/1-9/15; 14-day limit. 3 non-elec sites, $16 ($8 with federal senior pass); 52 elec sites, $20 ($10 with senior pass). RV limit in excess of 65 ft; 6 pull-through sites; 1 RV & 1 tent or 2 tents per site. Tbls, flush toilets, showers, dump, cfga, drkg wtr, beach, playground, picnic shelter ($50). Boating(ld), swimming, hiking trails, volleyball, fishing. Non-campers pay $4 day use fee for picnicking, beach, boat ramp, dump station. (417) 739-2792. NRRS.
GPS: 36.671199, -93.459728

BAXTER PARK

From Lampe at jct with SR 13, 4.8 mi W on CR H (signs); on White River arm of lake. 5/1-9/15; 14-day limit. 29 non-elec sites, $16 ($8 with federal senior pass); 25 elec/wtr sites, $21 ($10.50 with federal senior pass). RV limit in excess of 65 ft; 2 pull-through sites; 1 RV & 1 tent or 2 tents per site. Tbls, flush toilets, showers, dump, playground, beach.

Boating(ld), swimming, fishing, hiking trails, scuba diving, waterskiing. Non-campers pay $4 day use fee for picnicking, beach, boat ramp, dump station. (417) 779-5370. NRRS.
GPS: 36.567994, -93.498909

BIG M PARK

2 mi N of Eagle Rock on SR 86; 6 mi E on SR E; 2 mi S on CR M; on White River arm of lake. 5/1-9/15; 14-day limit. 37 non-elec sites, $16 ($8 with federal senior pass); 9 elec/wtr sites, $21 ($10.50 with senior pass); 14 full hookup sites, $23 ($11.50 with senior pass). RV limit in excess of 65 ft. Tbls, flush toilets, cfga, dump, drkg wtr, showers, beach, playground, picnic shelter. Boating(ld), fishing, swimming, sand volleyball court. Non-campers pay $4 day use fee for boat ramp, picnicking, beach, dump station. (417) 271-3190. NRRS.
GPS: 36.556262, -93.680817

CAMPBELL POINT PARK

From Shell Knob at jct with CR 39-5, 5.1 mi SE on SR YY; on White River arm of lake. 4/1-10/31; 14-day limit. 4 non-elec sites, $16 ($8 with federal senior pass); 28 elec sites, $20 ($10 with senior pass); 42 elec/wtr sites, $21 ($10.50 with senior pass); 1 full-hookup $23 ($11.50 with senior pass). RV limit in excess of 65 ft; 4 pull-through sites; 1 RV & 1 tent or 2 tents per site. Tbls, flush toilets, showers, cfga, drkg wtr, dump, beach, playground, picnic shelter ($50). Boating(ld), swimming, sand volleyball, basketball, hiking trails, scuba diving. Non-campers pay $4 day use fee for dump station, picnicking, boat ramp, beach, sand volleyball. (417) 858-3903. NRRS.
GPS: 36.597450, -93.553916

CAPE FAIR PARK

1 mi SW of Cape Fair on CR 76/82, following signs; at upper James River arm of lake. 4/1-10/31; 14-day limit. 13 non-elec sites, $16 ($8 with federal senior pass); 23 elec sites, $20 ($10 with senior pass); 46 elec/wtr sites, $21 ($10.50 with senior pass). RV limit in excess of

65 ft; 7 pull-through sites; 1 tent & 1 RV or 2 tents per site. Tbls, flush toilets, showers, cfga, drkg wtr, dump, playground, beach, picnic shelter ($50). Boating(l), fishing, hiking trails, scuba diving. Non-campers pay $4 day use fee for boat ramp, dump, beach, picnicking. (417) 538-2220. NRRS.
GPS: 36.723768, -93.526880

EAGLE ROCK PARK

From Eagle Rock, 3 mi S on SR 86; right before bridge (signs); at White River arm of lake. 5/1-9/15; 14-day limit. 37 non-elec sites, $16 ($8 with federal senior pass); 24 elec sites, $20 ($10 with senior pass); 1 elec/wtr site, $21 ($10.50 with senior pass); 1 full-hookup $23 ($11.50 with senior pass). RV limit in excess of 65 ft; 6 pull-through; 1 RV & 1 tent or 2 tents per site. Tbls, flush toilets, cfga, drkg wtr, showers, dump, beach, playground. Boating(ld), fishing, scuba diving, swimming, sand volleyball, waterskiing. Non-campers pay $4 day use fee for boat ramp, dump station, beach, picnicking, sand volleyball court. (417) 271-3215. NRRS.
GPS: 36.528916, -93.728303

INDIAN POINT PARK

From W of Branson at jct with SR 13, 3 mi W on SR 76; 2.8 mi S on Indian Point Rd; at White River arm of lake. 4/1-10/31; 14-day limit. 2 non-elec sites, $16 ($8 with federal senior pass); 21 elec sites, $20 ($10 with senior pass); 54 elec/wtr sites, $21 ($10.50 with senior pass). RV limit in excess of 65 ft; 1 RV & 1 tent or 2 tents per site. Group camping area with elec, $50. Tbls, flush toilets, showers, cfga, drkg wtr, dump, beach, playground, pay phone, picnic shelter with elec ($50). Boating(ld), swimming, scuba diving, fishing, basketball, hiking trails. Marina. Fish hatchery nearby. Non-campers pay $4 day use fee for boat ramp, dump station, beach, picnicking. (417) 338-2121. NRRS. **GPS: 36.629486, -93.344586**

LONG CREEK PARK

From Ridgedale at jct with US 65, 3 mi W on SR 86; S on CR 86/50 prior to bridge (signs); on Long Creek arm of lake. 5/1-9/15; 14-day limit. 10 non-elec sites, $16 ($8 with federal senior pass); 24 elec sites, $20 ($10 with senior pass); 13 elec/wtr sites, $21 ($10.50 with senior pass). RV limit 55 ft; 2 pull-through sites; 1 RV & 1 tent or 2 tents per site. Tbls, flush toilets, cfga, drkg wtr, dump, showers, beach, playground, picnic shelter ($50). Boating(ld), swimming, fishing, waterskiing. Non-campers pay $4 daily for boat ramp, dump, picnicking, beach, playground. Note: Closed for renovations in 2015; re-opening in 2016. (417) 334-8427. NRRS. **GPS: 36.520501, -93.305190**

MILL CREEK PARK

3 mi S of Kimberling City on SR 13; 1 mi W on CR RB; on White River arm of lake. 4/1-10/31; 14-day limit. 67 elec/wtr sites, $21 ($10.50 with federal senior pass). RV limit in excess of 65 ft; 19 pull-through sites; 1 RV & 1 tent or 2 tents per site. Tbls, flush toilets, showers, dump, cfga, drkg wtr, playground, beach, picnic shelter ($50). Boating(ld), scuba diving, swimming, hiking trails, sand volleyball, basketball, waterskiing. Non-campers pay $4 day use fee for boat ramp, dump station, picnicking, beach. (417) 779-5378. NRRS.
GPS: 36.594263, -93.440073

OLD HIGHWAY 86 PARK

From Ridgedale at jct with US 65, 7.6 mi W on SR 86; N on SR UU; on White River arm of lake. 4/1-10/31; 14-day limit. 77 elec/wtr sites, $21 ($10.50 with federal senior pass). RV limit in excess of 65 ft; 1 RV & 1 tent or 2 tents per site. Tbls, flush toilets, showers, cfga, drkg wtr, dump, playground, beach, pay phone, picnic shelter ($50). Boating(ld), fishing, swimming, scuba diving, hiking trails, sand volleyball, basketball. Non-campers pay $4 day use fee for boat ramp, beach, dump station, picnicking, sand volleyball court. (417) 779-5376. NRRS.
GPS: 36.55944, -93.31944

VIOLA PARK

From Viola, 5 mi S on SR 39; W on SR 39/48 (6 mi S of Shell Knob); on White River arm of lake. 4/1-9/15; 14-day limit. 11 non-elec sites, $16 ($8 with federal senior pass); 15 elec sites, $20 ($10 with senior pass); 24 elec/wtr sites, $21 ($10.50 with senior pass). RV limit in excess of 65 ft; 2 pull-through sites; 1 RV & 1 tent or 2 tents per site. Tbls, flush toilets, showers, dump, cfga, drkg wtr, playground, beach. Boating(ld), swimming, hiking trails, scuba diving, waterskiing. Non-campers pay $4 day use fee for boat ramp, dump station, beach, picnicking. (417) 858-3904. NRRS. **GPS: 36.560635, -93.594793**

⑩

WAPPAPELLO LAKE
GPS: 36.93, -90.2783

This 8,400-acre lake is 16 miles NE of Poplar Bluff and N of US 60, E of US 67, on CR T, 150 miles S of St. Louis. Campground checkout time 4 p.m. Campers required to register at the office for free sites. Bill Emerson Memorial Visitor Center provides picnicking, interpretation programs, special events during summer (573-222-8773). Overflow camping below the dam open only when all Corps and private campgrounds in surrounding area are full; $3 fee for primitive sites. Boat ramps at Cozart Point, Holiday Landing, Lost Creek, Otter Point, Pisos Point, Rockwood Point, Spillway, Sundowner & Walnut Cove Parks. Spillway Recreation area also has a fish cleaning station, picnic shelter, playground and interpretive trail. Daily lake information, (573) 222-8139/1-877-LAKEVIEW. Operations Manager, Wappapello Lake, 10992 Highway T, Wappapello, MO 63966-9603. (573) 222-8562.

BLUE SPRINGS CAMPGROUND

From just S of Greenville on BUS US 67, 3 mi SE on SR D; 1.8 mi S on SR BB to just past jct with CR 531; right (W) for 0.5 mi W on Blue Spring Rd to E shore of lake within Mark Twain National Forest. All year; 14-day limit. 2 free primitive sites in parking area. No facilities except grills. Boating(l), fishing. **GPS: 37.043540, -90.414627**

CHAONIA LANDING RECREATION AREA

From NW Poplar Bluff at jct with US 60B, N on SR W about 10 mi to W shore of lake. All year; 14-day limit. 9 sites without hookups, $10 ($5 with federal senior pass). 22-ft RV limit. Tbls, toilets, cfga, drkg wtr. Boating(ld), fishing. **GPS: 36.972534, -90.360484**

GREENVILLE RECREATION AREA

From Greenville, 2.5 mi S on US 67, turn right before bridge, following signs; near Little Lake Creek. 3/29-11/25; 14-day limit. $10 at 5 walk-to tent sites ($5 with federal senior pass). 8 non-elec sites, $14 ($7 with senior pass); 98 elec sites, $18 ($9 with senior pass). Overflow camping open when public & private campgrounds in area are full; $3 primitive sites, no facilities. RV limit in excess of 65 ft. Tbls, flush toilets, dump, showers, cfga, drkg wtr, amphitheater, picnic shelter ($50), playground. Boating(ld), horseshoe pits, historic trail, interpretive trail, volleyball courts, 3-mi paved bike trail between campground & city of Greenville. (573) 224-3884. NRRS during 3/18-11/21. **GPS: 37.100124, -90.456383**

ISLANDS CAMPING AREAS

Accessible by boat only. Located near dam, SW side, offshore from Wappapello State Park. 2 large islands. All year; 14-day limit. 6 primitive tent sites, $10 ($5 with federal senior pass. Honor pay at Rockwood Point boat ramp, Redman Creek fee both or project office. Pit toilets, fire rings. **GPS: 36.26602, -90.303454**

JOHNSON TRACT NATURAL AREA

From S of Greenville at jct with Old US 67, 2 mi S on SR D to parking lot on W side across from jct with CR 534. All year; 14-day limit. 2 free primitive hike-in sites. **GPS: 37.092517, -90.421021**

LOST CREEK LANDING

From dam near Wappapello, 11 mi N on SR D; 1 mi W on CR 524, then S on access rd to N shore of East Fork Lost Creek. All year; 14-day limit. 3 free primitive sites in parking area. No facilities except grills. Boating(l), fishing. **GPS: 37.0222744, -90.3064964**

NORTHERN PRIMITIVE CAMPING ZONE ·

Free primitive camping available on all Corps public lands S of Hwy 34 to PA 34 (access N of Greenville) on E side of the St. Francis River and all Corps public lands on the W side, N of where Highway FF intersects with Highway 67. All year; 14-day limit. Camping prohibited in the state wildlife area.

PEOPLES CREEK RECREATION AREA

From the dam, 1.7 mi N on SR D, then right on access rd, following signs. 3/3-11/25; 14-day limit. 3 tent sites, $16; 53 elec sites, $20 for 30-amp ($8 & $10 with federal senior pass); full hookups & 50-amp elec, $20 ($10 with federal senior pass). RV limit in excess of 65 ft. Tbls, flush toilets, showers, dump, cfga, drkg wtr, beach, fishing pier, 4 picnic shelters ($50). Boating(l), fishing, swimming. Group camping area. NRRS. 573-222-8562. **GPS: 36.950837, -90.280371**

POSSUM CREEK CAMPGROUND

From the dam, 3 mi N on SR D; 1.5 mi W on CR 521 & Possum Creek Rd. All year; 14-day limit. 2 free primitive sites at parking area. Pit toilet, cfga, no drkg wtr. Boating(l), fishing. **GPS: 36.964038, -90.302532**

REDMAN CREEK RECREATION AREA

From the dam, 1 mi S on CR T, following signs. About 3/22-11/4; 14-day limit. 105 elec sites, $24 ($12 with federal senior pass). 6 primitive boat-in tent sites, $10 ($5 with senior pass). Tbls, flush & pit toilets, dump, cfga, drkg wtr, showers, fish cleaning station, visitor center, playground, beach, 3 picnic shelters ($50). Boating(ld), fishing, volleyball courts, horseshoe pits, hiking trail, interpretive trail, tennis courts. Nearby boat rentals. (573) 222-8233. NRRS. **GPS: 36.918153, -90.284014**

SULPHUR SPRINGS CAMP

From Greenville, 1.3 mi S on US 67; 3.2 mi S on SR D; W on Road 17. All year; 14-day limit. 4 free primitive sites at parking area. Pit toilet, cfga, no drkg wtr. Boating(l), fishing.

OZARK TRAIL

The Ozark Trail transverses approximately 30 mi through the Wappapello Lake Project and passes within 100' of 19 designated parking areas S of U. S. Highway 67. Free primitive tent camping permitted on Corps land within 100' of the trail. No facilities.

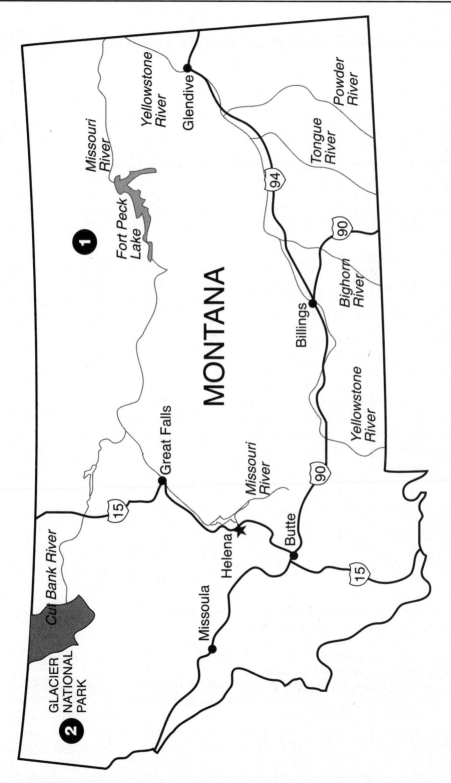

MONTANA

STATE INFORMATION:

CAPITAL: Helena
NICKNAME: Treasure State
STATEHOOD: 1889 - 41st State
FLOWER: Bitterroot
TREE: Ponderosa Pine
BIRD: Western Meadowlark

STATE TIDBITS:

• Montana's name comes from the Spanish word mountain.

• The first inhabitants of Montana were the Plains Indians.

• Montana has the largest migratory elk herd in the nation.

WWW.VISITMT.COM

Toll-free number for travel information:
1-800-847-4868.

MONTANA LAKES

To find campgrounds operated by the U.S. Army Corps of Engineers, match the lake's numbers on the preceding map page with numbered lake entries on the following pages. Campgrounds are listed alphabetically under the appropriate lakes. The following Montana impoundments have Corps of Engineers campgrounds.

Fort Peck Lake. This 240,000-acre lakes has 1,520 miles of shoreline and is 10 miles SW of Nashua on SR 117 in northeastern Montana, 112 miles W of the North Dakota state line and 76 miles S of Canada on the upper Missouri River.

Lake Koocanusa. A 46,500-acre lake 17 miles NE of Libby in northwestern Montana on SR 37, at the Kootenai River.

➊
FORT PECK LAKE
GPS: 48.0, -106.4167

This 240,000-acre lake has 1,520 mi of shoreline and is 10 mi SW of Nashua on SR 117 in northeastern Montana, 112 mi W of North

Dakota state line and 76 mi S of Canada on upper Missouri River. Power plant museum tours by appointment LD-MD; rest of year hourly every day 9-4:45; interpretive center & programs, paved nature trails, theater. Day use fees are not charged. Day use facilities: Beaver Creek Nature Area -- multi-use trails; First Dredge Park -- picnicking, group shelter, playground, beach; Flat Lake Park -- boat ramp, picnicking, group shelter; Kiwanis Park -- shelter, playground; Lewis & Clark Overlook -- group picnic shelter, interpretive trail; Milk River Observation Point -- hiking; Nelson Dredge Park -- boat ramp; Second Dredge Park -- beach. Camping areas not managed by the Corps include: James Kipp Recreational Area (Bureau of Land Management); Crooked Creek Marina (concessionaire); Hell Creek State Park; Rock Creek Marina (concessionaire); Rock Creek State Park; Hell Creek State Park. Lake Manager, Fort Peck Lake, P. O. Box 208, Ft. Peck, MT 59223-0208. (406) 526-3411/3224.

BONETRAIL RECREATION AREA

Recreation area W of the dam. From Fort Peck, about 3 mi NW on SR 24; left (W) for 60 mi on Maxness Rd, becoming gravel Willow Creek Rd, becoming Burke Ranch Rd (impassable when wet, dirt last 30 mi); at N shore of lake. All year; 14-day limit. 6 free primitive sites; 16-ft RV limit. Tbls, toilets, cfga, picnic shelter. Nearest dump station, 60 mi. **GPS: 47.69001, -107.17703**

CROOKED CREEK RECREATION AREA

From Winnett, N on all-weather gravel Dovetail Valentine Rd (also called Drage Ridge Trail) to its end; 0.5 mi E on 79 Trail Rd; N (left) on Crooked Creek Rd to site (signs). All year; 14-day limit. 20 free primitive sites; 25-ft RV limit. Picnic shelter, pit toilets, fire rings, drkg wtr, toilets, tbls. Marina nearby.
GPS: 47.432232, -107.936726

DEVILS CREEK RECREATION AREA

From Jordan, at jct with SR 200, NW on gravel Brusett Rd, following signs through badlands of Hell Creek Geological Formation to S shore of lake. All year; 14-day limit. 6 free primitive sites; 16-ft RV limit. Picnic shelter, pit toilets, fire rings, tbls, no drkg wtr. Nearest dump station, 50 mi.
GPS: 47.618025, -107.653452

DOWNSTREAM CAMPGROUND

From Fort Peck, 1 mi SE on Judith Rd; W of spillway below dam. About 4/25-10/30; 14-day limit. 1 walk-to tent site & 14 basic tent sites, $12 base ($5 with federal senior pass); 62 elec sites: 30-amp elec, $18, 50-amp elec, $20 ($9 & $10 with senior pass). No wtr hookups. RV limit in excess of 65 ft. Tbls, flush & pit toilets, cfga, drkg wtr, dump, playground, interpretive center, fish cleaning station, pay phone, picnic shelters with elec, $20. Group camping area, $184. Boating(l), fishing ponds, interpretive trail, hiking, basketball. (406) 526-3224. NRRS during 5/15-9/10.
GPS: 48.008243, -106.428525

DUCK CREEK RECREATION AREA

From near Fort Peck at jct with SR 117, 3.7 mi NW on SR 24; 2 mi S on Duck Creek Rd; 2 mi W on Rd 108, then SE on Rd 445 to lake. All year; 14-day limit. 9 free primitive sites. RV limit 40'. Pit toilets, fire rings, picnic shelter. Boating(l), fishing. **GPS: 47.977131, -106.554004**

FLAT LAKE RECREATION AREA

From Fort Peck, 5.7 mi E on SR 24. All year;

14-day limit. 3 free primitive sites. Picnic shelter, pit toilets, fire rings, no drkg wtr. Nearest dump station 6 mi. Boating(l), fishing.
GPS: 48.020851, -106-3742001

FLOODPLAIN RECREATION AREA

From Fort Peck, N on SR 117 (Yellowstone Rd) near jct with Judith Rd; on the right just before C.M. Russell National Willdlife Refuge office. All year; 14-day limit. 5 free primitive sites; 50-ft RV limit. Fire rings, drkg wtr, pit toilets. Boating(l), fishing.
GPS: 48.017997, -106.442800

FOURCHETTE BAY RECREATION AREA

From Malta at jct with SR 2, 60 mi S on gravel rds (last 20 mi impassable when wet). S of Malta on Hwy 365, then 0.4 mi E; S on Content Rd, through Content; right (S) on Sun Prairie Rd to Reynolds Rd, then S on Reynolds to site. At N shore of Forchette Creek arm of lake. All year; 14-day limit. 44 free primitive sites; 20-ft RV limit. Picnic shelters, fire rings, pit toilets, no drkg wtr. Nearest dump station, 60 mi. Boating(ld), fishing.
GPS: 47.670655, -107.664138

MCGUIRE CREEK RECREATION AREA

From dam at Fort Peck, 37 mi SE on SR 24; about 6 mi W on N. McGuire Creek Rd; at W side of McGuire Creek arm of lake. All year; 14-day limit. 10 free primitive sites; 16-ft RV limit. Fire rings, pit toilets, tbls, no drkg wtr. Nearest dump station, 45 mi. **GPS: 47.622877, -106.199008**

NELSON CREEK RECREATION AREA

From dam at Ft. Peck, 44 mi SE on SR 24; 7 mi W on all-weather gravel Nelson Creek Rd, following signs; at tip of Big Dry arm of lake within Hell Creek Geological Formation, called the bandlands. All year; 14-day limit. 16 free primitive sites; 40-ft RV limit. Picnic shelter, fire rings, drkg wtr, tbls, pit toilets. Nearest dump station, 45 mi. Boating(ld), fishing.
GPS: 47.564825, -106.226732

ROUNDHOUSE POINT CAMP

From Ft. Peck, N of dam on SR 117; right following signs . All year; 14-day limit. 3 free primitive sites. Fishing pier, pit toilets, walkway, fire rings, no drkg wtr. Nearest dump station 2 mi. Boating, fishing.

THE PINES RECREATION AREA

From near Fort Peck at jct with SR 117, 4 mi NW on SR 24; 12 mi SW on Maxness Rd, becoming Willow Creek Rd (all-weather gravel), then 15 mi S on gravel Pines Rd. All year; 14-day limit. 30 free primitive sites; 30-ft RV limit. Picnic shelter with elec & grill, fish cleaning station, fire rings, toilets, tbls, playground, no drkg wtr. Nearest dump station, 33 mi. Boating(ld), fishing.
GPS: 47.831036, -106.613088

WEST END CAMPGROUND

From jct with SR 24 just W of Fort Peck, 2 mi SW on Duck Creek Rd; right (S) on Duck Creek Boat Ramp Rd to site overlooking lake W of dam. MD-LD; 14-day limit. Primitive sites without hookups, $5 ($2.50 with federal senior pass); 13 sites with elec, $16 ($8 with senior pass); 35-ft RV limit. Picnic shelter, drkg wtr, flush & pit toilets, cfga, dump, showers. Nearest dump station, 3 mi. Boating(ld), fishing. **GPS: 47.983560, -106.520466**

➋
LAKE KOOCANUSA
LIBBY DAM
GPS: 48.42. -115.31

A 46,500-acre lake 17 mi;es NE of Libby in northwestern Montana on SR 37. At Kootenai River. Campsites available on project lands with some amenities. Visitor center provides powerhouse tours, interpretive programs, picnicking, dam tours. Murray Springs Fish Hatchery. Libby Dam Project, 17115 Highway 37, Libby, MT 59923-7828. (406) 293-5577.

ALEXANDER CREEK CAMP

From Libby, about 12 mi E on SR 37; 3.5 mi N on Big Bend Rd, becoming gravel FR 228. On W side of Kootenai River below dam at mouth of Alexander Creek. All year; 14-day limit. 2 free primitive sites. Pit toilet, tbls, cfga, no drkg wtr. Boating(l), fishing.
GPS: 48.391883, -115.329516

BLACKWELL FLATS RECREATION AREA

From Libby, about 12 mi E on SR 37; 3.5 mi N on gravel FR 228. On W side of Kootenai River, 3.5 mi below dam. All year; 14-day limit. 7 free primitive sites, some pull-through. Pit toilets, tbls, cfga, no drkg wtr. Boating(l), fishing.
GPS: 48.369627, -115.321148

DOWNRIVER CAMPING AREA

From Libby, about 14 mi E on SR 37, across David Thompson Bridge over Kootenai River; at E shore of river below bridge. 2 free primitive sites; third site above gravel boat ramp near wildlife ponds. Fire rings, tbls, trash cans. **GPS: 48.364789, -115.325246**

DUNN CREEK FLAT CAMP

From Libby, about 14 mi E on SR 37, across David Thompson Bridge over Kootenai River, then 2 mi N; at E shore of river, about 3 mi below dam. All year; 14-day limit. 13 free primitive sites, some pull-through sites. Basketball hoop, small amphitheater. Footpath from ramp to wildlife ponds.
GPS: 48.380736, -115.320588

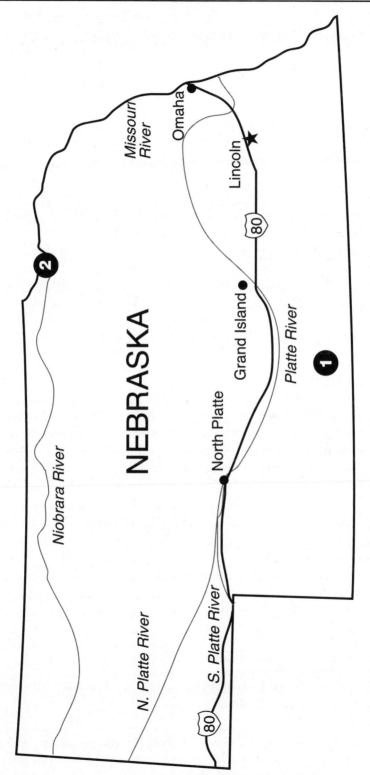

NEBRASKA

STATE INFORMATION:

CAPITAL: Lincoln
NICKNAME: Cornhusker State
STATEHOOD: 1867 - 37th State
FLOWER: Goldenrod
TREE: Eastern Cottonwood
BIRD: Western Meadowlark

STATE TIDBITS:

• Buffalo Bill Cody held his first rodeo in North Platte on July 4, 1882.

• Father Edward Flanagan founded Boys Town in Omaha in 1917.

• Kearney is located exactly between Boston and San Francisco.

WWW.VISITNEBRASKA.GOV

Toll-free numbers for travel information:
1-877-NEBRASKA.

Dept of Economic Development, Division of Travel and Tourism, PO Box 94666, Lincoln, NE 68509-4666. E-mail: tourism@visitnebraska.org

NEBRASKA LAKES

To find campgrounds operated by the U.S. Army Corps of Engineers, match the lake's numbers on the preceding map page with numbered lake entries on the following pages. Campgrounds are listed alphabetically under the appropriate lakes. The following Nebraka impoundments have Corps of Engineers campgrounds.

Harlan County Lake. A 13,250-acre lake 1 mile S of Republican City off US 136 in south-central Nebraska near the Kansas state line. It is Nebraska's second largest lake.

Lewis & Clark Lake. Located 4 miles W of Yankton, South Dakota, on Hwy 50 at the Nebraska state line. It is the smallest of the six Missouri River lakes; it has 90 miles of shoreline.

❶ HARLAN COUNTY LAKE
GPS: 40.0667, -99.2117

A 13,250-acre lake 1 mile S of Republican City off US 136 in south-central Nebraska near the Kansas state line. Nebraska's second largest lake. Campsites that are free sites in the off season may have reduced amenities. Visitor center. Camping also at North Shore Marina, Patterson Harbor Marina & Alma City Park. Operations Project Manager, Harlan County Lake, 70788 Corps Road A, Republican City, NE 68971-9742. (308) 799-2105.

CEDAR POINT/PATTERSON HARBOR PARK

From Republican City at jct with US 136, 5 mi S on CR A; at dam on the S side. All year; 14-day limit. 30 primitive sites, $10 ($5 with federal senior pass) during 5/15-9/15. Some sites open & free off-season. Tbls, pit toilets, cfga, drkg wtr, playground, beach, picnic shelter, change house. Boating(l), fishing, swimming, hiking. **GPS: 40.043247, -99.232239**

GREMLIN COVE PARK

From Republican City at jct with US 136, 1.7 mi S on CR 1815 (Berrigan Rd), then right (W) into park; at N side of dam. All year; 14-day limit. 70 primitive gravel sites, $12 ($6 with

federal senior pass) during 5/15-9/15. Some sites open & free off-season. Picnic shelter, change house, flush & pit toilets, cfga, drkg wtr, showers, playground, beach. Boating(l), fishing, swimming.
GPS: 40.086174, -99.2213785

HUNTER COVE PARK

From Republican City at jct with US 136, 1.2 mi S on CR 1815 (Berrigan Rd); 0.5 mi W on Corps Rd B, then S into park, following signs; at N side, E end of lake. 4/1-11/30; 14-day limit. 20 tent sites, $12 ($6 with federal senior pass); 47 non-elec RV/tent sites, $14 ($7 with senior pass) during 5/1-9/30; $12 in Oct, Nov & Apr; 84 elec sites, $16 base, $20 at premium locations ($8 & $10 with senior pass) during 5/1-9/30; $12 in Oct, Nov & Apr (holders of senior pass pay half rate off-season). RV limit in excess of 65 ft; 19 pull-through sites. Tbls, flush & pit toilets, cfga, showers, drkg wtr, dump, playground, beach, picnic shelters, amphitheater, fish cleaning station. Boat rentals at North Shore Marina. Off-road vehicles prohibited. Non-campers pay $3 day use fee at boat ramp. 308-799-2105. NRRS 5/1-11/29. **GPS: 40.083785, -99.229074**

METHODIST COVE PARK

From Alma at jct with US 183, 2.5 mi W on South St; near W end of lake. 4/1-11/30; 14-day limit. 82 non-elec sites, $12 & $14 during 5/1-9/30 ($6 & $7 with federal senior pass), $8 in Oct, Nov & Apr ($4 with senior pass); 48 elec sites, $20 base, $24 at premium locations during 5/1-9/30 ($10 & $12 with senior pass). RV limit in excess of 65 ft. Tbls, flush & pit toilets, showers, cfga, drkg wtr, dump, playground, fish cleaning station with grinder. Two group camping areas ($50). Boating(ld), fishing, hiking trails. Non-campers pay $3 day use fee for boat ramp. 308-799-9742. NRRS 5/1-9/30. **GPS: 40.086034, -99.329989**

NORTH OUTLET PARK

From Republican City, 2 mi S on Corps Rd A (CR 1815); left (E) on access rd; below dam

at N side of Republican River outlet. All year; 14-day limit. 30 sites without hookups, $10 during 5/15-9/15 ($5 with federal senior pass). During 9/15-5/14, some sites open & free. Picnic shelter, tbls, pit toilets, cfga, drkg wtr, playground. Basketball, hiking, fishing.
GPS: 40.070978, -99.207788

SOUTH OUTLET PARK

From Republican City, 3 mi S on Corps Rd A (CR 1815), across dam, then 0.25 mi E & 1 mi N on Corps Rd 1; below the dam at S shore of Republican River. All year; 14-day limit. 30 sites no hookups, $10 during 5/15-9/15 ($5 with federal senior pass). During 9/15-5/14, some sites open & free. Pit toilets.
GPS: 40.069681, -99.208217

❷
LEWIS & CLARK LAKE
GAVINS POINT DAM
GPS: 42.88, -97.48

Located 4 miles W of Yankton, South Dakota, on Hwy 50 at the Nebraska state line. It is the smallest of the six Missouri River lakes; it has 90 miles of shoreline. Visitor center just downstream from powerplant; exhibits, theater, prairie garden. Dam tours daily from 10 a.m. to 6 p.m. Memorial Day through Labor Day. Day use facilities: Overlook Park -- picnicking, group shelter, playground, hiking trail; Santee Park, boat ramp. Lake Manager, Gavins Point Project, P. O. Box 710, Yankton, SD 57078. (402) 667-7873. See SD listing.

COTTONWOOD RECREATION AREA

From Yankton, South Dakota, 4 mi W on SR 52, then S on Dam Toe Rd; E of dam on downstream side. About 4/21-10/16; 14-day limit. 77 elec sites (20/30/50-amp), $16 base, $18 at premium locations ($8 & $9 with federal senior pass). During off-season, some sites are open and free with reduced amenities & no wtr. RV limit in excess of 65 ft; 1 RV & 2 tents or 3 tents per site. Tbls, flush toilets, showers, dump, cfga, drkg wtr, playground,

fish cleaning station, picnic shelter. Boating(l), fishing. NRRS 5/21-9/6.
GPS: 42.859671, -97.482687

NEBRASKA TAILWATERS RECREATION AREA

From Yankton, South Dakota, 2 mi S on US 81, then 4 mi W on Nebraska SR 121; E of the dam on S side of river off Rt 121. About 5/15-10/15; 14-day limit. 13 non-elec sites, $12 ($6 with federal senior pass); 31 elec sites (30/50-amp), $16 ($8 with senior pass). RV limit in excess of 65 ft. Tbls, flush toilets, showers, dump, cfga, drkg wtr, fish cleaning station, picnic shelters, fishing pier, playground. Boating(l), fishing, hiking. NRRS.
GPS: 42.848695, -97.468783

Rio Grande
River

1

2

Santa Fe

25

Gallup

Canadian
River

40

40

Albuquerque

Gila
River

25

NEW MEXICO

Pecos River

Carlsbad

Las Cruces

CARLSBAD CAVERNS
NATIONAL PARK

10

NEW MEXICO

STATE INFORMATION:

CAPITAL: Santa Fe
NICKNAME: Land of Enchantment
STATEHOOD: 1912 - 47th State
FLOWER: Yucca
TREE: Piñon
BIRD: Roadrunner

NM

STATE TIDBITS:

• Santa Fe is the ending point of the 800 mile Santa Fe Trail.

• The Rio Grande is New Mexico's longest river and runs the entire state length.

• The Navajo, have a reservation that covers 14 million Acres.

WWW.NEWMEXICO.ORG

Dept of Tourism, Lamy Building, 491 Old Santa Fe Trail, Santa Fe, NM 87501. 800-545-2070; 505-827-7400. enchanntment@newmexico.org.

NEW MEXICO LAKES

To find campgrounds operated by the U.S. Army Corps of Engineers, match the lake's numbers on the preceding map page with numbered lake entries on the following pages. Campgrounds are listed alphabetically under the appropriate lakes. The following New Mexico impoundments have Corps of Engineers campgrounds.

Abiquiu Reservoir. A 5,200-acre lake 7 miles NW of Abiquiu off US 84 on SR 96, 60 miles NW of Santa Fe on the Rio Chama River.

Cochiti Lake. A 1,200-acre lake 50 miles NE of Albequerque and NW of I-25 on SR 22, 35 miles SW of Santa Fe.

①

ABIQUIU RESERVOIR

GPS: 36.24, -106.43

A 5,200-acre lake 7 miles NW of Abiquiu off US 84 on SR 96, 60 mi NW of Santa Fe. The lake is 6,400 feet above sea level on the Rio Chama River. Swimming permitted except where prohibited by signs. Visitor's center, picnicking. Day use facilities: Downstream Park -- picnicking; Overlook Park -- picnicking, interpretive trail; Rio Chama Recreation Area -- picnicking; Cerrito Recreation Area, picnicking, boat ramp, playground, interpretive & multi-use trails. 3-mile Vista Trail with connected hiking/biking loops; 7-mile Old Spanish Trail connects dam with Pueblo de Abiquiu. Operations Manager, Abiquiu Dam, P. O. Box 290, Abiquiu, NM 87510. (505) 868-2221.

RIANA RECREATION AREA

6 mi NW of Abiquiu on US 84; 1 mi SW on SR 96; N on access rd; at bluff overlooking SE shore of lake near dam. All year; 14-day limit; fees during 4/15-10/15. 15 walk-to tent sites (2-tent limit0, $7 ($3.50 with federal senior pass); 24 non-elec sites, $12 ($6 with senior pass); 15 elec/wtr sites, $16 ($8 with senior pass). Free primitive camping off-season. Tbls, flush & pit toilets, cfga, drkg wtr, showers, dump, playground, amphitheater. Boating(ld); fishing. Group camping area. RV limit in excess of 65'. Elev 6400 ft. 505-685-4371. NRRS. **GPS: 36.247025, -106.431041**

❷
COCHITI LAKE
GPS: 35.625, -106.3333

A 1,200-acre lake 50 miles NE of Albuquerque and NW of I-25 on SR 22, 35 mi SW of Santa Fe on the Rio Grande River. Within boundaries of Pueblo de Cochiti Indian Reservation. Visitor center with interpretive programs, picnicking. Ground fires and ORV prohibited. Swimming allowed except where prohibited by signs. Entire lake is a no-wake zone. Wind surfing popular. Day use areas with picnic shelters, boat ramps, fishing piers, multi-use trails. Operations Manager, Cochiti Lake, 82 Dam Crest Road, Pena Blanca, NM 87041. (505) 465-0307.

COCHITI RECREATION AREA

From Albuquerque, NE on I-25 to exit 259; N on SR 22 (Cochiti Hwy) through Pena Blanca to project office & campsites. All year; 14-day limit. 32 non-elec sites, $12 ($6 with federal senior pass); 48 elec sites (some wtr hookups), $20 ($10 with senior pass). 4 primary camping loops. RV limit in excess of 65 ft; 18 pull-through sites. Tbls, flush & pit toilets, cfga, drkg wtr, dump, showers, playground, fishing pier, covered shelters, beach, visitor center, pay phone. Boating(ld), swimming, fishing, interpretive trails, hiking. Juniper Loop has 34 sites (32 with elec, 7 with shade shelters); inside sites with wtr hookups; dump station; showers & flush toilets. Buffalo Grove Loop has 16 sites with 50-amp elec/wtr (7 pull-through), shade shelters, tbls, cfga, solar lighting, access to flush toilets & showers. Elk Run Loop has 16 non-elec sites (2 pull-through) with shade shelters, tbls, cfga, solar lighting; access to drkg wtr, flush toilets & showers. Ringtail Cat Loop has 14 non-elec sites with shad shelters, tbls, cfga, lantern posts, flush toilets, showers, dump; access to drkg wtr. Apache Plume group camping area with 22 sites, pit toilets, access to other loop amenities; available by reservation. Non-campers pay $3 day use fee for boat ramp.

3-night minimum stay on holiday weekends. 505-465-0307. NRRS.
GPS: 35.641517, -106.325555

TETILLA PEAK RECREATION AREA

From Albuquerque, NE on I-25 to exit 264; about 6 mi NW on SR 16, then right (NE) at Tetilla Peak turnoff to recreation area at E shore of lake. 4/1-10/30; 14-day limit. 10 non-elec sites, $12 ($6 with federal senior pass); 34 sites with elec (no wtr hookups), $20 ($10 with senior pass). RV limit in excess of 65 ft; 7 pull-through sites. Tbls, flush & pit toilets, cfga, drkg wtr, showers, dump, beach, picnic shelters; no day use fees. Boating(ld), fishing, swimming, hiking. 9-acre Cholla Campground with modern sites & hookups; Coyote Campground without hookups on partially paved access rd. 3-night minimum stay on holiday weekends. 505-465-0307. NRRS during 4/15-10/15.
GPS: 35.646190, -106.301737

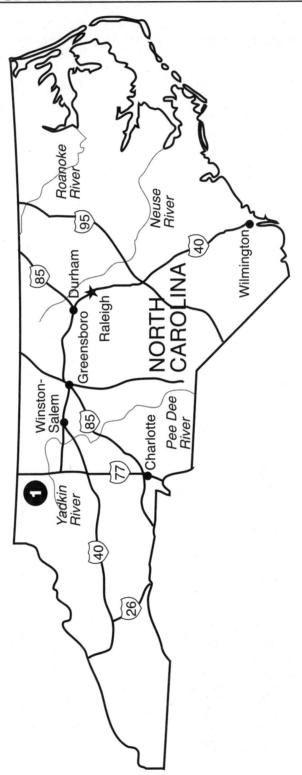

STATE INFORMATION:

CAPITAL: Raleigh
NICKNAME: Tar Heel State
STATEHOOD: 1789 - 12th State
FLOWER: Dogwood
TREE: Longleaf Pine
BIRD: Cardinal

STATE TIDBITS:

• Pepsi was invented and first served in New Bern in 1898.

• Krispy Kreme Doughnuts was founded in Winston-Salem in 1937.

• The oldest town in the state is Bath, incorporated in 1705.

WWW.VISITNC.COM

Toll-free number for travel information: 1-800-VISIT-NC. In state: 919/733-4172.

NORTH CAROLINA LAKES

To find campgrounds operated by the U.S. Army Corps of Engineers, match the lake's number on the preceding map page with the numbered lake entry on this page; the campgrounds are listed under it.

❶ W. KERR SCOTT RESERVOIR
GPS: 36.15, -81.2333

A 1,470-acre lake 3 miles W of Wilkesboro and S of US 421 off SR 268 in northwestern North Carolina; impoundment on Yadkin River. Visitors center, historic & cultural site, interpretive programs. Campground checkout time 3 p.m., visitors to 10 p.m. Off-road vehicles prohibited. Day use facilities: Berry Mountain Park -- picnicking, group shelter, playground, beach, trails, basketball court, showers; Blood Creek -- fishing pier, picnicking; Boomer Park -- boat ramp, picnicking, group shelter, playground, beach; Dam Site -- boat ramp, picnicking, interpretive trail; Dark Mountain -- fitness & multi-use trail; Fish Dam Creek -- picnicking, group shelter, playground, fitness trail; Keowee -- boat ramp, picnicking, playground, group shelter, fishing pier; Marleys Ford -- boat ramp, multi-use trail; Mountain View -- hiking; Smitheys Creek -- boat ramp, picnicking, playground, fishing pier; Tailwater Access -- multi-use trail, fishing pier. Trailhead for 6-mi Overmountain Victory National Historic Trail at Bandit's Roost Campground; 25 mi of mountain biking trails also available near the lake. Non-campers pay day use fees: $3 at boat launches, $4 at beaches, $3 dump station $4 other facilities; $25 picnic shelters. Project Manager, W. Kerr Scott Dam, 499 Reservoir Rd, Wilkesboro, NC 28697. (336) 921-3390.

BANDITS ROOST CAMP

From Wilkesboro at jct with US 421, 5.5 mi W on SR 268; 0.5 mi N on CR 1214, then right (E) on CR 1141 to campground; at SE shore of lake. 4/1-10/31; 14-day limit. 17 tent sites, $18 ($9 with federal senior pass); 85 elec/wtr RV sites, $24 base ($12 with senior pass). RV limit in excess of 65 ft; 5 pull-through sites. Tbls, flush & pit toilets, cfga, drkg wtr, showers, dump, playground, beach, pay phone, amphitheater, picnic shelter. Group tent camping area with elec, $85. Boating(ld), fishing, swimming, hiking trails, basketball. 336-921-3190. NRRS. **GPS: 36.123248, -81.246525**

FORT HAMBY CAMPGROUND

From Wilkesboro, 5 mi N on US 421; 1.5 mi S (left) on Recreation Rd; at NW shore of lake. 4/15-10/15; 14-day limit. 32 elec sites, $24 ($12 with federal senior pass). RV limit in excess of 65 ft. Tbls, flush & pit toilets, cfga, drkg wtr, showers, dump, amphitheater, picnic shelters, beach, playground. Group camping area with elec, $125. Boating(ld), fishing, hiking, swimming, basketball, horseshoe pits. 336-973-0104. NRRS. **GPS: 36.124576, -81.266561**

WARRIOR CREEK CAMP

From Wilkesboro, 8 mi W on SR 268, across bridge, then N on access rd; at S shore of lake. 4/15-10/15; 14-day limit. 49 elec/wtr sites (6 for tents), $20 base, $24 at premium locations ($10 & $12 with federal senior pass). RV limit in excess of 65 ft. Tbls, flush toilets, cfga, drkg wtr, showers, dump, beach, playground, pay phone, amphitheater. 2 group camping areas with elec, $85. Boating, biking/hiking trails, fishing, swimming. Boat ramp & fishing piers 1 mi. (336) 921-2177. NRRS.
GPS: 36.103486, -81.284119

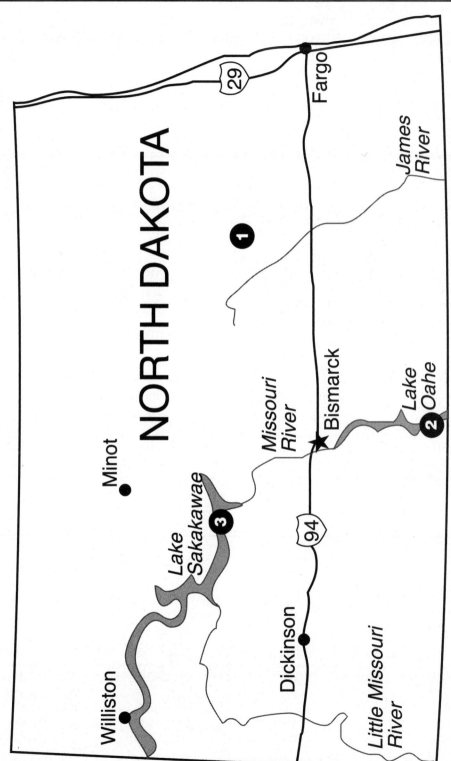

NORTH DAKOTA

STATE INFORMATION:

CAPITAL: Bismarck
NICKNAME: Peace Garden State
STATEHOOD: 1889 - 40th State
FLOWER: Wild Prairie Rose
TREE: American Elm
BIRD: Western Meadowlark

ND

STATE TIDBITS:

• The World's Largest Buffalo monument is located at Frontier Village in Jamestown.

• Devils Lake is the largest natural body of water in North Dakota.

• Fort Union Trading Post was the principal fur-trading depot from 1829 to 1867.

WWW.NDTOURISM.COM

Toll-free number for travel information: 800-435-5663. Home page: http://www.ndtourism.com

NORTH DAKOTA LAKES

To find campgrounds operated by the U.S. Army Corps of Engineers, match the lake's numbers on the preceding map page with numbered lake entries on the following pages. Campgrounds are listed alphabetically under the appropriate lakes. The following North Dakota impoundments have Corps of Engineers campgrounds.

Lake Ashtabula. A 5,234-acre lake 11 miles NW of Valley City, exit 69 on I-94, in east-central North Dakota, NW of Fargo on the Sheyenne River.

Lake Oahe. The lake has 2,250 miles of shoreline and is 6 miles N of Pierre, South Dakota, on SR 1804.

Lake Sakakawea. A 368,000-acre lake near Riverdale on SR 200, 75 miles N of Bismarck and W of US 83.

❶ LAKE ASHTABULA
BALDHILL DAM
GPS: 47.0367, -98.08

A 5,234-acre lake 11 miles NW of Valley City, exit 69 on I-94, in east-central North Dakota, NW of Fargo on Sheyenne River. Snowmobiling permitted in winter. Visitor center, interpretive programs, picnicking. Day use facilities: Sibley Landing -- boat ramp, hiking trail, fish cleaning station; Sundstrom's Landing -- boat ramp, picnicking, shelter, fishing pier, playground. 3 designated swimming areas, 7 boat ramps. Resource Manager, Lake Ashtabula, 2630 - 114th Avenue SE, Valley City, ND 58072-9795. (701) 845-2970.

ASHTABULA CROSSING EAST CAMPGROUND

From Valley City, 12 mi N on CR 21; right (N) before Ashtabula Bridge into campground on E shore of lake. 5/1-9/30; 14-day limit. 6 walk-to tent sites, $26 ($13 with federal senior pass); 31 elec sites, $26 ($13 with senior pass); double sites $52. RV limit in excess of 65 ft. Tbls, flush & pit toilets, cfga, drkg wtr, showers, dump, beach, playground, picnic shelter, pay phone. Boating(ld), fishing, swimming. (701) 845-2970. NRRS. **GPS: 47.158396, -98.003991**

ASHTABULA CROSSING WEST CAMPGROUND

From Valley City, 12.5 mi N on CR 21, crossing Ashtabula Bridge, then immediate right into campground on lake's W shore. 5/1-9/30; 14-day limit. 13 tent sites & 26 elec sites, $26 ($13 with federal senior pass). Tbls, flush & pit toilets, cfga, drkg wtr, dump, no showers, beach, visitor center, fishing pier, picnic shelter, fish cleaning stations, playground, store. Boating(d), fishing, hiking, backpacking, swimming. Self-pay station. NRRS MD-LD. **GPS: 47.161627, -98.007960**

EGGERT'S LANDING CAMP

From Valley City, 10 mi N on CR 21; 1 mi W on 22nd St SE, then S on access rd, following signs; at E shore of lake. 5/1-9/30; 14-day limit. 4 tent sites, 2 non-elec RV sites & 35 elec sites, $26 ($13 with federal senior pass). RV limit in excess of 65 ft. Tbls, flush & pit toilets, cfga, drkg wtr, showers, fishing pier, picnic shelter, fish cleaning station, beach, playground, pay phone. Biking, hiking, canoeing, boating(ld), fishing, swimming. 3-night minimum stay required on holiday weekends. 701-845-2970. NRRS. **GPS: 47.095524, -98.008518**

MEL RIEMAN RECREATION AREA

From Valley City at I-94 exit 292, under the railroad bridge, then 6 mi N on CR 21; left (W) on 26th St SE (becoming River Rd) & S along lakeshore to campground. 5/1-9/30; 14-day limit. 27 sites, all $26 ($13 with federal senior pass). 6 walk-to tent sites, 1 drive-to tent site, 20 elec sites (3 pull-through). RV limit in excess of 65 ft. Tbls, flush & pit toilets, cfga, drkg wtr, showers, playground, beach, fish cleaning station, pay phone, visitor center, no dump, picnic shelter $25. Boating(ld), fishing, horseshoe pits, canoeing, swimming, hiking. 701-845-2970. NRRS. **GPS: 47.033485, -98.071239**

❷ LAKE OAHE
GPS: 44.45. -100.3868

The lake has 2,250 miles of shoreline and is 6 miles N of Pierre, South Dakota, on SR 1804. Powerhouse tours daily during the summer. Park Manager, Lake Oahe, 28563 Powerhouse Rd., Room 105, Pierre, SD 57501-6174. Note: Most Corps campgrounds on the lake are now operated by the State of South Dakota as state park facilities. Future plans including shifting management of North Dakota campgrounds to that state's park system. (605) 224-5862/ (701) 255-0015.

BADGER BAY RECREATION AREA

From Hazelton, 13 mi W on gravel 63rd St SW to Livona, then 1 mi S on SR 1804; W following signs. All year; 14-day limit. 6 free primitive sites. Pit toilet, fire rings, no drkg wtr. Nearest dump station is 23 mi. **GPS: 46.495748, -100.554814**

BEAVER CREEK RECREATION AREA

From Linton, 16 mi W on SR 13; 1 mi S on SR 1804; at N side of lake's Beaver Bay. 5/1-9/30; 14-day limit. 2 primitive areas with 21 sites, $12 ($6 with federal senior pass), $10 during 5/1-5/14 & 9/13-9/30; 45 elec sites, some pull-through, $18 ($9 with senior pass), $14 during 5/1-5/14 & 9/13-9/30. Tbls, pit & flush toilets, cfga, drkg wtr (seasonal), showers (seasonal), dump, playground, beach, fish cleaning stations, picnic shelter ($25). Boating(ld), fishing, sand volleyball, nature trail, swimming, horseshoe pits, hiking. Self-pay station. (701) 255-0015. NRRS (5/15-9/12). **GPS: 46.249378, -100.532627**

CATTAIL BAY RECREATION AREA

From Strasburg, about 12 mi W on gravel 89th St SE; 0.5 mi S on Main Ave; 6 mi W on 90th St SW; 2 mi S on SR 1804; 3 mi SW on 91st St SW; at SE shore of lake's Cattail Bay. All year; 14-day limit. 6 free primitive sites. Pit toilets, fire rings, no drkg wtr. Nearest dump station 15 mi. **GPS: 46.091880, -100.592006**

HAZELTON RECREATION AREA

From Hazelton, 13 mi W on gravel 63rd St SW to Livona, then 1 mi N on SR 1804; at E shore of lake. 5/1-9/30; 14-day limit. 18 primitive sites, $10; 12 elec sites (30/50-amp), $14 ($5 & $7 with federal senior pass). 30-ft RV limit. Tbls, pit toilets, cfga, drkg wtr, playground, fish cleaning stations. Boating(ld), fishing, horseshoe pit. Self-pay station. Nearest dump station 25 mi. 701-255-00915. NRRS. **GPS: 46.520692, -100.542755**

❸

LAKE SAKAKAWEA
GARRISON DAM
GPS: 45.5017, -101.4317

A 368,000-acre lake near Riverdale on SR 200, 75 miles N of Bismarck and W of US 83. Powerplant tours daily in summer. Offroad vehicle area, national fish hatchery. Visitor center, interpretive programs, historic & cultural site. 35 recreation areas. Nesting area for least tern and piping plover and rest stop for whooping cranes.

Facilities not managed by the Corps: West Totten Trail Recreation Area -- boat ramps, pit toilet (McLean County); Sportsman's Centennial Park -- boat ramps, campground, playground, fish cleaning station, picnicking, group shelter, trails (McLean County); Ft. Stevenson State Park -- camping, boat ramp, dump, beach, volleyball court, picnicking; Indian Hills Recreation Area -- boat ramp, boat rental, camping, fish cleaning station, dump, showers, picnicking (Three Affiliated Tribes & State of N Dakota); Parshall Bay Recreation Area -- boat ramps, camping, fish cleaning station, group shelters, picnicking, playground, dump, showers (Montrail County Parks); Van Hook Recreation Area -- boat ramp, boat rental, camping, fish cleaning station, picnicking, group shelter, playground, dump, showers (Montrail County Parks); Pouch Point Recreation Area -- boat ramp, camping, group shelter, picnicking, playground, dump, showers (Three Affiliated Tribes); New Town Marina Recreation Area -- boat ramp, camping, fish cleaning station, picnicking, group shelter, playground, dump, showers (New Town Parks); White Earth Bay Recreation Area -- boat ramp, camping, group shelter, picnicking, playground, pit toilet; Little Beaver Bay Recreation Area -- boat ramp, camping, pit toilets, group shelter, picnicking (Williams County Water Resources District); Little Egypt Recreation Area -- camping, pit toilets (Williams County Water Resources District); White Tail Bay (Lund's Landing) Recreation Area -- boat ramp, boat rental, camping, picnicking, shower, flush & pit toilets (Williams County Water Resources District); Lewis and Clark State Park -- amphitheater, boat ramp, camping, fish cleaning station, hiking trail, dump, shower, picnicking, group shelter, playground; Lake Trenton Recreation Area -- boat ramp, camping, group shelter, picnicking, playground, showers, beach (Williams County Water Resources District); American Legion Park -- boat ramp, camping, group shelter, picnicking, pit toilets (American Legion Post 37); Tobacco Gardens -- boat ramp, camping, fish cleaning station, picnicking, group shelter, playground, dump, showers (McKenzie County Parks); Four Bears Recreation Area -- boat ramp, camping, fish cleaning station, group shelters, picnicking, playground, dump, showers (Three Affiliated Tribes); Skunk Creek Recreation Area -- boat ramp, camping, pit toilet (Three Affiliated Tribes); McKenzie Bay Recreation Area -- boat ramp, camping, boat rental, fish cleaning station, group shelter, picnicking, playground, dump, showers (Watford Cit Parks); Beaver Creek Bay Recreation Area -- boat ramp, camping, group shelters, picnicking, pit toilet (Zap Parks); Lake Shore Park -- boat ramp, boat rental, camping, fish cleaning station, group shelter, picnicking, playground, dump, showers (Beulah Parks); Beulah Bay Recreation Area -- boat ramp, camping, fish cleaning station, group shelter, picnicking, dump, showers (Beulah Parks); Hazen Bay Rec. Area -- boat ramp, camping, fish cleaning station, dump, group shelter, picnicking, showers (Hazen Parks); Lake Sakakawea State Park -- amphitheater, basketball court, boat ramp, boat rental, camping, fish cleaning station, hiking trail; group shelter, picnicking, playground, dump, showers, beach, volleyball court; Riverdale Overlook Recreation Area -- picnicking, group shelter.

Corps-managed day use facilities: Spillway Pond Recreation Area -- boat ramp, picnicking, group shelter, flush toilets, playground, grills, beach; Spillway Overlook Recreation Area -- picnicking, group shelters, pit toilets; Government Bay Rec. Area -- boat ramp, fish cleaning station, pit toilet; Little Missouri Bay Recreation Area is closed. Note: The Corps of Engineers in 2013 proposed that the State of North Dakota take over management of up to 35 federal recreation areas (including East Totten Trail and Downstream Campgrounds) around Lake Sakakawea and Lake Oahe by 2015. However, that proposal was not accepted by the governor's office, so the Corps continued management of those facilities. Consideration also is being given to transferring land to the Fort Berthold Indian Reservation and to closing Corps-managed campgrounds due to budget cuts. A non-profit citizens group, Friends of Lake Sakakawea, is closely monitoring the various proposals; for current status, check with that organization online or with the lake management offices. Lake Manager, Lake Sakakawea, Box 527, Riverdale, ND 58565-0527. (701) 654-7411.

DEEPWATER CREEK RECREATION AREA

From just N of Coleharbor on US 83, about 22 mi W on SR 37 (17 mi S of Parshall), then S on access rd (following signs) to shore of lake's Deepwater Creek Bay. 4/1-9/30; 14-day limit. 30 free primitive sites. Picnic shelter, pit toilets, drkg wtr, cfga. Boating(ld), fishing. **GPS: 47.733154, -102.129754**

DOUGLAS CREEK RECREATION AREA

From jct with US 83, 2 mi W of Emmet on SR 37; 7 mi SE on gravel rds; at Douglas Creek Bay section of lake. All year; 14-day limit. 17 free primitive sites. 25-ft RV limit. Pit toilets, cfga, tbls, drkg wtr. Boating(ld), fishing. **GPS: 47.578089, -101.577122**

DOWNSTREAM CAMPGROUND

Near Riverdale, below dam on W side of spillway. 5/1-9/30; 14-day limit. 16 tent sites, $12; 101 elec sites, $18 ($6 & $9 with federal senior pass). RV limit in excess of 65 ft. Tbls, flush & pit toilets, cfga, drkg wtr, amphitheater, fish cleaning station, picnic shelters, beach, playground, pay phone. Interpretive programs, horseshoe pits, boating(l), fishing, swimming, hiking, interpretive trails. (701) 654-7440. NRRS 5/15-9/7. **GPS: 47.480002, -101.428120**

EAST TOTTEN TRAIL RECREATION AREA

6 mi E of Garrison on SR 37; 2.5 mi S on US 83 (N on US 83 from Coleharbor), then qtr mi E to lake. 5/1-9/30; 14-day limit. 10 primitive sites, $10; 30 elec sites, $14 ($7 with federal senior pass). 25-ft RV limit. Tbls, pit toilets, cfga, drkg wtr, dump, fish cleaning station. Boating(ld), fishing. **GPS: 47.617912, -101.262039**

WOLF CREEK RECREATION AREA

1 mi E of Riverdale on SR 200; 2 mi N & 2 mi E on CR 15; 2 mi N on gravel 36th Ave N, following signs; at lake's S shore. All year; 14-day limit. 101 primitive sites, $10 ($5 with federal senior pass). Tbls, pit toilets, cfga, drkg wtr, dump, playground, fish cleaning station, picnic shelter. Boating(ld), fishing, horseshoe pits, volleyball court. Group camping area (contact office, 701-654-7411). No reservations. **GPS: 47.545598, -101.313386**

OHIO

OHIO

STATE INFORMATION:

CAPITAL: Columbus
NICKNAME: Buckeye State
STATEHOOD: 1803 - 17th State
FLOWER: Scarlet Carnation
TREE: Ohio Buckeye
BIRD: Cardinal

STATE TIDBITS:

• Neil Armstrong was the first man to walk on the moon. He was from Wapakoneta.

• Cincinnati had the first professional city fire department.

• Cleveland became the world's first city to be lighted electrically in 1879.

WWW.OHIO.GOV/TOURISM

Toll-free numbers for travel information: 1-800-BUCKEYE.

Ohio Division of Tourism, Box 1001, Columbus, OH 43266-0101. Phone 800-BUCKEYE. 614-466-8844.

OHIO LAKES

To find campgrounds operated by the U.S. Army Corps of Engineers, match the lake's number on the preceding map page with the numbered lake entry on this page; the only campground is listed under it.

①

BERLIN LAKE
GPS: 41.0467, -81.0

A 3,590-acre lake near Deerfield on US 224 and Bedell Rd SE of Akron on the Mahoning River. The lake provides flood protection for the Mahoning River Valley as well as for the Beaver and upper Ohio Rivers. Alcohol prohibited. Campfire programs at amphitheater the first Friday each month. Day use activities: Bonner Road -- boat ramp, toilets; Dam Area -- picnic shelters, toilets; Deer Creek -- picnicking, boat ramp, toilets. For daily lake information, call (330) 547-5445. Resource Manager, Berlin Lake, 7400 Bedell Road, Berlin Center, OH 44401-9707. (330) 547-3781.

MILL CREEK RECREATION AREA

From I-76 exit 54, 5.5 mi S on SR 534; 2 mi E on US 224; 0.8 mi S on Bedell Rd. MD-LD; 14-day limit. 241 sites without hookups, $14 base, $18 at premium sites ($7 & $9 with federal senior pass); 107 elec sites, $20 base, $24 with 50-amp elec ($10 & $12 with senior pass). RV limit in excess of 65 ft. Camping limited to 1 RV & 1 tent or 2 tents and one screen tent. Tbls, flush toilets, cfga, drkg wtr, showers, dump, amphitheater, beach, playground. Interpretive programs, kayaking, sailing, canoeing, biking, boating(ld), fishing, fitness trails, swimming, volleyball, waterskiing. Group tent camping area for up to 40 people & 8 vehicles, $20; group tent/RV area, $40. (330)547-8180. NRRS.
GPS: 41.010491, -80.986662

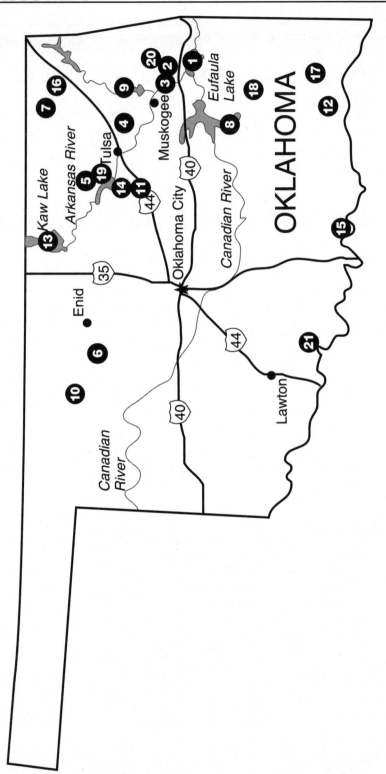

OKLAHOMA

STATE INFORMATION:

CAPITAL: Oklahoma City
NICKNAME: Sooner State
STATEHOOD: 1907 - 46th State
FLOWER: Mistletoe
TREE: Eastern Redbud
BIRD: Scissor-tailed Flycatcher

STATE TIDBITS:

• The National Cowboy Hall of Fame is located in Oklahoma City.

• Choctaw is the oldest chartered town in Oklahoma in 1893.

• Oklahoma has more man-made lakes than any other state.

WWW.TRAVELOK.COM

Toll-free number for travel information: 800-652-6552.

Tourism and Recreation Department, PO Box 52002, Oklahoma City, OK 73152. 405-230-9400 or 800-652-6552.

OKLAHOMA LAKES

To find campgrounds operated by the U.S. Army Corps of Engineers, match the lake's numbers on the preceding map page with numbered lake entries on the following pages. Campgrounds are listed alphabetically under the appropriate lakes. The following Oklahoma impoundments have Corps of Engineers campgrounds.

Robert S. Kerr Reservoir. This 4,200-acre pool at Arkansas River Lock & Dam 15 is 8 miles S of Sallisaw on US 59 S of I-40 in east-central Oklahoma, 33 miles W of Ft. Smith, Arkansas. It is part ofthe McCellan-Kerr Arkansas River Navigation System flowing SE through Arkansas and Oklahoma to the Mississippi River.

Webbers Falls Reservoir. A 10,900-acre lake 5 miles NW of Webbers Falls (30 miles SE of Muskogee). It is part of the McCellan-Kerr Arkansas River Navigation System flowing SE through Arkansas and Oklahoma to the Mississippi River.

Chouteau Pool. Located SE of Tulsa and 4 mi NW of Okay on the Arkansas River, the lock and dam is part of the McClellan-Kerr Arkansas River Navigation System.

Newt Graham Lake. Part of the McClellan Kerr Arkansas River Navigation System, Lock & Dam 18 is 7 m S of Inola and E of Tulsa.

Birch Lake. This 1,137-acre lake is 20 miles SW of Bartlesville off SR 123/11 and 1.5 mile S of Barnsdall, 35 miles NW of Tulsa.

Canton Lake. A 7,910-acre lake 75 miles NW of Oklahoma City and 2 miles N of Canton on SR 58A; at the North Canadian River.

Copan Lake. A 4,850-acre lake W of Copan on the Little Caney River, located 2 miles W of US 75 on SR 10, N of Tulsa near the Kansas state line.

Eufaula Lake. A 102,200-acre lake with 600 miles of shoreline, Eufaula is Oklahoma's largest lake. It is on the Canadian River, 27 miles upstream from the Arkansas River, 12 miles E of Eufaula on SR 75 and 31 miles S of Muskogee.

Fort Gibson Lake. A 19,900-acre lake 5 miles NW of Fort Gibson on SR 251A from the Muskogee Turnpike on the Grand (Neosho) River.

Fort Supply Lake. A 1.920-acre lake 15 miles NW of Woodward on US 183 and 1 mile SE of Fort Supply in northwestern Oklahoma near the panhandle; on Wood Creek.

Heyburn Lake. A 920-acre lake 13 miles SW of Sapulpa, 2 miles from US 65 and 25 miles SW of Tulsa off I-44.

Hugo Lake. A 13,250-acre lake 6 miles E of Hugo on US 70 about 30 miles N of Paris, Texas, in southeastern Oklahoma on the Kiamichi River.

Kaw Lake. A 17,000-acre lake 8 miles E of Ponca City off US 60, 70 miles NE of Enid on the Arkansas River; it has 168 miles of shoreline.

Keystone Lake. A 26,000-acre lake on the Arkansas River, 15 miles W of Tulsa on US 412 and SR 51; it has 330 miles of shoreline.

Lake Texoma. Located 5 miles N of Dennison, Texas, in south-central Oklahoma on the state line, Lake Texoma has 88,000 acres with 580 miles of shoreline; it is on the Red River at its confluence with the Washita River.

①

ARKANSAS RIVER
LOCK 8 DAM 15
ROBERT S. KERR RESERVOIR
GPS: 35.3467. -94.7767

This 42,000-acre pool of the Arkansas River is 8 miles S of Sallisaw on US 59 S of I-40 in east-central Oklahoma, 33 miles W of Ft. Smith, Arkansas. It is part of the McClellan-Kerr Arkansas River Navigation System flowing southeast through Arkansas and Oklahoma to the Mississippi River. It also follows portions of the Verdigris River in Oklahoma and the White River in Arkansas and includes the Arkansas Post Canal -- a short canal connecting the Arkansas and White Rivers. Day use facilities at the dam site include boat ramp, picnic area, beach. Off-season primitive camping is provided at Applegate Cove, in winter loop at Short Mountain Point, and in winter loop at Cowlington Point. Project Engineer, Robert S. Kerr Project Office, HC 61, Box 238, Sallisaw, OK 74955-9945. (918) 775-4475.

APPLEGATE COVE
RECREATION AREA

From I-40 at Sallisaw, 1 mi S on US 59; 3.5 mi W on Drake Rd; 4 mi S on Dwight Mission Rd; right into park, following signs. All year; 14-day limit. 27 sites with elec/wtr, $15 ($7.50 with federal senior pass). 50-ft RV limit. Tbls, flush toilets, showers, cfga, drkg wtr, beach, dump. Picnic shelter for up to 50 people & 10 vehicles, $50. Boating(ld), fishing, swimming. Non-campers pay day use fee at boat ramp & dump station. No reservations.
GPS: 35.399845, -94.866184

COWLINGTON POINT
RECREATION AREA

From Keota, 2 mi E on SR 9; 3 mi N on N. Star Rd to town of Star; 2 mi E on E1175 Rd (becoming D1171 Dr); left (N) into park, following signs; at SE shore of lake. All year; 14-day limit. 6 primitive sites, $10; 32 elec/wtr sites (30-amp), $15 ($5 & $7.50 with federal senior pass). 60-ft RV limit. Tbls, toilets, cfga, drkg wtr, dump, playground, beach, picnic shelter $50. Swimming, boating(l), fishing. Non-campers pay day use fees for boat ramp, dump station. No reservations.
GPS: 35.316579, -94.828191

SHORT MOUNTAIN COVE
RECREATION AREA

From Cowlington (12 mi S of Sallisaw), 0.5 mi E on CR 42; 1 mi N on CR N4630, following signs; at SE shore of lake just W of US 59. All year; 14-day limit. 42 elec/wtr sites, $15 ($7.50 with federal senior pass). 55-ft RV limit. Tbls, toilets, cfga, drkg wtr, dump, beach, picnic shelter $50. Nature trail, boating(ld), fishing, swimming. No day use fees. No reservations. **GPS: 35.322409, -94.781713**

❷
ARKANSAS RIVER LOCK & DAM 16
WEBBERS FALLS RESERVOIR
GPS: 35.5533, -95.1683

A 10,900-acre lake 5 miles NW of Webbers Falls (30 miles SE of Muskogee). It is part of the McClellan-Kerr Arkansas River Navigation System flowing SE through Arkansas and Oklahoma to the Mississippi River. Visitors may watch boats & barges go through locks from an observation platform. Project Manager, Rt. 2, Box 21, Gore, OK 74435-9404. (918) 489-5541.

BREWERS BEND RECREATION AREA

From Webbers Falls, 2 mi W on US 64; 3 mi N & 2 mi NW on N4410 Rd; right (E) into park, following signs. All year; 14-day limit. During 4/1-10/31, 8 non-elec sites $10; 34 elec/wtr sites $16 ($5 & $8 with federal senior pass). During 11/1-3/31, elec sites $13 ($6.50 with senior pass) & reduced fees on non-elec sites; no wtr hookups, flush toilets or showers in off-season. Tbls, flush toilets, cfga, drkg wtr, showers, dump, beach, amphitheater, change house, picnic shelter $25. Boating(l), fishing, swimming. No day use fees. (918) 487-5252. **GPS: 35.578383, -95.188343**

SPANIARD CREEK CAMP

From Muskogee at jct with Muskogee Turnpike (SR 351) & SR 10, 3 mi S on US 64; 4 mi E on E 103rd St (Elm Grove Rd), then 0.5 mi S, following signs across S 65th St E bridge & right into campground. All year; 14-day limit. During 4/1-10/31, one non-elec site, $14; 35 elec/wtr sites, $18 ($7 & $9 with federal senior

pass). During 11/1-3/31, elec sites $15 ($7.50 with senior pass) & reduced fee at non-elec site; no wtr hookups, flush toilets or showers in off-season. No day use fees. No reservations. **GPS: 35.598056, -95.266850**

❸
ARKANSAS RIVER LOCK & DAM 17
CHOUTEAU POOL
GPS: 35.8583, -95.3717

Located SE of Tulsa and 4 miles NW of Okay on the Arkansas River, the lock and dam is part of the McClellan-Kerr Arkansas River navigation system. Boat ramps at Afton Landing, Coal Creek and Tullahassee Loop Parks; non-campers pay day use fee at Afton for boat ramp & dump station. Picnicking, horseback riding. Lake Manager, Ft. Gibson, Fort Gibson Lake, 8568 State Highway 251A, Ft. Gibson, OK 74434. (918) 682-4314. See Newt Graham L&D No. 18 later in the Oklahoma section.

AFTON LANDING RECREATION AREA

From Wagoner at jct with US 69, 5 mi W on SR 51; left (S) on access rd just before Verdigris River bridge about 2 mi (signs); at N shore of river loop & W shore of main river. All year; 14-day limit. Now a Corps "Class B" park without showers, flush toilets. 2 non-elec sites, $10; 22 elec/wtr sites, $14 for 30-amp, $16 for 50-amp ($5 & $7 & $8 with federal senior pass). Tbls, pit toilets, cfga, drkg wtr, dump, picnic shelter $50. Boating(l), fishing. Non-campers pay $3 day use fee for boat ramp & dump station. **GPS: 35.946441, -95.486575**

TULLAHASSEE LOOP RECREATION AREA

From Tullahassee, 1 mi W on SR 51B; about 4 mi N on 477th E Ave to oxbow loop of Verdigris River. All year; 14-day limit. Free primitive undesignated sites. Pit toilets, fire rings, tbls, drkg wtr. Boating(l), fishing. **GPS: 35.890041, -95.447481**

❹ ARKANSAS RIVER LOCK & DAM 18
NEWT GRAHAM LAKE
GPS: 36.05, -95.5383

Part of the McClellan-Kerr Arkansas River Navigation System Lock & Dam 18 is 7 miles S of Inola and E of Tulsa. The Corps manages two park areas -- Bluff Landing Campground and Highway 33 Landing boat ramp/day use park. Lock Engineer, 8568 SR 251A, Fort Gibson, OK 74434. (918) 682-4314.

BLUFF LANDING CAMPGROUND

From Broken Arrow, 12.7 mi E on 71st St; left (N) on 3695h E Ave to S shore of Verdigris River oxbow. All year; 14-day limit. 7 non-elec sites, $14 ($7 with federal senior pass); 25 elec/ wtr sites, $18 for 30-amp, $20 for 50-amp ($9 & $10 with senior pass). During 11/1-3/31, some sites available at same rates. Tbls, flush toilets, cfga, drkg wtr, dump. Boating(l), fishing. Non-campers pay $3 day use fee for boat ramp, dump station.
GPS: 36.069221, -95.561378

❺ BIRCH LAKE
GPS: 36.535, -96.1583

This 1,137-acre lake is 20 miles SW of Bartlesville off SR 123/11 and 1.5 miles S of Barnsdall, 35 mi NW of Tulsa. Campground checkout time 4 p.m. Non-campers pay day use fee of $1 per person ($4 vehicle) at swimming beaches, $3 at boat ramps, $4 for other facilities (or $30 annually). Lake Manager, Skiatook/Birch Lake, 14004 Lake Rd, Skiatook, OK 74070. (918) 396-3170.

BIRCH COVE A RECREATION AREA

From Barnsdall at jct of SR 11 & 8th St, 3 mi S on 8th St (becoming CR 2409), across spillway, then 0.7 mi W on Birch Cove Rd, following signs. 4/1-10/31; 14-day limit. 85 elec sites (no wtr hookups), $18 ($9 with federal senior pass); 5 pull-through, 3 handicap sites. RV limit in excess of 65 ft. Tbls, flush & pit toilets, cfga, drkg wtr, amphitheater, playground, beach, change house, dump, two picnic shelters with elec ($80 & $100). Boating(ld), fishing, handicap accessible fishing area, swimming. Non-campers pay day use fee at boat ramp; beach & fishing dock not open to non-campers. NRRS.
GPS: 36.521243, -96.166549

BIRCH COVE B RECREATION AREA

From Barnsdall at jct of SR 11 & 8th St, 3 mi S on 8th St (becoming CR 2409), across spillway, then 0.7 mi W on Birch Cove Rd, following signs. All year; 14-day limit. 12 sites with wtr/ elec, $14 ($7 with federal senior pass). Tbls, pit toilets, cfga, drkg wtr, dump. Beach, showers, flush toilets, playground, fishing dock at Birch Cove A open to registered campers. Boating(l), fishing, swimming, hiking Non-campers pay day use fee at boat ramp. No reservations.
GPS: 36.518268, -96.171983

TWIN COVE RECREATION AREA

From Barnsdall, 1.5 mi S on 8th St (becoming CR 2409); right on lake access rd before spillway. 4/1-9/30; 14-day limit. 11 sites no hookups, $8 ($4 with federal senior pass). Tbls, pit toilets, cfga, drkg wtr, showers, dump, beach, playground, change house at beach. Boating(l), fishing(d), swimming, hiking. Group picnic shelters $25. Non-campers pay day use fee for beach, boat ramp.
GPS: 36.537416, -96.169810

❻ CANTON LAKE
GPS: 36.0917, -98.5917

A 7,910-acre lake 75 miles NW of Oklahoma City and 2 miles N of Canton on SR 58A; at the North Canadian River. The Corps operates 5 multi-use recreation areas. 3 parking areas with fishing jetties are at the dam. Visitor center, nature trail, outdoor amphitheater, active prairie dog town. Swimming allowed in all areas except around boat ramps & docks. Non-campers pay day use fees at beaches ($1), boat ramps ($3 self-deposit) and other facilities ($4). Note: In 2015, lake levels were quite low, making most boat ramps unavailable. Lake Manager, Canton Lake, HC 65, Box 120, Canton, OK 73724-9512. (580) 886-2989.

BIG BEND RECREATION AREA

From Canton, 1.8 mi W on SR 51; 4 mi N on paved N2460 Rd; 0.1 mi right (E) on E0620 Rd, then left (N) into campground at W shore of lake. 4/1-10/31; 14-day limit. 2 camping areas. At Loop A, primitive sites $15; elec/wtr sites $20 for 30-amp, $22 for 50-amp ($7.50, $10 & $11 with federal senior pass). At Loop B, primitive sites $15; 42 elec/wtr sites $20 ($7.50 & $10 with senior pass). 45-ft RV limit. During Nov & early March, some sites may be open and free without amenities. Pit & flush toilets, tbls, cfga, drkg wtr, dump, playground, picnic shelter $40. Boating(d), fishing, waterskiing. (580) 886-3576. NRRS. **GPS: 36.119209, -98.615770**

BLAINE PARK

From Canton, 0.7 mi W on SR 51; 1.7 mi N on SR 58A, below dam. 4/1-10/31; 14-day limit. 16 primitive sites, $10 ($5 with federal senior pass). Off-season, some sites are open & free, but no utilities (pit toilets). Tbls, flush & pit toilets, cfga, drkg wtr, playground, no showers. Boating(l), ball field, hiking, fishing. Note: During early 2015, park was closed temporarily for work on auxiliary spillway; check current status with lake office before arrival. **GPS: 36.080698, -98.599055**

CANADIAN RECREATION AREA

From Canton, 0.7 mi W on SR 51; 1.5 mi N on SR 58A; 0.8 mi W on secondary road. 4/1-10/31; 14-day limit. Loop B, 53 elec/no wtr sites $18 ($9 with federal senior pass); elec/wtr sites, $22 ($11 with senior pass). 10 sites have 50-amp elec. RV limit in excess of 65 ft.

Two group camping areas with elec, $209-266. Group shelter, $40. At reserved sites, 2-night minimum stay required on peak season weekends, 3 nights on holiday weekends. Note: 77-site Loop A damaged by tornado in 2012; re-opening summer of 2015 for $22 wtr/elec; check current status with lake office before arrival. Campground closed off-season during winter of 2013/14. Non-campers pay $3 daily for day area with boat ramps. (580) 886-3454. NRRS during 4/1-10/30. **GPS: 36.089858, -98.60895**

FAIRVIEW GROUP CAMP

Follow directions to Canadian Campground; after registering, return to SR 58A, then N across dam; at fork, continue right (E), then N on SR 58 to Longdale; continue 1 mi N, then 2.5 mi W on E0600 secondary rd, following signs to campground at jct with N472 Rd. 4/1-9/30; 14-day limit. Group camping area without elec for up to 100 people and 45 vehicles & 4 RVs with several tents, $50. Large shelter, 7 tbls, 4 gravel pads. 580-886-3454. NRRS. **GPS: 36.145000, -98.597660**

LONGDALE RECREATION AREA

From Longdale at jct with SR 58, 2 mi W on paved E0610 Rd; at E shore of lake. All year; 14-day limit. 35 primitive RV/tent sites, $11 during 4/1-10/31 ($5.50 with federal senior pass); free off-season but no amenities or wtr. Gatehouse closed by low lake level in 2015; self-pay registration required. 40-ft RV limit. Tbls, pit toilets, cfga, drkg wtr, playground, beach, picnic shelter $40. Boating(l), fishing, swimming, waterskiing. (580) 274-3454. NRRS during 4/1-10/31. **GPS: 36.130312, -98.581030**

SANDY COVE RECREATION AREA

From Canton, 0.7 mi W on SR 51; 5 mi N on SR 58A; left (N) on access rd; on SE shore of lake. 4/1-10/31; 14-day limit (closed off-season). 35 elec sites (no wtr hookups), $18 ($9 with federal senior pass). 40-ft RV limit. Tbls, flush & pit toilets, cfga, drkg wtr, showers, playground, beach, no dump, pay phone, picnic shelter $40. No day use fees. (580) 274-3576. NRRS. **GPS: 36.10658, -98.56853**

⑦ COPAN LAKE
GPS: 36.91, -95.94

A 4,850-acre lake W of Copan on the Little Caney River, located 2 miles W of US 75 on SR 10, N of Tulsa near the Kansas state line. Campground checkout time 4 p.m. Day use areas: Copan Point -- boat ramp, picnicking, group shelter ($25), beach, hiking trails; Osage Plains -- boat ramp. Non-campers pay $3 day use fees at boat ramps, $1 person at beach. Lake Manager, 39120 State Hwy 10, Copan, OK 74022. (918) 532-4334.

POST OAK RECREATION AREA

From just S of Copan on US 75, 3 mi W (over dam) on SR 10; 1.2 mi N on SR 10; then E on access rd; at SE shore of Copan Lake. 4/1-10/30; 14-day limit. 17 back-in elec sites (30-amp), $16 base, $18 at 2 full-hookup handicap sites ($8 & $9 with federal senior pass). RV limit in excess of 65 ft. Tbls, flush & pit toilets, cfga, new playground, dump, pay phone. (918) 532-4334. NRRS. **GPS: 36.89753, -95.96973**

WASHINGTON COVE RECREATION AREA

From NW corner of Copan, 0.3 mi W on W 800 Rd; 1 mi N on N3970 Rd; left on access rd, following signs; at SE shore of lake. 4/1-10/30; 14-day limit. 101 wtr/elec sites (30-amp), $16 ($8 with federal senior pass). RV limit in excess of 65 ft. Tbls, flush & pit toilets, cfga, drkg wtr, showers, pay phone, playground, dump, group picnic shelter $25. Ball fields, boating(ld), fishing, volleyball, hiking, horseback riding. Non-campers pay day use fees. (918) 532-4129. NRRS. **GPS: 36.907880, -95.957469**

⑧ EUFAULA LAKE
GPS: 35.3083, -95.3617

A 102,200-acre lake with 600 miles of shoreline, Eufaula is Oklahoma's largest lake. It is on the Canadian River, 27 miles upstream from the Arkansas River, 12 miles E of Eufaula on SR 71 and 31 miles S of Muskogee. Powerhouse tours by appointment. Visitor center.

Recreation facilities not managed by the Corps of Engineers include: Eufaula Cove Marina (concession); Arrowhead State Park (State of Oklahoma); Belle Starr Marina (concession); Highway 9 Landing Marina (concession marina); Eufaula Wildlife Management Area; Gaines Creek Unit -- primitive camping & boat ramp at Hickory Point area (State of Oklahoma); Crowder Point, Eufaula State Park; Evergreen Marina (concession); Juniper Point -- camping, boat ramp.

Corps-operated day use facilities: Ben O Carroll Overlook -- shelter, hiking trail; Cardinal Point -- boat ramp, picnicking, group shelter; Gaines Creek -- boat ramp; Hickory Point -- boat ramp, picnicking; Holiday Cove -- boat ramp. Non-campers pay day use fees at Highway Landing and Porum Landing beaches; other swimming areas free; fees also charged non-campers at Corps boat ramps. Lake Manager, Eufaula Lake, 102 E BK 200 Rd, Stigler, OK 74462. (918) 799-5843.

BELLE STARR RECREATION AREA

From I-40 S of Checotah, 7 mi S on US 69 to SR 150 jct; 2 mi E on Texanna Rd (E 1140 Rd); 2 mi S on N4200 Rd (Belle Starr Rd), following signs; on right. 4/1-9/30; 14-day limit. 111 elec/wtr sites, $18 for 30-amp elec, $20 for 50-amp ($9 & $10 with federal senior pass). RV limit in excess of 65 ft; 36 pull-through sites. Tbls, flush toilets, cfga, drkg wtr, showers, dump, playground, change house at beach, two picnic shelters $50. Boating(ld), fishing, hiking, swimming, hiking trails. Non-campers pay day use fees for beach, dump, boat ramp. NRRS. **GPS: 35.332567, -95.539679**

BROOKEN COVE RECREATION AREA

From Enterprise, 5 mi N on SR 71 toward dam, then NW following signs. 4/1-9/30; 14-day limit. 73 elec sites (no wtr hookups), $18 for 30-amp elec, $20 for 50-amp ($9 & $10 with federal senior pass); 8 pull-through sites. 60-ft RV limit. Tbls, flush toilets, cfga, drkg wtr, dump, beach, showers, playground, 2 group picnic shelters $50. Boating(ld), fishing, swimming, hiking trails. Non-campers pay day use fee for boat ramp. NRRS. **GPS: 35.288244, -95.400252**

DAMSITE EAST RECREATION AREA

From Enterprise, 7 mi N on SR 71; cross dam, then follow SR 71 curving SE; right (S) on second rd into small campground; below dam near N shore of Canadian River. 4/1-10/31; 14-day limit. 10 elec sites, $13 ($6.50 with federal senior pass). During off-season, some sites open & free but no amenities. Tbls, toilets, cfga, drkg wtr. Fishing, boating. **GPS: 35.305289, -95.353485**

DAM SITE SOUTH RECREATION AREA

From Enterprise, 7 mi N on SR 71; across dam from Damsite East, then W, following signs. 4/1-9/30; 14-day limit. 5 tent sites & 8 primitive RV/tent sites, $12; 44 elec sites (no wtr hookups), $18 base, $20 at premium locations ($6, $9 & $10 with federal senior pass). 55-ft RV limit. Tbls, flush toilets, cfga, drkg wtr, showers, dump, playground, beach with change house. Hiking trails, swimming, boating(ld), fishing. Non-campers pay day use fee for boat ramp, beach, dump. Group picnic shelter, $50. NRRS. **GPS: 35.299471, -95.370147**

ELM POINT RECREATION AREA

From McAlester at jct with US 69, 12 mi NE on SR 31, then NW on Elm Point access rd, following signs. 3/1-10/31; 14-day limit. 17 elec sites (no wtr hookups), $13 ($6.50 with federal senior pass), $9 off-season but no utilities or restrooms. No reservations. **GPS: 35.010842, -95.600088**

GENTRY CREEK RECREATION AREA

From Checotah, 9 mi W on US 266, then S on access rd following signs. 4/1-10/31; 14-day limit. 16 primitive RV/tent sites, $13; 15 elec sites, $18 ($6.50 & $9 with federal senior pass). 50-ft RV limit; 3 pull-through sites. Tbls, flush toilets, cfga, drkg wtr, showers, dump. Boating(l), fishing. NRRS. **GPS: 35.495347, -95.671123**

MILL CREEK BAY RECREATION AREA

From Eufaula at jct with US 69, 6 mi W on SR 9; 2 mi S on CR N4110; just N of lake bridge, turn right into campground. 3/1-10/31; 14-day limit. 12 primitive sites, $9 ($4.50 with federal senior pass). Pit toilets, tbls, cfga, drkg wtr, shelter. Boating(ll), fishing. Non-campers pay $3 day use fee for boat ramp. **GPS: 35.257430, -95.700220**

OAK RIDGE RECREATION AREA

From Eufaula at jct with US 69, 6 mi S to just across Canadian River bridge, then turn NE on SR 9A into campground on right. 3/1-10/31; 14-day limit. 5 primitive sites, $9; 8 elec sites (no wtr hookups), $13 ($4.50 & $6.50 with federal senior pass). Off-season, some sites may be open & free but no amenities. Tbls, toilets, cfga, drkg wtr. Boating(ld), fishing. **GPS: 35.215689, -95.602536**

9

FORT GIBSON LAKE
GPS: 35.98, -95.29

A 19,900-acre lake 5 miles NW of Ft. Gibson on SR 251A from the Muskogee Turnpike on the Grand (Neosho) River. Park attendants collect camping fees 4/1-9/30, and campers pay by self-deposit off-season. Campsites that are free in the off-season may have reduced amenities. Day-use facilities include boat ramps at Dam Site East, Harbor Cliff, Sunset Valley Mallard Bay, Mission Bend, Taylor Ferry North and Toppers Park. Swimming beaches at Rocky Point and Taylor Ferry. Non-campers pay $3 day use fees for boat ramps, $1 person at beaches. Facilities not operated by the Corps of Engineers include Jackson Bay Marina (concession); Long Bay Landing (concession); Mazie Landing Marina (concession); Pryor Creek Park; Taylor Ferry Marina (concession); Sequoyah Bay Park; Sequoyah State Park. Lake Manager, Fort Gibson Lake, 8568 State Highway 251A, Ft. Gibson, OK 74434-0370. (918) 682-4314.

BLUE BILL POINT CAMP

From Wagoner at jct with SR 51, 6 mi N on US 69; 3 mi E/NE on E680 Rd & E670 Rd, following signs; at shore of lake's Flat Rock Bay. All year; 14-day limit. 3 primitive sites, $11-$14; 40 elec/wtr sites, $16 for 30-amp elec, $20 for 50-amp elec ($5.50-$7 at primitive sites, $8 & $10 at elec sites with federal senior pass). Fees not reduced off-season. RV limit in excess of 65 ft. Tbls, pit & flush toilets, cfga, drkg wtr, dump, picnic shelter with elec, $50. Boating(ld), fishing. Non-campers pay $3 day use fee for boat ramp, dump station. NRRS. **GPS: 36.043131, -95.333623**

DAM SITE CAMPGROUND

From Okay, 6 mi E on SR 251A; S on access rd below dam on W side of outlet. All year; 14-day limit. 48 elec/wtr sites, $15 for 30-amp, $20 for 50-amp ($7.50 & $10 with federal senior pass). RV limit in excess of 65 ft. Tbls, flush toilets, cfga, drkg wtr, showers, dump, pay phone, two picnic shelters with elec, $50. Boating(l), fishing. Non-campers pay $3 day use fee for boat ramp, dump station. NRRS. **GPS: 35.868071, -95.234055**

FLAT ROCK CREEK CAMP

From Wagoner, 8 mi N on US 69; 3 mi E on E660 Rd; 2 mi S on S320 Rd; 1 mi W on E670 Rd. 3/1-11/30; 14-day limit. 2 primitive sites, $14; 36 elec/wtr sites, $18 for 30-amp, $20 for 50-amp ($7, $9 & $10 with federal senior pass). RV limit in excess of 65 ft. Tbls, flush & pit toilets, cfga, drkg wtr, dump, picnic shelter

$50. Boating(l), fishing. Non-campers pay day use fee for boat ramp, dump station. NRRS 4/1-9/30. **GPS: 36.047178, -95.327739**

JACKSON BAY RECREATION AREA

From Wagoner, about 3.5 mi S on SR 16; 4 mi E on 100th St N; 2 mi N on S340 Rd; left on access rd. Free primitive sites near shore of lake. All year; 14-day limit. Tbls, pit toilet, cfga, no drkg wtr. Boating(l), fishing. **GPS: 35.909266, -95.2910742**

MISSION BEND RECREATION AREA

From just S of Mazie on US 69, 4 mi E on W630 Rd; 1 mi N on S433 Rd (Rocking Rd); 1.5 mi E on W620 Rd (Mission Bend Rd); 1 mi N on S4345 Rd; right on access rd, following signs; at W shore of Neosho River. All year; 14-day limit. Free designated sites. Tbls, cfga, no toilets, no drkg wtr. Boating(l), fishing. **GPS: 36.129010, -95.268452**

ROCKY POINT CAMPGROUND

From Wagoner at jct with SR 51, 5 mi N on US 69; 1.8 mi E on SR 251D Rd; 1 mi N on N4310 Rd, following signs. All year; 14-day limit. 3 primitive sites, $14; 57 elec/wtr sites, $18 for 30-amp, $20 for 50-amp ($7, $9 & $10 with federal senior pass). RV limit in excess of 65 ft. Tbls, flush & pit toilets, cfga, drkg wtr, dump, beach with change house, showers, picnic shelter with elec, $50. Non-campers pay $3 day use fee for beach, boat ramp, dump station. NRRS. **GPS: 36.03306, -95.31639**

TAYLOR FERRY SOUTH CAMP

From Wagoner at jct with US 69, 8 mi E on SR 51; S before bridge on access rd. All year; 14-day limit. 6 non-elec sites, $14; 85 elec/wtr sites, $16 for 30-amp elec, $20 for 50-amp ($7, $8 & $10 with federal senior pass). RV limit in excess of 65 ft. Tbls, flush & pit toilets, cfga, drkg wtr, showers, dump. Boating(l), fishing, picnic shelters. Non-campers pay $3 day use fee for boat ramp, dump station. (918) 485-4792. NRRS. **GPS: 35.935930, -95.281554**

WAHOO BAY RECREATION AREA

From Okay at jct with SR 16, 0.5 mi E on SR 251A; 2 mi N on Sequoyah Bay Rd; 1 mi E on 100th St N; 0.5 mi S on S340 Rd, then E to bay on SW shore of lake. Free primitive designated sites. Pit toilet, cfga, tbls, no drkg wtr. **GPS: 35.879165, -95.277445**

WILDWOOD CAMPGROUND

From Hulbert, 5 mi W on SR 80. All year; 14-day limit. 30 elec/wtr sites, $18 for 30-amp, 30 for 50-amp ($9 & $10 with federal senior pass). RV limit in excess of 65 ft; 9 pull-through sites. Tbls, pit & flush toilets, cfga, drkg wtr, dump, showers, picnic shelter with elec, $50. Boating(l), fishing. Non-campers pay $3 day use fee for boat ramp, dump station. NRRS. **GPS: 35.918785, -95.210357**

⑩ FORT SUPPLY LAKE
GPS: 36.55, -99.5667

A 1,820-acre lake 15 miles NW of Woodward on US 183 and 1 mile SE of Fort Supply in northwestern Oklahoma near the panhandle, Fort Supply is on Wolf Creek. Visitor center features exhibits of Indian arrowheads, old camp supply artifacts, wildlife display. The Corps operates two multi-use recreation areas. Lake Manager, Fort Supply Lake, Route 1, Box 175, Fort Supply, OK 73841. (580) 766-2701.

BEAVER POINT CAMPGROUND

From E edge of Fort Supply at US 270, 2 mi S on N1930 Rd; 1 mi SE across dam to Crappie Cove section. 4/1-10/31; 14-day limit. 16 primitive sites, $12 ($6 with federal senior pass). Pit toilets, some tbls, no drkg wtr, beach. Boating(l), fishing, swimming. Rest of Beaver Point and all of Wolf Creek Public Use Areas are for day use and lake access; camping is prohibited. Non-campers pay $3 day use fee for boat ramp. **GPS: 36.543614, -99.554876**

SUPPLY PARK CAMPGROUND

From E edge of Fort Supply at US 270, 2 mi S on N1930 Rd; at 4-way stop, turn left on access rd (E0320 Rd); along lakeshore W of dam. All year; 14-day limit. 16 non-elec sites, $16; 94 elec sites, $21 for 30-amp, $23 for 50-amp ($8, $10.50 & $11.50 with federal senior pass). Off-season fees by self-deposit; showers & waterborne restrooms closed off-season until 4/1; pit toilets open. RV limit in excess of 65 ft; 14 pull-through sites. Tbls, flush & pit toilets, cfga, drkg wtr, showers, dump, playground, pay phone, picnic shelter with elec, $160. Non-campers pay day use fees (self-deposit) for boat ramp, beach. Non-camper fee also for using dump station. Handicap accessible fishing area. (580) 755-2001. NRRS during 5/1-9/14. **GPS: 36.548940, -99.575250**

⑪ HEYBURN LAKE
GPS: 35.9467, -96.305

A 920-acre lake 13 miles SW of Sapulpa, 2 miles from US 66 and 26 miles SW of Tulsa off I-44. The lake is on Polecat Creek with 52 miles of shoreline and has four campgrounds. Lake Manager, Heyburn Lake, 27349 W. Heyburn Lake Rd, Kellyville, OK 74039-9615. (918) 247-6391.

HEYBURN CAMPGROUND

From SR 66 just W of Heyburn, 3 mi N on S273rd Ave W; 0.5 mi W on W151st St; at W side of dam. 4/1-10/31; 14-day limit. 45 wtr/elec sites: 30-amp sites $14, 50-amp sites $15, premium sites with close lake access $16 ($7, $7.50 & $8 with federal senior pass). 10 pull-through. Tbls, flush toilets, showers, cfga, drkg wtr, dump, playground, beach, amphitheater, change house, picnic shelter ($25). Group camping area, $100. Boating(ld), fishing, swimming. Non-campers pay $3 day use fee for beach, boat ramp, dump. (918) 247-6601. NRRS during 3/30-9/28. **GPS: 35.947005, -96.307440**

ROCKY POINT CAMPGROUND

From Bristow, 10 mi N on SR 48; 3.5 mi E on SR 33; 2 mi S on 305th W. Ave; 2 mi E on W141st St S; S on access rd; at N side of lake just E of Sheppard Point. $7. All year; 14-day limit. Primitive tent sites along equestrian trail; no services. Check in at Sheppard Point Campground.

SHEPPARD POINT CAMP

From I-44 exit 211 just W of Sapulpa, about 7 mi E on SR 33; 2 mi S on 305th W. Ave; 1 mi E on W141st St S, then right (S) on access rd; at N side of lake. 4/1-10/31; 14-day limit. 17 tent sites, $10 ($5 with federal senior pass); 21 elec/wtr RV/tent sites, $14 base, $16 at premium locations ($7 & $8 with federal senior pass). RV limit in excess of 65 ft. Some equestrian sites. Tbls, flush toilets, cfga, drkg wtr, dump, playground, beach, 2 group picnic shelters ($50 elec, $25 non-elec). Boating(ld), hiking, fishing, swimming, horseback riding. (918) 247-4551. NRRS during 4/1-9/28. **GPS: 35.953241, -96.312971**

SUNSET BAY CAMPGROUND

From SR 66 just E of Heyburn, 3 mi N on S257th W Ave; right (W) on Heyburn Lake Rd; at NE side of dam (6 mi W of Kellyville). All year; 14-day limit. 14 primitive sites, $8 ($4 with federal senior pass). Non-campers pay $3 day use fee for boat ramp, beach, dump station. **GPS: 35.951469, -96.289823**

⑫ HUGO LAKE
GPS: 34.0167. -95.3767

A 13,250-acre lake 6 miles E of Hugo on US 70 about 30 miles N of Paris, Texas, in southeastern Oklahoma on the Kiamichi River; it has 110 miles of shoreline. In addition to the campgrounds, boat ramps are at Frazier Point, Salt Creek, Sawyer Bluff and Wilson Point, which also has picnic facilities, a playground and beach. 9 horse stalls available on Raccoon Rd in Kiamichi Park

for equestrian campers. Lake Manager, Hugo Lake, P. O. Box 99, Sawyer, OK 74756-0099. (580) 326-3345.

HUGO LAKE GROUP CAMP

From just E of Sawyer at jct with US 70, 3.5 mi N on SR 147, then l mi W & 0.6 mi S (2.6 mi on county road). All year; 14-day limit Four group camping areas, each with 5 elec/wtr sites, group shelter, $75. Tbls, flush toilets, cfga, drkg wtr, dump, playground, beach, change house. Boating(ld), boating, fishing, swimming. NRRS. **GPS: 34.0575, -95.38472**

KIAMICHI PARK

From Hugo, 6.8 mi E on US 70; 1 mi N on CR N4285, then left on access rd, following signs; at S shore of lake near Hugo Lake State Park. 3/1-12/31; 14-day limit. 24 non-elec sites, $12 ($6 with federal senior pass); 37 elec sites (no wtr hookups), $15 ($7.50 with senior pass); 62 elec/wtr sites, $18 ($9 with senior pass); 5 full-hookups, $22 ($11 with senior pass). RV limit in excess of 65 ft. Tbls, flush toilets, cfga, drkg wtr, showers, dump, playground, change house, beach, two picnic shelters ($25). Nature trail, equestrian trail, archery range, equestrian trail, paved biking/hiking trail. Non-campers pay $3 day use fee for boat ramp, beach, dump station. One camping loop remains open in winter for archery deer hunters. NRRS during 3/30-9/29. Call lake office for off-season reservations. **GPS: 34.021938, -95.421799**

RATTAN LANDING CAMP

From Rattan, 4 mi W on SR 3/7, then S on access rd before bridge; at E shore of Kiamichi River above lake. All year; 14-day limit. 13 elec/wtr sites, $12 ($6 with federal senior pass). Tbls, toilets, cfga, drkg wtr. Boating(l), fishing. Non-campers pay $3 day use fee for boat ramp. **GPS: 34.197374, -95.483766**

VIRGIL POINT CAMPGROUND

From just E of Hugo on US 70, 2 mi N on SR

147; right on E2040 Rd, then immediate left (S) on access rd; at SE shore of lake. All year; 14-day limit. 52 elec/wtr sites, $15 base, $22 at premium locations ($7.50 & $11 with federal senior pass). 55-ft RV limit. Tbls, flush toilets, cfga, drkg wtr, showers, dump,. Boating(l), fishing, hiking, biking. NRRS during 4/1-9/30. Reserve off-season sites by phoning lake office. GPS: 34.048784, -95.379449

KAW LAKE
ARKANSAS RIVER
GPS: 36.7017, -96.933

A 17,000-acre lake 8 miles E of Ponca City off US 60, 70 miles NE of Enid on the Arkansas River. 168-mile shoreline. Campground checkout time 4 p.m. Day use facilities: Burbank Landing -- boat ramp; Fisherman's Bend -- picnicking; Pioneer Park -- boat ramp, marina, picnicking, group shelter, beach; Traders Bend -- boat ramp. Two 12-mile trails: Eagle View Hiking Trail between Osage Cove and Burbank Landing, and Five Fingers Equestrian Trail south from Sarge Creek to Burbank Landing. Two concessions operate marinas: McFadden Cove and Pioneer Cove. Lake Manager, Kaw Lake, 9400 Lake Road, Ponca City, OK 74604-9629. (580) 762-5611.

BEAR CREEK COVE RECREATION AREA

From Newkirk, 7 mi E on Peckham Rd (E. River Rd); 3 mi S on Bear Creek Rd to area where Bear Creek enters lake along E shore. 3/1-11/30; 14-day limit. 22 elec/wtr sites, $15 ($7.50 with federal senior pass). 40-ft RV limit. Tbls, flush toilets, cfga, dump, drkg wtr, picnic shelter. Boating(ld), fishing. (580) 362-4189. NRRS during 5/1-9/30.
GPS: 36.839859, -96.910722

COON CREEK COVE RECREATION AREA

From Ponca City, 4 mi N on US 77; 6 mi E on SR 11, 1 mi N on Rocky Ridge Rd; at W

shore where Coon Creek enters lake. 3/1-ll/30; 14-day limit. 12 primitive sites, $12; 54 elec/wtr sites, $16 & $18 ($6, $8 & $9 with federal senior pass). 55-ft RV limit. Tbls, flush toilets, cfga, drkg wtr, dump. Boating(ld), fishing, hiking trails. Non-campers pay $3 day use fee for boat ramp. (580) 362-2466. NRRS during 4/1-9/30. GPS: 36.782583, -96.919498

MCFADDEN COVE RECREATION AREA

From Ponca City at US 77, 7 mi E on Lake Rd; after curve to S, left (E) on access rd; at SE shore of lake N side of dam. 3/1-11/30; 14-day limit. 15 non-elec sites, $14 ($7 with federal senior pass). Tbls, toilets, cfga, drkg wtr, picnic shelter. Boating(ld), fishing. Non-campers pay day use fee at boat ramp. No reservations.
GPS: 36.704760, -96.934203

OSAGE COVE RECREATION AREA

From Ponca City at US 77, 9 mi E on Lake Rd, across dam on Kaw Dam Rd; 0.5 mi E on E 20th Rd; 2 mi N on Osage Cove Rd, 1 mi W on Osage Park Rd to SE shore of lake. 3/1-11/30; 14-day limit. 94 elec sites (no wtr hookups), $18 ($9 with federal senior pass). 60-ft RV limit. 1 RV & 1 tent or 2 tents per site. Tbls, flush toilets, showers, cfga, drkg wtr, dump, playground, amphitheater, picnic shelter. Group camping areas with elec, $75-$100. Hiking, nature trail, boating(ld), fishing, horseback riding. Non-campers pay day use fee for boat ramp, dump station. (580) 762-9408. NRRS (4/1-9/30). GPS: 36.71317, -96.89835

SANDY PARK

From Ponca City at US 77, 9 mi E on Lake Rd, across dam on Kaw Dam Rd; 0.5 mi below dam on E side. 4/1-10/1; 14-day limit. 12 elec sites (no wtr hookups), $16 ($8 with federal senior pass). Tbls, toilets, cfga, drkg wtr. Boating(l), fishing. Boat ramp free.
GPS: 36.696289, -96.924072

SARGE CREEK COVE RECREATION AREA

From Kaw City, 2.8 mi E on SR 11 across bridge, then S on access rd, following signs; at Sarge Creek arm on east-central section of lake. 3/1-11/30; 14-day limit. 51 elec/wtr sites, $18 ($9 with federal senior pass). 60-ft RV limit. Sites 1-7 with horse pens available for equestrians. Tbls, flush toilets, cfga, drkg wtr, dump, playground, amphitheater, picnic shelter. Group camping area with elec, $100. Equestrian trail, ATV trail, hiking, fishing, boating(ld). Non-campers pay day use fees at boat ramp, dump. (580) 269-2303. NRRS (4/1-9/30). **GPS: 36.76665, -96.808197**

WASHUNGA BAY RECREATION AREA

From Kaw City, 2.6 mi E on SR 11 across bridge; 0.6 mi NE on county rd; 4.5 mi W on E. Ferguson Rd, across a second bridge, then right into park, following signs; at SW mouth of Washunga Bay section of lake. 3/1-11/30; 14-day limit. 11 non-elec sites, $12 ($6 with federal senior pass); 24 elec/wtr sites, $16 base, $18 at premium locations ($8 & $9 with senior pass). 60-ft RV limit. 1 RV & 1 tent or 2 tents per site. Tbls, flush toilets, cfga, drkg wtr, dump, showers. Boating(ld), fishing, hiking. Non-campers pay day use fee at boat ramps, dump. (580) 269-2220. NRRS (5/1-9/15). **GPS: 36.791691, -96.838732**

⑭

KEYSTONE LAKE
ARKANSAS RIVER
GPS: 36.15. -96.2533

A 26,000-acre lake on the Arkansas 15 miles W of Tulsa on US 412 and SR 51 with 330 miles of shoreline. Powerhouse tours by reservation. The lake has 16 recreation areas, 11 boat ramps, 2 ORV areas, 5 trails and nine swimming beaches. Non-campers are charged day use fees at Corps boat ramps and beaches. Day use facilities: Swift County Park -- boat ramp below dam; Cowskin Bay N -- boat ramp; Osage Ramp -- boat ramp; Pawnee Cove -- boat ramp, New Mannford Ramp -- boat ramp (City of Mannford); Keystone Ramp -- boat ramp, picnicking, beach. Privately operated facilities include Keyport Marina & Westport Marina. City of Mannford now leases Salt Creek Cove North Recreation Area from the Corps & plans to sub-lease it for a proposed Jellystone Camp Resort and commercial marina development. The State of Oklahoma operates Keystone State Park. The state has canceled its lease of Walnut Creek State Parks, and in 2015 the Corps was operating the campground there and seeking a lease partner to manage the facility. Visitor center. Lake Manager, Keystone Lake, 23115 W Wekiwa Road, Sand Springs, OK 74063-9312. (918) 865-2621.

APPALACHIA BAY CAMP

From Sand Springs, 10.1 mi W on US 64; 2 mi SW on Appalachia Bay Rd. All year; 14-day limit. 28 very primitive sites, $8 ($4 with federal senior pass). Tbls, toilets, cfga, drkg wtr, beach. Boating(l), fishing, swimming, ATV trail. Non-campers pay day use fee for boat ramp, beach & use of ATV facility. **GPS: 36.185256, -96.296153**

BRUSH CREEK CAMPGROUND

From Sand Springs, 8 mi W on US 64; 0.25 mi S on SR 151; right (SE) on W. Wekiwa Rd, then left (S) into campground; below dam, N side of spillway at Brush Creek. All year; 14-day limit. 5 elec sites, $15 base; $20 at 15 premium elec/wtr sites ($7.50-$10 with federal senior pass). Tbls, flush toilets, cfga, drkg wtr, dump, showers. Fishing, boating. Non-campers pay day use fee for dump station. **GPS: 36.150169, -96.247305**

COWSKIN BAY SOUTH CAMP

13 mi NW of Sand Springs on US 64; 1 mi NW on Old Keystone Rd (Old US 64) past town of Westport. All year; 14-day limit. 30 free primitive undesignated sites. No RV size limit. Tbls, toilets, cfga, drkg wtr. Boating(ld), fishing. **GPS: 36.229361, -96.374803**

KEYSTONE RAMP RECREATION AREA

From Mannford, about 3 mi E on SR 51, then N on Tower Rd (becoming Coyote Trail), following signs. All year; 14-day limit. 6 free primitive undesignated sites. Pit toilets, no drkg wtr. No day use fees. Fishing, boating(l).
GPS: 36.158425, -96.287098

WALNUT CREEK STATE PARK

From town of Prue (NW of Tulsa), 2 mi W on CR 1200; 2 mi S on CR 1521 to park on N shore of lake. 4/1-10/30; 14-day limit. 140 sites, including 8 full hookups & 71 elec/wtr sites. Contact lake office for fees. Tbls, flush toilets, cfga, drkg wtr, beaches, showers, picnic shelter. Boating(ld), fishing, swimming, ball fields, volleyball, horseback riding, hiking, nature trail, mountain biking. Closed in 2014 as state park, operated in 2015 by Corps of Engineers.
GPS: 36.238321, -96.280832

WASHINGTON IRVING SOUTH

From Sand Springs, 10.1 mi W on US 64, across lake bridge to Bears Glen exit; left at stop sign onto Frontage Rd for 1 block; right at first paved rd for 2 mi to park entrance at W shore of lake. 4/1-10/31; 14-day limit. 2 primitive sites, $10 ($5 with federal senior pass); 38 elec sites (no wtr hookups), $16 base, $17 at premium locations ($8 & $8.50 with federal senior pass). RV limit in excess of 65 ft. Tbls, flush toilets, cfga, drkg wtr, showers, dump, beach, playground. Hiking, nature trail, swimming, boating(ld), fishing (918) 865-9312. Non-campers pay day use fees for boat ramp, beach, dump station. NRRS (4/1-9/15).
GPS: 36.197985, -96.258645

⑮
LAKE TEXOMA
DENNISON DAM
GPS: 33.76, -96.46

Located 5 miles N of Denison, Texas, in south-central Oklahoma on the state line,

Lake Texoma has 88,000 acres with 580 miles of shoreline; it is on the Red River at its confluence with the Washita River. The Corps manages 54 parks, including 10 campgrounds with more than 700 campsites. Some 25 mi of equestrian trails are available, along with the 14-mile Cross Timbers hiking trail. Off-road vehicles prohibited. Lake Manager, Lake Texoma, 351 Corps Road, Denison, TX 75020. (903) 465-4990. See Texas listings.

BUNCOMBE CREEK CAMP

From Kingston, 4 mi W on SR 32; 7 mi S on SR 99; 2 mi E on Willis Beach Rd, following signs; at N side of lake along E shore of Buncombe Creek Cove. 4/15-9/30; 14-day limit; closed off-season. $20 at 54 elec/wtr 30-amp sites. 45-ft RV limit. Pit & flush toilets, tbls, cfga, drkg wtr, dump, showers, picnic shelter. Nature trail, hiking, boating(ld), fishing. (580) 564-2901. NRRS (4/1-9/30).
GPS: 33.896762, -96.809742

BURNS RUN EAST CAMP

From Colbert, 4 mi W on SR 75A to Cartwright, then W on Main St & SW on Boat Club Rd, following signs; on E shore of Burns Run Cove, just NW of Denison Dam. All year; 14-day limit. During 4/1-9/30, 3 primitive tent sites, $15; 25 elec/wtr 30-amp sites, $20; 19 elec/wtr 50-amp sites, $24 ($7.50, $10 & $12 with federal senior pass). During 10/1-3/31, all available sites (no wtr hookups), $12 ($6 with federal senior pass); wtr at frost-free hydrant near park entrance; no showers or bathroom facilities; payment by honor deposit. RV limit in excess of 65 ft. Tbls, flush & pit toilets, cfga, drkg wtr, showers, dump, beach, playground, 4 picnic shelters with elec ($50). Nature trail, hiking, boating(ld), fishing, swimming. Non-campers pay day use fee for boat ramp, dump station. (580) 965-4660. NRRS (4/1-9/30).
GPS: 33.848517, -96.580102

OKLAHOMA

BURNS RUN WEST CAMP

From Colbert, 4 mi W on SR 75A to Cartwright, then 1 mi W on Main St; 2 mi N on Boat Club Rd; 3 mi W & S on West Burns Run Rd; at SE shore of lake, W of Burns Run Cove. 4/1-9/30; 14-day limit (closed off-season). 11 tent sites, $12; 84 elec/wtr 30-amp sites, $20 base; 21 elec/wtr 50-amp sites, $24 ($6, $10 & $12 with federal senior pass). RV limit in excess of 65 ft; 43 pull-through. Tbls, flush & pit toilets, cfga, drkg wtr, showers, dump, playground, beach, 2 picnic shelters with elec ($50). 5 group camping areas with elec, $100. Boating(l), fishing, swimming, waterskiing, hiking. Non-campers pay day use fee for boat ramp, dump station. (580) 965-4922. NRRS (4/1-9/30). **GPS: 33.864750, -96.592441**

CANEY CREEK CAMPGROUND

From Kingston, 3 mi S on Donahoo St (Rock Creek Rd); 2 mi E on E Lasiter Rd; 2 mi S on Muncrief Rd (N3510 Rd); on N shore of lake at mouth of Caney Creek Cove. All year; 14-day limit. During 4/1-9/30, 10 non-elec sites $15; 23 elec/wtr 30-amp sites $20, 19 elec/wtr 50-amp sites $22 ($7.50, $10 & $11 with federal senior pass). During 10/1-3/31, all available RV sites $12 ($6 with senior pass); no wtr hookups, but frost-free hydrant at park entrance; payment by honor deposit. RV limit in excess of 65 ft. Tbls, flush & pit toilets, cfga, drkg wtr, dump, playground, beach, picnic shelter with elec ($50). Non-campers pay day use fee at dump station. (580) 564-2632. NRRS (4/1-9/30). **GPS: 33.929982, -96.705512**

DAM SITE NORTH AREA

From Colbert, 5 mi W (through Cartwright) & S on SR 75A; at Oklahoma side of dam (5 mi N of Denison, TX). Camping no longer permitted.

JOHNSON CREEK CAMP

From Durant, 10 mi W on US 70; N side of road before causeway. All year; 14-day limit. During 4/1-9/30, 53 paved elec/wtr sites (9 have covered tbls), $20 for 30-amp sites, $22 for 50-amp ($10 & $11 with federal senior pass); double sites $40. During 10/1-3/31, 20 elec sites (no wtr hookups) are $12 ($6 with senior pass); shower & bathroom facilities closed; wtr from frost-free hydrant near park entrance; payment by honor deposit. RV limit in excess of 65 ft. Tbls, pit & flush toilets, cfga, drkg wtr, dump, picnic shelter with elec ($50). Boating(ld), fishing, hiking. Non-campers pay day use fee for dump station, boat ramp. (580) 924-7316. NRRS (5/1-9/7). **GPS: 33.998419, -96.570125**

LAKESIDE CAMPGROUND

From Durant, 10 mi W on US 70; 4 mi S on Streetman Rd. All year; 14-day limit. During 4/1-9/30, 4 tent sites, $15; 109 elec/wtr 30-amp sites, $20; 26 elec/wtr 50-amp sites, $22 ($7.50, $10 & $11 with federal senior pass). During 10/1-3/31, all available elec RV sites (no wtr hookups), $12 ($6 with senior pass); shower & bathroom facilities closed; wtr from frost-free hydrant near B Area entrance; payment by honor deposit. RV limit in excess of 65 ft. Tbls, flush & pit toilets, cfga, drkg wtr, dump, playground, fish cleaning stations, picnic shelter with elec ($50). Equestrian trail, boating(ld), fishing, waterskiing. Non-campers pay day use fee for boat ramp, dump stations. (580) 920-0176. NRRS (4/15-9/30). Note: new 50-amp elec service is planned. **GPS: 33.938928, -96.552744**

PLATTER FLATS CAMPGROUND

From Durant, 5 mi S on US 69; 6 mi W on Platter Rd N; 2 mi N on Platter Rd; 1 mi SW on Trail Ride Rd; on NE shore of lake at Rock Creek Cove. All year; 14-day limit. During 4/1-9/30, $15 at 3 non-elec sites; $20 at 43 elec/wtr 30-amp sites; $22 at 19 elec/wtr 50-amp sites ($7.50, $10 & $11 with federal senior pass). Sites A1-A57 available for equestrians but open to all. During 10/1-3/31, 58 elec sites (no wtr hookups), $12 ($6 with senior pass); shower & bathroom facilities closed; wtr from frost-free hydrant near park entrance; payment by honor deposit. RV limit in excess of 65 ft. Tbls, pit & flush toilets, cfga, drkg wtr, dump, two picnic shelters ($50). Equestrian trails, hiking, boating(l), fishing. (580) 434-5864. NRRS (4/1-9/30). **GPS: 33.921889, -96.547637**

16

OOLOGAH LAKE
GPS: 36.4233. -95.6783

A 29,500-acre lake 2 miles SE of Oologah on SR 88, 25 miles NE of Tulsa and NW of I-44. Campground checkout time 4 p.m. Day use facilities include Corps boat ramps at Allens Point, Big Creek Park, Clermont I Park, Redbud Bay and Winganon Ramp. Overlook Park has picnicking. 18-mi Will Rogers Country Centennial Trail on E side of the lake with horseback riding & hiking. Project Officer, 8400 E. Hwy 88, Oologah, OK 74053-0700. (918) 443-2250.

BIG CREEK RAMP CAMP

From Nowata, 5.1 mi E on US 60; 2 mi N on SR 28; 1 mi W on EO200 Rd; on Verdigris River N of lake. All year; 14-day limit. 16 free primitive sites. Pit toilets, tbls, cfga, drkg wtr. Boating(l), fishing. **GPS: 36.729929, -95.541149**

BLUE CREEK RECREATION AREA

From Foyil, 4 mi W on EW400 Rd; 1.2 mi N on NS4180 Rd; 1.5 mi W on gravel EW390 Rd, following signs; at SE shore of lake. 4/1-10/31; 14-day limit. 1 tent site & 36 non-elec RV/tent sites, $16; 22 elec sites (no wtr hookups), $20 ($8 & $10 with federal senior pass). RV limit in excess of 65 ft. Tbls, flush & pit toilets, cfga, drkg wtr, playground, dump, showers, picnic shelter ($50). Bridle trail; horses allowed in one loop. Boating(l), fishing, swimming, waterskiing. Non-campers pay day use fee for dump station, boat ramp. (918) 341-4244. NRRS. **GPS: 36.452308, -95.593817**

HAWTHORN BLUFF RECREATION AREA

From Oologah at jct with US 169, 1.5 mi E on SR 88; right on access rd, following signs.

4/1-10/31; 14-day limit. 15 non-elec sites, $16; 41 elec sites (30-amp, no wtr hookups), $20 ($8 & $10 with federal senior pass). RV limit in excess of 65 ft. Tbls, flush & pit toilets, cfga, drkg wtr, dump, playground, beach, amphitheater, pay phone, change house, three group picnic shelters ($50). Hiking trail, interpretive trail, fishing, sailing, boating(ld), fishing, swimming, waterskiing. Non-campers pay day use fees for boat ramp, dump station, beach. (918) 443-2319. NRRS (4/1-9/30). **GPS: 36.429328, -95.6787773**

REDBUD BAY RECREATION AREA

From Oologah, 3.2 mi E on SR 88; at E side of dam. 4/1-10/31; 14-day limit. 12 elec/wtr sites, $16 ($8 with federal senior pass). Tbls, toilets, cfga, drkg wtr. Marine dump station & concessionaire services. Boating(ld), fishing. No reservations. Non-campers pay day use fee for boat ramp. **GPS: 36.418382, -95.665748**

SPENCER CREEK RECREATION AREA

From Foyil, 6 mi N on NS4200 Rd; 2 mi W on EW350 Rd; 1 mi N on NS4180 Rd, then left (W) on access rd, following signs. 22 non-elec sites, $16; 29 elec sites (30-amp, no wtr hookups), $20 ($8 & $10 with federal senior pass). RV limit in excess of 65 ft. Tbls, flush & pit toilets, cfga, drkg wtr, dump, showers, playground, beach, pay phone, group picnic shelter ($50). Non-campers pay day use fees for boat ramp, beach, dump station. (918) 341-3690. NRRS during 4/1-9/30. **GPS: 36.519294, -95.560241**

VERDIGRIS RIVER RECREATION AREA

From Oologah at jct with US 169, 3.1 mi E on SR 88, below the dam, then right (S) on access rd; at Verdigris River. All year; 14-day limit. 8 non-elec sites, $12 ($6 with federal senior pass). Tbls, toilets, cfga, drkg wtr. Boating(l), fishing, picnic shelter. No day use fees. **GPS: 36.420851, -95.686895**

⑰
PINE CREEK LAKE
GPS: 34.025. -95.0783

A 3,800-acre lake 8 miles N of Valliant off SR 98 in southeastern Oklahoma near the Texas state line on Little River. Campground checkout time 4. p.m. The only day use facilities outside main recreation areas are a picnic area at the dam & hiking trail near the office complex. Note: Roadway across Pine Creek Dam closed in 2015 (possibly until May 2016) for work on dam & outlet areas. Lake Manager, Pine Creek Lake, 175 White Dove Lane, Valliant, OK 74764-9615. (405) 933-4239.

LITTLE RIVER PARK

From Wright City, 6 mi N on Old State Hwy 98; 8.5 mi W on SR 3 across bridge, then SE on Little River Park Rd, following signs; on W shore of lake. 3/1-10/31; 14-day limit. 25 non-elec sites, $12; 30 elec/wtr sites: $15 for 30-amp service, $22 for 50-amp sites, $23 full hookups ($6, $7.50, $11 & $11.50 with federal senior pass). RV limit in excess of 65 ft; 4 pull-through sites. Tbls, pit toilets, cfga, drkg wtr, showers, dump, playground, beach, picnic shelter. Group camping area with elec, $65. Nature trail, boating(l), fishing, swimming, hiking. Non-campers pay day use fees for dump station, boat ramp ($3), beach. (580) 876-3720. NRRS. **GPS: 34.170110, -95.124350**

LOST RAPIDS PARK

From Wright City, 6 mi N on SR 98; 6 mi W on SR 3, then S before causeway, following signs; at E shore of lake. 3/1-10/31; 14-day limit. 13 non-elec sites, $10; 17 elec/wtr sites, $15 ($5 & $7.50 with federal senior pass). RV limit in excess of 65 ft. Group camping area, $65. Tbls, flush toilets, cfga, drkg wtr, no showers, picnic shelter, dump. Boating(ld), fishing. Non-campers pay day use fee for boat ramp ($3), dump station. (580) 876-3720. NRRS. **GPS: 34.177433, -95.104110**

PINE CREEK COVE PARK

From just N of Valliant at jct with Old State Hwy 98, 8 mi N on Pine Creek Rd, following signs; on SW shore of lake near dam. 3/1-10/31; 14-day limit. 1 primitive site, $12; 40 elec/wtr sites: 30-amp sites $15, 50-amp sites $22, $23 at prime locations ($6, $7.50, $11 & $11.50 with federal senior pass). RV limit in excess of 65 ft. Tbls, flush toilets, cfga, drkg wtr, showers, dump, playground, beach, picnic shelter. Group camping area with elec, $65. Boating(ld), fishing, swimming, hiking, ball fields. Non-campers pay day use fees for boat ramp ($3), beach, dump station. (580) 933-4215. NRRS. **GPS: 34.113084, -95.083923**

TURKEY CREEK PARK

At town of Ringold on N end of lake. From Little River Park at jct with SR 3, 1 mi W on SR 3; 0.5 mi E on E1950 Rd to Burwell; about 3 mi N of Burwell on County Line Rd (N4430 Rd); 1.5 mi E on Pine Creek Park Rd, following signs. 4/1-9/30; 14-day limit. 22 non-elec sites, $10; 8 elec/wtr sites, $15 ($5 & $7.50 with federal senior pass). RV limit in excess of 65 ft. Tbls, flush toilets, cfga, drkg wtr, dump, playground, picnic shelter ($40). Non-campers pay day use fees for boat ramp ($3), dump station. (580) 876-3720. NRRS. **GPS: 34.185937, -95.151343**

⑱
SARDIS LAKE
GPS: 34.61. -95.34

A 14,360-acre lake on Jackfork Creek 3 miles N of Clayton on SR 2/43 and S of Wilborton & US 270 in SE Oklahoma. It has 117 miles of shoreline. Lake Manager, Sardis Lake, HC 60, Box 4195, Clayton, OK 74536. (918) 569-4131.

POTATO HILLS CENTRAL RECREATION AREA

From Clayton at jct with US 271, 3.3 mi N on SR 2; W into campground on access rd; at E shore of lake. 4/1-10/31; 14-day limit. 80 elec/

wtr sites, $18 ($9 with federal senior pass). RV limit in excess of 65 ft. Tbls, flush toilets, cfga, drkg wtr, showers, dump, playground. Two group camping areas with elec, $150. Nature trail, hiking, fishing, boating(ld). (918) 569-4146. NRRS. **GPS: 34.670868, -95.324818**

POTATO HILLS SOUTH RECREATION AREA

From Clayton at jct with US 271, 2.5 mi N on SR 2; 0.5 mi W on CR 1625, then N on access rd; at E shore of lake. 4/1-10/31; 14-day limit. 18 non-elec sites, $10 ($5 with federal senior pass). RV limit in excess of 65 ft. Tbls, flush toilets, cfga, drkg wtr, playground, beach, change house, two picnic shelters ($30). Nature trail, hiking, swimming, boating(ld). Non-campers pay day use fee for boat ramp, beach. (918) 569-4549. NRRS. **GPS: 34.662582, -95.330933**

SARDIS COVE RECREATION AREA

From N of Clayton at jct with SR 2, 8.3 mi W on SR 43. 4/1-10/31; 14-day limit. 23 non-elec sites, $10 ($5 with federal senior pass); 22 elec sites (no wtr hookups), $15 ($7.50 with federal senior pass). Tbls, toilets, cfga, drkg wtr, dump. Boating(ld), fishing. Non-campers pay day use fee for boat ramp, dump station. (918) 569-4637. **GPS: 34.649202, -95.453328**

⑲ SKIATOOK LAKE
GPS: 36.3517, -96.0917

The lake is W of Skiatook on SR 20 and NW of Tulsa on Harmony Creek. Campground checkout time 4 p.m. Corps day use parks: Hominy Landing -- boat ramp, toilets; Overlook -- picnicking; Osage -- boat ramp; Quapaw -- fishing pier; Skiatook Point -- boat ramp. Marina concessions on the lake are Cross Timbers and Crystal Bay. Osage County manages Black Dog Park, a boat launch and fishing area. Visitor center. Boat ramps at Twin Points & Hominy Landing Recreation Areas were closed in early 2015 due to drought.

Lake Manager, Skiatook Lake, 14004 Lake Rd, Skiatook, OK 74070. (918) 396-3170.

BULL CREEK PENINSULA CAMP

From NE edge of Hominy, about 8.5 mi E on CR 2130, across lake bridge, following signs. All year; 14-day limit. 41 non-elec sites, $8 ($4 with federal senior pass). Tbls, toilets, cfga. Boating(ld), fishing. Non-campers pay day use fee at boat ramp. (918) 396-2444. **GPS: 36.416621, -96.219721**

TALL CHIEF COVE CAMP

From Skiatook, 2 mi W on SR 20; 1.7 mi S on W.C Rogers Blvd; 3 mi S on Lake Rd, following signs; right (W) on Tall Chief Cove Rd. 4/1-10/31; 14-day limit. 50 elec/wtr sites, $20 ($10 with senior pass). RV limit in excess of 65 ft. Tbls, pit & flush toilets, cfga, drkg wtr, showers, dump, pay phone, amphitheater, playground, beach, picnic shelter ($50). Interpretive trail, swimming, fishing, boating(ld). Non-campers pay day use fee for boat ramp, beach, dump station. (918) 288-6820. NRRS. **GPS: 36.319863, -96.114771**

TWIN POINTS CAMPGROUND

From Skiatook, about 10 mi W on SR 20, across main lake bridge, then right (N) on access rd, following signs. 4/1-10/31; 14-day limit. 49 elec/wtr 20/30/50-amp sites, $20 ($10 with federal senior pass). RV limit in excess of 65 ft. Tbls, flush & pit toilets, cfga, drkg wtr, dump, showers, playground, beach. Hiking, swimming, fishing, boating(ld).Non-campers pay day use fee for boat ramp, beach, dump station. NRRS. **GPS: 36.390369, -96.217570**

⑳ TENKILLER FERRY LAKE
GPS: 35.5933, -95.0367

A 12,900-acre lake 7 miles NE of Gore on SR 100, 22 mi SE of Muskogee. The lake has 130 miles of shoreline and frequently experiences low water levels. The Corps, concessionaires and the state park system operate 14 campgrounds around the lake. Corps-operated day use facilities: Carlisle Cove -- boat ramp; Cato Creek Landing -- boat ramp, picnicking, hiking trail; Chicken Creek South -- boat ramp, shelter, beach; Horseshoe Bend -- boat ramp; Overlook Park -- group shelter, playground, hiking trail. Facilities not operated by the Corps include: Barnacle Bill's -- camping, boat ramp, marina; Blackgum Landing -- boat ramp; Burnt Cabin Marina & Resort; Cherokee Landing State Park; Sixshooter Resort & Marina; Caney Ridge Marina; Cookson Bend Resort & Marina; Elk Creek Landing Marina; Pettit Bay Marina; Pine Cove Marina; Snake Creek Marina; Strayhorn Landing Marina, and Tenkiller State Park. Visitor center. Tenkiller Project Office, Rt. 1, Box 259, Gore, OK 74435-9547. (918) 487-5252.

CARTERS LANDING RECREATION AREA

From Tahlequah, 4 mi SW on US 62; 6.6 mi S (left) on SR 82; 2 mi NE (left) on E. Carters Landing Rd; on shore of upper Illinois River about 2.5 mi N of lake. All year; 14-day limit. 15 sites no hookups, $7; 10 elec/wtr sites, $11 ($3.50 & $5.50 with federal senior pass). 30-ft RV limit. Picnic shelter $25 with $10 reservation fee. Non-campers pay $3 day use fee at boat ramp. (918) 487-5252.
GPS: 35.798219, -94.896142

CHICKEN CREEK POINT RECREATION AREA

From Cookson, 4 mi S on SR 100; 1.5 mi NW (right) on Chicken Creek Rd, following signs. All year; 14-day limit. 102 elec sites: During 4/1-10/31, elec/wtr sites $16 (30-amp) & $18 (50-amp); $8 & $9 with federal senior pass. During 11/1-3/31, sites $13 (30-amp) & $15 (50-amp) but no wtr hookups, showers or flush toilets. RV limit in excess of 65 ft. 1 RV & 2 tents or 3 tents per site. Tbls, flush toilets, cfga, drkg wtr, showers, dump, playground, beach, 2 picnic shelters ($25). Boating(ld),

fishing, swimming. Non-campers pay $3 day use fees for beach, dump station, boat ramp. Note: In 2014-15, campground closed for winter on 12/1. NRRS during 4/1-9/30.
GPS: 35.682242, -94.960155

COOKSON BEND RECREATION AREA

From Cookson, 2 mi W on W. Cookson Bend Rd, following signs; on E shore of lake. All year; 14-day limit. 65 non-elec sites, $10 during 4/1-10/31 ($5 with federal senior pass); $7 during 11/1-3/31 ($3.50 with senior pass). 62 elec sites (some with wtr hookups), $16 for 30-amp & $18 for 50-amp during 4/1-10/31 ($8 & $9 with senior pass). Some elec sites $13 & $15 during 11/1-3/31 ($6.50 & $7.50 with senior pass); no wtr hookups, showers or flush toilets off-season. RV limit in excess of 65 ft; 7 sites are 50-amp. Tbls, flush & pit toilets, cfga, drkg wtr, showers, dump, beach, playground, 2 picnic shelters($25). Boating(ld), swimming, fishing. Marina. Non-campers pay $3 day use fee for boat ramp, beach, dump station. NRRS during 4/1-9/30. **GPS: 35.706395, -94.954834**

ELK CREEK LANDING RECREATION AREA

From Coookson, 4 mi N on SR 100; left (W) before Illinois River bridge on access rd (560 Rd); at N end of lake, E shore. All year; 14-day limit. 21 non-elec sites, $10 during 4/1-10/31 ($5 with federal senior pass); $7 during 11/1-3/31 ($3.50 with senior pass). 18 elec 30-amp sites (no wtr hookups), $16 during 4/1-10/31 ($8 with senior pass); $13 during 11/1-3/31 ($6.50 with senior pass); no showers or flush toilets in off-season. RV limit in excess of 65 ft. Tbls, flush & pit toilets, cfga, drkg wtr, showers, dump, playground, beach, 2 picnic shelters ($10). Boating(ld), fishing, swimming. Marina. Non-campers pay $3 day use fees for boat ramp, beach, dump station. Note: In 2014, campground closed for season on 12/1. NRRS during 4/1-9/30.
GPS: 35.754793, -94.901190

PETTIT BAY RECREATION AREA

From Tahlequah, 4 mi S on US 62; 4.6 mi S (left) on SR 82; 2 mi S (right) on Indian Rd; 1 mi SE (left) on W870 Rd. All year; 14-day limit. Pettit Bay was operated as two parks with a marina between them; now it is a single park with 2 camping areas: Pettit I is on N side of the recreation area; it has non-reservable non-elec & elec sites; Pettit II on the S and has reservable sites, all with hookups. 13 non-elec sites, $10 during 4/1-10/31 ($5 with federal senior pass); $7 during 11/1-3/31 ($3.50 with senior pass). 72 elec sites (7 wtr hookups). During 4/1-10/31, 30-amp elec is $16, 50-amp elec $18, 7 full hookups $20 ($8, $9 & $10 with senior pass). During 11/1-3/31, 30-amp elec is $13, 50-amp elec is $15. No wtr hookups, showers or flush toilets during off-season. RV limit in excess of 65 ft. Tbls, flush & pit toilets, cfga, drkg wtr, dump, showers, playground, beach, 3 picnic shelters ($10 to $50). Boating(ld), fishing, swimming. Marina. Non-campers pay $3 day use fee for boat ramp, beach, dump station. NRRS during 4/1-9/30. **GPS: 35.754628, -94.946616**

SIZEMORE LANDING RECREATION AREA

From Tahlequah, 4 mi SE on US 62; 4.6 mi S (left) on SR 82; 3.5 mi S (right)on Indian Rd; 1 mi left at sign on Sizemore Rd. All year; 14-day limit. 32 primitive sites, $5 ($2.50 with federal senior pass). 30-ft RV limit. Tbls, pit toilets, cfga, no drkg wtr, picnic shelter ($10). No reservations. Non-campers pay $3 day use fee for boat ramp. No drkg wtr. **GPS: 35.718730, -94.963524**

SNAKE CREEK COVE RECREATION AREA

From Gore, 15 mi N on SR 100, then W (left) on access road; at Snake Creek Cove. All year; 14-day limit. 111 elec sites: During 4/1-10/31, 30-amp sites $16, five 50-amp sites $18, four full hookups $20 ($8, $9 & $10 with federal senior pass). Sites are $13, $15 & $17 during 11/1-3/31, but no showers or flush toilets off-season. In 2014, campground closed for winter on 12/1. RV limit in excess of 65 ft. Tbls, flush & pit toilets, cfga, drkg wtr, dump, playground, beach, 3 picnic shelters for up to 50 people & 21 vehicles ($25). Boating(ld), fishing, swimming. Marina. Non-campers pay $3 day use fee for boat ramp, dump station, beach. NRRS during 4/1-9/30. **GPS: 35.649019, -94.969661**

STANDING ROCK LANDING RECREATION AREA

From Cookson, 1 mi N on S. Molly Brown Mountain Rd; 2 mi N on S550 Rd to park; at E shore of lake. All year; 14-day limit. Free primitive sites. Tbls, toilets, cfga, no drkg wtr. Boating(l), fishing. **GPS: 35.751367, -94.920314**

STRAYHORN LANDING RECREATION AREA

From Gore, 7 mi NE on SR 100; 1.5 mi N on SR 10A; 0.3 mi E (right) at sign on access road. All year; 14-day limit. 38 elec 30-amp sites, $16 during 4/1-10/31, $20 for 2 full hookups ($8 & $10 with federal senior pass). During 11/1-3/31, sites $13 & $17 ($6.50 & $8.50 with senior pass); no flush toilets or showers in off-season. RV limit in excess of 65 ft. Tbls, flush & pit toilets, cfga, drkg wtr, dump, playground, beach, 3 picnic shelters ($25-$50). Boating(l), fishing, swimming, hiking. Marina. NRRS during 4/1-9/30. **GPS: 35.615708, -95.061264**

㉑
WAURIKA LAKE
GPS: 34.235, -95.055

A 10,100-acre lake 6 miles NW of Waurika on SR 5, 25 miles NE of Wichita Falls, Texas. It is on Beaver Creek, a tributary of the Red River, in southwestern Oklahoma. It has 80 miles of shoreline. Visitor center. 13-mile Walker Creek Trail for hiking & equestrian activities. Lake Manager, Waurika Lake, 5900 Waurika Dam Rd, Waurika, OK 73573. (580) 963-2111.

CHISHOLM TRAIL RIDGE RECREATION AREA

From Hastings, 5.2 mi E on SR 5; merge onto gravel county rd, then 3 mi N on Advent Rd & 0.9 mi W on Chisholm Trail Rd. 5/1-9/30; 14-day limit. 95 elec/wtr sites, $14 base or $18 at premium locations ($7 & $9 with federal senior pass). 60-ft RV limit; 14 pull-through sites. Tbls, flush & pit toilets, cfga, drkg wtr, change house at beach, playground. Fishing, boating(ld), swimming, nature trail. Non-campers pay day use fee for boat ramp, dump station. (580) 439-8040. NRRS.
GPS: 34.253776, -98.033903

KIOWA RECREATION AREA

From jct with SR 5 at E edge of Hastings, 3 mi N on CR N240 Rd; 1.5 mi E on Kiowa Park Rd (E1900 Rd); at W shore of lake. 3/1-10/31; 14-day limit. 164 elec/wtr sites, $14 base, $18 at premium locations ($7 & $9 with federal senior pass). 60-ft RV limit; 47 pull-through sites. Tbls, flush & pit toilets, cfga, drkg wtr, dump, beach, playground, change house, pay phone, fishing pier. Two group camping areas with elec, $100. Nature trail, fishing, hiking, boating(ld), swimming. (580) 963-9031. Non-campers pay day use fee for boat ramp, dump station. NRRS.
GPS: 34.261012, -98.078728

MONEKA PARK

From Waurika, 64 mi N on SR 5; 0.8 mi N on County N2780 Rd, then left on Dam Access Rd; just below dam on E shore of Beaver Creek. 3/1-10/31; 14-day limit. 38 primitive sites, $8 ($4 with federal senior pass). Tbls, toilets, cfga, no drkg wtr. Nature trail, fishing. No day use fees.
GPS: 34.227629, -98.052206

WICHITA RIDGE RECREATION AREA

From just E of Hastings at jct with SR 5, 4 mi N on County N2740 Rd (Corum Rd); across bridge, then left into park at NW shore of lake. All year; 14-day limit. 16 sites without hookups & 1 site with wtr, $8; 10 elec sites (2 wtr hookups), $12 ($4 & $6 with federal senior pass). Tbls, toilets, cfga, drkg wtr, dump, picnic shelter ($20). Nature trail, equestrian trail, boating(ld), fishing, hiking. Non-campers pay day use fee for boat ramp, dump station. No reservations. GPS: 34.308509, -98.107942

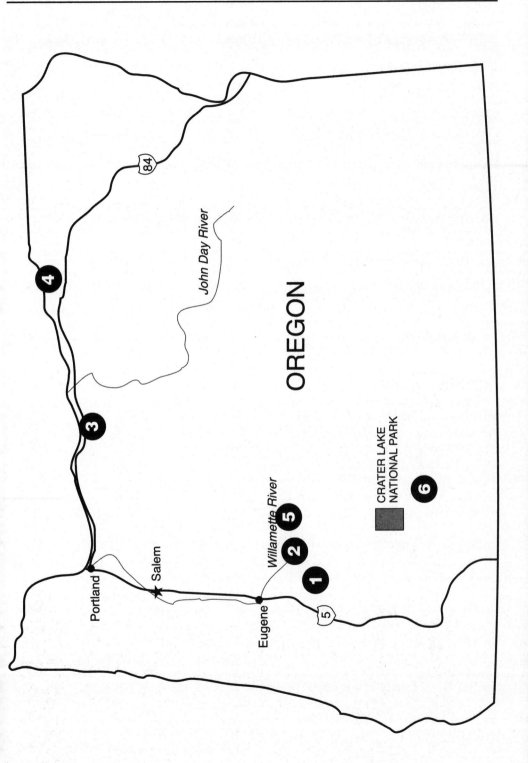

OREGON

STATE INFORMATION:

CAPITAL: Salem
NICKNAME: Beaver State
STATEHOOD: 1859 - 33rd State
FLOWER: Oregon Grape
TREE: Douglas Fir
BIRD: Western Meadowlark

STATE TIDBITS:

• Oregon has more ghost towns than any other state.

• Pilot Butte, a cinder cone volcano, exists within the city limits of Bend.

• At 8,000 feet deep Hells Canyon is the deepest river gorge in North America.

WWW.TRAVELOREGON.COM

Toll free number for travel information: 1-800-547-7842.

Tourism Division, 775 Summer St. NE, Salem, OR 97310

OREGON LAKES

To find campgrounds operated by the U.S. Army Corps of Engineers, match the lake's numbers on the preceding map page with numbered lake entries on the following pages. Campgrounds are listed alphabetically under the appropriate lakes. The following Oregon impoundments have Corps of Engineers campgrounds.

Cottage Grove Lake. This 1,100-acre lake is 5 miles S of Cottage Grove off I-5 (exit 172) on London Rd, 20 miles S of Eugene.

Dorena Lake. This 1,700-acre lake is 6 miles E of Cottage Grove off I-5 exit 174 on Row River Rd, 20 miles S of Eugene.

Lake Umatilla. Located on the Columbia River off SR 14 near Rufus, Oregon, 25 miles E of The Dalles, Oregon. It is 216 miles upstream from the mouth of the Columbia River at Lake Celilo.

Lake Wallula. A 38,800-acre surface lake with 242 miles of shoreline, Lake Wallula is N of the junction of I-82 and US 730 and 1 mile N of Umatilla.

Lookout Point Lake. 22 miles SE of Eugene on SR 58, Lookout Point is a popular recreation area with a newly remodeled campground and three day use areas.

Lost Creek Lake. This 3,430-acre lake is 30 miles NE of Medford on SR 62 and the Rogue River.

❶

COTTAGE GROVE LAKE
GPS: 43.80, -123.05

This 1,100-acre lake is 5 miles S of Cottage Grove off I-5 (exit 172) on London Rd, 20 miles S of Eugene. Visitor hours to 10 p.m. Off-road vehicles & alcohol prohibited. Interpretive programs. For guided tours, call (541) 942-5631. Day use facilities: Lakeside Park -- boat ramp, picnicking, beach; Shortridge Park -- picnicking; Wilson Creek Park -- boat ramp, picnicking, beach. Project Manager, Cottage Grove Lake, 75819 Shortridge Hill Rd, Cottage Grove, OR 97424. 541-942-5631.

PINE MEADOWS CAMPGROUND

From dam S of Cottage Grove, 1 mi SW on Reservoir Rd, N side. 5/15-9/15; 14-day limit.

85 sites without hookups, $18 ($9 with federal senior pass). RV limit in excess of 65 ft; 26 pull-through sites. Tbls, flush & pit toilets, showers, dump, cfga, drkg wtr, beach, playground, amphitheater, fishing pier, pay phone. Boating, fishing, swimming, waterskiing. At reserved sites, 2-night minimum stay required on weekends, 3 nights on holiday weekends. (541) 942-5631. NRRS.
GPS: 43.700365, -123.056864

PRIMITIVE CAMPGROUND

S of Pine Meadows Campground on Reservoir Rd; at E shore of lake just N of Wilson Creek. 5/15-9/15; 14-day limit. 15 primitive sites with pit toilets, fire rings, tbls, drkg wtr; no hookups or showers. $12 ($6 with federal senior pass). At reserved sites, 2-night minimum stay required on weekends, 3 nights on holiday weekends. NRRS.
GPS: 43.695199, 123.064057

❷ DORENA LAKE
GPS: 43.78, -122.9533

This 1,700-acre lake is 6 miles E of Cottage Grove off I-5, exit 174, on Row River Rd, 20 miles S of Eugene. Visitors to 10 p.m. Off-road vehicles & alcohol prohibited. Visitor center, interpretive programs, guided tours upon request. Day use facilities: Harms Park -- boat ramp, picnicking, hiking trail access; Bake-Stewart Park -- picnicking. The Bureau of Land Management operates the Row River National Recreation Trail, which runs 15.6 miles along an abandoned rail line from Cottage Grove to Dorena Lake, Culp Creek and the nearby Umpqua National Forest; the paved hiking/biking trail crosses three historic covered bridges. Project Manager, Dorena Lake, 75819 Shortridge Hill Road, Cottage Grove, OR 97424. (541) 942-5631.

SCHWARZ CAMPGROUND

East of Cottage Grove, from below dam at jct with Row River Rd, 0.2 mi SE on Shoreview

Dr, then E at W shore of Row River near outlet. About 4/23-9/14; 14-day limit. 72 sites without hookups, $16 ($8 with federal senior pass). RV limit in excess of 65 ft; 3 pull-through sites. Tbls, flush & pit toilets, dump, showers, cfga, drkg wtr, playground. Boating, fishing, hiking, interpretive trail, waterskiing, biking, pay phone. Six group camping areas without hookups, $140. At reserved sites, 2-night minimum stay required on weekends, 3 nights on holiday weekends. (541) 942-1418. NRRS.
GPS: 43.785975, -122.960905

❸ LAKE UMATILLA
JOHN DAY LOCK & DAM
GPS: 45.773561, -120.141278

Located on the Columbia River off SR 14 near Rufus, Oregon, 25 miles E of The Dalles, Oregon. It is 216 miles upstream from the mouth of the Columbia River at Lake Celilo. The lake's visitor center features a fish viewing window and self-guided tours. Corps-managed day use facilities include: Giles French Park -- boat ramp; Plymouth Park -- boat ramp, picnicking, beach; Railroad Island Park -- boat ramp; Rock Creek Park -- boat ramp, picnicking; Roosevelt Park -- boat ramp; Sundale Park -- boat ramp. Day use fees charged at boat ramps, dump stations. Facilities not managed by the Corps: Boardman Park -- nature trails, volleyball courts, tennis courts, hiking & biking trail, playground, concerts (Boardman Township); Irrigon Park & Marina -- boat ramp, picnicking, playground, beach; Umatilla National Wildlife Refuge -- boat ramp, hiking, biking, horseback riding. Resource Manager, Lake Umatilla, P. O. Box 564, The Dalles, OR 97058-9998. (503) 296-1181. See WA listings.

ALBERT PHILIPPI RECREATION AREA

On E side of the John Day River, 3.5 mi upstream from Lepage Park. Boat-in access only; anchor in river. All year; 14-day limit. Formerly free, now $3 day use fee, paid at

Lepage Park. About 35 undesignated primitive tent sites. Pit toilets, tbls, cfga, drkg wtr, showers. Fishing, boating, waterskiing, hiking. Park was closed temporarily by budget cuts during 2013 & 2014; check current status with lake office before arrival.

GILES FRENCH RECREATION AREA

Below dam on Oregon side. From I-84 exit 109, N toward river on John Day Dam Rd, then right into park. All year; 14-day limit Free primitive dispersed camping in grassy areas below dam. Portable toilets, tbls, cfga, no drkg wtr. Boating(l), fishing.
GPS: 45.700462, -120.730938

LEPAGE PARK

From John Day Dam, 9 mi E on I-84 to exit 114, then S; at confluence of John Day & Columbia Rivers. 4/1-10/31; 14-day limit. 20 walk-to tent sites, $15 base ($7.50 with federal senior pass), $17 at gazebo sites ($8.50 with senior pass). 22 RV/tent sites with elec, $22 base; $25 at riverfront sites ($11 & $12.50 with senior pass). Primitive overflow sites $12 ($6 w senior pass). 55-ft RV limit; 8 pull-through sites. Tbls, flush & pit toilets, dump, showers, cfga, drkg wtr, beach, fish cleaning stations. Boating(l), fishing, waterskiing, swimming. Non-campers pay $5 day use fee for dump station, $3 for boat ramp. Off-road vehicles prohibited. NRRS during 4/1-10/31.
GPS: 45.726746, -120.650284

PATTERSON PARK

From Umatilla, about 3 mi W on US 730 (Columbia River Hwy) to Irrigon; 2 mi W on S Main Ave W (becoming CR 971), then N on Patterson Ferry Rd (CR 930) about 0.75 mi to park. Free. 5/15-9/15; 7-day limit. Primitive undesignated sites. Toilets, no drkg wtr. Boating, fishing. GPS: 45.914592, -119.554977

QUESNEL PARK

From about 6 mi E Arlington to I-84 exit 151, 0.75 mi N , 3 mi E of Lepage Park off I-84 exit

151 (Threemile Canyon exit), 0.75 mi N to park at lakeshore. All year; 14-day limit. Free primitive camping. Pit toilets, cfga, no drkg wtr. Also known as Three Mile Canyon Park. Windsurfing, boating(l), fishing.
GPS: 45.810110, -119.970746

❹
LAKE WALLULA
MC NARY DAM
GPS: 45.9367, -119.2978

A 38,800-acre surface lake with 242 miles of shoreline, Lake Wallula is N of the junction of I-82 and US 730 and 1 mi N of Umatilla. Visitor center with interpretive displays, fish viewing rooms. Corps-operated facilities: Lewis and Clark Commemorative Trail -- hiking/equestrian trail, picnicking, swimming; Locust Grove/Martindale Park -- fishing, hiking, hunting; McNary Beach Park -- picnicking, group shelter, cold showers, swimming, hiking trails; McNary Beach Park -- picnicking, hiking trails, nature group shelter, cold showers, swimming; McNary Wildlife Nature Area -- picnicking, hiking trails, nature trail, wildlife management trail, pond trail; Oregon Boat Launch -- boat ramp, docks, pit toilet; Pacific Salmon Visitor Center -- audiovisual program, lectures, interpretive displays; Spillway Park -- picnicking; Warehouse Beach -- picnicking, swimming; Washington Boat Launch -- boat launch; West Park -- picnicking, group shelters; Yakima Rver Delta Wildlife Nature Area -- hiking trails, bird watching. Resource Manager, Western Project, Monument Drive, Burbank, WA 99323. (541) 922-4388. See WA listings.

Facilities not operated by the Corps include: Chiawana Park & Road 54 Park -- picnicking, group shelters, hiking trails, playground, biking trail (City of Pasco Parks, WA); Columbia Park Marina -- camping area closed, swimming, hiking trails, playground, golf course, boat ramps (City of Kennewick Parks, WA); Hat Rock State Park -- picnicking, hiking trails, boat ramp, horseshoe pits, ponds; Howard Amon Park -- picnicking, group shelters, swimming, hiking trails, playground, tennis courts, sports fields, biking trail (City of Richland Parks, WA); Leslie R. Grove Park -- picnicking, group shelters, swimming, hiking trails, playground, biking trail, multi-purpose courts, sports fields (City of Richland Parks, WA); Madame Dorion Memorial Park -- primitive camping, dump station, picnicking (U.S. Fish & Wildlife Service); McNary Yacht Club -- marina, boat ramp; Pasco Boat Basin -- picnicking, boat ramp, playground (City of Pasco, WA); Peninsula Habitat Management Unit -- fishing, hiking, hunting (U.S. Fish & Wildlife Service, WA); Sacajawea State Park (WA) -- picnicking, horseshoe pits, sports fields, group shelters, swimming, interpretive center, playground, boat ramp; Two Rivers Park -- picnicking, hiking trail, swimming, playground, boat ramp (Benton County Parks, WA); Walla Walla Yacht Club -- boat ramp; Wye Park -- picnicking, shelters, playground (Richland Parks, WA).

SAND STATION RECREATION AREA

From Umatilla, 10.5 mi E on US 730. All year; 14-day limit. 15 free primitive sites (10 tent only) on beach, designated areas only. Pit toilets, tbls, no drkg wtr, cfga, beach. Swimming, fishing. 8 acres. **GPS: 45.922453, -119.118644**

❺ LOOKOUT POINT LAKE
GPS: 43.87097, -122.68164

22 miles SE of Eugene on SR 58, Lookout Point is a popular recreation area with a newly renovated campground and three day use areas with boat ramps, picnic facilities and hiking trails. Project Manager, Lookout Point Lake, 40386 West Boundary Rd, Lowell, OR 97452. 541-937-2131.

IVAN OAKES CAMPGROUND

From Lowell, 6.3 mi E on West Boundary Rd (North Shore Dr) & on gravel rd along N shore of lake to park. $12. MD-LD; 14-day limit. 24 sites. Tbls, pit toilets, cfga, drkg wtr. Boating(l), fishing. **GPS: 43.875335, -122.671973**

❻ LOST CREEK LAKE (PORT)
GPS: 44.27, -122.60

This 3,430-acre lake is 30 miles NE of Medford on SR 62 and the Rogue River. Powerhouse tours by appointment. Free electrical cook stoves at group picnic sites. Visitor center at McGregor Park. Cole M. Rivers Fish Hatchery downstream from the dam. The lake has more than 20 developed parks, including campgrounds, picnic areas, trailheads, boat ramps and group use areas. Visitor center with interpretive displays, interactive exhibits, interpretive boardwalk trail. Facilities not managed by the Corps include Joseph H. Stewart Park State Recreation Area and Takelma Recreation Area with group picnicking & boat ramp. Lost Creek Marina offers boat launching, rentals & moorage as well as a restaurant and a store. Park Manager, Rogue River Basin Projects, 100 Cole M. Rivers Drive, Trail, OR 97541-9607. (541) 878-2255.

FIRE GLEN CAMPGROUND

From Prospect, about 8 mi SW on SR 62; right (W) for 0.8 mi on Lewis Rd, then SW by trail to lakeshore. All year; 14-day limit. Free. 4 primitive tent sites for up to 8 people. Hike-in or boat-in access only. Pit toilet, no drkg wtr. **GPS: 42.693683, -122.634925**

FOUR CORNERS CAMPGROUND

From Trail, about 6 mi E on SR 62; 1.4 mi
N on Takelma Dr; 0.5 mi N on logging road,
E side of lake. All year; 14-day limit. Hike-in
or boat-in access only. Free primitive tent
camping for 4 tents & 8 people. Pit toilet cfga,
no drkg wtr. Boating, fishing, hiking.
GPS: 42.689117, -122.669300

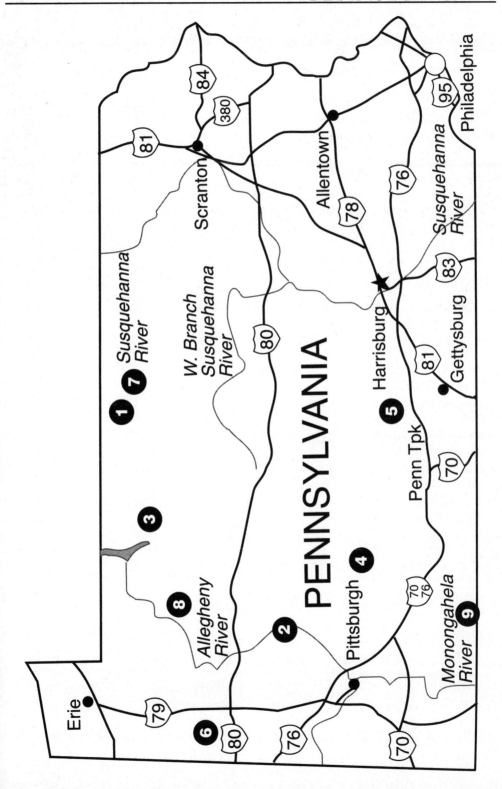

PENNSYLVANIA

STATE INFORMATION:

CAPITAL: Harrisburg
NICKNAME: Keystone State
STATEHOOD: 1787 - 2nd State
FLOWER: Mountain Laurel
TREE: Eastern Hemlock
BIRD: Ruffed Grouse

STATE TIDBITS:

• The Rockville Bridge in Harrisburg is the longest stone arch bridge in the world.

• The first daily newspaper was published in Philadelphia on Sept. 21, 1784.

• In 1909 the first baseball stadium was built in Pittsburgh.

WWW.VISITPA.COM

Tourism Office, Dept. of Community and Economic Development, 4th Floor, Commonwealth Keystone Building, 400 North St., Harrisburg, PA 17120. 800-237-4363 or 717-787-5453. Information: 800-VISIT-PA.

PENNSYLVANIA LAKES

To find campgrounds operated by the U.S. Army Corps of Engineers, match the lake's numbers on the preceding map page with numbered lake entries on the following pages. Campgrounds are listed alphabetically under the appropriate lakes. The following Pennsylvania impoundments have Corps of Engineers campgrounds.

Cowanesque Lake. This 1,085-acre lake is 2.2 miles W of Lawrenceville on SR 49 and N of Williamsport on the Cowanesque River just upstream from the confluence with the Tioga River.

Crooked Creek Lake. This 350-acre lake is S of Kittanning and Ford City on the E side of SR 66, 48 miles NE of Pittsburgh.

East Branch Clarion River Lake. The 1,160-acre lake is 36 miles N of DeBois off US 219 and is 105 miles SE of Erie, E of Allegheny National Forest.

Loyalhanna Lake. This 400-acre lake is S of Saltsburg and W of SR 981, 32 miles E of Pittsburgh.

Raystown Lake. This 8,300-acre lake is the largest in Pennsylvania. It is just SW of Huntington, E of Johnstown, N of the Pennsylvania Turnpike and E of US 220.

Shenango River Lake. This 3,560-acre lake is 2 miles N of Hermitage and US 62 off SRs 18 and 518; it is 6 miles N of I-80, 21 miles NE of Youngstown, Ohio.

Tioga-Hammond Lakes. The 685-acre Hammond Lake is a "twin" lake with 498-acre Tioga Lake; they are 5 miles S of Tioga on SR 287 in north-central Pennsylvania, 72 miles W of Binghamton, New York. Tioga is on the Tioga River, Hammond along Crooked Creek.

Tionesta Lake. A 480-acre SW of Tionesta on SR 36, 60 miles SE of Erie near the southwestern corner of the Allegheny National Forest.

Youghiogheny River Lake. This 2,850-acre, 16-mile lake is S of Confluence off SR 281 and N of US 40 in southwestern Pennsylvania, spanning the Mason-Dixon Line between Pennsylvania and Maryland.

❶
COWANESQUE LAKE
GPS: 41.9817, -77.1717

This 1,085-acre lake is 2.2 miles W of Lawrenceville on SR 49 and N of Williamsport on the Cowanesque River just upstream from confluence with the Tioga River. Campground checkout time 3 p.m. (a late fee applies). Visitors to 10 p.m. Corps-operated day use facilities: Lawrence Park -- picnicking, group shelter; South Shore Park -- boat ramp, picnicking, group shelter, playground, hiking trail, beach. Non-campers pay $3 day use fee at boat ramps. Operations Manager, Tioga-Hammond/Cowanesque Lakes, RR 1, Box 65, Tioga, PA 16946-9733. (570) 835-5281.

TOMPKINS CAMPGROUND

From Lawrenceville, 5 mi W on Bliss Rd, then S (W of the town of Nelson); on N shore of lake. 5/15-9/30; 14-day limit. 16 walk-to tent sites & 24 non-elec RV/tent sites, $20 ($10 with federal senior pass); 34 elec/wtr sites, $32 ($16 with senior pass); 52 full-hookup sites, $34 ($17 with federal senior pass). 55-ft RV limit. Amphitheater, fish cleaning station, tbls, flush & pit toilets, cfga, drkg wtr, showers, dump, coin laundry, beach, playground, pay phone. Store. Group camping areas with 7 sites & 24 sites, $140 base. Swimming, hiking trail, interpretive trail (4 mi through reclaimed farm fields & woods), boating(ld), ball field. Picnic shelters $35-$80. (570) 827-2109. NRRS. **GPS: 41.98083, -77.18944**

❷
CROOKED CREEK LAKE
GPS: 40.715, -79.51

This 350-acre lake is S of Kittanning and Ford City on E side of SR 66, 48 miles NE of Pittsburgh. It is 6.7 miles above the creek's junction with the Allegheny River. Winter activities include two ice skating ponds, sled area and cross country skiing. Day use facilities: Beach Area -- picnicking, beach, hiking trail; Crooked Creek Park -- picnicking, group shelter, playground; Outflow Area -- picnicking, hiking trail. Visitor center with interpretive programs. 141-mi Baker Trail crosses Crooked Creek Lake. Non-campers pay $4 day use fees at most recreation areas, including boat ramps & beaches. Resource Mgr, Crooked Creek Lake, 114 Park Main Rd, Ford City, PA 16226-8815. (724) 763-2761.

CROOKED CREEK CAMP

From Ford City, 5 mi S on SR 66; 1 mi E on SR 2019 to park manager's office. 5/15-LD; 14-day limit. 46 non-elec sites, $15 ($7.50 with federal senior pass). Tbls, toilets, cfga, drkg wtr, dump, playground, beach. Group camping area (MD-LD). Interpretive programs, boating(dl), fishing, swimming, hiking, waterskiing, biking, ball field. Non-campers pay $4 day use fee for boat ramp, beach. No reservations. **GPS: 40.721770, -79.503722**

CROOKED CREEK
PRIMITIVE GROUP AREA

From Ford City, 5 mi S on SR 66; E on SR 2019 to park manager's office; call or visit for information. 5/15-LD. Group camping area on W side of lake off Township Rd 460, $35-$45. Tbls, toilets, cfga, drkg wtr, dump, picnic shelter, beach, playground. Boating(ld), fishing, swimming, hiking, waterskiing. Non-campers pay $4 day use fee for boat ramp, beach.

❸
EAST BRANCH
CLARION RIVER LAKE
EAST BRANCH DAM
GPS: 41.5583, -78.5967

1,160-acre lake is 36 miles N of De Bois off US 219 and is 105 miles SE of Erie, E of Allegheny National Forest. Winter activities include ice fishing. Daily lake information, (814) 965-4762. Visitor center. Overlook Pavilion for picnics, $35. Facilities not managed by the Corps include Elk State Park, Bendigo State

Park, Clear Creek State Park and Elk State Forest. Boat ramp fees waived. Resource Manager, 631 E Branch Dam Road, Wilcox, PA 15870-9709. (814) 965-2065.

EAST BRANCH RECREATION AREA

From Wilcox at jct with US 219, 1 mi E on Rasselas Rd; right (SE) for 5 mi SE on Glen Hazel Rd; exit E (left) past resource mgr office to campground. About 4/15-10/15; 14-day limit. 16 sites no hookups, $15 ($7.50 with federal senior pass); 16 elec sites, $20 ($10 with senior pass). Tbls, flush toilets, showers, dump, playground, cfga, drkg wtr, picnic shelter. Boating(ld), fishing, hiking, waterskiing. (814) 965-2065. Note: Campground closed in 2015 during dam repairs; check lake office for status before arrival. **GPS: 41.564209, -78.594727**

❹ LOYALHANNA LAKE
GPS: 40.2367, -79.4517

This 400-acre lake is S of Saltsburg and W of SR 981, 32 mi;es E of Pittsburgh. For daily lake information, call (724) 639-3785. Dam picnic area features group shelters, picnicking, playground and trails. Non-campers pay $4 day use fee at beaches & boat ramps. Resource Manager, Loyalhanna Lake, 440 Loyalhanna Dam Road, Saltsburg, PA 15681-9302. (724) 639-9013.

BUSH RECREATION AREA

From Saltsburg, 2 mi SE on SR 981; 1 mi S on Bush Rd; at E side of lake. 5/15-9/15; 14-day limit. 32 primitive sites, $19 ($9.50 with federal senior pass); 12 elec/wtr sites, $25 ($12.50 with senior pass). Tbls, flush toilets, dump, coin showers, drkg wtr, playground. Boating(l), interpretive programs, fishing, waterskiing. Picnic shelter ($45). **GPS: 40.438176, -79.436672**

KISKI GROUP CAMPING AREA

From Bush Recreation Area, 0.3 mi N on Bush

Road. 5/5-10/15; 14-day limit. Primitive group camping area for organized groups only. Call office at 724-639-9013.

❺ RAYSTOWN LAKE
GPS: 40.43333, -78.04

This 8,300-acre lake is the largest in Pennsylvania. It is just SW of Huntingdon, E of Johnstown, N of Pennsylvania Turnpike and E of US 220. Facilities for handicapped include special fishing at Aitch and Shy Beaver Recreational Areas. Other day use facilities: Aitch -- boat ramp, picnicking, group shelter; Baker's Hollow -- biking & hiking trail; Corbins Island -- boat ramp, picnicking, group shelter; James Creek -- boat ramp; Raystown Dam -- picnicking, shelter; Raystown Visitor Center -- hiking trail; Ridenour Overlook -- multi-purpose trail; Shy Beaver -- boat ramp, picnicking; Snyders Run -- boat ramp; Tatman Run -- boat ramp, picnicking, group shelter, playground, beach; Weaver Falls -- boat ramp, picnicking, group shelter, playground. Branch Camp is leased by the Corps to a private manager. Checkout time 4 p.m. Resource Manager, Raystown Lake, 6145 Seven Points Rd, Hesston, PA 16647. (814) 658-3405. Raystown.

NANCY'S CAMP

From Marklesburg, 1.5 mi SW on SR 26, then 1 mi SE & N to trail. Access by boat-in or hike-in only; between marker 15 & 16 on W shore. All year; 14-day limit. 50 lakefront tent sites, $12 ($6 with federal senior pass). Campers have access to showers at Seven Points change house near marker 9. Pit toilets, fire rings, drkg wtr. Self-registration at honor vault. Most campers boat in from launch at James Creek.

SEVEN POINTS CAMPGROUND

From McConnelstown, 1.2 mi SW on SR 26; 2 mi SE past Hesston & S of administration building. 4/1-10/31; 14-day limit. 261 total sites. 6 tent sites, $23; 30-amp elec/wtr sites, $25; 50-amp elec/wtr sites $27 base, $32 at waterfront locations (50% discounts with federal senior pass). Reservations required during peak 5/14-9/6 period. RV limit in excess of 65 ft. Tbls, flush toilets, showers, cfga, drkg wtr, picnic shelter ($), amphitheater, pay phone, dump, beach, playground, coin laundry. Visitor center, interpretive trail, boating(lr), fishing, swimming, waterskiing, hiking/biking trails, kayaking(r). Marina. NRRS during 5/14-9/1. **GPS: 40.386280, -78.080499**

SUSQUEHANNOCK CAMPGROUND

From Seven Points campground, l mi NE past the administration building, then SE on Susquehannock Rd; on peninsula. About 5/21-10/30; 14-day limit. 24 primitive tent sites & 36 RV/tent sites, $14 base, $17 at waterfront sites ($7 & $8.50 with federal senior pass). RV limit in excess of 65 ft, but most sites are quite small, suitable for folding trailers or pickup campers. Pit toilets, tbls, cfga, well drkg wtr, coin laundry. Hiking & biking trails, boating, fishing, waterskiing. Campers have access to Seven Points day use areas & showers. (814) 658-6806. NRRS. **GPS: 40.388957, -78.050276**

❻
SHENANGO RIVER LAKE
GPS: 41.265, -80.4633

This 3,560-acre lake is 2 miles N of Hermitage and US 62 off SRs 18 and 518; it is 6 miles N of I-80, 21 miles NE of Youngstown, Ohio. Non-campers pay day use fees up to $4 for dump stations, $3 for boat ramps; $3 entry fee paid at Shenango campground by non-campers. Picnic shelters, $40. Campground checkout time 4 p.m. Alcohol prohibited. 250-acre area for ORV. Exact change required for all cash transactions. Day use facilities: Chestnut Run -- group shelter, picnicking, beach; Clark Recreation Area -- picnicking, shelter, boat ramp; Golden Run Wildlife Area -- boat ramp, interpretive trail; Hartford Rd Access -- boat ramp; Mahaney Recreation Area -- shelter, picnicking, playground, interpretive trail, boat ramp; Parkers Landing -- boat ramp. For

daily lake information call (724) 962-4384. Resource Manager, Shenango River Lake, 2442 Kelly Road, Hermitage, PA 16148-9703. (724) 962-7746.

SHENANGO RECREATION AREA

From Hermitage at jct with US 62, 4.6 mi N on SR 18; 0.8 mi W on W Lake Rd, then S; at N shore of lake. About 5/15-9/7, but campground open earlier & later most years; 14-day limit. 330 total sites. 215 non-elec sites, $19 base, $34 at premium locations ($9.50 & $17 with federal senior pass). 110 elec sites, $24 ($12 with senior pass). RV limit in excess of 65'; 4 pull-through sites. Picnic shelter, $40. Interpretive programs, firewood for a fee, amphitheater, interpretive trails, horseshoe pits. At reserved sites, 2-night minimum stay required on weekends, 3 nights on holiday weekends. (724) 646-1124. NRRS 5/15-9/7. **GPS: 41.28889, -80.43833**

❼
TIOGA-HAMMOND LAKES
GPS: 41.9017, -77.145

685-acre Hammond Lake is a "twin" lake with 498-acre Tioga Lake; they are 5 miles S of Tioga on SR 287 in north-central Pennsylvania, 72 miles W of Binghamton, New York. Tioga is on the Tioga River, Hammond along Crooked Creek. The lakes are joined by a gated connecting channel. Display gardens. Campground checkout time 3 p.m. (late fee applies). Lambs Creek Park day use facilities -- boat ramp, group shelter, hiking/biking trail. Non-campers pay $3 day use fee at boat ramps. Operations Manager, Tioga-Hammond/ Cowanesque Lakes, RR 1, Box 65, Tioga, PA 16946-9733. (570) 835-5281.

IVES RUN RECREATION AREA

From Tioga, 5 mi S on SR 287; exit E on Ives Run Lane, following signs; at E shore of Hammond Lake. About 4/15-10/31; 14-day limit (5/1 opening in 2015). 57 non-elec sites

$20 ($10 with federal senior pass); 131 elec/wtr sites, $32, full hookups $34 ($16 & $17 with senior pass). RV limit in excess of 65 ft; 5 pull-through sites; 1 RV & 1 tent or 2 tents per site. Tbls, flush & pit toilets, showers, dump, coin laundry, cfga, drkg wtr, amphitheater, fish cleaning station, playground, beach, pay phone, picnic shelters with elec ($40-$80). Archery, boating(l), fishing, interpretive trails, hiking, swimming, ball field. Store. NRRS. GPS at hookup sites, 41.888265, -77.177206; GPS at non-hookup sites, 41.881700, -77.187377

8

TIONESTA LAKE
GPS: 41.47, -79.4467

A 480-acre lake SW of Tionesta on SR 36, 60 miles SE of Erie near the southwestern corner of the Allegheny National Forest. Visitor center at dam with interpretive programs on Sundays during summer. Non-campers pay $3 at boat ramps. Picnic shelters, $45 with elec, $35 non-elec. Resource Manager, 477 Spillway Rd, Tionesta, PA 16353-9613. (814) 755-3512.

LACKEY FLATS CAMPGROUND

By boat-in only. All year; 14-day limit. 17 free primitive tent sites. Pit toilets, cfga, no drkg wtr. Boating, fishing, waterskiing.

GLASNER RUN CAMPGROUND

By boat-in only. All year; 14-day limit. 10 free primitive sites. No facilities. Boating, fishing, waterskiing. **GPS: 41.485587, -79.385641**

KELLETTVILLE CAMPGROUND

From just N of Kellettville at jct with SR 666, SE across bridge on FR 127 (The Branch Rd); campground is 17 mi upstream from dam at Tionesta Creek. About 4/15-9/30; 14-day limit. 20 primitive sites, $12 ($6 with federal senior pass). Pit toilets, cfga, drkg wtr, low-volume flush toilets, dump. 5 acres. Boating, fishing, hiking. **GPS: 41.542365, -79.25774**

OUTFLOW RECREATION AREA

From Tionesta, 1 mi S on SR 36 (Colonel Drake Hwy), then SE into campground. All year; 14-day limit. 39 sites without hookups, $14 during 4/15-10/31 ($7 with federal senior pass); free off-season, but reduced amenities (pit toilets, no wtr). 39 sites without hookups; 35-ft RV limit. Tbls, flush toilets, cfga, drkg wtr, showers, playground, beach, picnic shelter. Boating(l), fishing, swimming, hiking. **GPS: 41.474161, -79.440111**

TIONESTA RECREATION AREA

From Tionesta, 0.5 mi S on SR 36 (Colonel Drake Hwy); left on Beach Rd & continue E on Jonston Rd along S shore of Allegheny River into campground. About 5/18-9/9; 14-day limit. 107 full-hookup sites, $30 ($15 with federal senior pass). RV limit in excess of 65 ft. Tbls, flush toilets, showers, dump, cfga, drkg wtr, pay phone, playground, beach. Boating(l), swimming, hiking, waterskiing. 2 handicap sites reserved for campers with disabilities. Group camping area for organized youth, scout or church groups with prior approval. NRRS. **GPS: 41.483795, -79.447825**

9

YOUGHIOGHENY RIVER LAKE
GPS: 39.7983, -79.3683

This 2,840-acre, 16-mile lake is S of Confluence off SR 281 and N of US 40 in southwestern Pennsylvania, spanning the Mason-Dixon Line between Pennsylvania and Maryland. Trout stockings April-September. Non-campers pay $3 day use fees at boat ramps, $1 per person at beaches. Interpretive programs. Resource Manager, Youghiogheny River Lake, R.D. 497 Flanigan Road, Confluence, PA 15424-1902. (814) 395-3166. See Maryland listings.

MILL RUN CAMPGROUND

From I-68 exit 4 at Friendsville, MD, 3.5 mi
NE on SR 53; 1 mi W on Mill Run Rd, S of
Mill Run Reservoir in Maryland. All year;
14-day limit. Non-elec sites, $15 during 5/1-
9/7, self-register ($7.50 with federal senior
pass). Free rest of year for self-contained RVs;
no amenities. Tbls, flush toilets, cfga, drkg
wtr, dump, coin laundry, beach, playground.
Boating(l), fishing, swimming, waterskiing.
GPS: 39.71586, -79.384933

OUTFLOW CAMPGROUND

From Confluence, 0.7 mi SW on SR 281; at
lake. All year; 14-day limit. Some non-elec sites
$15 with self-registration during about 4/15-
5/15 & about 9/15-10/4 ($7.50 with federal
senior pass). During peak season of 5/15-
9/13, 10 tent sites & 15 non-elec RV/tent sites
are $20 ($10 with senior pass); 36 elec sites,
$25 ($12.50 with senior pass). During about
10/4-4/15, camping free with self-contained
RVs, but no amenities. 60-ft RV limit; 1 RV &
1 tent or 2 tents per site. Tbls, flush toilets,
showers, dump, cfga, drkg wtr, playground,
amphitheater, fishing pier, picnic shelter.
Biking trail & rentals, hiking, boating(ld),
fishing. 2 walk-to group camping areas. NRRS
(MD-LD). **GPS: 39.805066, -79.366286**

STATE INFORMATION:

CAPITAL: Columbia
NICKNAME: Palmetto State
STATEHOOD: 1788 - 8th State
FLOWER: Yellow Jessamine
TREE: Sabal Palm
BIRD: Carolina Wren

SC

STATE TIDBITS:

• The first battle of the Civil War took place at Fort Sumter in 1861.

• The Upper Whitewater Falls is the highest cascade in eastern America.

• Johnston is known as the "Peach Capital of the World."

WWW. DISCOVERSOUTHCAROLINA.COM

Department of Parks, Recreation and Tourism, 1205 Pendleton St., Columbia, SC 29201; 803 734-1700.

SOUTH CAROLINA LAKES

To find campgrounds operated by the U.S. Army Corps of Engineers, match the lake's numbers on the preceding map page with numbered lake entries on the following pages. Campgrounds are listed alphabetically under the appropriate lakes. The following South Carolina impoundments have Corps of Engineers campgrounds.

Hartwell Lake. A 56,000-acre surface area lake with 962 miles of shoreline located 5 miles N of Hartwell, Georgia, on US 29 SW of Greenville on the Georgia-South Carlina state line.

J. Strom Thurmond Lake. A 71,000-acre lake with 1,200 miles of shoreline adjacent to the W side of Clarks Hill, SW of Greenville on US 221 and the Georgia state line. It is the largest Corps of Engineers lake east of the Mississippi River.

❶ HARTWELL LAKE
GPS: 34.35489, -82.912041

A 56,000-acre surface area lake with 962 miles of shoreline located 5 miles N of Hartwell, Georgia, on US 29 SW of Greenville on the Georgia-South Carolina state line. Guided tours of dam and power plant available. Alcohol prohibited in campgrounds. Golf carts, off-road vehicles, motorized scooters, etc., also are prohibited. The Corps manages nine campgrounds with a total of 524 campsites (Milltown Campground in Georgia was closed in 2014). In 2015, it continues to operate several day use areas and boat ramps on the lake. Day use areas in South Carolina include: Asbury Access -- boat ramp, picnicking; Broyles -- boat ramp, toilets, shelter ($40), drkg wtr, playground, beach; Friendship -- boat ramp, toilets; Richland Creek -- boat ramp, toilets; River Forks -- boat ramp, toilets, picnicking, shelter ($40), drkg wtr, beach, playground; Singing Pines -- boat ramp, picnicking, shelter ($40), drkg wtr, beach, playground, fishing pier; Twelve Mile -- boat ramp, picnicking, shelter ($40), drkg wtr, beach, playground; Twin Lakes -- boat ramp, toilets, picnicking, shelter ($40), beach, playground; Weldon Island -- picnicking, shelter ($40), toilets, no boat ramp (closed in 2015). Project Manager, Hartwell Lake and Powerplant, 5625 Anderson Hwy, Hartwell, GA 30643. (706) 856-0300 or 888-893-0678. See Georgia listings.

CONEROSS CAMPGROUND

From Townville, 1.5 mi N on SR 24; E on Coneross Creek Rd, following signs; at Seneca River arm of lake. 5/1-9/30; 14-day limit. 106 total sites. 12 primitive sites, $18; 94 elec/wtr (30/50-amp), $24 base, $26 at premium locations ($9, $12 & $13 with federal senior pass. 36 pull-through, 1 handicap. RV limit in excess of 65 ft; 1 RV and/or as many tents that fit on pad at hookup sites; 3 vehicles permitted at each site. Tbls, flush toilets, showers, dump, playground, beach, cfga, drkg wtr, pay phone. Boating(ld), swimming, fishing. NRRS.
GPS: 34.593297, -82.892200

CRESCENT GROUP CAMP

From Anderson, 14 mi S on US 29 (8 mi N of Hartwell, GA). 5/1-10/31. Two group camping areas (all with 50-amp elec): Loop A for up to 100 people and 30 vehicles with 10 sites, $120; Loop B for up to 100 people and 66 vehicles with 22 sites, up to $264. Loop B features a picnic shelter for up to 100 people. Both loops reserved, $384. 38-ft RV limit. Tbls, flush toilets, showers, dump, drkg wtr, cfga, beach. Boating(l), fishing. NRRS.
GPS: 34.38111, -82.81639

OCONEE POINT CAMPGROUND

From Townville, 1.5 mi N on SR 24; 2.5 mi E on Coneross Creek Rd; 3 mi S on Friendship Rd, following signs; at Seneca River arm of lake. 5/1-9/30; 14-day limit. 70 elec/wtr sites 30/50-amp), 16 pull-through, $26 ($13 with federal senior pass); double sites $52. 25-ft RV limit at 3 sites, larger for other sites; 1 RV & as many tents that will fit on pad. Tbls, flush toilets, showers, dump, playground, beach, cfga, drkg wtr, pay phone. Swimming, boating(l), fishing. NRRS.
GPS: 34.601493, -82.870131

SPRINGFIELD CAMPGROUND

From Anderson, 4.5 mi W on SR 24; 4 mi S on SR 187, follow signs on Providence Church Rd. 4/1-10/31; 14-day limit. 79 elec/wtr sites (75 waterfront, 28 pull-through), 30/50-amp, $26 ($13 with federal senior pass); double sites $52. 40-ft RV limit; 1 RV & any tents fitting on pad. Tbls, flush toilets, showers, dump, playground, beach, cfga, pay phone, drkg wtr. Boating(ld), swimming, fishing. NRRS.
GPS: 34.445937, -82.821647

TWIN LAKES CAMPGROUND

From Clemson, 5.5 mi SE on US 76; 3 mi SW on State Rd S-4-56 (E. Queen St), veering right onto Twin Lake Rd & follow signs to campground; at NE shore of lake. 4/1-11/30 (33 sites open all year); 14-day limit. 102 elec/wtr sites (89 waterfront). 30-amp elec/wtr, $24; 50-amp, $26; double sites $52 ($12, $13 & $26 with federal senior pass). 60-ft RV limit; 1 RV & any sites fitting on pad. Tbls, flush toilets, showers, cfga, drkg wtr, dump, playground, beach. Boating(ld), fishing, swimming. Non-reservable picnic shelter; 2 reservable shelters in day use area. NRRS.
GPS: 34.627629, -82.850797

❷
J. STROM THURMOND
GPS: 33.50. -81.96

A 71,000-acre lake with 1,200 miles of shoreline adjacent to the W side of Clarks Hill, SW of Greenville on US 221 and the Georgia state line. It is the largest Corps of Engineers lake east of the Mississippi River. The lake extends 39.4 miles up the Savannah River, 29 miles up the Little River and 6.5 miles up the Broad River -- all in Georgia -- as well as 17 miles up the Little River in South Carolina. Exhibits on display in visitor center at 510 Clarks Hill Hwy, Clarks Hill, SC (864-333-1147); tours of dam just S of visitor center. $4 cay use fees charged non-campers; $3 boat ramp. In addition to developed day use areas, the Corps manages 29 access areas with boat ramps. The Corps operates 13 campgrounds with 554 sites, five major day use areas and numerous other recreational facilities.

South Carolina day use areas: Below dam --

boat ramp, toilets, drkg wtr, picnicking, shelter ($75), 5 small shelters ($10), fishing pier, playground; Clark Hill Park -- tbls, shelters ($25, $75 & $125), small shelters ($10-20), toilets, drkg wtr, fish cleaning station, boat ramp, 2 beaches; Parksville -- boat ramp, fish cleaning station, 2 shelters ($50 & $125), toilets; Calhouse Falls -- boat ramp; Mount Carmel -- boat ramp; Mount Pleasant -- boat ramp. Checkout time 2 p.m. Alcohol prohibited in campgrounds. For current lake conditions, call 1 (800) 333-3478, ext. 1147.

Management of five Thurmond campgrounds was scheduled to be turned over to the non-profit Lake Thurmond Campgrounds agency for five years, but in 2013 that agreement was terminated because the Corps learned it did not have authority to make it. The agreement included Petersburg, Ridge Road, Raysville and Winfield Campgrounds in Georgia and Modoc Campground in South Carolina. Later in 2013, the Corps announced it would close Leroys Ferry and Mt. Carmel Campgrounds in South Carolina.

Leroys Ferry and Mt. Carmel were closed in 2014, but in early 2015, the Corps was negotiating with McCormick County in South Carolina for lease of the two campgrounds.

Raysville in Georgia was closed in 2014 but was leased to McDuffie County for operation during 2015. Lincoln County, Georgia, agreed to 5-year leases and is now managing the Broad River, Clay Hill and Hesters Ferry Campgrounds.

To check current status of any parks, contact the lake's resource manager, J. Strom Thurmond Lake, Rt. 1, Box 12, Clarks Hill, SC 29821-9701. (864) 333-1100/(800) 533-3478. See GA listings.

HAWE CREEK CAMPGROUND

From McCormick at jct with US 221, 0.5 mi SW on US 378 past jct with SR 439, then 4 mi S on Chamberlains Ferry Rd. 4/1-9/30; 14-day limit. 28 elec/wtr sites (30/50-amp), $24 base, $26 at premium locations ($12 & $13 with federal senior pass). 45-ft RV limit; 6 pull-through sites. Tbls, flush toilets, cfga, drkg wtr, showers, dump. Boating(l), fishing. (864) 443-5441. NRRS.
GPS: 33.837075, -82.338206

LEROYS FERRY CAMPGROUND

From Willington, 2 mi SW of Willington on SR S-33-135, following signs; 2 mi S on Leroys Ferry Rd. All year; 14-day limit. $6. 10 primitive sites. Pit toilets, campfire grill areas. No reservations. Note: This campground was closed for 2014 & 2015 seasons (boat ramp open); check current status with lake office before arrival.
GPS: 33.921143, -82.489746

MODOC CAMPGROUND

From Modoc, 1 mi S on US 221, then E following signs. 4/1-11/30; 14-day limit. 1 non-elec site, $18; 69 wtr/elec sites, most 30/50-amp, $22 base, $26 at premium locations ($9, $11 & $13 with federal senior pass. 29 pull-through; double sites, $52. 45-ft RV limit. Tbls, flush & pit toilets, dump, showers, cfga, drkg wtr, playground, beach, picnic shelter, pay phone, coin laundry. (864) 333-2272. NRRS.
GPS: 33.724322, -82.215532

MOUNT CARMEL CAMPGROUND

From Mount Carmel, 4.3 mi SW, following signs. 4/1-9/6; 14-day limit. 5 non-elec sites, $18; 39 elec/wtr sites (30/50-amp), $24 base, $26 at premium locations ($9, $12 & $13 with federal senior pass). 40-ft RV limit; 12 pull-through sites. Picnic shelter, fish cleaning station. (864) 391-2711. Note: This campground closed for 2015 season (boat ramp open); check current status with lake office before arrival.

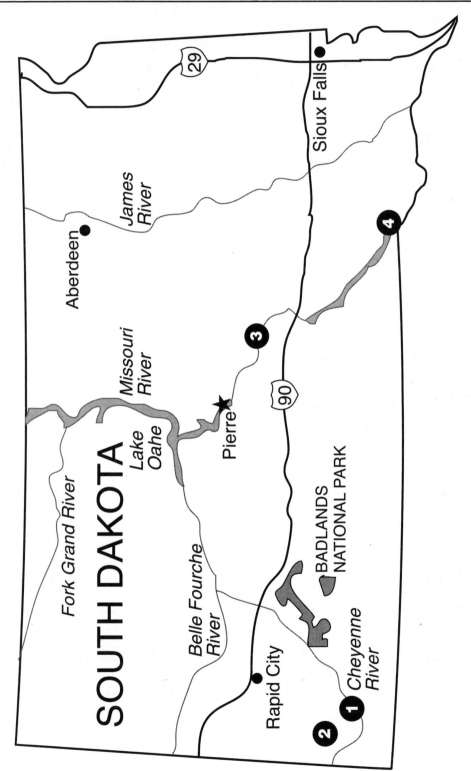

STATE INFORMATION:

CAPITAL: Pierre
NICKNAME: Mt. Rushmore State
STATEHOOD: 1889 - 40th State
FLOWER: Pasque Flower
TREE: White Spruce
BIRD: Ring-Necked Pheasant

SD

STATE TIDBITS:

• Yankton was the original Dakota Territorial capital city.

• The U.S.S. South Dakota was the most decorated battleship during World War II.

• The Dakota, Lakota and Nakota tribes make up the Sioux Nation.

WWW.TRAVELSD.COM

Toll-free number for travel information: 1-800-S-DAKOTA.

Dept of Tourism, Capitol Lake Plaza, Pierre, SD 57501-5070; 605-773-3301. E-mail: SDINFO@state.sd.us

SOUTH DAKOTA LAKES

To find campgrounds operated by the U.S. Army Corps of Engineers, match the lake's numbers on the preceding map page with numbered lake entries on the following pages. Campgrounds are listed alphabetically under the appropriate lakes. The following South Dakota impoundments have Corps of Engineers campgrounds.

Cold Brook Lake. 1 mile NW of Hot Springs off US 385 in SW South Dakota; on Fall River.

Cottonwood Springs Lake. 5 miles W of Hot Springs in SW South Dakota.

Lake Shape. 2 miles SW of Fort Thompson and 60 miles SE of Pierre.

Lewis & Clark Lake. 4 miles W of Yankton on Hwy 50 at the Nebraska state line. It is the smallest of the six Missouri River lakes, having 990 miles of shoreline.

❶
COLD BROOK LAKE
GPS: 43.4533. -103.4883

1 mile NW of Hot Springs off US 385 in SW South Dakota; on Fall River. Archery range, visitor center. Corps of Engineers, Cold Brook Lake & Cottonwood Springs, P. O. Box 664, Hot Springs, SD 57747. (605) 745-5476.

COLD BROOK CAMPGROUND

From Hot Springs, 0.5 mi N on Germond St, then follow signs to campground at N end of lake. All year; 14-day limit. 13 small sites, $8 ($4 with federal senior pass). Free during 9/15-5/15 with reduced amenities. 32-ft RV limit. Tbls, pit toilets, cfga, drkg wtr, playground, picnic shelters, beach. Boating(ld), fishing, swimming, archery, basketball. Group camping area, picnic shelters.
GPS: 43.461649, -103.491586

❷
COTTONWOOD SPRINGS LAKE
GPS: 44.84. -103.27

5 mi W of Hot Springs in SW South Dakota. Corps of Engineers, Cold Brook Lake & Cottonwood Springs, HC 69, Box 74, Hot Springs, SD 57747. (605) 745-5476.

COTTONWOOD SPRINGS

From Hot Springs, 5 mi W on SR 18, then 2 mi N on CR 17, then right on access rd. 5/15-9/15; 14-day limit. 18 sites, $10 ($5 with federal senior pass). RV limit 30 ft. Pit toilets, tbls, cfga, drkg wtr, picnic shelters, playground. Boating(l), fishing, hiking.
GPS: 43.439381, -103.572450

❸
LAKE SHARPE
BIG BEND DAM
GPS: 44.0383, -99.4467

2 miles SW of Fort Thompson & 60 miles SE of Pierre. Dam named for the Missouri River bend 7 mi upstream. Powerhouse tours daily during summer and during off-season by appointment. Visitor center with exhibits and artifact displays. Day use activities: Good Soldier Park -- boat ramp, picnic shelter, playground; Right Tailrace -- boat ramp, picnic shelter, playground; Spillway Dike -- boat ramp, picnic shelter; Spillway Overlook -- picnicking. Lake Manager, Lake Sharpe, HC 69, Box 74, Chamberlain, SD 57325-9407. (605) 245-2255.

OLD FORT THOMPSON CAMP

1 mi SW of Fort Thompson on SR 47; at Old Fort Thompson Rd below dam on E side of the spillway. All year; 14-day limit. Free. 13 primitive sites. Picnic shelter, showers, pit toilets, cfga, drkg wtr, showers, playground. Dump station half mi.
GPS: 44.059399, -99.445503

NORTH SHORE RECREATION AREA

From SW of Fort Thompson at jct with SR 47, 1.5 mi NW on BIA Rd 8, past the project office. All year; 14-day limit. 24 primitive sites, free. 2 handicap sites. Fish cleaning station, picnic shelter, pit toilets, cfga, drkg wtr, playground, beach. Ball field, basketball, swimming, boating(l), fishing. Dump station 1 mi.
GPS: 44.065201, -99.475403

LEFT TAILRACE CAMPGROUND

From Fort Thompson, 3 mi S on SR 47; below dam on S side of spillway. May-Sept; 14-day limit. 81 elec sites (35 pull-through), 2 handicap sites, $16. 35-ft RV limit. Picnic shelter, fish cleaning station, amphitheater, horseshoe pits. **GPS: 44.041016, -99.440186**

❹
LEWIS & CLARK LAKE
GAVINS POINT DAM
GPS: 42.88, -97.48

Located 4 miles W of Yankton, South Dakota, on Hwy 50 at the Nebraska state line. It is the smallest of the six Missouri River lakes; it has 90 miles of shoreline. Visitor center just downstream from powerplant; exhibits, theater, prairie garden. Dam tours daily from 10 a.m. to 6 p.m. Memorial Day through Labor Day. Day use facilities: Overlook Park -- picnicking, group shelter, playground, hiking trail; Santee Park, boat ramp. Lake Manager, Gavins Point Project, P. O. Box 710, Yankton, SD 57078. (402) 667-7873. See SD listing.

COTTONWOOD RECREATION AREA

From Yankton, 4 mi W on SR 52, then S on Dam Toe Rd; E of dam on downstream side. About 4/21-10/16; 14-day limit. 77 elec sites (20/30/50-amp), $16 base, $18 at premium locations ($8 & $9 with federal senior pass). During off-season, some sites are open and free with reduced amenities & no wtr. RV limit in excess of 65 ft; 1 RV & 2 tents or 3 tents per site. Tbls, flush toilets, showers, dump, cfga, drkg wtr, playground, fish cleaning station, picnic shelter. Boating(l), fishing. NRRS 5/21-9/6. **GPS: 42.859671, -97.482687**

NEBRASKA TAILWATERS RECREATION AREA

From Yankton, 2 mi S on US 81, then 4 mi W on Nebraska SR 121; E of the dam on S side of river off Rt 121 in Nebraska. About 5/15-10/15; 14-day limit. 13 non-elec sites, $12 ($6 with

federal senior pass); 31 elec sites (30/50-amp), $16 ($8 with senior pass). RV limit in excess of 65 ft. Tbls, flush toilets, showers, dump, cfga, drkg wtr, fish cleaning station, picnic shelters, fishing pier, playground. Boating(l), fishing, hiking. NRRS.
GPS: 42.848695, -97.468783

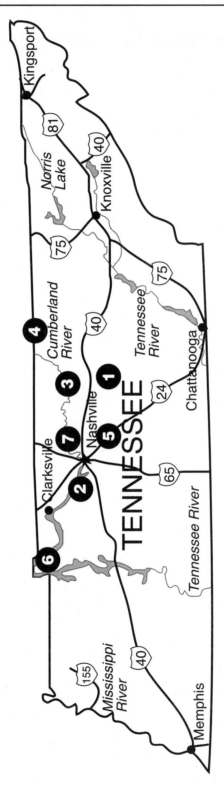

TENNESSEE

STATE INFORMATION:

CAPITAL: Nashville
NICKNAME: Volunteer State
STATEHOOD: 1796 - 16th State
FLOWER: Iris
TREE: Tulip
BIRD: Mockingbird

TN

STATE TIDBITS:

• When Tennessee became a state in 1796, the total population was 77,000.

• Tennessee has more than 3,800 documented caves.

• Bristol is known as the Birthplace of Country Music.

WWW.TNVACATION.COM

Tennessee Department of Tourist Development. Vacation guide: 800-462-8366 or info@tnvacation.com

TENNESSEE LAKES

To find campgrounds operated by the U.S. Army Corps of Engineers, match the lake's numbers on the preceding map page with numbered lake entries on the following pages. Campgrounds are listed alphabetically under the appropriate lakes. The following Tennessee impoundments have Corps of Engineers campgrounds.

Center Hill Lake. An 18,200-acre surface area lake located south of I-40 on SR 96, NW of Smithville and 64 miles E of Nashville.

Cheatham Lake. A 7,450-acre, 67-mile lake 12 miles NW of Ashland City off SR 12, NW of Nashville on the Cumberland River.

Cordell Hull Lake. An 11,960-acre lake 2.5 miles NE of Carthage off SR 263 and 49 miles E of Nashville on the Cumberland River. It is 72 miles long with 381 miles of shoreline.

Dale Hollow Lake. This 27,700-acre lake is 4 miles E of Celina and NE of Nashville on bth sides of the Kentucky/Tennessee state line on

the Cumberland and Obey Rivers. It has 620 miles of shoreline.

J. Percy Priest Lake. This 14,200-acre lake is 10 miles E of Nashville off I-40.

Lake Barkley. This 57,920-acre lake is S of junction I-24 and US 62 and E of Paducah, Kentucky. It has 1,004 miles of shoreline.

Old Hickory Lake. This 22,500-acre lake is 2 miles W of Hendersonville, S of US 31E and 10 miles NE of Nashville.

❶
CENTER HILL LAKE
GPS: 36.1017, -85.82

An 18,220-acre surface area lake located south of I-40 on SR 96, NW of Smithville and 64 miles E of Nashville. Wildlife exhibit. Alcohol prohibited. Campground checkout time 3 p.m. Free primitive camping available at five locations on the lake; a camping permit is required; boat-in tent camping at East shore, Davies Island East & Davies Island West; vehicle camping at White County Access & Cane Hollow Access. Corps day use areas: Buffalo Valley -- boat ramp, showers, interpretive trail; Hurricane Bridge -- boat ramp, shelter, picnicking; Johnsons Chapel -- boat ramp, picnicking; White County Access -- boat ramp. 4 reservable picnic shelters,

$50. Resource Manager, Center Hill Lake, 158 Resource Lane, Lancaster, TN 38569-9410. (931) 858-3125/(615) 548-4521.

CANE HOLLOW RECREATION AREA

From Cookeville, 6 mi S on SR 135 (Burgess Falls Rd); right across Burgess Falls Dam; 2 mi S on CR 2214; 0.5 mi W on Browntown Rd; continue 1 mi W on Wildcat Rd, then right (NW) on Cane Hollow Rd to Falling Water River arm of lake. All year; 14-day limit. Primitive undesignated sites, free with camping permit from lake office. Pit toilet, drkg wtr, cfga. Boating(l), fishing. **GPS: 36.032733, -85.621339**

FLOATING MILL CAMPGROUND

From I-40 exit 273 at Silver Point, 3.5 mi S on SR 56; right at store on Floating Mill Rd, following signs. About 4/15-10/15; 14-day limit. 6 non-elec tent sites, $14; 9 non-elec RV/tent sites $16; 39 tent sites with 30-amp elec, $18 base, $20 at premium locations; 44 elec RV sites (30-amp), $20 base, $24 at premium locations; 13 RV elec/wtr sites (50-amp), $22 or $24 at premium locations. All sites half price with federal senior pass. 60-ft RV limit. Tbls, flush toilets, showers, dump, pay phone, amphitheater, fish cleaning station, drkg wtr, cfga, coin laundry, playground, beach, picnic shelter ($50). RV limit 60'. At reserved sites, 2-night minimum stay required on weekends, 3 nights on holiday weekends. (931) 858-4845. NRRS. **GPS: 36.04489, -85.76347**

LONG BRANCH CAMPGROUND

From I-40 exit 268 at Buffalo Valley, 5 mi W on SR 96; 2 mi W on Center Hill Dam Rd, across dam; 1 mi N on SR 141, on right (signs); below dam on Caney Creek River. 4/1-10/30; 14-day limit. 60 elec sites: 57 are 30-amp, 3 are 50-amp. 3 handicap sites. Elec/wtr sites, $20; full hookups, $22; elec/wtr premium locations, $24 ($10, $11 & $12 with federal senior pass). Picnic shelter, $50. RV limit in excess of 65 ft. Tbls, flush toilets, showers, dump, coin laundry, cfga, drkg wtr, fish cleaning station, playground.

Boating(l), canoeing, fishing. (615) 548-8002. NRRS. **GPS: 36.099299, -85.831836**

RAGLAND BOTTOM CAMP

From Smithville, 7.1 mi NE on US 70, across lake bridge; left on Ragland Bottom Rd for 1.1 mi (signs). 4/20-10/15; 14-day limit. 16 basic tent sites, $14; 10 premium elec/wtr tent sites & 20 elec/wtr RV sites, $20; 9 full-hookup RV sites, $22; premium elec/wtr locations, $24 ($7, $10, $11 & $12 with federal senior pass. RV limit in excess of 65 ft. Tbls, flush toilets, showers, dump, cfga, drkg wtr, coin laundry, playground, beach, picnic shelter ($50). Boating(l), swimming, fishing, hiking, waterskiing, interpretive trails. (931) 761-3616. NRRS. **GPS: 35.977633, -85.720675**

WHITE COUNTY ACCESS

From Yatestown at jct with SR 136 (Old Kenton Rd), about 6 mi W on Three Island Rd (through village of Center Point); at E shore of Cany Fork River below Center Hill Lake. All year; 14-day limit. Primitive undesignated sites, free with permit from lake office. Pit toilet, cfga, drkg wtr. Boating(l), fishing. **GPS: 35.858170, -85.668941**

❷
CHEATHAM LAKE
CHEATHAM LOCK & DAM
GPS: 36.2303, -87.2228

A 7,450-acre, 67-mile lake 12 miles NW of Ashland City off SR 12, NW of Nashville on the Cumberland River. Day use fees of $4 are charged to non-campers except at Sycamore and Bush Creek Recreation Areas. Group picnic shelters are $25 & $50. Corps day use facilities include: Bluff Creek -- boat ramp, picnicking; Brush Creek -- boat ramp, fishing pier, shelter, playground, restrooms, accessible fishing trail with pier; Cheatham Dam left bank -- boat ramp, shelter, playground, tailwater fishing platform, restrooms; Cheatham Dam right bank -- boat ramps, fishing pier, fish cleaning station, 4 shelters, picnicking, 2 playgrounds, 2 volleyball courts, softball field, restrooms, beach; Cleast Ferry -- boat ramps on left bank & right bank; Johnson Creek - boat ramp, picnicking, chemical toilet; Pardue -- boat ramp, picnicking, playground; Sycamore Creek -- boat ramp, shelter, picnicking, playground, restrooms. Campers may use Cumberland River Bicentennial Trail, a 6.5-mi rails-to-trails facility ending at Lock A. Resource Manager, Cheatham Lake, 1798 Cheatham Dam Road, Ashland City, TN 37015-9805. (615) 254-3734/792-5697.

HARPETH RIVER BRIDGE CAMP

From Ashland City, about 10 mi W on SR 49; right before bridge into campground; at S shore of Harpeth River, E of bridge. About 4/30-10/15; 14-day limit. 15 elec/wtr sites, $18 ($9 with federal senior pass). Tbls, toilets, cfga, drkg wtr, playground. Boating(l) fishing, courtesy float. (615) 792-4195. No reservations. **GPS: 36.284263, -87.145282**

LOCK A CAMPGROUND

From Ashland City, 8 mi W on SR 12 to Cheap Hill; 4 mi SW (left) on Cheatham Dam Rd; at right bank of lake just upstream from dam. 4/1-10/30; 14-day limit. 45 elec/wtr sites (30/50-amp), 7 for tents only, 2 handicap sites. Tent sites & RV sites, $19 base; premium RV sites $23 ($9.50 & $11.50 with federal senior pass). Tbls, flush toilets, showers, dump, coin laundry, fish cleaning station, drkg wtr, cfga, playground, beach, picnic shelter. Boating(ld), horseshoe pits, nature trail, swimming, hiking trails (6.5-mi Cumberland Bicentennial Trail), volleyball courts, interpretive trail, basketball, courtesy floats. (615) 792-3715. NRRS (4/1-9/15). **GPS: 36.316995, -87.196035**

CORDELL HULL LAKE
GPS: 36.29, -85.9417

An 11,960-acre lake 2.5 miles NE of Carthage off SR 263 and 49 miles E of Nashville on the Cumberland River. It is 72 miles long

with 381 miles of shoreline. Wildlife exhibit at visitor center. Golf carts, off-road vehicles, electric scooters, etc., are prohibited. Non-campers pay $4 day use fee. Picnic shelters, $50. Trails include 6-mi Bearwaller Gap hiking trail; Cordell Hull horseback riding trails; half-mi Turkey Creek Nature Trail, and Bear Wheels mountain biking trail. Boat ramps are at Brimstone, Buffalo, Butlers Landing, Flynns Lick, Holleman Bend, Horseshoe Bend, Lock Tailwater, Martins Creek, Smith's Bend, Sullivans Bend and Whites Bend. Other day use areas are Cordell Hull Dam -- boat ramp, fishing pier, shelter, picnicking, toilets, playground, interpretive trail; Donaldson Park -- boat ramp, shelter, toilets, picnicking, playground, fitness trail; Indian Creek -- archery range; Moody's Place -- boat ramp, fishing pier; Overlook -- hiking trail; Roaring River -- boat ramp, fishing pier, shelter, toilets, picnicking, playground, beach, fitness trail; Wartrace Creek -- boat ramp, shelter, toilets, picnicking, beach. Campgrounds may charge $1 per day extra on weekends and holiday weekends. Resource Manager, Cordell Hull Lake, 71 Corps Lane, Carthage, TN 37030-9710. (615) 735-1034.

DEFEATED CREEK CAMP

From Carthage, 4 mi W on SR 25; 2 mi N on SR 80 (Pleasant Shade Hwy); 2.5 mi E on SR 85 (Turkey Creek Hwy), then S on Marina Lane, following signs. About 3/15-11/1; 14-day limit. 155 elec sites (63 full hookups, 35 pull-throughs). Elec/wtr sites $15 base, $18 at premium locations; full hookups $26 ($7.50, $9 & $13 with federal senior pass). A $1 per night additional fee may be charged on weekends and holidays. RV limit in excess of 65 ft. Picnic shelters ($50-$100). Tbls, flush toilets, showers, dump, cfga, drkg wtr, coin laundry, playground, beach, pay phone. Marina. Tennis & volleyball courts, boating(ld), fishing, hiking, swimming, biking. Trailhead for 6-mi Bearwaller Gap Trail. Non-campers pay $3 day use fee. (615) 774-3141. NRRS. **GPS: 36.302005, -85.909288**

SALT LICK CREEK CAMP

From Carthage, 4 mi W on SR 25; 2 mi N on SR 80 (Pleasant Shade Hwy); about 7 mi E on SR 85 to Gladice; right (SE) for 1 mi on Smith Bend Rd, then 1 mi SE on Carl Dixon Lane, following signs; at N shore of lake. About 4/15-10/15; 14-day limit. 145 elec/wtr sites (31 full hookups, 15 pull-through), $15 base, $26 full hookups ($7.50 with federal senior pass). A $1 per night additional fee may be changed on weekends and holiday weekends. RV limit in excess of 65 ft. Tbls, flush toilets, showers, dump, coin laundry, cfga, drkg wtr, beach, playground, pay phone, picnic shelter ($50). Visitor center. Boating(l), fishing, swimming, horseback riding, swimming. Non-campers pay $3 day use fee. (931) 678-4718. NRRS. **GPS: 36.323917, -85.791228**

❹ DALE HOLLOW LAKE
GPS: 36.5367, -85.4486

This 27,700-acre lake is 4 miles E of Celina and NE of Nashville on both sides of the Kentucky/Tennessee state lines on the Cumberland and Obey River. It has 620 miles of shoreline. National fish hatchery just below dam. Visitor center with interpretive programs, historic and cultural site. Alcohol prohibited. Free primitive camping available at 34 locations and more than 70 campsites around the lake, both in Tennessee and Kentucky; camping permits required; reservations now available through National Recreation Reservation Service (NRRS) for those sites at a $3 minimal fee per night. Non-campers pay $4 day use fees at most Corps parks. Day use facilities: Pleasant Grove -- toilets, boat ramp, shelter, picnicking, playground; Wolf Creek Bridge -- boat ramp. Group picnic shelters are $30, $40 & $50. 18-mi Oak Ridge Trail for hiking, horseback riding, primitive camping by permit. Accordion Bluff Hiking Trail, 7.5 mi connecting Lillydale & Willow Grove Campgrounds. Resource Manager, Dale Hollow Lake, 540 Dale Hollow Dam Road, Celina, TN 38551-9708. (931) 243-3136.

DALE HOLLOW DAM CAMP

From Celina, 2 mi NE on SR 53; 1 mi SE (right) on Dale Hollow Dam Rd, then 2nd right on Campground Rd, following signs; on N shore of Obey River below spillway. About 4/1-10/31; 14-day limit. 78 sites. 1 non-elec site, $17; 6 elec sites, $18; 46 elec/wtr sites, $21; 24 premium sites, $24 ($8.50, $9, $10.50 & $12 with federal senior pass). 60-ft RV limit; 16 pull-through sites, 2 handicap sites. Tbls, flush toilets, showers, dump, coin laundry, fishing pier, playground, fish cleaning stations, amphitheater, picnic shelters ($200, $250). Boating(ld), volleyball, hiking trails, biking, basketball. Dale Hollow National Fish Hatchery. (931) 243-3554. NRRS. **GPS: 36.53778, -85.4575**

LILLYDALE RECREATION AREA

From Oakley (a small town 5 mi N of SR 111 on SR 294), 7 mi N on SR 294 Willow Grove Rd), 1.5 mi N on Lilly Dale Rd; at S shore of lake (across lake from Dale Hollow State Resort Park). About 4/25-9/15; 14-day limit. 114 individual sites. 15 island walk-in primitive tent sites, $10 ($5 with federal senior pass); 14 other tent & 5 non-elec RV/tent sites, $15, or $21 for elec or premium location ($7.50 & $10.50 with senior pass); elec/wtr 30-amp sites (including 1 accessible paved site), $21 ($10.50 with senior pass); elec/wtr 50-amp sites, $24 ($12 with senior pass). 65-ft RV limit; 3 pull-through sites. Pavilion, amphitheater, tbls, flush & pit toilets, showers, dump, coin laundry, pay phone, playground, beaches, picnic shelter ($40). Boating(ld), biking, 2 volleyball courts, 7.5-mi hiking trail, courtesy float, basketball, volleyball, waterskiing. Non-campers pay $4 day use fee. (931) 823-4155. NRRS. **GPS: 36.602575, -85.301574**

OBEY RIVER PARK

3 mi S of Byrdstown on SR 111 (signs); on S side of Obey River arm of lake. About 4/15-10/15; 14-day limit. 131 total sites. 22 basic tent sites, $15 base, $21 at premium locations

($7.50 & $10.50 with federal senior pass). Also 18 non-elec RV/tent sites, $15 base, $21 at premium locations; 68 elec/wtr sites, $21 base, $24 for 50-amp ($7.50, $10.50 & $12 with senior pass). 55-ft RV limit. Tbls, flush toilets, showers, dump, coin laundry, cfga, drkg wtr, playground, beach, pay phone, amphitheater, 2 picnic shelters ($40). Hiking, boating(l), basketball, volleyball, swimming, fishing. Non-campers pay $4 day use fee. (931) 864-6388. NRRS. **GPS: 36.531356, -85.167968**

WILLOW GROVE CAMP

From Oakley, 10 mi N & W on SR 294 (Willow Grove Rd); at S shore of lake. About 5/15-9/1; 14-day limit. 83 sites. 21 basic tent sites, $15, $18 at premium locations; 61 wtr/elec RV sites (all 30/50-amp), $18 base, $24 at premium locations ($7.50, $9 & $12 with federal senior pass). 1 handicap site with wtr/50-amp elec. 50-ft RV limit. Tbls, flush toilets, showers, dump, coin laundry, amphitheater, playground, beach, pay phone, picnic shelters ($50-$200). Scuba diving, boating(ld), waterskiing, swimming, hiking trails, volleyball, biking. (931) 823-4285. NRRS. **GPS: 36.587397, -85.342022**

5
J. PERCY PRIEST LAKE
GPS: 36.1583, -86.6133

This 14,200-acre lake is 10 miles E of Nashville off I-40. Alcohol and off-road vehicles prohibited. Visitor center with exhibits. Campground checkout time 2 p.m. Non-campers pay $4 day use fees; guests of campers pay $3 entry fee. The lake has 3 Corps campgrounds and primitive island camping. Group picnic shelters, $40 at Anderson Road & Cook Park, free at East Fork. Pool Knobs Archery Trail with practice targets. 18-mi Twin Forks Horse Trail. Other Corps day use areas: Cook -- toilets, boat ramp, fishing pier, picnicking, playground, beach, 1.6-mi interpretive nature trail; Dam Site Center & Overlook -- toilets, fitness trail; East Fork -- toilets, boat ramp, picnicking, equestrian trail; Fall Creek -- boat ramp; Hurricane Creek -- boat ramp; Jefferson Springs -- shelter, boat ramp, toilets, picnicking; Lamat Hill -- boat ramp; Mona -- boat ramp; Smith Springs -- toilets, boat ramp, shelter, picnicking; Stewart Creek -- boat ramp, fishing pier, multi-use trail; Tailwater Left Bank -- fishing pier, fitness trail; Tailwater Right Bank -- fishing pier; Vivrett Creek -- picnicking, boat ramp; West Fork -- boat ramp. Resource Manager, J. Percy Priest Lake, 3737 Bell Road, Nashville, TN 37214-2660. (615) 889-1975.

ANDERSON ROAD CAMP

From Nashville, 5 mi E on I-40 to exit 219; 5 mi S on Ferry Pike (becoming Bell Rd); 1 mi E on Smith Spring Rd; 1 mi N on Anderson Rd. About 5/15-9/8; 14-day limit. 26 primitive sites, $14 base, $16 at premium locations; 10 sites with 30/50-amp elec/wtr, $24 ($7, $8 & $12 with federal senior pass). RV limit in excess of 65 ft; 14 pull-through sites; 1 RV & 1 tent or 2 tents per site. Tbls, flush toilets, showers, dump, drkg wtr, cfga, coin laundry, playground, beach, 2 picnic shelters ($40 plus $4 per vehicle day-use fee). Boating(ld), swimming, fitness trail, hiking. Non-campers pay $4 day use fees for boat ramp, picnicking, dump station, beach. (615) 361-1980. NRRS. **GPS: 36.105636, -86.603594**

POOLE KNOBS CAMPGROUND

From Lavergne, SE on US 41, then 2 mi N on Fergus Rd; 4 mi NE on Jones Mill Rd. 5/1-9/30; 14-day limit. 87 sites. 7 basic tent sites, $14 base, $16 at premium locations ($7 & $8 with federal senior pass); 55 elec/wtr RV sites (30/50-amp), $18 base, $24 at premium locations ($9 & $12 with senior pass); 1 tent site with elec/wtr, $18 ($9 with senior pass); 33 non-elec RV/tent sites, $14 base, $16 at premium locations ($7 & $8 with senior pass). RV limit in excess of 65 ft; 56 pull-through sites; 1 RV & 1 tent or 2 tents per site. Tbls, flush toilets, showers, cfga, drkg wtr, dump,

coin laundry, picnic shelters, beach. Group camping area, $50. Boating(l), canoeing, fishing, swimming. Non-campers pay $4 day use fees (615) 459-6948. NRRS.
GPS: 36.055032, -86.514577

SEVEN POINTS CAMPGROUND

From I-40 exit 221B, S (right) on Old Hickory Blvd (sign), then E (left) on Bell Rd; 1 mi S (right) on New Hope Rd; 1 mi E (left) on Stewarts Ferry Pike (signs). 4/1-10/30; 14-day limit. 58 wtr/elec sites, $20 base, $24 at premium locations ($10 & $24 with federal senior pass). RV limit in excess of 65 ft; 4 pull-through sites, 6 handicap sites; 1 RV & 1 tent or 2 tents per site. Tbls, flush toilets, cfga, drkg wtr, showers, dump, coin laundry, playground, beach, 2 picnic shelters ($40-$120). Boating(ld), fishing, swimming, canoeing. (615) 889-5198. NRRS. **GPS: 36.134088, -86.570560**

❻
LAKE BARKLEY
BARKLEY LOCK 8 DAM
GPS: 37.0217. -88.22

This 57,920-acre lake is S of junction I-24 and US 62 and E of Paducah, Kentucky. It has 1,004 miles of shoreline. Visitor center with various exhibits. Tennessee day use areas: Blue Creek -- boat ramp; Dover -- picnicking, shelter ($35), boat ramp; Dyers Creek -- picnicking, shelter ($35), drkg wtr, playground, volleyball court, boat ramp; Hickman Creek -- boat ramp; Linton -- picnicking, shelter ($35), boat ramp, playground, toilets. Resource Manager, Lake Barkley, 200 Barkley Dam Overlook, Grand Rivers, KY 42045-0218. (502) 362-4236. See Kentucky listings.

BUMPUS MILLS CAMPGROUND

From Clarksville, 20 mi W on US 79; 10 mi NW on SR 120 through Bumpus Mills; W on Tobaccoport Road (sign); 1 mi on gravel rd (continue straight at "Y" and sign, down hill). About 5/3-9/3; 14-day limit. 15 elec/wtr sites,

$17 base, $20 at premium locations ($8.50 & $10 with federal senior pass). RV limit 65 ft; 2 pull-through sites. Tbls, flush toilets, cfga, drkg wtr, showers, dump, coin laundry, beach, playground. Boating(ld), fishing, hiking, swimming. 270-362-4236. NRRS.
GPS: 36.622658, -87.867563

❼
OLD HICKORY LAKE
GPS: 36.295. -86.6117

This 22,500-acre lake is 2 miles W of Hendersonville, S of US 31E and 10 miles NE of Nashville. Visitor center displays, exhibits and video and interpretive programs. Visitors may be charged day use fee at the campgrounds. Non-campers pay $4 fees at 3 day use areas. Picnic shelters are $35 except at Old Hickory Beach ($50) and Rockland Recreation Area ($35-$160). Day use parks: Avondale -- picnicking, shelter, boat ramp, toilets; Cedar Creek -- picnicking, shelter, beach, sand volleyball, boat ramp, playground, toilets; Laguardo -- picnicking, shelter, beach, playground, boat ramp, toilets; Lock 3 -- beach, picnicking, boat ramp, toilet (no fees); Lone Branch -- picnicking, shelter, boat ramp, toilet; Nate Calwelll -- picnicking, shelter, boat ramp, portable toilet; Old Hickory Beach -- picnicking, shelter, boat ramp, playground, toilet, beach; Shutes Branch -- picnicking, shelter, boat ramp, fishing platform, toilet. Resource Manager, Old Hickory Lake, No. 5 Power Plant Road, Hendersonville, TN 37075-3465. (615) 822-4846/847-2395.

CAGES BEND CAMPGROUND

From Hendersonville, 5.5 mi NE on SR 31E; SE on Benders Ferry Rd (signs). 4/1-10/31; 14-day limit. 43 elec/wtr sites, $20 base, $24 at premium locations & for 50-amp elec ($10 & $12 with federal senior pass). RV limit in excess of 65 ft; 1 pull-through site, 4 handicap sites. Tbls, flush toilets, showers, cfga, drkg wtr, dump, coin laundry, picnic shelters, playground. Boating(ld), fishing, waterskiing.

(615) 824-4989. NRRS. Reservations required.
GPS: 36.304539, -86.516513

CEDAR CREEK CAMPGROUND

From jct with CR 109, 6 mi W on US 70, then
N following signs. 4/1-10/31; 14-day limit.
59 elec/wtr sites, $20 base, $24 at premium
locations ($10 & $12 with federal senior pass).
RV limit in excess of 65 ft. Tbls, flush toilets,
showers, dump, cfga, drkg wtr, coin laundry,
beach, playground, picnic shelter ($35).
Boating(ld), fishing, swimming, waterskiing.
Non-campers pay $4 day use fee. (615) 754-
4947. NRRS. **GPS: 36.276844, -86.510795**

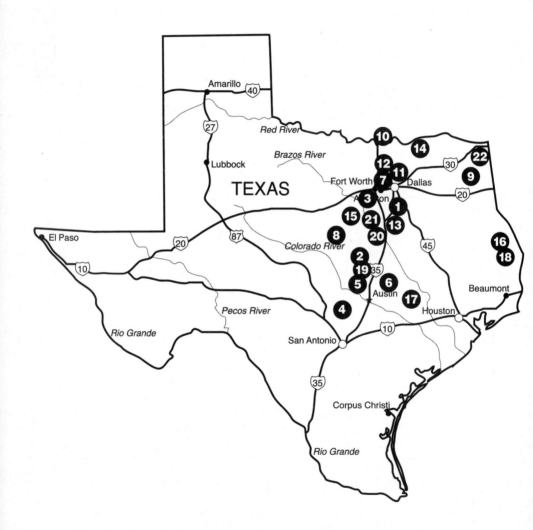

TEXAS

STATE INFORMATION:

CAPITAL: Austin
NICKNAME: Lone Star State
STATEHOOD: 1845 - 28th State
FLOWER: Bluebonnet
TREE: Pecan
BIRD: Mockingbird

STATE TIDBITS:

• Texas comes from the Hasinai Indian word tejas meaning friends or allies.

• The world's first rodeo was held in Pecos on July 4, 1883.

• More wool comes from the state of Texas than any other state.

WWW.TRAVELTX.COM

TEXAS LAKES

To find campgrounds operated by the U.S. Army Corps of Engineers, match the lake's numbers on the preceding map page with numbered lake entries on the following pages. Campgrounds are listed alphabetically under the appropriate lakes. The following Texas impoundments have Corps of Engineers campgrounds.

Bardwell Lake. A 3,500-acre lake on Waxahachie Creek with 25 miles of shoreline S of Ennis, 35 miles SE of Dallas and W of I-45.

Belton Lake. This 12,300-acre lake is 5 miles NW of Belton on FM 2271; adjacent to Fort Hood Army Base and N of Austin. It has 136 miles of shoreline.

Benbrook Lake. 3,770-acre lake 12 miles SW of Fort Worth on S side of Benbrook; on Clear Fork of Trinity River.

Canyon Lake. 8,230-acre lake with 80 miles of shoreline, located NE of San Antonio and 16 miles NW of New Braunfels off FM 306 on the Guadalupe River.

Georgetown Lake. This 1,310-acre lake is on North Fork of the San Gabriel River, part of the Brazos River System. It is 25 miles N of Austin off I-35 and 2 miles W of Georgetown on FM 2338, where it includes the Middle and South Forks.

Granger Lake. This 4,400-acre lake is 30 miles NE of Austin off SR 95 and 6.5 miles E of Granger on FM 971, then 1 mile S on local road.

Grapevine Lake. This 7,380-acre lake is on Denton Creek just NW of Grapevine (Dallas-Fort Worth Airport) off SR 26, 23 miles NE of Fort Worth.

Hords Creek Lake. This 510-acre lake is 8.7 miles W of Coleman and 55 miles S of Abilene.

Lake O' The Pines. This 19,780-acre lake is 9 miles W of Jefferson and 25 miles NW of Marshall on the Big Cypress Bayou.

Lake Texoma. This 89,000-acre lake is 5 miles NW of Denison on SR 91 and 88 miles N of Dallas/Ft. Worth on the Oklahoma state line. Lake Texoma has 580 miles of shoreline; it is on the Red River at its confluence with the Washita River.

Lavon Lake. A 21,400-acre lake 30 miles NE of Dallas and 3 miles E of Wylie off SR 78.

Lewisville Lake. A 28,980-acre lake just N of and adjacent to Lewisville (E of Mill St and I-35E) and NW of Dallas; on Elm Fork of Trinity River as well as Stewart, Panther, Cottonwood, Doe Branch, Little Elm, Pecan and Hickory Creeks.

Navarro Mills Lake. This 5,070-acre lake is 71 miles S of Dallas and 11 miles SW of Corsicana off SR 31; at Richland Creek.

Pat Mayse Lake. A 5,990-acre lake 1 mile S of Chicota off FM 197 and 12 miles N of Paris in northeastern Texas; 100 miles W of Texarkana on Sanders Creek, a tributary of the Red River.

Proctor Lake. This 4,610-acre lake has 38 miles of shoreline; it is 8 miles NE of Comanche off US 67 on FM 1476 and 97 miles SW of Fort Worth.

Sam Rayburn Lake. This 114,500-acre lake is 15 miles N of Jasper on US 96 in east-central Texas on the Angelina River. It is 89 miles N of Beaumont and 30 miles W of the Louisiana state line.

Somerville Lake. An 11,460acre lake with 85 miles of shoreline, located 1 mile W of Somerville on SR 36, on Thornberry Ave and 84 miles E of Austin.

B.A. Steinhagen Lake. This 13,700-acre lake is 15 miles SW of Jasper off FM 1746 in east-central Texas, 75 miles N of Beaumont.

Stillhouse Hollow Lake. A 6,430-acre lake 5 miles SW of Belton on FM 1670, S of Fort Hood and 80 miles N of Austin. It has 58 miles of shoreline.

Waco Lake. This 8,900-acre lake is on the NW side of Waco off FM 1637 at the Brazos River.

Whitney Lake. This 23,560-acre lake is 5.5 miles SW of Whitney on SR 23 and 79 miles S of Fort Worth on the Brazos River.

Wright Patman Lake. This 33,750-acre lake is 9 miles SW of Texarkana and the junction of US 82 off US 59.

Fort Worth District - Non-campers are charged $3 day use fees at most boat ramps in the district, $4 for use of dump stations, showers and recreational facilities. Visitor's to 10 p.m., and a fee may be charged. Note: Recreation areas such as campgrounds have been operated jointly at some lakes by the Corps of Engineers and a non-profit agency -- the Our Land and Waters Foundation. The future of that relationship is in question after an internal legal review determined the Corps does not have authority to allow cooperating agencies to retain user fees. Following that review, the Fort Worth District re-assumed operation of the parks, but some parks are once again being operated jointly. Texas Corps campgrounds involved in this issue include all those at Benbrook Lake and Sam Rayburn Reservoir, along with the following: Lavon Lake's Lavonia Park, Lakeland Park, Clearlake Park, East Fork, Ticky Creek and Avalon day use; Lewisville Lake's Westlake, Oakland and Hickory Creek Parks.

❶

BARDWELL LAKE
GPS: 32.2667, -96.6333

A 3,500-acre lake on Waxahachie Creek with 25 mi of shoreline S of Ennis, 35 mi SE of Dallas and W of I-45. Campground checkout time 2 p.m. Night emergency exits at gated campgrounds. Ground fires prohibited. In 2013, boat ramps were closed due to low lake water. Non-campers pay $4 day use fees for boat ramps, picnicking, beaches, showers, multi-use trails, dump stations, fishing. No charge to visit campers. Day use areas: Love

Park -- boat ramp, picnicking, toilets, volleyball court, horseshoe pit, group shelter, $100; Buffalo Creek Wetlands -- hiking trail; Little Mustang Creek -- boat ramp. Lake Manager, Bardwell Lake Office, 4000 Observation Drive, Ennis, TX 75119-9563. (972) 875-5711.

HIGH VIEW PARK

From Bardwell, 1.7 mi NE on SR 34, then SW prior to lake bridge on High View Marina Rd; on SW side of lake. Night-time exit provided. All year; 14-day limit. 18 elec/wtr sites (30-amp), $14; 21 elec/wtr sites (50-amp), $16 ($7 & $8 with federal senior pass). 65-ft RV limit. Tbls, flush & pit toilets, dump, showers, cfga, drkg wtr. Boating(ld), fishing, swimming. Non-campers pay $4 day use fees. Group picnic area, $50. 155 acres NRRS. (972) 875-5711. **GPS: 32.270941, -96.666909**

MOTT PARK

From Bardwell, 1 mi NE on SR 34, then SE (right) 1.4 mi on FM 985, then NE on access rd; at SE shore of lake. 7 non-elec sites, $14; 33 elec/wtr (30-amp) sites, $16 ($7 & $8 with federal senior pass). Night exit provided. 4/1-9/30; 14-day limit. 65-ft RV limit; 14 pull-through sites. Tbls, flush toilets, showers, dump, cfga, drkg wtr, beach. Boating(ld), fishing, swimming. Group camping area, $80. Non-campers pay $4 day use fees. 270 acres. NRRS. Note: Overnight camping closed temporarily by flooding late in Apr 2015. **GPS: 32.257542, -96.663079**

WAXAHACHIE CREEK PARK

From Bardwell, 1.2 mi NE on SR 24; 1.6 mi NW (left) on Bozek Lane, then right (NE) on Brightwater Lane; at NW shore of lake. All year; 14-day limit. 7 primitive sites, $14, $16 at premium locations ($7 & $8 with federal senior pass). 69 elec/wtr (30-amp) sites, including 4 equestrian sites, $16 base, $18 at premium locations ($8 & $9 with senior pass). 65-ft RV limit; 14 pull-through sites. Tbls, flush & pit toilets, showers, dump, cfga, drkg wtr.

Boating(l), fishing, nature trail, equestrian trail. Group camping with elec, $120. Boat rentals nearby. Non-campers pay $4 day use fees. Night exit provided. 205 acres. Note: Camping temporarily closed by flooding late in April 2015. NRRS. **GPS: 32.293046, -96.69114**

❷
BELTON LAKE
GPS: 31.1, 97.4833

This 12,300-acre lake is 5 miles NW of Belton on FM 2271; adjacent to Fort Hood Army Base and N of Austin. It has 136 miles of shoreline. Campground checkout time 2 p.m. Restored historic bridge; nature area with hiking trail; wildlife viewing areas; visitor center; interpretive programs. Non-campers pay $4 vehicle day use fee for picnicking, beaches, dump station; $3 for boat ramps. Group shelters: $40 weekdays, $60 weekends at Frank's; $60 weekdays, $100 weekends at Overlook; $40 weekdays, $70 weekends at Temple's Lake; $100 weekdays, $175 weekends at Turkey Roost; $40 weekdays, $70 weekends at Sunset & Coveside. Day use areas: boat ramps at Arrowhead Point, Iron Bridge, Leona, McGregor, Rogers, Sparta & Temple Lake. Temple Lake also has toilets, fishing pier, playground, beach, multi-purpose trail. Most boat ramps & all docks unusable in 2015 due to low lake water; check current status with lake office before arrival. Resource Manager, Little River Project Office, 3110 FM 2271, Belton, TX 76513-6522, 254-939-2461; or stop at 3740 FM 1670, Belton, at N end of Stillhouse Hollow Dam.

CEDAR RIDGE PARK

From jct with SR 317 N of Belton, 2 mi NW on SR 36; 2 mi SW on Cedar Ridge Park Rd. Park access codes provided to campers for late entry. All year; 14-day limit, but sites 1-40 were closed during 2014-15 winter. 68 elec/wtr sites, $22 (1 double site $36); 8 screened shelters ($30) for those without camping equipment. 4 elec/wtr tent sites, $16; 30/50-amp elec/wtr RV sites,

$22. (All sites half price with federal senior pass). RV limit in excess of 65 ft; 2 pull-through sites, 49 handicap sites. Tbls, flush toilets, showers, dump, cfga, drkg wtr, coin laundry, beach, playground, fishing pier. Basketball & volleyball courts, horseshoe pits, swimming, boating(ld), fishing, hiking. For Turkey Roost group camping area, see listing below. 2 picnic shelters with elec/wtr, $40-$70. Marina. Free Wi-fi for campers at activity bldg. Center for camper parties & meetings. 254-986-1404. NRRS. **GPS: 31.169491, -97.442851**

IRON BRIDGE PARK

From jct with SR 317 NW of Belton, 10 mi NW on SR 36, crossing lake bridge; 0.5 mi E on Deer Ridge Rd; 2 mi NE on gravel Iron Bridge Park Rd, following sign; at NE shore of lake. 5 isolated primitive sites, free. All year; 14-day limit. Pit toilet, tbls, cfga, no drkg wtr. Picnic area, boating, fishing. Boat ramps very shallow; small flat-bottom boats recommended (not usable in 2015). **GPS: 31.280532, -97.4722270**

LIVE OAK RIDGE PARK

From N of Belton at jct with SR 317, 1.7 mi NW on FM 2305 (W. Adams Ave); left (S) 2 mi on FM 2271 (Morgans Point Rd); adjacent to dam & spillway. All year; 14-day limit. 48 elec/wtr sites, covered tbls, grills; 14 handicap sites. $18 at 30-amp sites, $22 for 50-amp ($9 & $11 with federal senior pass). RV limit in excess of 65 ft. Tbls, flush toilets, cfga, drkg wtr, coin laundry, amphitheater, dump, playground. Activity center for parties & meetings, free wireless Internet access for campers at activity bldg. Boating(l), fishing, hiking. 254-780-1738. NRRS. **GPS: 31.116870, -97.473037**

OWL CREEK PARK

From jct with SR 317 NW of Belton, 6.5 mi NW on SR 36, across lake bridge; 1.1 mi W on Owl Creek Rd; right on access Rd. About 20 free, undesignated primitive sites. No drkg wtr. Tbls, pit toilet, cfga, picnicking. Boating(l),

fishing. All year; 14-day limit. **GPS: 31.217706, -97.51307**

TURKEY ROOST GROUP CAMPGROUND

At Cedar Ridge Park. Horseshoe pits, picnic shelter, group camping only. Must be by reservation made in person at the Little River Project Office or through NRRS. Contact the office for maximum number of RVs and tents permitted. 6 sites, 2 double sites with 50-amp elec. Friday-Sunday nights, $175; Monday-Thursday nights $100. Open all year. Tbls, flush toilets, cfga, drkg wtr, showers. NRRS.

WESTCLIFF PARK

From jct with SR 317 N of Belton, 3.7 mi NW on FM 439 (Lake Rd); 0.2 mi NW on Sparta Rd, then NE on Westcliff Park Rd; at SE shore of lake. All year; 14-day limit (sites 1-19 closed 12/1-3/1). 31 sites with covered tbls, grills, lantern poles. 26 wtr/elec sites, $22; 4 basic tent only sites, $10 ($11 & $5 with federal senior pass); elec tent sites $16 ($8 with senior pass). 65-ft RV limit; 20 pull-through sites, 4 handicap sites with elec, 8 handicap sites with wtr/elec. Tbls, flush & pit toilets, showers, dump, cfga, drkg wtr, playground, beach, picnic shelter. Swimming, boating(l), fishing, hiking. Free Wi-fi for campers at activity building. NRRS. **GPS: 31.1114496, -97.517020**

WHITE FLINT PARK

From jct with SR 317 NW of Belton, 5.5 mi NW on SR 36, across bridge, then right into park; on NW shore of lake. Access codes provided to registered campers for late night entry. All year; 14-day limit. 13 elec/wtr (30/50-amp) sites (covered tbls, grills), $22 ($11 with federal senior pass). 6 handicap sites, 12 screened shelters for those without camping gear, $30. RV limit 60 ft. Flush & pit toilets, showers, dump, cfga, drkg wtr. Boating(ld), fishing. NRRS. **GPS: 31.230436, -97.472398**

WINKLER PARK

From jct with SR 317 NW of Belton, 7.5 mi NW on SR 36; exit right (SE) 2 mi past White Flint Park on Deer Ridge, then 3.5 mi SE to park; at NW shore of lake. All year; 14-day limit. 14 semi-primitive sites, wtr hookups, $10-$12 ($5-$6 with federal senior pass). 35-ft RV limit. Covered tbls, flush toilets, cfga, drkg wtr, showers. Boating, fishing. Register, pay fees at nearby White Flint Park. Now by reservation, NRRS. **GPS: 31.251516, -97.473278**

❸ BENBROOK LAKE
GPS: 32.65, -97.45

3,770-acre lake 12 miles SW of Forth Worth on S side of Benbrook. On Clear Fork of Trinity River. Campground checkout time 2 p.m. Non-campers pay day use fees of $3 for boat ramps, $2 showers, $4 dump stations. Picnicking & swimming allowed in all undeveloped areas. Trailheads to 14-mi equestrian & hiking trail; equestrian camping at one site in Holiday Campground & throughout Westcreek Circle. Bridle trails also in & N of Rocky Creek Park. For 2105, all boat ramps closed except Mustang's due to low lake water. Marina at Rocky Creek not operating during 2015. Resource Manager, Benbrook Lake, 7001 Lakeside Dr, Ft. Worth, TX 76126. (817) 292-2400.

HOLIDAY CAMPGROUND

From N side of Benbrook at jct with I-20, 5.7 mi SW on US 377; qtr mi E on Stevens Dr; 1 mi SE on Lakeview Dr. 105 sites, 43 are 30-amp elec, 31 are 30/50-amp; 5 have 30/50-amp & wtr in enclosed screened shelters; 26 non-elec sites. Site 65 for equestrians. Walk-to tent sites, non-elec tent sites & non-elec equestrian site $14; elec sites $28; screened shelters $40 ($7, $14 & $20 with federal senior pass). RV sites have covered tbls, cookers. RV limit in excess of 65 ft; 40 pull-through sites. Covered tbls, flush toilets, cfga, drkg wtr, showers, dump, pay phones, fishing pier. Boating(ld),

fishing, hiking, horseback riding trails. Non-campers pay day use fees: $3 for boat launch, swimming beach, picnicking; $2 for showers, $4 for dump station. Horse rentals nearby. NRRS. **GPS: 32.618168, -97.497053**

MUSTANG PARK
BEAR CREEK CAMPGROUND

From N side of Benbrook at jct with I-20, 6.4 mi SW on US 377; 1.4 mi SE on FM 1187; 2.6 mi NW CR 1042, past entrance to Mustang Point area; at S shore of Bear Creek. All year; 14-day limit (but closed during winter of 2014-15, re-opened 4/1/2015). 40 elec/wtr sites (6 have 50-amp, 2 with sewers, $28 ($14 with federal senior pass). RV limit in excess of 65 ft; 10 pull-through sites. Covered tbls, cookers, drkg wtr, showers, dump, picnic shelter, fishing pier. Group camping at 6 sites with wtr/elec, $125. Boating(l), fishing. Night-time exit provided. Non-campers pay day use fees. NRRS. **GPS: 32.603365, -97.495637**

MUSTANG PARK
MUSTANG PT. CAMPGROUND

Adjacent to Bear Creek Campground at Mustang Park. No designated sites, primitive area; 9 areas have covered tbls, but open shoreline camping for tents & RVs. 4/1-9/30; 14-day limit. $14 ($7 with federal senior pass). Tbls, toilets, cfga, drkg wtr, beach. Campers can use showers at other campgrounds for $2. Boating(l), fishing, swimming.

MUSTANG PARK
WEST CREEK CIRCLE
BEAR CREEK CAMPGROUND

From N side of Benbrook at jct with I-20, 6.4 mi SW on US 377; 1 mi SE on FM 1187; SE 1 mi to Ben Day-Murrin Rd (CR 1025), then E 1 mi to the park. Limited-development camping at Bear Creek shoreline. Free primitive camping, including equestrian camping (future equestrian facilities planned). 1 pit toilet, cfga, tbls, no drkg wtr. Boating(l), fishing. Trailhead to 14 mi of hiking &

equestrian trails. Fee for use of showers, dump station, boat launch, beach at Bear Creek Campground. **GPS: 32.600717, -97.498963**

ROCKY CREEK CAMPGROUND

From Benbrook, S on US 377; 7 mi SE on FM 1187; 3.6 mi N on CR 1089; at jct with CR 1150, exit S to park. All year; 14-day limit; closed winter of 2014-15, but re-opened 4/1/2015. 11 sites, $14 ($7 with federal senior pass). Covered tbls, nearby drkg wtr, cfga, tbls, open picnicking. Dump nearby. Boating(l), fishing. **GPS: 32.592756, -97.453011**

❹ CANYON LAKE
GPS: 29.8667, -98.2

8,230-acre lake with 80 miles of shoreline, located NE of San Antonio and 16 miles NW of New Braunfels off FM 306 on the Guadalupe River. Campground checkout time 2 p.m. Non-campers pay $4 day use fee for dump station, picnicking, beaches; $3 & $4 at boat ramps. No park access after 10 p.m. Trails include partially built Overlook Park Trail, Madrone Hiking Trail from Canyon Park, Canyon Dam Trail, 3.5-mi Hancock Horse Trail. Other Corps day use areas: Canyon Beach -- picnicking, beach, toilet; Comal Park -- 2 boat ramps, picnicking, beach, playground, toilets; Guadalupe -- fishing pier, hiking trail; Little Jacobs Creek -- boat ramp, picnicking. Due to low lake levels, several boat ramps were closed during 2015. Resource Manager, Canyon Lake, 601 COE Road, Canyon Lake, TX 78133-4129. (830) 964-3341.

CANYON PARK

From Canyon City, 3.2 mi NW on FM 306, then SW (right) on Canyon Park Rd; at NW shore of Canyon Lake. 4/1-9/30; 14-day limit. 150 primitive sites, $12 ($6 with federal senior pass). Pit toilets, cfga, drkg wtr, picnic shelter ($75). Boating(dl), hiking/biking trails, swimming. Boat rentals nearby. **GPS: 29.895806, -98.232300**

CRANES MILLS PARK

From Startzville, 2.8 mi NW on FM 2673; at SW shore of lake. All year; 14-day limit. 34 tent sites (29 with 15-amp elec), $20; 30 elec/wtr RV sites (20/30/50-amp), $26 ($10 & $13 with federal senior pass). Tbls, flush toilets, cfga, dump, playground. Boating(ld), fishing. 2 fishing piers open & close with wtr levels. NRRS. **GPS: 29.891034, -98.291684**

NORTH PARK

From Canyon City, 1.2 mi NW on FM 306, then 1 mi SE on North Park Rd; near dam. Open only Fri & Sat nights during 4/1-9/30. 19 primitive sites. $12 ($6 with federal senior pass). Pit toilets, tbls, cfga, drkg wtr. Popular scuba diving area, but no boat ramp. **GPS: 29.874039, -98.202976**

POTTERS CREEK PARK

From Canyon City, 6.2 mi NW on FM 306; 2 mi S on Potters's Creek Rd; at NW shore of lake. All year; 14-day limit. Park open 7am-10pm. Five camping loops containing 114 elec/wtr RV/tent sites (covered tbls, fire rings, standing grills), $26 ($13 with federal senior pass); double sites $40, triple sites $60. 1 loop of 10 tent sites, $20 ($10 with senior pass). 7 screened shelters, $40. 60-ft RV limit. Tbls, flush toilets, showers, dump, fishing pier, recycle station, beach, playground, picnic shelters ($100). Boating(ld), swimming, fishing, hiking, jet skiing, waterskiing, campfire programs, interpretive programs, biking. No day use by non-campers. NRRS 4/1-9/30. **GPS: 29.906176, -98.264905**

❺ GEORGETOWN LAKE
GPS: 30.675, -97.725

This 1,310-acre lake is on North Fork of the San Gabriel River, part of the Brazos River System. It is 25 miles N of Austin off I-35 and 2 miles W of Georgetown on FM 2338, where it includes the Middle and South Forks. Fee at developed campgrounds for extra vehicles.

Campground checkout time 2 p.m. Overlook Park, open daily, has a fishing pier & hiking trailhead. Non-campers pay day use fee of $4 for picnicking, boat ramps, dump stations. Most boat docks closed in 2015 due to low lake water. Resource Manager, Lake Georgetown, 500 Lake Overlook Rd, Georgetown, TX 78633. (512) 930-5253.

CEDAR BREAKS PARK

From just S of Georgetown at jct with I-35, 3.5 mi SE on FM 2338; 1 mi N on D.B. Wood Rd; 2 mi NW on Cedar Breaks Rd, following signs; at NW shore of lake, just E of dam. Late night emergency exit provided. All year; 14-day limit. 64 elec/wtr sites (30/50-amp), covered tbls, $26 ($13 with federal senior pass). 55-ft RV limit. Flush toilets, showers, cfga, drkg wtr, dump, fishing pier, 41 covered shelters in day use area. Boating(ld), fishing, hiking trails. NRRS. **GPS: 30.661231, -97.737336**

CEDAR HOLLOW CAMP

Access either by boat or hike in on the Good Water Hiking Trail; between mileposts 4 & 5. Primitive area, free. Tbl, fire ring, lantern stand, pit toilet, no drkg wtr. Open all year; 14-day limit.

JIM HOGG PARK

From just S of Georgetown at jct with I-35, about 7 mi SE on FM 2338; 2 mi N on Jim Hogg Rd, at SW shore of lake opposite Cedar Breaks Park. Night exit provided. All year; 14-day limit; several sites closed 11/1-3/1. 148 elec/wtr back-in sites, $22 for 30-amp, $26 for 30/50-amp; 10 double sites with 30/50 amp elec/wtr, $28-$36; 5 double screened sites 30/50-amp elec/wtr, $32-$40. 50% discounts with federal senior pass. 55-ft RV limit. Tbls, flush toilets, showers, dump, cfga, drkg wtr. Boating(ld), fishing, hiking trails. (512) 819-9046). NRRS. **GPS: 30.685450, -97.742218**

RUSSELL PARK

From SE of Georgetown at jct with I-35, 7.5 mi SE on FM 2338; 3 mi NW on FM 2338 (past exit to Jim Hogg Park); 0.7 mi E on FM 3405; 2 mi N on CR 262. All year; 14-day limit; most sites closed 11/1-3/1. 17 non-elec tent sites, $12; 10 non-elec screened shelters containing bunks (no mattresses), $24 ($6 & $12 with federal senior pass). 3 elec overnight group screened shelters, $75. Toilets, showers, drkg wtr. Group picnic shelter, $75 open Fri-Sun & holidays; weekdays by appt. **GPS: 30.677316, -97.759153**

SAWYER CAMP

Access by boat or hike in on the Good Water Hiking Trail; between mileposts 6 & 7. Primitive tent area, free. Tbls, fire rings, lantern stands, pit toilet, no drkg wtr. Open all year; 14-day limit.

TEJAS PARK

NW of lake's project office. From jct with SR 2338, 5.5 mi W on FM 3405, then SE on CR 258. All year; 14-day limit; 6 sites closed 11/1-3/1. $6. 12 primitive tent only sites, 3 walk-in/boat-in sites. Fire rings, tbls, drkg wtr, pit toilets. Group tent camping, $14. Boating, fishing, hiking. Register at Russell Park gatehouse. **GPS: 30.695668, -97.828166**

WALNUT SPRINGS CAMP

Access by water or hike in on the Good Water Hiking Trail; between mileposts 15 & 16. Free primitive tent area. Tbls, fire rings, lantern stands, pit toilet, no drkg wtr. All year; 14-day limit.

6

GRANGER LAKE
GPS: 30.7033, -97.3167

This 4,400-acre lake is 30 miles NE of Austin off SR 95 and 6.5 miles E of Granger on FM 971, then 1 mi S on local road. Non-campers pay day use fees of $4 at 5 boat ramps, beaches, picnicking, hiking, biking, horseback riding, fishing, dump stations. Friendship Park open for day use Fri-Sun & holidays during 3/1-9/30 (boat ramp, beach, picnicking, fishing, group shelter). Resource Manager, Granger Lake, 3100 Granger Dam Road, Granger, TX 76530-5067. (512) 859-2934.

FOX BOTTOM
PRIMITIVE CAMPING AREA

Hike in from West Trailhead on CR 496 on the Comanche Bluff Hiking Trail, which starts at the park and ends at Taylor Campground; or boat-in from Taylor Park (paying boat ramp fee for number of days prior to departure); or 0.5 mi downstream from Box 7 primitive boat launch via jon boat or canoe. All year; 14-day limit. 8 free primitive sites, each with tent pad, lantern hanger, fire pit; no drkg wtr available; 2 central tbls & fire pit; compost toilet; group fire ring. Advance phone registration required (512-859-2668). **GPS: 30.663774, -97.382421**

TAYLOR PARK

From Circleville at jct with SR 95, about 5 mi NE on FM 1331, then qtr mi N on Granger Dam Rd & NW on Fox Park Rd. 3/1-9/30; 14-day limit. 48 elec/wtr sites, $20 (4 double sites with elec for 1 RV, $24); $10 & $12 with federal senior pass. 50-ft RV limit. Tbls, flush toilets, dump, showers, cfga, drkg wtr, beach, playground. Biking, hiking, boating(ld), fishing, waterskiing. Comanche Bluff Hiking Trail starts at the park; trail museum. Non-campers pay $4 day use fees for boat ramp (open all year), beach, picnicking, hiking, horseback riding, fishing, dump station. NRRS. **GPS: 30.665832, -97.371322**

WILLIS CREEK PARK

From Granger at jct with Hwy 95, 0.8 mi E on FM 971; 4 mi SE on CR 348; NE on CR 346. All year; 14-day limit. 10 primitive sites (5 for equestrians), $10; 23 elec/wtr sites, $20; 4 full hookups, $24 ($5, $10 & $12 with federal senior pass). 50-ft RV limit. Pit toilets, tbls, cfga, drkg wtr, showers, dump, picnic

shelter ($50 - open Fri-Sun & holidays). Group camping area with elec/wtr, $50. Boating(ld), fishing, horseback riding, sailing, waterskiing, swimming. Non-campers pay $4 day use fees for boat ramp, beach, picnicking, hiking, horseback riding, fishing, dump station. NRRS. **GPS: 30.695331, -97.389089**

WILSON H. FOX CAMPGROUND

From Taylor Park, 1 mi NE on FM 1331, then NW; adjacent to S side of dam. All year; 14-day limit. 49 wtr/elec sites, including 5 screened shelters. Four 30-amp sites, $20; 35 elec/wtr 50-amp sites, $22; screened shelters, $34; five double 50-amp sites, $36 ($10, $11, $17 & $18 with federal senior pass). Pit toilets, tbls, showers, dump, cfga, drkg wtr, playground, beach, fish cleaning station, fishing pier, group picnic shelter ($50 - open Fri-Sun & holidays). Boating(ld), fishing, swimming. Non-campers pay $4 day use fees for boat ramps, beach, picnicking, hiking, horseback riding, fishing, dump station; closed for day use 10/1-3/31. NRRS. **GPS: 30.683282, -97.349714**

❼
GRAPEVINE LAKE
GPS: 32.9667, -97.05

This 7,380-acre lake is on Denton Creek just northwest of Grapevine (Dallas-Fort Worth Airport) off SR 26, 23 miles NE of Fort Worth. Golf course below the dam. Alcoholic beverages prohibited. ORV area and an equestrian trail are provided. Former Corps campgrounds Silver Lake (now Vineyards Campground) and Meadowmere Park are managed by the City of Grapevine; Twin Cove Park has been leased to the City of Flower Mound. (For details about camping at these parks, see our new "Guide to Western County & City Parks" book) Camping provided only at Murrell Park, and it is open only for primitive tent camping. Non-campers pay day use fee at boat ramps. During 2015, Farris, Murrell, Vineyards, Katie's Woods & McPherson Slough boat ramps remain closed by low lake water; Meadowmere low-wtr ramp, Lakeview North, Dove Loop & Trawick open. Resource Manager, Grapevine Lake, 110 Fairway Drive, Grapevine, TX 76051-3495. (817) 865-2600.

MURRELL PARK

From Grapevine at jct with SR 121, 4.5 mi N on FM 2499; 0.2 mi W (sign) on FM 3040; 0.4 mi W on McKamey Creek Rd, then S on Simmons Rd. All year; 14-day limit. Group camping area (some free for use by boy scouts, church groups, etc.). 22 primitive tent sites. $10 ($5 with federal senior pass). Pit & portable toilets, tbls, cfga, drkg wtr, playground. Hiking, biking, boating. Boat ramp closed in 2015 due to low lake wtr. NRRS. **GPS: 32.9975, -97.08917**

❽
HORDS CREEK LAKE
GPS: 31.85, -99.5667

This 510-acre lake is 8.7 miles W of Coleman and 55 miles S of Abilene. Friendship day use park offers boat ramps, fishing pier, picnicking, beach. Resource Manager, Hords Creek Lake, 230 Friendship Park Rd, Coleman, TX 76834. (915) 625-2322. Note: Due to low water levels in 2015, this entire lake is a no-wake zone, and all boat ramps are closed except at Friendship Park; designated swimming beaches also closed. Open fires prohibited, even in fire pits, fire rings or uncovered BBQ pits.

FLATROCK PARK

From Coleman, 8.7 mi W on Hwy 153; S across dam on Hords Creek Rd, then W on Flat Rock Park Rd, following signs; on S shore of lake. 4/1-9/30; 14-day limit. 39 elec/wtr 30-amp sites, $16; 10 elec/wtr 50-amp sites, $20 base, $22 premium locations, $32 double; 4 full hookups, $22 ($8, $10, $11, $16 & $11 with federal senior pass); 2 double elec/wtr 30-amp sites, $32; 1 double full-hookup site, $44. 6 screened shelters $22 base, $26 with elec & A/C. RV limit in excess of 65

ft; 10 pull-through sites. Tbls, flush toilets, cfga, drkg wtr, dump, showers, beach, fish cleaning station. Two group camping areas with shelters, $100-$130. Boating(ld), fishing, swimming. Campground remodeled for 2015. NRRS. **GPS: 31.826790, -99.566082**

LAKESIDE PARK

From Coleman, 8 mi W on Hwy 153 past Friendship Park, then S on Lakeside Rd, following signs; on N shore of lake. All year; 14-day limit. 44 elec/wtr 30-amp sites, $16 base, $20 at premium locations; 16 elec/wtr 50-amp sites, $20 base, $22 at premium locations; 6 screened overnight shelters, $22 or $26 with a/c; 8 wtr/elec 50-amp sites, $26. RV limit in excess of 65 ft; 9 pull-through. Tbls, flush toilets, showers, dump, cfga, drkg wtr, beach, fish cleaning station, picnic shelters ($40). Group camping areas, up to $260. Boating(ld), horseshoe pits, fishing, swimming. NRRS. **GPS: 31.845533, -99.579644**

❾
LAKE O' THE PINES
GPS: 32.765, -94.967

This 19,780-acre lake is 9 miles W of Jefferson and 25 miles NW of Marshall on the Big Cypress Bayou. Campground checkout time 2 p.m. Fee campgrounds have emergency night-time exits. Operation of ORV, golf carts and motorized scooters prohibited in parks unless properly licensed in the state. Activities include watching wintering bald eagles. Non-campers pay day use fees: $3 for boat ramps, $4 for dump stations, picnicking, beaches. Day use areas: Cedar Springs -- boat ramp; Copeland Creek -- boat ramp; Hurricane Creek -- boat ramp, picnicking; Lakeside -- shelter, boat ramp, picnicking, beach; Lone Star -- boat ramp; Oak Valley -- boat ramp; Outlet Area -- boat ramp; Overlook Area -- boat ramp, fishing pier, picnicking; Pine Hill -- boat ramp. In 2015, the following boat ramps were closed: Overlook, Oak Valley, Johnson Creek. Visitor center. Resource Manager, Lake O' The Pines, 2669 FM 726, Jefferson, TX 75657. (903) 665-2336.

ALLEY CREEK CAMPGROUND

From Jefferson, 4 mi NW on SR 49; 12 mi W on FM 729 across 3 lake bridges; after third bridge, turn S on Alley Creek Rd, following signs. 3/1-9/30; 14-day limit. 30 tent sites, $18; 23 elec RV sites, $26 base, $28 for premium location; 6 elec RV/tent sites, $30 (double sites $44); group elec area (12 sites), $175. Holders of federal senior pass pay half rates. RV limit in excess of 65 ft. Tbls, flush toilets, showers, dump, playground, beach. Boating(ld), swimming, fishing, waterskiing. During 2015, beach & tent area 1 were closed. (903) 755-2637. NRRS. **GPS: 32.798377, -94.590086**

BRUSHY CREEK CAMPGROUND

From Jefferson, 4 mi NW on SR 49; 3.5 mi W on FM 729; 4.8 mi SW on FM 726 past dam, on right (sign); at SE shore of lake. 3/1-11/30; 14-day limit. 25 non-elec tent sites, $16 & $18; 12 elec tent sites, $20; 40 elec RV sites, $26 base, up to $42 for premium locations. Holders of federal senior pass pay half rates. RV limit in excess of 65 ft. Tbls, flush toilets, cfga, drkg wtr, showers, dump, playground, beach. Boating(ld), fishing, swimming, waterskiing. For 2015, beach, tent area 2 & lower rd to tent area 1 closed. (903) 777-3491. NRRS. **GPS: 32.743212, -94.535948**

BUCKHORN CREEK PARK

From Jefferson, 4 mi NW on SR 49; 3.5 mi W on FM 729; 2.4 mi SW on FM 726, on right (sign) before the dam. 3/1-9/30; 14-day limit. 38 tent sites, $18; 72 elec RV sites, $26 base, up to $44 for premium locations (holders of federal senior pass pay half price). RV limit in excess of 65 ft. Tbls, flush toilets, showers, cfga, drkg wtr, dump, playground, beach. Boating(ld), fishing, swimming, waterskiing, hiking trails. During 2015, RV2 Loop, tent 2 loop & restrooms closed. (903) 665-8261. NRRS. **GPS: 32.757252, -94.495736**

CEDAR SPRINGS PARK

From Avinger, 4 mi SW on SR 155, across lake, then left on Upshur County Landing Rd; at NW shore of lake. 28 primitive sites; 48 acres. Free. All year; 14-day limit. Pit toilets, drkg wtr, cfga, tbls. Boating(ld), fishing. **GPS: 32.841479, -94.696355**

HURRICANE CREEK PARK

From Jefferson, 4 mi NW on SR 49; 4 mi W on FM 729 past FM 726, then 0.25 mi S following signs; at E shore of Hurricane Creek arm of lake. All year; 14-day limit; reduced facilities in winter. 23 primitive sites. Free. Pit toilets, drkg wtr, tbls, cfga. Boating(ld), fishing. **GPS: 32.785908, -94.511433**

JOHNSON CREEK CAMP

From Jefferson, 4 mi NW on SR 49; 8.5 mi W on FM 729, on left after crossing bridge over Johnson Creek; at NE shore of lake. All year; 14-day limit. 38 tent sites, $18 base, $20 with elec; 31 elec RV sites, $26 base, $30 premium locations ($9, $10, $13 & $15 with federal senior pass). RV limit in excess of 65 ft. Tbls, flush toilets, showers, cfga, drkg wtr, playground, beach, fish cleaning station, fishing pier, amphitheater, picnic shelter ($75). Group camping area with 12 elec sites, $150-$175. Boating(ld), swimming, hiking, volleyball court, waterskiing. (903) 755-2435. NRRS. **GPS: 32.78667, -94.55056**

⑩
LAKE TEXOMA
GPS: 33.8333, -96.5667

This 89,000-acre lake is 5 miles NW of Denison on SR 91 and 88 miles N of Dallas/Ft. Worth on the Oklahoma state line. Lake Texoma has 580 miles of shoreline; it is on the Red River at its confluence with the Washita River. ORV prohibited. The Corps operates 10 campgrounds with more than 700 campsites. Lake Manager, Texoma Lake, 351 Corps Road, Denison, TX 75020. (903) 465-4490. See Oklahoma listings.

DAM SITE SOUTH RECREATION AREA

From Denison, 5 mi N on SR 91; turn right on Denison Dam Rd; below dam on S side of Red River. 4/1-9/30; 14-day limit. 5 tent sites & 8 primitive RV/tent sites, $12; 44 elec sites (no wtr hookups), $18 base, $20 at premium locations ($6, $9 & $10 with federal senior pass). 55-ft RV limit. Tbls, flush toilets, cfga, drkg wtr, showers, dump, playground, beach with change house. Hiking trails, swimming, boating(ld), fishing. Non-campers pay day use fee for boat ramp, beach, dump. Group picnic shelter, $50. NRRS.
GPS: 35.299471, -95.370147

JUNIPER POINT EAST CAMP

From just W of Gordonville at jct with FM 901, about 4 mi N on US 377; before Willis Bridge over lake, turn right on access rd, following signs; at S shore of lake. 4/1-9/30; 14-day limit. 14 elec/wtr 30-amp sites, $20; 17 elec/wtr 50-amp sites, $22 ($10 & $11 with federal senior pass). Off-season, camp at nearby Juniper Point West. Tbls, flush toilets, cfga, drkg wtr, dump, beach, showers, picnic shelter ($50). Boating(ld), fishing, swimming. 903-523-4022. NRRS (4/1-9/30).
GPS: 33.859021, -96.830428

JUNIPER POINT WEST CAMP

From just W of Gordonville at jct with FM 901, about 4.2 mi N on US 377; just past Juniper Point East turnoff before Willis Bridge over lake; turn left on access rd, following signs; at S shore of lake. All year; 14-day limit. During 4/1-9/30, 3 primitive tent sites, $15; 13 elec/wtr 30/50-amp sites $22 ($7.50 & $11 with federal senior pass). During 10/1-3/31, all elec sites open, but shower & restroom facilities closed, and no wtr hookups after 11/1; fill fresh wtr tanks from frost-free hydrant near park entrance; off-season fee $12 ($6 with federal senior pass). Tbls, flush & pit toilets, cfga, drkg wtr, dump, showers. Boating(ld), fishing, hiking. Cross Timbers Hiking Trail begins at Juniper Point West and follows the lake's S shoreline about 15 mi; free wilderness tent camping along trail, but no wtr. 903-523-4022. NRRS 4/1-9/30.
GPS: 33.861102, -96.834773

PRESTON BEND RECREATION AREA

From Pottsboro, 9 mi N on FM 120; on peninsula between lake's main channel & Little Mineral Creek arm. 4/1-9/30; 14-day limit. 12 primitive tent sites, $15; 26 elec/wtr 30-amp sites, $20 ($7.50 & $10 with federal senior pass). RV limit in excess of 65 ft. Tbls, flush & pit toilets, cfga, drkg wtr, dump, showers, beach, picnic shelter. (903) 786-8408. Note: Historically, some elec campsites open off-season & wtr available from frost-free hydrant; but since winter of 2013-14, park has closed in Oct. NRRS 4/1-9/30.
GPS: 33.87833, -96.64722

⑪ LAVON LAKE
GPS: 33.0333, -96.4833

A 21,400-acre lake 30 mi NE of Dallas and 3 mi E of Wylie off SR 78. Alcohol prohibited. Besides the following campgrounds, the Corps also leases Collin Park to Collin Park Marina. Non-campers pay day use fees: $3 at some boat ramps, $4 for dump stations, beach, picnicking. Day use areas: Avalon -- toilets, boat ramp, shelter, picnicking, beach (park closed in 2015 until further notice); Bratonia -- toilets, boat ramp (closed in 2015 due to low wtr); Brockdale -- toilets, boat ramp; Caddo -- picnicking, toilets, boat ramp, fishing ponds; Elm Creek -- toilets, boat ramp (closed in 2015 by low wtr); Highland -- toilets, boat ramp (closed in 2015 by low wtr); Large Avalon/ Hackberry Ridge -- picnicking, day use shelter; Little Ridge (day use only) -- showers; Pebble Beach -- toilets, boat ramp, picnicking, beach; Stilling Basin -- boat ramp, fishing pier; Tickey Creek -- boat ramp open 2015; Twin Groves -- boat ramp (closed 2015 by low wtr). Caddo Lakeland & Pebble Beach Parks closed until further notice. Resource Manager, Lavon Lake, 3375 Skyview Drive, Wylie, TX 75098-0429. (972) 442-3014/3141.

CLEAR LAKE PARK

From Princeton, 9 mi S on FM 982 (changes into CR 735); 1 mi S then E on CR 436. 4/1-9/30; 14-day limit. 23 elec/wtr sites (30-amp), $30 ($15 with federal senior pass). RV limit in excess of 65 ft. Tbls, flush toilets, dump, showers, playground, beach. Boating(ld), fishing, swimming. Group camping with elec & shelter, cookers, toilets, volleyball, horseshoes, $150. Non-campers pay $4 boat ramp fee. NRRS. **GPS: 33.056335, -96.488800**

EAST FORK PARK

From just E of Wylie, 1.5 mi NE on SR 78; 0.5 mi N on FM 389; right at fork onto Forrest Ross Rd to camp; at S shore of lake, W of dam. All year; 14-day limit. 50 elec/wtr sites (30/50-amp), $30; 12 wtr-only tent sites, $14 ($15 & $7 with federal senior pass). 55-ft RV limit. Flush toilets, showers, dump, cfga, drkg wtr, pay phone, playground. Group camping area with 6 elec sites & shelter, $150. 11 equestrian sites with stalls, $30. Boating(ld), fishing, horseback trails, swimming. Non-campers pay $4 for boat ramp. NRRS. **GPS: 33.038169, -96.514109**

LAVONIA PARK

From SR 78 just SW of Lavon, 2 mi N on CR 486 (Lake Rd); at E side of dam. All year; 14-day limit. 15 tent sites, wtr only, $14; 38 full hookups (30-amp), $30; $7 & $15 with federal senior pass. 60-ft RV limit. Tbls, flush toilets, showers, dump, cfga, drkg wtr, playground, beach. Boating(l), swimming, fishing. NRRS. **GPS: 33.042013, -96.443835**

⑫ LEWISVILLE LAKE
GPS: 33.0667, -97.0167

A 28,980-acre lake just N of and adjacent to Lewisville (E of Mill St and I-35E) and NW of

Dallas; on Elm Fork of Trinity River as well as Stewart, Panther, Cottonwood, Doe Branch, Little Elm, Pecan & Hickory Creeks. ORV prohibited. Campground checkout time 2 p.m. Observation drive-through of fee parks is not permitted on weekends from Easter through Labor Day weekend. The Corps has leased camping areas to other entities and companies. They include Lewisville Lake Environmental Learning Center; Smithville's Lake Park; Pilot Knoll Park at Highland Village; Willow Grove Park, Lake Dallas; Hidden Cove Park, The Colony (see details in our new book, "Guide to Western County & City Parks." Corps day use areas: Oakland -- boat ramp, toilets, shelter, picnicking, playground (western half of park closed until further notice); Westlake -- picnic shelter, toilets, boat ramp, picnicking. Westlake/Oakland parks & boat ramps closed 10/1-3/31. Non-campers pay $4 day use fees. Shelters are $75-$100. Resource Manager, Lewisville Lake, 1801 N Mill Street, Lewisville, TX 75067-1821. (469) 645-9100.

HICKORY CREEK CAMPGROUND

From Lewisville, 4 mi N on I-35E, across lake bridge, then exit 457B (from the N, use exit 458) toward Lake Dallas; take overpass W over I-35E; 0.2 mi W on Turbeville Rd; 0.5 mi S on Pt. Vista Rd, on right. All year; 14-day limit. 131 sites (10 pull-through). 10 primitive walk-to tent sites, $14; 80 elec/wtr (30-amp) sites, $28; 44 elec/wtr (50-amp) sites, $30 ($7, $14 & $15 with federal senior pass). Night-time exit available. 65-ft RV limit. Tbls, flush & pit toilets, showers, dump, amphitheater, pay phone, cfga, drkg wtr, playground, beach, coin laundry. Boating(ld), fishing, swimming, hiking/biking trail. (940) 497-2902. NRRS. **GPS: 33.109580, -97.045594**

⑬ NAVARRO MILLS LAKE
GPS: 31.95, -96.7

This 5,070-acre lake is 71 miles S of Dallas and 11 miles SW of Corsicana off SR 31; at Richland Creek. Campground checkout time 1 p.m. ORV prohibited. Non-campers pay $3 to launch boats at Liberty Hill, Oak Park & Wolf Creek; $4 to use dump stations at all four campgrounds. Pelham boat ramp closed indefinitely due to low wtr. No day use fees for boat ramp & picnicking at Brushie Prairie Park. Resource Manager, Navarro Mills Lake, 1175 FM 677, Purdon, TX 76679. (254) 578-1431.

LIBERTY HILL CAMPGROUND

From Dawson at jct with SR 31, 4 mi NW on FM 709, on right; at S shore of lake. All year; 14-day limit. 99 elec/wtr sites, 3 primitive sites. $18 at 92 elec/wtr sites during 3/1-10/31; $14 during 11/1-2/28 ($9 & $7 with federal senior pass). 5 wtr/elec sites & screened shelters, $26 during 3/1-10/31; $22 during 11/-2/28 ($13 & $11 with senior pass). 6 full hookups, $22 during 3/1-10/31; $18 during 11/1-2/28 ($11 & $9 with senior pass). 6 double elec/wtr sites, $36 during 3/1-10/31; $28 during 11/1-2/28 ($18 & $14 with senior pass). 3 primitive sites, $16 during 3/1-10/31; $12 during 11/1-2/28 ($8 & $6 with senior pass). RV limit in excess of 65 ft. Tbls, flush toilets, showers, dump, cfga, drkg wtr, playground, beach, picnic shelter ($80). Boating(ld), swimming, fishing. Marina, store. Non-campers pay $3 for boat ramp, $4 dump station, $1 swimming. NRRS. **GPS: 31.946245, -96.716745**

OAK PARK

From Dawson, 4.3 mi NE on SR 31, 1.5 mi N on FM 667, on left; at NE shore of lake. All year; 14-day limit. 42 elec/wtr sites, $18 during 3/1-10/31; $14 during 11/1-2/28 ($9 & $7 with federal senior pass). 6 full hookups, $22 during 3/1-10/31; $18 during 11/1-2/28 ($11 & $9 with senior pass). RV limit in excess of 65 ft. Tbls, flush toilets, showers, dump, cfga, drkg wtr, playground, beach, fishing pier, picnic shelter ($80). Boating(ld), fishing, swimming, hiking, interpretive trails. Non-campers pay $3 for boat ramp, $4 dump station, $1 swimming. NRRS. **GPS: 31.965161, -96.690159**

PECAN POINT PARK

From Dawson, 3.5 mi NE on SR 31; 3.2 mi N on FM 667; 2 mi SW on FM 744; 2 mi SE on FM 1578; right on CR 3360 Rd to park entrance on right; at N shore of lake. 4/1-9/30; 14-day limit. 30 non-elec sites, $10; 5 elec/wtr sites (50-amp), 11 pull-through, $12 ($5 & $6 with federal senior pass). RV limit in excess of 65 ft. Tbls, flush toilets, showers, cfga, drkg wtr, dump. Boating(l), biking, hiking, waterskiing. Non-campers pay $4 for dump station. NRRS. **GPS: 31.965416, -96.740874**

WOLF CREEK PARK

From Dawson, 3.5 mi NE on SR 31; 3.2 mi N on FM 667; 2.5 mi W on FM 639, then 1 mi S on NW 3140 Rd into park; at N shore of lake. 4/1-9/30; 14-day limit. 20 non-elec sites, $14; 2 non-elec double sites, $28; 50 elec/wtr sites (30/50-amp), $16 ($7, $14 & $8 with federal senior pass). RV limit in excess of 65 ft; 12 pull-through. Tbls, flush & pit toilets, showers, dump, cfga, drkg wtr, pay phone, fishing pier, picnic shelter ($80). Boating(ld), fishing. Non-campers pay $4 for dump station, $3 for boat ramp. NRRS. **GPS: 31.973726, -96.725918**

⓮ PAT MAYSE LAKE
GPS: 33.8533, -95.5483

A 5,990-acre lake 1 mile S of Chicota off FM 197 and 12 miles N of Paris in northeastern Texas; 100 miles W of Texarkana. On Sanders Creek, a tributary of the Red River. ORV prohibited. Gated campgrounds provide emergency late night exits. Lake Manager, Pat Mayse Lake, 1679 FM 906 W, Powderly, TX 75473-3337. (903) 732-3020.

LAMAR POINT

From Powderly, about 5 mi S on US 270; about 6 mi W on FM 1499; 5.5 mi N on FM 1500; at S shore of lake. Lake access only; camping no longer permitted.

PAT MAYSE EAST CAMP

From Chicota, 0.8 mi W on FM 197; 2 mi S on CR 35850, then SE on park access rd to N shore of lake. All year; 14-day limit. 26 wtr/elec 30-amp sites, $15 ($7.50 with federal senior pass). Tbls, toilets, cfga, drkg wtr, dump, beach. Boating(l), fishing. Non-campers pay day use fees for boat ramp, beach, dump station. **GPS: 33.839980, -95.583115**

PAT MAYSE WEST CAMP

From Chicota, 2.3 mi W on FM 197; 1 mi S on CR 35810; then E & S on Pat Mayse W Park Rd. All year; 14-day limit. 5 non-elec sites, $12; 83 wtr/elec sites, 30-amp, $18 ($6 & $9 with federal senior pass). RV limit in excess of 65 ft. Tbls, flush & pit toilets, cfga, drkg wtr, dump, beach, showers, pay phone. Fishing, boating(ld), swimming. Non-campers pay use fees for boat ramp, dump station. (903) 732-4955. NRRS 4/1-9/30.
GPS: 33.844810, -95.606418

SANDERS COVE CAMPGROUND

From Chicota, 3.2 mi E on FM 906, then SW on entrance rd; at E shore of lake. All year; 14-day limit. 4 non-elec sites, $12; 85 elec/wtr sites, $18 for 30-amp, $22 for 50-amp ($6, $9 & $11 with federal senior pass). Tbls, flush & pit toilets, showers, cfga, drkg wtr, dump, beach, pay phone, picnic shelter ($25). Group camping area (5 non-elec sites), $75. RV limit in excess of 65 ft. Boating(ld), fishing, swimming. Non-campers pay use fees for boat ramp, dump station, beach. (903) 732-4956. NRRS 4/1-9/30.
GPS: 33.841210, -95.534406

⑮
PROCTOR LAKE
GPS: 31.9667, -98.5

This 4,610-acre lake has 38 miles of shoreline; it is 8 miles NE of Comanche off US 67 on FM 1476 and 97 miles SW of Ft. Worth. Gated campgrounds provide emergency late night exits. High Point Park closed; day use horse & hiking trail parking allowed at entrance. Boat ramps closed temporarily in 2015 due to lake level. Resource Manager, Proctor Lake, 2180 FM 2861, Comanche, TX 76442-7248. ((254) 879)2424.

COPPERAS CREEK PARK

From Proctor at jct with FM 1476, 5.5 mi S through Hasse on US 377; 2.5 mi N on FM 2861 (CR 410); N on access rd to S shore of lake. All year; 14-day limit. 67 elec/wtr sites, $16 for 30-amp, $20 at 2 premium 50-amp sites; $22 at 7 full hookups ($8, $10 & $11 with federal senior pass). Double elec/wtr sites $42. Two group camping areas, $100 & $130. RV limit in excess of 65 ft. Tbls, flush & pit toilets, showers, dump, cfga, drkg wtr. Boating(ld), fishing, hiking trails. (254) 879-2498. NRRS 3/1-9/30. **GPS: 31.964091, -98.502924**

PROMONTORY PARK

From Comanche at jct with US 377, 12 mi N on SR 16; 5 mi E on FM 2318; at NW side of lake. 4/1-9/30; 14-day limit. 30 primitive sites, $8; 52 elec/wtr sites, $16 (double sites $32); 5 premium elec/wtr sites (50-amp), $20 ($4, $8, $16 & $10 with federal senior pass). 1 quad site with 50-amp/wtr $50 (no senior discount). 4 overnight screened shelters, $22; 1 screened shelter with RV site, $38. Tbls, pit & flush toilets, showers, dump, cfga, drkg wtr, beach. Boating(ld), swimming, hiking trails, horseback riding, fishing. Three group camping areas, $50-$130. RV limit in excess of 65 ft; 4 pull-through sites. (254) 893-7545. (254) 893-7545. NRRS.
GPS: 31.981843, -98.489717

SOWELL CREEK PARK

From Proctor at jct with US 377, 2 mi W on FM 1476; S before dam on recreation road. All year; 14-day limit. 60 sites with elec/wtr, $16 base for 30-amp, $20 at 11 premium sites (50-amp); 14 full hookups, $26; four double elec/wtr sites $32 ($8, $10, $13 & $16 with federal senior pass). RV limit in excess of 65 ft. Tbls, flush toilets, showers, dump, cfga, drkg wtr, beach. 2 group camping areas with open groups shelter, $190. Boating(ld), fishing, hiking trails, swimming. (254) 879-2322. NRRS 4/1-9/30. **GPS: 31.990097, -98.458668**

⑯ SAM RAYBURN LAKE
GPS: 31.1067, -94.1072

This 114,500-acre lake is 15 miles N of Jasper on US 96 in east-central Texas on the Angelina River. It is 89 miles N of Beaumont and 30 miles W of the Louisiana state line. Equestrian trail. Campground checkout time 2 p.m. $3 extra vehicle fee may be charged. Non-campers pay day use fees at developed campgrounds: $4 for boat ramps, for dump stations & beaches. Camping no longer available at Etoile Park. Several campsites at Mill Creek, Hanks Creek, San Augustine & Rayburn Parks were closed in April 2015 due to high wtr; check current status with lake office before arrival. Resource Manager, Sam Rayburn Reservoir, 7695 RR 255 W, Jasper, TX 75951. (409) 384-5716.

EBENEZER PARK

From Jasper, 12 mi N on US 96, 8 mi W on Recreation Rd 255 across dam, then N; on CR 49; at S shore of lake. Equestrian sites open all year; other sites open 3/1-LD; 14-day limit. 13 equestrian sites, all with wtr: 7 have 30-amp elec, 6 have 50-amp; each site includes hitching posts, tbl, fire ring, hardened RV pullout; corrals provided. 1.5 mi of Corps equestrian trail, 20 mi of national forest trails nearby. 17 non-elec sites, $14; wtr/30-amp elec sites $26; wtr/50-amp elec sites, $28 ($7, $13 & $14 with federal senior pass). 50-ft RV limit; 1 RV & 1 tent or 2 tents per site. Tbls, toilets, dump, cfga, drkg wtr, beach. Swimming, horseback riding. Nearest boat ramp at Twin Dikes Park (4 mi). NRRS. **GPS: 31.069688, -94.125999**

HANKS CREEK PARK

From Huntington, 12 mi SE on FM 2109; 2 mi NE on FM 2801, following signs; on NW shore of lake. All year; 14-day limit. 37 elec/ wtr 30-amp sites, $26; 7 elec/wt 50-amp sites, $28 ($13 & $14 with federal senior pass). 60-ft RV limit. 8 screened shelters with adjacent RV sites & open group shelter, $38. Tbls, flush & pit toilet, dump, showers, drkg wtr, cfga, beach, playground, pay phone, picnic shelter ($50). Group camping area with elec, $150. Boating(ld), swimming, fishing, volleyball, horseshoe pits, mountain biking. Entry gates closed at 9pm; late arrivals are turned away; registered campers must make late entry arrangements before leaving campground. Non-campers pay $4 at dump station & beach. NRRS 3/1-9/30. **GPS: 31.1274040, -94.402986**

MILL CREEK PARK

From Brookeland, 2 mi W on SR Loop 149; 1 mi W on Spur 165. All year; 14-day limit. 59 elec/wtr 30-amp sites, $26; 51 elec/wtr 50-amp sites, $28 ($13 & $14 with federal senior pass). RV limit in excess of 65 ft. Tbls, flush & pit toilets, showers, dump, playground, cfga, drkg wtr, beach, pay phone group shelter ($50). Horseshoe pits, volleyball court, boating(l), swimming, fishing. Non-campers pay $4 at dump station & beach. NRRS 3/1-9/30. **GPS: 31.151873, -94.005547**

RAYBURN PARK

From Pineland at jct of US 96, 10 mi N on FM 83; 11 mi S on FM 705; 1.5 mi W on FM 3127; on N shore of lake. Sites 26-50 open all year; sites 1-10 & 55-65 open 3/1-LD; 14-day limit. 25 primitive sites (1 double), no hookups, no access to showers/restrooms; pit toilets, $14 ($7 with federal senior pass); during 2015, those primitive sites were closed for budget reasons. 16 back-in 30-amp elec/wtr sites, $26; 8 pull-through 50-amp elec/wtr sites, $28 ($13 & $14 with federal senior pass). RV limit in excess of 65 ft. Tbls, flush toilets, showers, dump, playground, beach, cfga, drkg wtr, pay phone. Non-campers pay $4 at dump station; no picnicking fee. NRRS 3/1-8/1. **GPS: 31.06183, -94.107154**

SAN AUGUSTINE PARK

From Pineland at jct with US 96, 6 mi W on FM 83; 4 mi S on FM 1751; at E shore of lake. Sites 29-33, 50-70 & 87-100 open all year; other sites open 3/1-LD; 14-day limit. 5 elec/wtr tent sites, $16; 95 elec/wtr 30-amp RV sites, $26 ($8 & $13 with federal senior pass). RV limit in excess of 65 ft. Tbls, flush toilets, showers, dump, cfga, drkg wtr, playground, beach, pay phone, fish cleaning station, picnic shelter with elec ($50). Boating(l), swimming, horseshoe pits, interpretive trail, volleyball courts, fishing, basketball. Non-campers pay $4 for dump station. NRRS 3/1-9/30. **GPS: 31.199170, -94.078890**

TWIN DIKES PARK

From Jasper, 13 mi N on US 96; 5 mi W on FM 255, then N; on S shore of lake. 3/1-LD weekend; 14-day limit. 24 non-elec sites, $14; 6 elec/wtr 30-amp sites, $26; 4 elec/wtr 50-amp sites, $28; 6 full hookups (30-amp), $28 ($7, $13, $14 with federal senior pass). 3 sites with screened shelters & full hookups, $38. 60-ft RV limit; 1 RV & 2 tents or 2 tents per site. Tbls, flush toilets, cfga, drkg wtr, showers, dump, beach, pay phone, picnic shelter ($50). Boating(ld), swimming, fishing. Non-campers pay $4 for dump station. NRRS 3/1-9/30. **GPS: 31.071094, -94.056530**

⑰

SOMERVILLE LAKE
GPS: 30.3333, -96.5333

An 11,460-acre lake with 85 miles of shoreline, located 1 mile W of Somerville on SR 36 on Thornberry Ave and 84 miles E of Austin. Three camping areas are leased by the Corps to other operators. They include Big Creek Park and Marina (now private), Overbrook Park and Marina, operated by the City of Somerville, and Welch Park (now private). Visitor center, wildlife viewing. Resource Manager, Somerville Lake, 1560 Thornberry Dr, Somerville, TX 77879. (979) 596-1622

ROCKY CREEK CAMPGROUND

From Somerville, SE on SR 36; 4.5 mi W on FM 1948; on peninsula at S shore of lake. All year; 14-day limit. 35 elec/wtr tent sites and 30 elec/wtr 30-amp RV sites, $26 during 3/1-9/30, $24 rest of year; 127 elec/wtr 30/50-amp sites, $28 during 3/1-9/30, $26 rest of year ($13, $12, $14 & $13 with federal senior pass). RV limit in excess of 65 ft. Tbls, pit & flush toilets, showers, dump, playground, picnic shelter ($125 during 3/1-9/30, $100 rest of year). Boating(l), amphitheater, fishing, nature trail. NRRS. **GPS: 30.297907, -96.569159**

YEGUA CREEK CAMPGROUND

From Somerville, SE on SR 36; 2 mi W on FM 1948; right into park; at SE shore of lake. All year; 14-day limit. 76 elec/wtr 20/30/50-amp sites, $28 during 3/1-9/30; $26 rest of year ($14 & $13 with federal senior pass). RV limit in excess of 65 ft. Tbls, flush & pit toilets, showers, dump, playground. Hiking, interpretive trails, boating(l), fishing. NRRS. **GPS: 30.306967, -96.540416**

⑱

B. A. STEINHAGEN LAKE
TOWN BLUFF DAM
GPS: 30.7833, -94.1667

This 13,700-acre lake is 15 miles SW of Jasper off FM 1746 in E-central Texas, 75 miles N of Beaumont. ORV prohibited. Non-campers pay day use fees: $3 for boat ramp, $2 for showers, $4 dump station. Day use parks: Bluffview -- picnicking, group shelter ($45), fishing pier, playground, fitness trail; East End -- fishing pier, picnicking. All Corps boat ramps open in 2015. Non-campers pay $3 for using boat ramps. Resource Manager, Town Bluff Dam & B. A. Steinhagen Lake, 890 FM 92, Woodville, TX 75979-9631. (409) 429-3491.

CAMPERS COVE CAMPGROUND

From Woodville, 12.1 mi SE on US 190; 2.5 mi

SE on FM 92, then N 0.6 mi on CR 4130. 4/1-9/30; 14-day limit. 25 sites. Free. Campground closed until further notice.
GPS: 30.822646, -94.201959

MAGNOLIA RIDGE PARK

From Woodville, 11 mi E on US 190; 1.5 mi NW on FM 92, then NE on park entrance rd. All year; 14-day limit. 8 primitive sites, $10 ($5 with federal senior pass); 32 elec/wtr 30-am sites, $16 base, $18 at premium locations ($8 & $9 with senior pass). 1 site with screened shelter, elec/wtr $25. RV limit in excess of 65 ft. Tbls, flush toilets, showers, dump, cfga, drkg wtr, playground, beach, picnic shelter ($45). Store. Children's fishing pond, boating(ld), interpretive trails, biking, hiking. (409) 283-5493.**GPS: 30.870579, -94.234688**

SANDY CREEK CAMPGROUND

From Jasper, 10 mi W on US 190; 1.3 mi S on FM 777; 2.5 mi W on CR 155; at SE shore of lake. 6 primitive tent sites, $10; 34 elec/wtr 30-amp sites, $16; 35 elec/wtr 50-amp sites, $18 ($5, $8 & $9 with federal senior pass). All year; 14-day limit. 2 sites with screened shelters & 30-amp elec/wtr, $25. RV limit in excess of 65 ft. Tbls, flush & pit toilets, cfga, drkg wtr group picnic shelter with elec ($50). Boat rentals nearby. Non-campers pay $4 for dump station, swimming beach, $2 for showers. (409) 384-6166. NRRS. **GPS: 30.827537, -94.153883**

⑲ STILLHOUSE HOLLOW LAKE
GPS: 31.0333. -97.5333

A 6,430-acre lake 5 miles SW of Belton on FM 1670, S of Fort Hood and 80 miles N of Austin. It has 58 miles of shoreline. Campground checkout time 2 p.m. Visitor center, interpretive programs. Chalk Ridge Falls Environmental Learning Center below the dam includes hiking trail along Lampasas River, a spring-fed creek with waterfall and several wildlife viewing points. Other day use areas: Cedar Gap -- boat ramp; Overlook -- picnicking, fitness trail; Rivers Bend -- boat ramp, picnicking; Stillhouse -- toilets, boat ramp, 2 shelters ($40 weekdays, $70 weekends), picnicking, playground, beach. Non-campers pay $4 day use fees for dump stations, picnicking, beaches; $3 for boat ramps. During 2015, courtesy docks & beaches not usable. Resource Manager, Stillhouse Hollow Lake, 3740 FM 1670, Belton, TX 7651. (254) 939-2461.

DANA PEAK CAMPGROUND

From jct with US 190, 0.3 mi S on Simmons Rd; 5 mi W on FM 2410; 5 mi S on Comanche Gap Rd; at N shore of lake. All year; 14-day limit. 8 primitive tent sites, $10; 5 elec/wtr tent sites, $16; 22 elec/wtr RV/tent sites $22 ($5, $8 & $11 with federal senior pass). 2 double sites with elec/wtr, $36. RV limit in excess of 65; 2 pull-through. Tbls, flush & pit toilets, showers, dump, beach, playground,group shelter ($40 weekdays, $70 weekends). Boating(ld), swimming, biking, horseback riding, interpretive trails, fishing. NRRS.
GPS: 31.024869, -97.604073

UNION GROVE CAMPGROUND

From N of Salado at jct with I-35, 5.3 mi W on FM 2484; 1 mi N on Union Grove Park Rd; at S shore of lake. All year; 14-day limit. 7 elec/wtr tent sites, $16; 30 wtr/elec RV/tent sites, $22; 2 double sites $36 ($8, $11 & $18 with federal senior pass). 3 screened overnight shelters, $30. RV limit in excess of 65 ft; 4 pull-through sites. Tbls, pit & flush toilets, showers, dump, cfga, drkg wtr, beach, playground, fishing pier. Boating(ld), crabbing, fishing, swimming. NRRS. **GPS: 31.101737, -97.620757**

⑳ WACO LAKE
GPS: 31.6. -97.2167

This 8,900-acre lake is on the NW side of Waco off FM 1637 at the Brazos River. It is the largest state in America located entirely within a city's boundaries. ORV prohibited, Wildlife viewing area, fossil pit. Day use facilities include Bosque Park -- fishing pier & fishing below the dam; Lacy Point Access -- boat ramp, multi-use trail; Twin Bridges -- 2 beaches, picnicking, boat ramp, group shelter with horseshoe pits & sand volleyball ($150), playground; Flat Rock -- boat ramp; Airport Beach -- beach, picnicking, boat ramp, group shelter ($150), playground; Koehne -- boat ramp, picnicking; Waco Dam -- multi-use trail. Non-campers pay day use fees of $4 for beaches, boat ramps, picnicking, dump stations. Resource Manager, Waco Lake, 3801 Zoo Park Dr, Waco, TX 76708-9602. (254) 756-5359.

AIRPORT PARK

From I-35 exit 338 (Lake Shore Dr), W on Lake Shore (FM 3051); cross FM 3051 & FM 1637, then right (NW) on Airport Rd; left on Skeet Eason Rd to park (just W of regional airport); on NE shore of lake. All year; 14-day limit. 15 basic tent sites, $12 ($14 for wtr); 38 wtr/elec sites (some with 50-am), $20; 21 full hookups, $24 ($6, $7, $10 & $12 with federal senior pass). Group camping area with shelter & elec/wtr (6 sites full hookups), 6-foot barbecue grill, 12-foot serving bar, toilets, $275. RV limit in excess of 65 ft. Tbls, flush toilets, cfga, drkg wtr, showers, dump, beach, 8 screened shelters ($30). Boating(ld), fishing, swimming, hiking. Floating restaurant at the nearby marina. $4 gray wtr dump. NRRS. **GPS: 31.599907, -97.239588**

MIDWAY PARK

From Waco & I-35 exit 330, 5 mi W on SR 6; exit on Fish Pond Rd and circle under SR 6, then stay on access road; on E shore of South Bosque River. All year; 14-day limit. 5 primitive tent sites $12; 22 elec/wtr 30-amp sites, $20 ($36 at 4 double sites); 11 full hookups $24 ($6, $10 & $12 with federal senior pass). RV limit in excess of 65 ft. Tbls, flush toilets, showers, playground, dump, cfga, drkg wtr, multi-use play area for children. Hiking, fishing, boating(l), swimming. NRRS. **GPS: 31.5256, -97.2250**

REYNOLDS CREEK PARK

From Waco I-35 exit 330, 7 mi W on SR 6 across lake; 1 mi NE on Speegleville Rd, pass 4-way stop sign; approximately 1 mi on right; on W shore of lake. 4/1-9/30; 14-day limit (all year at 10 equestrian sites). 6 primitive tent sites $12; 51 elec/wtr sites (some 50-amp), $20 ($6 & $10 with federal senior pass). Tbls, flush toilets, showers, dump, cfga, drkg wtr, pay phone, picnic shelter with elec ($20). Interpretive programs, amphitheater, hiking trails, boating(l), horseback trails. Formerly known as Speegleville I Park. NRRS. **GPS: 31.582566, -97.266458**

SPEEGLEVILLE PARK

From Waco I-35, 6 mi N on SR 6; after crossing lake on Twin Bridges, exit left on access rd, past Twin Bridges Park about 0.25 mi; continue on Overflow Rd to park entrance; on W shore of lake. All year; 14-day limit. 30 elec/wtr sites, $20 ($10 with federal senior pass). 2 screened picnic shelters, $30. NRRS. **GPS: 31.555902, -97.239347**

㉑
WHITNEY LAKE
GPS: 31.85. -97.3667

This 23,560-acre lake is 5.5 miles SW of Whitney on SR 22 and 79 miles S of Fort Worth on the Brazos River. Dam tours available. Checkout time 2 p.m. ORV prohibited. The Corps manages 10 parks, and three others are operated by Hill County and private individuals. The Corps leases Ham Creek Park to a private marina. Additional facilities are at Lake Whitney State Park. Hopewell Trail is a 12.5-mile equestrian and multi-use trail through wildlife areas. Equestrian camping available at Plowman Creek Park. Day use facilities are at Lofers Bend -- 2 swimming beaches, boat ramp, picnicking, 2 sand volleyball courts; McCown Valley -- 7 picnic sites, 6 beach shelters, picnic sites, swimming beach, 2 sand volleyball courts. Whitney Lake's Corps campgrounds require non-campers to pay day use fees for boat ramps, dump stations, beaches. Resource Manager, Whitney Lake, 285 County Road 3602, Clifton, TX 76634. (254) 694-3189.

CEDAR CREEK PARK

From Whitney, 5.5 mi NW on FM 933; 2.2 mi SW & SE on FM 2604; on E side of lake. 20 free basic sites with wtr nearby, fire rings, 1 toilet, group shelter. All year; 14-day limit. **GPS: 31.990085, -97.373333**

CEDRON CREEK PARK

From Whitney, 2.4 mi NW on FM 933; 6 mi SW on FM 1713 across Katy Bridge on left, following signs; at W side of lake. 4/1-9/30; 14-day limit. 57 elec/wtr 30-amp sites, $16 ($8 with federal senior pass). 45-ft RV limit. Tbls, flush toilets, showers, dump, pay phone, picnic shelter. Group camping area with 8 wtr/elec sites, $140. Horseshoe pits, boating(l), fishing, swimming, waterskiing. NRRS. **GPS: 31.969767, -97.418454**

KIMBALL BEND PARK

From NW of Blum at jct with FM 933, 6 mi SW on SR 174, across bridge, then NW into park; N of lake on W side of Brazos River. Access boat ramp by road under bridge. All year; 14-day limit. 35 free sites. Tbls, 1 toilet, cfga, drkg wtr. Boating(l), waterskiing, fishing. **GPS: 32.123054, -97.494736**

LOFERS BEND EAST PARK

From Whitney, 5.7 mi S on SR 22, then W on access rd, following signs; at SE shore of lake. All year; 14-day limit. 6 wtr-only sites, no elec, $12 during 3/1-9/30, $10 off-season ($6 & $5 with federal senior pass). 60 elec/wtr 30-amp sites, $16 during 3/1-9/30, $14 off-season ($8 & $7 with senior pass). 45-ft RV limit. Tbls, flush toilets, showers, dump, cfga, drkg wtr, playground, pay phone. Store, marina. Group camping area with elec, $105. Boating(l), swimming, waterskiing, fishing. NRRS. **GPS: 31.879498, -97.36951**

LOFERS BEND WEST PARK

Adjacent to Lofers Bend E; on main stem of Brazos River. 4/1-9/30; 14-day limit. 22 wtr-only sites, no elec, $12; 39 elec/wtr 30-amp sites, $16; 6 elec/wtr 50-amp sites, $20 ($6, $8 & $10 with federal senior pass). 45-ft RV limit; 5 pull-through sites. Picnic shelter ($50). Group camping area with elec, $80. NRRS. **GPS: 31.879498, -97.36951**

MCCOWN VALLEY PARK

From Whitney, 2.4 mi NW on FM 933; 4 mi SW on FM 1713, veering right on SR 1731 Spur W (becoming CR 1241) to park; at E shore of lake. All year; 14-day limit. 7 wtr-only sites, no elec, $12 during 3/1-9/30, $10 off-season; 31 elec/wtr 30-amp sites, $16 during 3/1-9/30, $14 off-season; 14 elec/wtr 50-amp sites & 20 elec equestrian sites, $20 during 3/1-9/30, $18 off-season ($6, $5, $8, $7, $10 & $9 with federal senior pass). 5 camping cabins, $24; $30 with 30-amp RV hookups, $30; cabins without hookups, $24. 50-ft RV limit. Tbls, flush & pit toilets, cfga, drkg wtr, showers, dump, playground, beach, picnic shelter ($45). Horseshoe pits, equestrian trails, boating(l), biking, hiking, swimming, horseback riding. Horse stalls, store. NRRS. **GPS: 31.946254, -97.397221**

PLOWMAN CREEK PARK

From downtown Kopperl, 2 blocks SE; 0.5 mi W & S on CR 1242 to park; at W shore of Brazos River N of lake. All year; 14-day limit. 12 wtr-only sites, no elec, $12 during 3/1-9/30, $10 off-season; 21 elec/wtr 30-amp sites, $16 during 3/1-9/30, $14 off-season ($6, $5, $8 & $7 with federal senior pass). 10 elec equestrian sites, $16 during peak season, $14 off-season ($8 & $7 with senior pass); primitive camping in equestrian trailhead area, $10 ($5 with senior pass). 45-ft RV limit. Tbls, flush toilets, showers, cfga, drkg wtr, playground. Basketball court, hiking, biking, fishing, boating(l). NRRS. **GPS: 32.064119, -97.494972**

RIVERSIDE PARK

From Whitney, 5 mi S on SR 22; facilities on both sides of Brazos River, but camping only on the SW shore, downstream from Whitney Dam. All year; 14-day limit. Free. 5 primitive camping/picnic sites. Tbls, pit toilet, cfga, fishing platform on W side; 1 toilet on E side.
GPS: 31.864535, -97.364662

SOLDIER BLUFF PARK

From Whitney, 6 mi S on SR 22, then N into park on access rd; at SE shore of lake just W of dam. All year; 14-day limit. Free. 14 primitive sites camping/picnic. Designated grassy campsites & 4 long-term parking areas. 1 portable toilet & pit toilets, picnic shelter, tbls, cfga, drkg wtr. Fishing.
GPS: 31.865157, -97.374980

STEELE CREEK CAMPGROUND

From SR 174 at Morgan, 7 mi E on FM 927, 1 mi SE on FM 56; 0.3 mi E on CR 1295, then right (E) on CR 1304; N into park at S shore of Brazos River. All year; 14-day limit. Free. 21 camping/picnic sites with tbls, ground cookers, central wtr, 2 pit toilets, cfga. Boating(l), fishing, waterskiing.
GPS: 32.009459, -97.446612

WALLING BEND

From NW of Laguna Park at jct with SR 22, 2 mi W on FM 56; 2.5 mi NE on FM 2841; at W shore of lake. All year; 14-day limit. Free. 10 primitive camping/picnic sites. Tbls, pit toilets, picnic shelter, cfga, drkg wtr. Boating(l), fishing, waterskiing.
GPS: 31.897308, -97.397715

㉒
WRIGHT PATMAN LAKE
GPS: 33.305, -94.16

This 33,750-acre lake is 9 miles SW of Texarkana and the junction of US 82 off US 59. Visitor center, wildlife viewing area. Campground checkout time 2 p.m. Besides camping facilities, the Corps operates four day-use areas at the lake: North Shore Park (day use fees) -- picnicking, beach, 3 sand volleyball courts, basketball court, showers, boat ramp, playground, picnic shelter ($25); Oak Park -- picnicking, RV dump station, playground, volleyball court, picnic shelter ($60), pit toilet; Spillway -- picnicking; Malden Lake Day Use Area (day use fee) -- picnicking, boat ramp; Elliott Bluff -- picnicking, boat launch, fishing pier; Sportsman's Cove -- boat ramp, picnicking, toilets & showers, picnic shelter; Spillway -- picnicking. Free boat ramps at Hwy 59 Park, Jackson Creek, Herron Creek, Overcup, Thomas Lake. Non-camper pay $4 for dump station, $1-$2 for showers, $3 for boat launch at Malden Lake, Elliott Bluff. Eight free primitive camping areas are scattered around the lake; most have no facilities and are hike-in access, but a few have fire rings, and two are drive-to access (listed below); for locations, get maps from the lake office. Leased facilities include Atlanta State Park, Cass County Park, Berry Farm, Kelly Creek Marina, Big Creek Landing & Campground, Sulphur Point Concession Area, and Highway 59 Park. Project Manager, Wright Patman Lake, 64 Clear Springs Park, Texarkana, TX 75504-1817. (903) 838-8781.

BASSETT CREEK & GLENNS MILL CAMPGROUNDS

From Bassett, 1 mi NE on US 67; 1 mi S on CR 4223; on N side of Bassett Creek. All year; 14-day limit. Free primitive camping. Campfire rings, no other amenities.
GPS: 33.3114, -94.5457

BLUE LAKE CAMPGROUND

From Bassett, half mi SW on US 67; 1 mi SE on CR 4269; at shore of Mudd Lake. All year; 14-day limit. Free primitive camping. Campfire rings, no other amenities.
GPS: 33.291382, -94.550614

CLEAR SPRINGS PARK

From Texarkana, 9 mi S on US 59; 0.5 mi W on FM 2148; 2 mi W on park road. All year; 14-day limit. 88 elec/wtr sites. 15 primitive tent sites, $14; 25 elec/wtr 30-amp sites, $22; 41 elec/wtr 30-amp full hookups, $24; 19 elec/wtr 50-amp sites $24; 3 premium elec/wtr 50-amp deck sites $26. All sites 50% discount with federal senior pass. RV limit in excess of 65 ft. Tbls, flush toilets, showers, dump, cfga, drkg wtr, playground, beach, fish cleaning station, 3 screened shelters ($32 each). 12-site group camping area with screened shelter, $22 per site, $90 for shelter. Horseshoe pits, nature trails, swimming, volleyball courts, basketball, fishing, biking, boating(ld). During April 2015, Loop A closed by high wtr. NRRS.
GPS: 33.35833, -94.19167

JACKSON CREEK PARK

From Douglassville at jct with SR 8, 4.1 mi E on SR 77; 1.5 mi N on FM 2791; 3 mi N on CR 2116; at S shore of lake at Poorboy Landing. All year; 14-day limit. Free. 10 primitive sites. 25-ft RV limit. Pit toilet, fire rings, tbls, no drkg wtr. Boating(l), fishing.
GPS: 33.224881, -94.302880

MALDEN LAKE PARK

From Maud at jct with US 67, 8.4 mi S on SR 8; before bridge, on left. All year; 14-day limit. 29 elec/wtr 30-amp sites, $22; 10 elec/wtr 50-amp sites, $24 ($11 & $12 with federal senior pass. Coded gate locks provided for late entry by registered campers. 55-ft RV limit. Tbls, flush toilets, showers, dump, pay phone, visitor center, restaurant, playgrounds, beach. Boating(ld), biking, canoeing, fishing, swimming. NRRS.
GPS: 33.27472, - 94.34778

PINEY POINT PARK

From Texarkana, 12 mi S on US 59; first right past Sulphur River bridge, following signs; just N of Rocky Point Park at SE shore of lake. 3/1-11/30; 14-day limit. 42 sites with 30-amp elec/wtr, $24 ($12 with federal senior pass). 6 sites with 50-amp elec/wtr, $26 ($13 with federal senior pass). 41 primitive tent sites, $12 ($6 with federal senior pass). 55-ft RV limit. Tbls, flush & pit toilets, dump, showers, cfga, drkg wtr. Picnic shelter for up to 75 people & 31 vehicles, $55. Coded gate entrance provided for registered campers. Nature trail, volleyball courts, waterskiing, boating(ld), fishing, hiking, waterskiing. NRRS.
GPS: 33.29861, -94.16806

ROCKY POINT PARK

Just S of Piney Point campground, S of dam. All year; 14-day limit. 100 sites with 30-amp elec/wtr, $16 ($8 with federal senior pass). 83 elec/wtr 50-amp sites, $24; 9 full hookups 30-amp, $26; 26 elec/wtr 50-amp sites, $26; 6 full hookups 50-amp, $28. RV limit in excess of 65 ft. Tbls, flush toilets, showers, dump, fish cleaning station, amphitheater, playground, beach, pay phone, group picnic shelter ($55). Interpretive trails, boating(ld), swimming, fishing, hiking, volleyball court. NRRS.
GPS: 33.287069, -94.168925

THOMAS LAKE PARK

From Bryans Mill at jct with FM 1766, about 1.5 mi NE on CR 2472; at "Y," veer right for 1 mi, then left 1 mi to S shore of Thomas Lake (just W of Wright Patman Lake). All year; 14-day limit. Free primitive camping; no facilities except tbls; no toilet, no drkg wtr. Boating(l), fishing. **GPS: 33.265963, -94.471232**

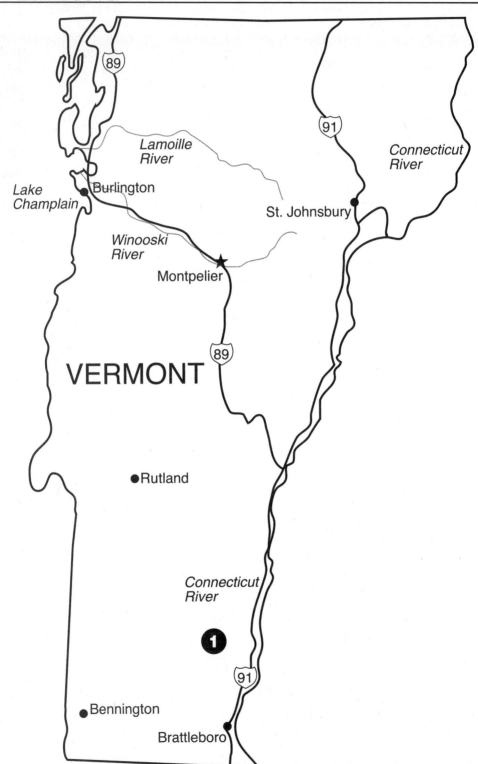

VERMONT

STATE INFORMATION:

CAPITAL: Montpelier
NICKNAME: Green Mountain State
STATEHOOD: 1791 - 14th State
FLOWER: Red Clover
TREE: Sugar Maple
BIRD: Hermit Thrush

VT

STATE TIDBITS:

• Montpelier, Vermont is the smallest state capital in the U.S.

• At various times, Vermont was claimed by both New Hampshire and New York.

• Until 1996, Vermont was the only state without a Wal-Mart.

WWW.VERMONTVACATION.COM

Department of Tourism and Marketing, One National Life Dr., 6th Floor, Montpelier, VT 05620. 800-VERMONT.

VERMONT LAKES

To find campgrounds operated by the U.S. Army Corps of Engineers, match the lake's number on the preceding map page with the numbered lake entry on this page; the only campground is listed under it.

①

BALL MOUNTAIN LAKE
GPS: 43.105, -72.775

A 75-acre lake NW of Jamaica off SR 30/100 and NW of Brattleboro on the West River, a tributary to the Connecticut River. The lake releases water for recreational whitewater activities in April and September. Non-campers pay $4 day use fees at Winhall Brook. Day use: Ball Mountain Dam Recreation Area -- picnicking, cross-country skiing, multi-purpose trail; Ball Mountain Rt 30 Access -- cross-country & multi-purpose trails; Overlook -- picnicking, multi-purpose trail. Camping is available from the third Friday in May through Columbus Day. In winter, cross-country skiing, snowshoeing and snowmobiling is available at the campgrounds 10 miles of trails. Project Manager, Ball

Mountain Lake, 88 Ball Mountain Road, Jamaica, VT 05343-9713. (802) 874-4881.

WINHALL BROOK PARK

From Jamaica, 1.5 mi NW on SR 30/100; 2 mi NW on Ball Mountain Lane; NW of dam & project offices. About 5/15-10/15; 14-day limit. 88 non-elec sites, $20; 23 elec/wtr sites, $26 ($10 & $13 with federal senior pass). Lean-to shelters, $24. 60-ft RV limit; 1 RV & 1 tent or 2 tents per site. Tbls, flush toilets, showers, dump, playground, beach, cfga, drkg wtr, amphitheater, visitor center. Boating(l) horseshoe pits, hiking, biking, basketball, swimming, fishing, interpretive programs. Day use fee for non-campers. (802) 824-4570. NRRS. **GPS: 43.16333, -72.80972**

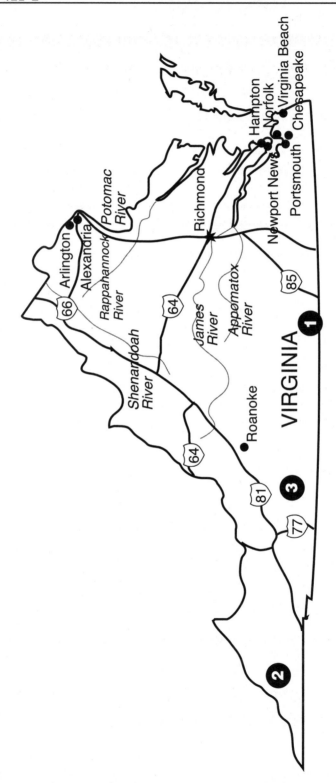

VIRGINIA

STATE INFORMATION:

CAPITAL: Richmond
NICKNAME: Old Dominion State
STATEHOOD: 1788 - 10th State
FLOWER: Dogwood
TREE: Flowering Dogwood
BIRD: Cardinal

STATE TIDBITS:

• The Blue Ridge Mountains are located in Virginia.

• The American Revolution ended with the surrender of Cornwallis in Yorktown.

• The first Thanksgiving in North America was held in Virginia in 1619.

WWW.VIRGINIA.ORG

Virginia Tourism Corporation, 901 E. Byrd St, Richmond, VA 23219. 800-VISIT VA.

VIRGINIA CAMPGROUNDS

To find campgrounds operated by the U.S. Army Corps of Engineers, match the lake's numbers on the preceding map page with numbered lake entries on the following pages. Campgrounds are listed alphabetically under the appropriate lakes. The following Virginia impoundments have Corps of Engineers campgrounds.

John H. Kerr Reservoir. A 50,000-acre lake with 900 miles of shoreline and an additional 50,000 acres of property, it is on the Virginia/ North Carolina state line near Boydton, 20 miles W of Spring Hill on I-85 and 20 miles N of Henderson, NC, on I-85.

John W. Flannagan Lake. A 1,145-acre lake with almost 40 miles of shoreline, it is near the Kentucky state line NW of Haysi on SR 63 and NW of Bristol.

Philpott Lake. A 2,880-acre lake with 100 miles of shoreline, Philpott is NW of Martinsburg off US 220, SR 57 and Philpott Dam Rd.

❶ JOHN H. KERR RESERVOIR
GPS: 36.594702, -78.311058

A 50,000-acre lake with 900 miles of shoreline and an additional 50,000 acres of property, it is on the Virginia/North Carolina state line near Boydton, 20 miles W of Spring Hill on I-85 and 20 mi N of Henderson, NC on I-85. No powerhouse tours currently. Alcoholic beverages, dirt bikes and ORV are prohibited. Checkout time 4 p.m. Also known as Buggs Island Lake. Interpretive programs at Joseph S.J. Tanner Environmental Education Center (open April-Oct). Nature & interpretive trails. Besides its campgrounds, the lake has several day use areas: Bluestone Access -- boat launch; Buffalo Springs -- picnicking, toilets, drinking water, picnic shelter, interpretive trail; Eagle Point -- boat ramp; Eastland Creek -- boat launch; Grassy Creek -- boat ramp, picnicking, pit toilet, beach, picnic shelter; Island Creek-- boat ramp, toilet; Ivy Hill -- boat ramp, picnicking, beach, toilet, picnic shelter ($35); Longwood -- boat ramp; Palmer Point -- boat ramp, picnicking, beach ($4 day use fee), picnic shelter ($25); Staunton View -- boat ramp, picnicking, hiking trail; Tailrace -- boat ramp, fishing pier, shelter, picnicking, multi-use trail. Non-campers pay $4 day use fees at most Corps-operated recreation areas; picnic shelter reservations, $35. Note: Campsites at Ivy Hill Park have been closed due to budget cuts. John H. Kerr Reservoir Management Center, 1930 Mays Chapel Road, Boydton, VA 23917-9725. (434) 738-6143/6144.

BUFFALO PARK

From Clarksville, 8 mi W on US 58 past jct with SR 49, across bridge, then 3 mi N on CR 732 (Buffalo Springs Rd) and E on CR 869 (Carters Point Rd) to its end; at W shore of lake. 5/1-9/30; 14-day limit. 19 non-elec sites, $20; 11 elec/wtr sites, $26 ($10 & $13 with federal senior pass). RV limit in excess of 65 ft. Tbls, flush & pit toilets, showers, dump, cfga, drkg wtr, beach playground, picnic shelter ($35 plus $4 per vehicle day use fee). Boating(ld), swimming, fishing. Non-campers pay $4 day use fee. (434) 738-6143. Walk-in reservations only; phone or Internet reservations not accepted.
GPS: 36.663023, -78.631672

LONGWOOD PARK

From Clarksville at jct of US 58/15, 2.5 mi S on US 15; on the W side at Beaver Pond Creek arm of lake. 4/1-10/31; 14-day limit (no longer open off-season). 32 non-elec sites, $20; 34 elec/wtr sites, $26 ($10 & $13 with federal senior pass). RV limit in excess of 65 ft. Tbls, flush & pit toilets, showers, dump, playground, beach, cfga, drkg wtr, picnic shelter ($35 plus day use fees). Boating(l), swimming, fishing. Group camping areas $75 & $100. Non-campers pay $4 day use fee for boat launch, picnicking, swimming, dump station. (434) 738-6143. NRRS.
GPS: 36.576904, -78.549671

NORTH BEND PARK

From Boydton, 5 mi E on US 58; 6 mi S on SR 4 (Buggs Island Rd); right at the dam for 200 yds on Mays Chapel Rd; at NE shore of lake. All year; 14-day limit. 106 sites no hookups, $20 during 4/1-10/31, $20 off-season but no wtr; 138 elec/wtr sites, $26 during 4/1-10/31,

$20 off-season but no wtr. Holders of federal senior pass pay half price. RV limit in excess of 65 ft. Tbls, flush & pit toilets, showers, dump, playground, beach, fishing pier, pay phone, cfga, drkg wtr. Interpretive trails, hiking, biking, boating(ld), fishing, swimming. Non-campers pay $4 fee for boat launch, picnicking, fishing pier, beach, dump. Group camping areas, $75-$100. Visitor center. NRRS.
GPS: 36.588827, -78.319516

RUDDS CREEK RECREATION AREA

From Boydton, 3 mi W on US 58; on S side of road before lake bridge; at Roanoke River. 4/1-10/31; 14-day limit. No longer open off-season. 24 non-elec sites, $20; 75 elec/wtr sites, $26 ($10 & $13 with federal senior pass). RV limit in excess of 65 ft. Tbls, flush & pit toilets, amphitheater, pay phone, showers, dump, playground, beach, cfga, drkg wtr, picnic shelter ($35). Boating(ld), fishing, swimming, interpretive trails. (434) 738-6143. NRRS.
GPS: 36.656000, -78.441192

❷
JOHN W. FLANNAGAN LAKE
GPS: 37.240021. -82.378006

A 1,145-acre lake with almost 40 miles of shoreline, it is near the Kentucky state line NW of Haysi on SR 63 and NW of Bristol. No camping reservations accepted. Boat launches are at the spillway launch area, Junction Area (fees) and Cranesnest Area. Dam & spillway areas provide picnic shelter, playground, fishing pier, multi-use trail. Note: Cranesnest access rd closed for flood damage repair in April 2015; check current status before arrival. Resource Manager, John W. Flannagan Dam & Reservoir, 192 White Water Rd, Rt. 1, Box 268, Haysi, VA 24256. (276) 835-9544.

CRANESNEST Nº1 & Nº2 CAMP

From Clintwood, 2 mi SE on SR 83, then N on SR 693 along Cranes Nest River. About MD-LD; 14-day limit. 24 sites; non-elec, $12,

elec sites $14 ($6 & $7 with federal senior pass). Tbls, flush toilets, cfga, drkg wtr, showers, dump, playground, picnic shelter, amphitheater. Boating, fishing.
GPS: 37.161890, -82.412224

CRANESNEST Nº3 CAMP

From Cranesnest #1 & #2, 1 mi NE. 11 elec sites. About 5/17-9/2; 14-day limit. Non-elec sites $12, elec sites $14 ($6 & $7 with federal senior pass). Tbls, toilets, cfga, drkg wtr. Boating(l), fishing, hiking.
GPS: 37.171192, -82.804542

LOWER TWIN CAMPGROUND

From Haysi, 6 mi NW on SR 63; 3 mi N on SR 739, 3 mi W on SR 611; exit SE on SR 683. About 5/17-9/2; 14-day limit. 33 sites. 18 non-elec sites, $12, 15 elec sites, $14 ($6 & $7 with federal senior pass). Amphitheater, tbls, toilets, showers, cfga, drkg wtr, playground, dump. Boating(l), fishing, hiking.
GPS: 37.230183, -82.373568

POUND RIVER CAMPGROUND

From Clintwood, 0.2 mi W on SR 83; 2 mi N on SR 631; 1.2 mi E on SR 754. About 5/17-9/2; 14-day limit. 27 sites, some pull-through. Non-elec sites $14, elec sites $16 ($7 & $8 with federal senior pass). Tbls, flush toilets, cfga, drkg wtr, showers, dump, playground. Boating(l), fishing.
GPS: 37.186762, -82.458867

❸

PHILPOTT LAKE
GPS: 36.7833, -80.0283

A 2,880-acre lake with 100 miles of shoreline, Philpott is NW of Martinsburg off US 220, SR 57 and Philpott Dam Rd. Visitor center. Campground checkout time 4 p.m. Alcoholic beverages prohibited. Free loan of fishing rod and tackle provided at the visitor center and parks. Day use parks: Bowens Creek, boat ramp, courtesy dock, beach, picnicking, flush toilets, playground ($4 day use fee); Runnet Bag Park -- boat ramp (no fee); Ryans Branch

-- boat ramp (no fee); Twin Bridges -- boat ramp, picnicking, pit toilet (no fee). Project Manager, Philpott Lake, 1058 Philpott Dam Road, Basset, VA 24055-8618. (276) 629-2703/7385.

DEER ISLAND CAMPGROUND

Access by boat only. S of Salthouse Branch Park on Deer Island, 2 mi N of dam. All year; 14-day limit. 21 primitive tent sites, $20 during 4/1-10/30, $10 off-season ($10 & $5 with federal senior pass). Get camping permits at Salt Branch or Bowens Creek, or off-season at Goose Point entrance and Ramp 1 honor vaults. Pit toilets, tbls, cfga, drkg wtr. Fishing, boating. **GPS: 36.807481, -80.041806**

GOOSE POINT PARK

From Martinsville, N on US 220, 11 mi N on SR 57; access on CR 822 (winding access roads). All year; 14-day limit. 10 non-elec sites, $20 3/26-10/30 (not open off-season); 53 elec/wtr sites, $25 during 4/1-10/31, $20 off-season at 9 sites but no wtr hookups (heated restrooms/showers). Fees $10, $12.50 & $10 with federal senior pass. 60-ft RV limit. Tbls, flush toilets, showers, dump, cfga, drkg wtr, beach, playground, amphitheater, picnic shelter. Boating(ld), fishing, swimming, hiking. $4 day use fee for non-campers using boat ramp, swimming area, playground, dump. (276) 629-1847. NRRS 4/1-10/31.
GPS: 36.80422, -80.05916

HORSESHOE POINT PARK

From Henry (NW of Martinsville off US 220), 2 mi W on Henry Rd (CR 605); about 3 mi W on Horseshoe Point Rd, following signs; at E shore of lake. 5/1-9/30; 14-day limit. 34 non-elec sites, $20; 15 elec/wtr & waterfront sites, $25 ($10 & $12.50 with federal senior pass). 40-ft RV limit. Tbls, flush toilets, showers, cfga, drkg wtr, beach, playground, picnic shelter. Boating(ld), swimming, fishing. $4 per vehicle day use fee for non-campers using boat ramp, courtesy dock, picnic area, swimming area,

playground, dump station. (276) 365-7385.
NRRS. **GPS: 36.83416, 80.07235**

JAMISON MILL PARK

From Henry (NW of Martinsville off US 220),
5 mi NW on CR 605 (Henry Rd); 2 mi S on
CR 778 (Nicholas Creek Rd); right on Jamison
Mill Rd, following signs; at NE shore of lake
near Nicholas Creek arm. 4/1-10/31; 14-day
limit. 7 non-elec sites & overflow area, $20; 5
elec/wtr sites, $25 ($10 & $12.50 with federal
senior pass). Some pull-through sites. Tbls,
flush toilets, showers, cfga, drkg wtr, dump.
Boating(l), fishing, hiking. No reservations
accepted; no day use fees. 540-365-2217.
GPS: 36.850557, -80.065119

PHILPOTT PARK

From Bassett at jct with Hwy 220, 6 mi W
on SR 57; right on Philpott Dam Rd for 1 mi;
near dam, S side. 4/1-10/30. Group camping
area with elec/wtr, by permit only, $100. Tbls,
flush toilets, showers, cfga, drkg wtr, picnic
shelter ($75). Hiking trails, exhibit museum,
boating(l). Non-campers, $3 for boat ramp; no
other day use fees.
GPS: 36.77611, -80.03694

SALTHOUSE BRANCH PARK

From Henry (NW of Martinsville off US 220),
3 mi W on CR 605 (Henry Rd); 2 mi SW on
CR 798 (Knob Church Rd), then left (S) on
CR 603 (Salthouse Branch Rd), following
signs. All year; 14-day limit. During 4/1-
10/31, 21 boat-in, 32 non-elec tent sites & 14
non-elec RV sites, $20; 43 elec/wtr sites, $25.
Off-season, elec sites (no wtr hookups but
heated restrooms & showers), $20. Rates with
federal senior pass, $10, $12.50 & $10. 17 pull-
through sites. 50-ft RV limit. Amphitheater,
tbls, flush & pit toilets, cfga, drkg wtr, showers,
dump, beach, picnic shelter ($75). Interpretive
trail, hiking trail, boating, fishing, swimming.
(276) 365-7005. NRRS.
GPS: 36.814258, -80.037321

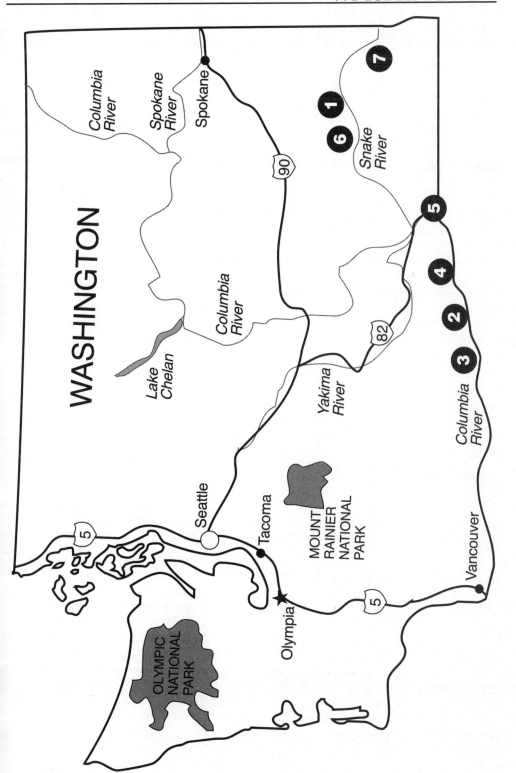

WASHINGTON

STATE INFORMATION:

CAPITAL: Olympia
NICKNAME: Evergreen State
STATEHOOD: 1889 - 42nd State
FLOWER: Pink Rhododendron
TREE: Western Hemlock
BIRD: Eastern Goldfinch

STATE TIDBITS:

• Starbucks, the biggest coffee chain in the world was founded in Seattle.

• Washington state has more glaciers than the other 47 contiguous states combined.

• Washington is the birthplace of both Jimi Hendrix and Bing Crosby.

WWW.EXPERIENCEWA.COM

For travel information: 800-544-1800.

Washington State Tourism, PO Box 42500 Olympia, WA 98504-2500

WASHINGTON CAMPGROUNDS

To find campgrounds operated by the U.S. Army Corps of Engineers, match the lake's numbers on the preceding map page with numbered lake entries on the following pages. Campgrounds are listed alphabetically under the appropriate lakes. The following Washington impoundments have Corps of Engineers campgrounds.

Lake Bryan. From Starbuck, 9 miles NE on Little Goose Dam Rd along the Snake River.

Lake Ceiilo, The Dalles Lock & Dam. This dam is 192 miles upriver from the mouth of the Columbia River and two miles E of the city of The Dalles, Oregon.

Lake Sacajawea. 9,200-acre reservoir at full pool. Located 5.5 miles E of Burbank, 2.4 miles N on Monument Dr.

Lake Umatilla. Located on the Columbia River off SR 14 near Rufus, Oregon, 25 miles E of The Dalles, Oregon.

Lake Wallula. A 38,800-acre surface area lake with 242 miles of shoreline N of junction I-82/US 730, 1 mile N of Umatilla.

Lake West, Lower Monument Dam. Located off US 260 S of Kahlotus on the Snake River.

Lower Granite Lake. From Lewiston, Idaho/Clarkston, Washington, 19 miles W on US 12; 2 miles N on Ledgerwood Spur Rd, 16 miles N on Kirby Mayview Rd, 12 miles E on Casey Creek Rd.

❶

LAKE BRYAN
LITTLE GOOSE DAM
GPS: 45.58329,-114.697266

From N of Starbuck, 9 mi NE on Little Goose Dam Rd along the Snake River. Semi-primitive and primitive camping. No open fires permitted from 6/10-10/10 (charcoal and gas grills permitted). Corps-operated recreation areas include Illia Dunes -- swimming, trails; Lamba Creek Recreation Area -- picnicking; Rice Bar Recreation Area -- picnicking and the former Central Ferry State Park (closed for 2013). Visitor center. Park Manager, Clarkston Natural Resource Office, 100 Fair Street, Clarkston, WA 99403-1943. (509) 751-0240/0250.

ILLIA LANDING

From town of Illia on S shore of Snake River, 1 mi NE on Almota Ferry Rd to park. All year; 14-day limit. Free primitive camping area, undesignated sites. Pit toilets, tbls, cfga, drkg wtr. Boating(ld), fishing.
GPS: 46.698244, -117.473770

LITTLE GOOSE DAM

From Starbuck, 10 mi NE on Little Goose Dam Rd; at Snake River mile 71. All year; 14-day limit. Free primitive camping on N & S shores W of dam; undesignated sites. Tbls, toilets, cfga, drkg wtr at visitor center (which features a fish viewing room), fish cleaning station. Fishing.
GPS: 46.578245, -118.041615

LITTLE GOOSE LANDING

From Starbuck, 9 mi NE on Little Goose Dam Rd; 1 mi E of Little Goose Dam. All year; 14-day limit. Free primitive camping area, undesignated sites. Pit toilets, tbls, cfga, no drkg wtr. **GPS: 46.585939, -118.005341**

WILLOW LANDING

From Central Ferry State Park S of Hay, 1 mi S on SR 127; 4 mi E on Deadman Rd; 5 mi N on Hasting Hill Rd. All year; 14-day limit. Free primitive camping area. Pit toilet, cfga, tbls, no drkg wtr. Boating(ld), fishing.
GPS: 46.682274, -117.749448

❷
LAKE CELILO
THE DALLAS
LOCK & DAM
GPS: 45.614638, -121.140790

The dam forming 24-mile-long Lake Celilo is 192 miles upstream from the mouth of the Columbia River and two miles E of the city of The Dalles, Oregon. It extends 1.5 miles from the Oregon shore to the navigation lock on the Washington shore. A visitor center provides interpretive displays. Several recreation areas on both sides of the river furnish boating, picnicking and camping opportunities. Resource Manager, The Dalles Lock & Dam, PO Box 564, The Dalles, OR 97058-0564. 541-296-1181.

AVERY PARK

From US 197 on the Washington shore about 3 mi N of The Dalles, Oregon, 6 mi E on SR 14 at milepost 93. All year except during Indian salmon harvest periods; 14-day limit. About 12 undesignated sites. Tbls, pit toilets, cfga, no drkg wtr. Boating(l), fishing. **GPS: 45.662180, -121.036410**

❸
LAKE SACAJAWEA
ICE HARBOR DAM
GPS: 46.2489, -118.8794

9,200-acre reservoir at full pool. Located 5.5 miles E of Burbank, 2.4 miles N on Monument Dr. Campground checkout time 12 p.m. Visitor center features interpretive displays and a fish viewing room open daily April through October. Alcoholic beverages prohibited. No tours of the powerhouse/navigation lock due to security measures. Road over dam and powerhouse closed. Visitor center open 9-5 during 4/1-10/31. Day use facilities include: Big Flat Park, boat ramp; Ice Harbor Dam, picnicking, pit toilets, phone, boat ramp; Levey Park, swimming, picnicking, flush toilets, drinking water, playgrounds, volleyball court, group shelter; Resource Manager, Ice Harbor Project, 1215 E Ainsworth, Pasco, WA 99301. (509) 547-2048/543-6060.

CHARBONNEAU PARK

From Burbank, 8.3 mi E on SR 124; 1.5 mi N on Sun Harbor Dr; left on Charbonneau Rd. 5/15-9/8; 14-day limit. 37 RV/tent sites with 50-amp elec/wtr, $22 ($11 with federal senior pass); 14 of the sites on shoreline at $24 ($12 with federal senior pass). 15 sites with 50-amp full hookups, $28 ($14 with federal senior

pass); 15 primitive overflow sites without elec, wtr or fire pits, $10 ($5 with federal senior pass). Lower fees are charged Mon-Thurs: elec sites $11; elec at shoreline $12; full hookups $14. 60-ft RV limit. Sun shelters, tbls, flush toilets, dump, showers, cfga, drkg wtr, pay phone, playground, beach, marine dump station, picnic shelter ($90), overlook group shelter ($110). Boating(ld), fishing, swimming, volleyball. (509) 547-9252. NRRS.
GPS: 46.258317, -118.843328

FISHHOOK PARK

From Burbank, 18 mi E on SR 124; 4 mi N on Fishhook Park Rd. 5/15-9/8; 14-day limit. 41 RV/tent sites with 50-amp elec/wtr, $22 ($11 with federal senior pass); 10 of the sites on shoreline at $24 ($12 with federal senior pass); full hookup sites $28 ($14 with senior pass). 1 primitive shoreline site without hookup, $16 ($8 with federal senior pass). 20 walk-to tent sites, $16 ($8 with senior pass); 2 of these sites have sun shelters, $24 ($12 with senior pass). Boat camping $12. Lower fees charged Mon-Thurs: $11 for elec/wtr, $12 for elec/wtr shoreline sites; $14 full hookups; $8 tent sites. 45-ft RV limit. Tbls, flush toilets, showers, dump, playground, cfga, drkg wtr, beach, pay phone, picnic shelter with elec ($75). Boating, swimming, fishing. NRRS.
GPS: 46.315917, -118.765984

WALKER PARK

From 26 mi E of Burbank: 8.6 mi N on SR 124 to Clyde; turn left, then 4 mi NW on Lower Monument Rd; left 1 mi before the dam, then 1 mi E; on S shore of Snake River. All year; 14-day limit. Free primitive camping at undesignated sites. Pit toilets, no drkg wtr. Birdwatching, fishing, boating(ld), hunting.

WINDUST PARK

From Kahlotus, 4 mi SW on Pasco/Kahlotus Rd; 5.2 mi SE on Burr Canyon Rd; on N shore of Snake River. Free primitive camping about 5/15-LD; park open all year; no wtr, portable toilets off-season; 14-day limit. 24

grass sites & boat camping; 40-ft RV limit. Covered sun shelters, tbls, cfga, drkg wtr, beach, playground, picnic shelter. Boating(l), swimming, fishing.
GPS: 46.533237, -118.579962

❹
LAKE UMATILLA
JOHN DAY LOCK & DAM
GPS: 45.773561, -120.141278

Located on the Columbia River off SR 14 near Rufus, Oregon, 25 miles E of The Dalles, Oregon. Corps parks now under lease include Crow Butte, operated by the Port of Benton County; Boardman Park, with nature trails, volleyball courts, tennis courts, hiking/biking trail, playground operated by Boardman Twp; Irrigon Park & Marina, with boat ramps, picnicking, playground, beach operated by the Irrigon (OR) Park District. Resource Manager, Lake Umatilla, P. O. Box 564, The Dalles, OR 97058-9998. (503) 296-1181. See Oregon listings.

CLIFFS PARK

From just N of Maryhill at jct with US 97, about 4 mi W on SR 14; S on John Day Rd by old aluminum plant; follow until paved rd becomes gravel. Free camping area. All year; 14-day limit. Primitive undesignated sites. Tbls, toilets, cfga, no drkg wtr. Boating(l), fishing, waterskiing. **GPS: 45.726256, -120.701678**

PARADISE PARK

From Plymouth (at shore of river just S of SR 14), W on Christie Rd, then S on access rd to river. About 5/15-9/15; 7-day limit. Free primitive, undesignated sites. Pit toilets, tbls, cfga, no drkg wtr. Boating(l), fishing.
GPS: 45.922408, -119.410191

PLYMOUTH PARK

From US 82 bridge N of Columbia River, 1 mi W on SR 14; 1 mi S on Plymouth Rd into town, then 0.5 mi W on Christie Rd & S on park access rd; at shore of lake & river below McNary Dam. 4/1-10/31; 14-day limit. 32 elec sites: wtr/elec, $22 ($11 with senior pass), full hookups, $24 ($12 with senior pass). 40-ft RV limit; 29 pull-through sites. Overflow tent camping available on weekends and holidays, $14 ($7 with senior pass). Tbls, flush & pit toilets, cfga, drkg wtr, beach, playground, coin laundry. Boating(l), swimming, fishing, waterskiing. Non-campers pay $5 for dump station, $3 boat launch. (509) 783-1270. NRRS. **GPS: 45.933136, -119.347132**

ROCK CREEK PARK

From The Dalles, 3 mi N on US 197, across river into Washington; 35 mi E on SR 14; left on Rock Creek Rd 1.5 mi, then left into park. All year; 14-day limit. Free primitive undesignated sites. Tbls, portable toilets (Apr-Sept), cfga, no drkg wtr. Boating(l), fishing. **GPS: 45.7640038, -122.3242595**

ROOSEVELT PARK

From The Dalles, OR, 3 mi N on US 197, across river into Washington, then 50 mi E on SR 14, following signs; on Columbia River. All year; 14-day limit. Free primitive undesignated sites; park RVs on asphalt near lawns. Pit toilets all year; flush toilets during 4/1-9/30. Swimming beach, boating(l), picnic sites, drkg wtr, windsurfing, fishing.

SUNDALE PARK

From I-82 exit 131 N of Plymouth, 61 mi W on SR 14 to milepost 128; left at sign. All year; 14-day limit. Free primitive undesignated sites. No facilities, no drkg wtr. Boating(l), fishing. **GPS: 4543134, -120.18924**

❺

LAKE WALLULA
MCNARY DAM
GPS: 45.9367. -119.2978

A 38,800-acre surface area lake with 242 miles of shoreline N of junction I-82/US 730,

1 mile N of Umatilla. Interpretive displays and fish viewing rooms at visitor center. Alcohol prohibited by state law. Several day-use parks are available. They include: Columbia Park, closed until further notice by City of Kennewick; Chiawana Park and Road 54 Park (leased to city of Pasco), picnicking, hiking trails, playground, biking trail; Hover Park (leased to Benton County Parks), hiking, fishing; Howard Amon Park (leased to City of Richland), boat ramp, swimming, playground, trails; Leslie R. Grove Park (City of Richland Parks), boating, swimming, playground, hiking trails; Locust Grove/Martindale, fishing, hiking, hunting; McNary Beach Park, picnicking, hiking trail, playground, beach, drkg wtr, toilets, cold showers; McNary Wildlife Nature Area, nature trail, hiking trails, picnicking; McNary Yacht Club, marina; Sacajawea State Park, boat ramp, day use activities; Pasco Boat Basin (leased to City of Pasco), picnicking, playground, boat ramp; Two Rivers Park (Benton County Parks), boat ramp, swimming, hiking trails, playground; Walla Walla Yacht Club, marina; Wye Park (leased to City of Richland), picnicking, playground, fishing, boat ramp; Yakima River Delta Wildlife Nature Area, hiking trails, bird watching, fishing. Madame Dorion Memorial Park was transferred from the Corps to the US Fish & Wildlife Service in 2012; it was closed to camping. Park Manager, Western Project, 2339 Ice Harbor Drive, Burbank, WA 99323. (541) 922-2268/4388. See OR listings.

HOOD CAMPGROUND

From Pasco, 3 mi S on US 12/395 to jct with SR 124 E of Burbank; continue 65 yds to park. 5/15-9/8; 14-day limit. 46 RV/tent sites with elec/wtr, $22 ($11 with federal senior pass); 21 shoreline sites with elec/wtr, $24 ($12 with senior pass); 20 overflow sites without hookups, $11 ($5.50 with senior pass). Some sites have 50-amp elec. Lower fees Mon-Thurs: $11 with elec, $12 elec shoreline sites, $12 boat camping. 65-ft RV limit. Tbls, flush toilets, showers, dump, playground, cfga, drkg wtr, pay phone, amphitheater, beach, picnic shelter ($110). Horseshoe pits, basketball court, boating(l), swimming, fishing, hiking. 509-547-7781. NRRS. GPS: 46.2122, -119.0136. **GPS: 46.215625, -119.013519**

6
LAKE WEST
LOWER MONUMENT DAM
GPS: 46.5779, -118.5374

Located off US 260 S of Kahlotus on the Snake River. Four free primitive camping areas. Fish viewing rooms at Little Goose and Lower Granite Dams. Fish viewing rooms at Little Goose and Lower Granite Dams. Visitor center. No open fires 6/10-10/10. Day use areas include Lower Monumental Lock & Dam, boat ramp; Lyons Ferry Recreation Area, trails; Matthews Recreation Area, boat ramp; North Shore Recreation Area, picnicking, and Skookum Habitat Management Area, fishing and boat ramp. Lyons Ferry Park (formerly a state park on Corps property), 8 mi N of Starbuck on Hwy 261, was closed indefinitely in 2011 after being operated by the Port of Columbia. Resource Manager, 5520 Devil's Canyon Rd, Kahlotus, WA 99335. (509) 282-3219.

AYER BOAT BASIN

From Burbank, 26 mi E on SR 124; 24 mi N through Clyde & Pleasant View to town of Ayer, then 0.5 mi SW at river mile 51. All year; 14-day limit. Free primitive camping at undesignated sites. 40-ft RV limit. Covered shelters, pit toilets, cfga, no drkg wtr. Boating(ld), fishing.
GPS: 46.587473, -118.371634

DEVILS BENCH PARK

From Kahlotus, 6 mi S on SR 263 (Devil's Canyon Rd); left on access rd; at N shore of lake just above Lower Monument Dam. All year; 14-day limit. Free primitive camping at 6 undesignated sites. Pit toilets, cfga, tbls, no drkg wtr. Fishing, boating(ld).
GPS: 46.567227, -118.537111

RIPARIA CAMPGROUND

From Hay, 14 mi SW on Little Goose Dam Rd about qtr mi S of jct with Riparia Rd, then right (S) on access rd to N shore of Snake River (about 3 mi W of Little Goose Dam). All year; 14-day limit. Free primitive camping at undesignated sites. 40-ft RV limit. Pit toilets, tbls, cfga, no drkg wtr. Boating(l), fishing.
GPS: 46.577393, -118.090813

TEXAS RAPIDS CAMPGROUND

From Starbuck, 6 mi NE on Little Goose Rd (2 mi W of Little Goose Dam); at S shore of Snake River. All year; 14-day limit. Free primitive camping at undesignated sites. Pit toilets (flush toilets in summer), cfga, no drkg wtr, shade shelters, tbls. Boating(l), fishing.
GPS: 46.563028, -118.100726

7
LOWER GRANITE LAKE
GPS: 46.6006, -117.4283

From Lewiston, Idaho/Clarkston, WA, 19 miles W on US 12; 2 miles N on Ledgerwood Spur Rd, 16 miles N on Kirby Mayview Rd, 12 miles E on Casey Creek Rd. No open fires during 6/10-10/10 (charcoal & gas grills permitted). Interpretive programs, visitor center, Clearwater & Snake River National Recreation Trail. Fish viewing rooms at Little Goose and Lower Granite Dams. Lower Granite Dam also has visitor center that features movies, interactive displays, guided tours. Day use areas include: Chestnut Beach Park, picnicking, beach, biking trail; Chief Looking Glass Park (leased to City of Asotin), picnicking, flush toilets, cold showers, playground, swimming area, tennis court, basketball court; Clearwater Park (leased to City of Lewiston), picnicking, flush toilets, softball, fishing pond, portable toilets, burling pond; Greenbelt Ramp, phone, swimming area, flush toilets, hiking & biking trails, fishing pier, boat ramp; Lewiston Levee Parkway, picnicking, grills, flush toilets, interpretive center, biking, hiking, wildlife

viewing, playground; North Lewiston Ramp
(leased to Nez Perce County), hiking trails,
camping, picnicking, boat ramp; Southway
Ramp (leased to Nez Perce County), hiking
trails, camping, handicap fishing, boating, pit
toilet, boat ramp; Swallows Park, picnicking,
covered shelters, tot lot playground, fire pits,
flush toilets, swimming area, hiking & biking
trails, phone, playground, volleyball court.
Park Manager, Clarkston Natural Resource
Office, 100 Fair Street, Clarkston, WA 99403-
1943. (509) 751-0240/0250.

BLYTON LANDING

From Clarkston at jct with US 12, N on SR
193 across Snake River bridge, then 20 mi
W on Wawawai River Rd (Old Hwy 193). All
year; 14-day limit. Free primitive camping at
undesignated sites. Pit toilets, cfga, tbls, no
drkg wtr. Fishing, boating(ld).

NISQUALLY JOHN LANDING

From Clarkston at jct with US 12, N on SR
193 across Snake River bridge, then 15 mi W
on Wawawai River Rd (Old Hwy 193). Free
primitive camping at undesignated sites. All
year; 14-day limit. Pit toilets, cfga, tbls, no
drkg wtr. Boating(ld), fishing. No wood fires
6/10-10/10; charcoal & propane okay.

OFFIELD LANDING

1 mi E of Lower Granite Dam on Wawawai
Ferry Rd at Lower Granite Lake, Snake
River milepost 108, S shore. All year; 14-day
limit. Free primitive RV/tent camping at
undesignated sites. Pit toilets, cfga, tbls, shade
shelter, no drkg wtr. Boating(ld), fishing.
GPS: 46.652220, -117.418249

WAWAWAI LANDING

28 mi W of Clarkston on CR 9000 (North
Shore Snake River Rd) or 19 mi SW of
Pullman on Wawawai Rd. All year; 14-day
limit. Free primitive camping at about 9
undesignated sites. Pit toilets, cfga, shade
shelters, tbls. Boating(ld), fishing.
GPS: 46.634277, -117.378273

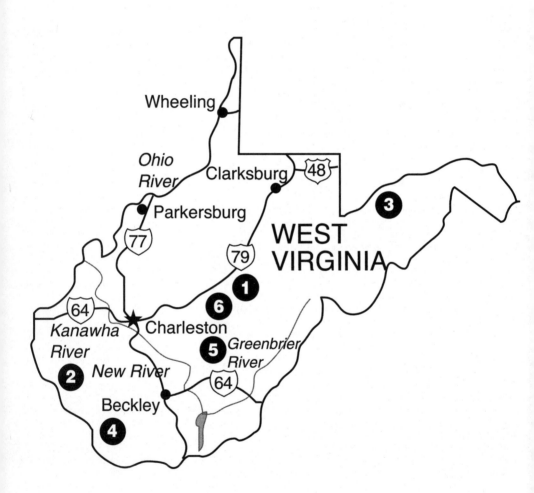

STATE INFORMATION:

CAPITAL: Charleston
NICKNAME: Mountain State
STATEHOOD: 1863 - 35th State
FLOWER: Rhododendron
TREE: Sugar Maple
BIRD: Cardinal

WV

STATE TIDBITS:

- Approximately 15% of the nation's total coal production comes from West Virginia.

- West Virginia was the first state to have a sales tax. It became effective July 1, 1921.

- The first rural free mail delivery was started in Charles Town on October 6, 1896.

WWW.WVTOURISM.COM

Toll-free number for travel information:
1-800-CALL-WVA.

Dept of Commerce, Division of Tourism, 90 MacCorkle Ave SW, Charleston, WV 25303. 1-800-CALL-WVA or 304-558-2200.

WEST VIRGINIA LAKES

To find campgrounds operated by the U.S. Army Corps of Engineers, match the lake's numbers on the preceding map page with numbered lake entries on the following pages. Campgrounds are listed alphabetically under the appropriate lakes. The following West Virginia impounds have Corps of Engineers campgrounds.

Burnsville Lake. A 978-acre E of Burnsville and I-79 on SR 5 in central West Virginia on the Little Kanawha River; it has 30 miles of shoreline.

East Lynn Lake. A 1,005-acre lake 12 miles S of Wayne on Twelvepole Creek off SR 37 in southwestern West Virginia.

Jennings Randolph Lake. A 952-acre lake 5 miles N of Elk Garden, E of Morgantown and W of Kyser in northeastern West Virginia; on the North Branch of the Potomac River.

R.D. Bailey Lake. A 630-acre lake near Justice, 4 miles E of Gilbert on US 52 and SR 97 on the Guandotte River.

Summersville Lake. A 2,790-acre lake located S of Summersville off US 19, 69 miles E of Charleston and W of Mt. Nebo on SR 129 in south-central WEst Virginia; on the Gauley River.

Sutton Lake. A 1,440-acre lake located 1 mile E of Sutton off US 19, NE of Charleston in central West Virginia on the Elk River. It has 40 miles of shoreline.

❶
BURNSVILLE LAKE
GPS: 38.34, -80.6183

A 968-acre lake E of Burnsville and I-79 on SR 5 in central West Virginia on the Little Kanawha River; it has 30 miles of shoreline. Campground checkout time 5 p.m. Civil War site nearby; reenactment every two years. Visitor center, interpretive programs, artifacts. Day use areas include Bulltown Overlook, interpretive trail, and Falls Mill Park, multi-use trail, waterfall, picnicking, toilets, ball field. Resource Manager, 2550 South Main St, Burnsville, WV 26335. (304) 853-2371. Lake information, (304) 853-2398.

BULLTOWN CAMPGROUND

From I-79 exit 67 near Flatwoods, 10 mi N on US 19 through Flatwoods & Napier, across lake bridge, on left; follow signs. About 4/20-12/1; 14-day limit. 22 wtr/elec 30-amp sites, $24; 48 wtr/elec 50-amp sites, $26; 134 full hookups 50-amp, $30 ($11, $13 & $15 with federal senior pass). 5 elec handicap sites. RV limit in excess of 65 ft. Tbls, flush toilets, showers, dump, cfga, drkg wtr, playground, beach, pay phone, coin laundry, picnic shelter. Boating(l), fishing, biking & hiking trails, horseshoe pits, interpretive trail & shelter, bridle trails, basketball, waterskiing. (304) 452-8006. NRRS during 5/23-9/1.
GPS: 38.793674, -80.560287

RIFFLE RUN CAMPGROUND

From I-79 exit 79 near Burnsville, E on 5th St into town, S on Main St, then E on Shaver Fork Rd (CR 5/11) to park at NE shore of lake. About 4/20-12/1; 14-day limit. 6 primitive sites, $20; 54 full hookups, $30. ($10 & $15 with federal senior pass). Tbls, flush toilets, dump, coin laundry, cfga, drkg wtr, showers, playground, picnic shelter. Boating(l), fishing, hiking, horseshoe pits, ball fields. (304) 853-2583. No reservations.
GPS: 38.839808, -80.608787

❷
EAST LYNN LAKE
GPS: 38.145, -82.385

A 1,005-acre lake 12 miles S of Wayne on Twelvepole Creek off SR 37 in southwestern West Virginia. Visitor center. Day use areas: Below dam -- toilets, picnicking, playground, hiking trail; Damsite -- toilets, boat ramp, fishing pier, picnicking, playground, hiking trail; Lakeside -- toilets, boat ramp, picnicking, hiking trail; Lick Creek -- toilets, boat ramp, fishing pier, shelter, picnicking, playground. Non-campers pay $3 at boat ramps. Bridge on East Fork Rd near SR 37 and the beach reduced to one lane in 2014, with a 6-ton weight limit. Resource Manager, East Lynn Lake, 683 Overlook Trail Rd, East Lynn, WV 25512. (304) 849-2355.

EAST FORK CAMPGROUND

From East Lynn, 2 mi S on SR 37, then 10 mi E of dam on SR 37; at East Fork Twelvepole Creek, following signs. About 5/10-10/18; 14-day limit. 166 elec sites, $16 base, $24 for elec/wtr ($9 & $12 with federal senior pass). RV limit in excess of 65 ft. Tbls, flush & pit toilets, showers, cfga, drkg wtr, playground, beach, coin laundry, amphitheater, pay phone. Horseshoe pits, nature trail, swimming, ball field, hiking, boating(ld), fishing, basketball, volleyball. (304) 849-5000. NRRS about 5/10-9/2. **GPS: 38.078265, -82.314377**

❸
JENNINGS RANDOLPH LAKE
GPS: 39.4803, -79.0717

A 952-acre 5 miles N of Elk Garden, E of Morgantown and W of Kyser in northeastern West Virginia; on North Branch of Potomac River. Campground checkout time is noon. Day use areas include Howell Run -- boat ramp, shelters ($50), picnicking, playground, hiking trail, horseshoe pits; Maryland Overlook -- picnicking, hiking trail; West Virginia Overlook -- toilets, picnicking, playground, beach. Resource Manager, Jennings Randolph lake, P. O. Box 247, Elk Garden, WV 26717. (301) 359-3861/(304) 355-2346.

ROBERT W. CRAIG CAMP

From Elk Garden, 5 mi NE on SR 46; exit N at sign. 5/1-10/11; 14-day limit. 9 non-elec sites, $18; 73 elec sites, $22 ($9 & $11 with federal senior pass). 55-ft RV limit. Tbls, flush toilets, showers, dump, playground, cfga, drkg wtr, beach, amphitheater, picnic shelter ($50), pay phone. Horseshoe pits, interpretive trail, hiking trail, boating(l), fishing, basketball, ball field, archery. RV limit 55'. NRRS.
GPS: 39.416792, -79.114587

④ R. D. BAILEY LAKE
GPS: 37.6069, -81.7781

A 630-acre lake near Justice, 4 miles E of Gilbert on US 52 and SR 97 on the Guyandotte River. ORV prohibited. Visitor center offers picnicking, picnic shelter with grill, hiking trail. Other day use areas include: Big Branch -- picnicking, shelter with grills, playground, horseshoe pits, basketball court; Dam Overlook -- picnicking, picnic shelter, playground, hiking trail; Downstream Area -- boat ramp, picnicking, hiking trails; Guyandotte Point -- picnicking, playground, shelters $45-$50, boat ramp. Non-campers pay $3 at boat ramps. Resource Manager, R. D. Bailey Lake, P. O. Box 70, Justice, WV 24851-0070. (304) 664-3229.

GUYANDOTTE POINT RECREATION AREA

From the dam, 1.1 mi to US 52, then 2.2 mi S; 5.8 mi SE on SR 97 toward Baileysville. Camping is in 2 areas along the Guyandotte River, the first being Reedy Creek about 3 mi from the campground entrance, with 31 50-amp elec sites, 6 full hookups. The other camping area after 1 more mile along the river is Locust Branch, with 63 sites. Each camping area has showers & comfort stations. 2 other camping areas were closed. MD-LD; 14-day limit. 94 paved 50-amp elec sites, $20 base ($10 with federal senior pass), $24 for 6 full hookups ($12 with senior pass). 1 double elec site $24; 1 double full-hookup site $34 ($12 & $17 with senior pass). 5 pull-through sites. Free primitive camping area open during pre-season & post-season periods, closed Jan & Feb. Tbls, flush toilets, showers, dump, cfga, drkg wtr, coin laundry, playground, beach. Boating(l), hiking, fishing, swimming, campfire programs, waterskiing.
GPS: 37.591209, -81.717183

⑤ SUMMERSVILLE LAKE
GPS: 38.22, -80.89

A 2,790-acre lake located S of Summersville off US 19, 69 miles E of Charleston and W of Mt. Nebo on SR 129 in south-central West Virginia on the Gauley River. Picnic shelters, Civil War site nearby, whitewater rafting below dam, visitor center. Checkout time 5 p.m. Trout stocked below dam in spring and fall. Day use facilities: Damsite Park -- 3 picnic shelters ($45), playground; Salmon Run -- boat ramp, picnicking, multi-use trails, fishing pier; Long Point -- boat ramp, multi- use trail. Non-campers pay $3 at boat ramps, $4 day use. Facilities leased by the Corps include Summersville Marina, with boat launch & campground. Resource Manager, Summersville Lake, 2981 Summersville Lake Rd, Summersville, WV 26651. (304) 872-3412/5809.

BATTLE RUN RECREATION AREA

From S of Summersville at jct with US 19; 3.4 mi W on SR 129 across dam, then N (right) at sign. 5/1-Columbus Day; 14-day limit. 7 walk-in tent sites, $20; 110 elec 30-amp sites, $30 ($10 & $15 with federal senior pass). RV limit in excess of 65 ft. Tbls, flush toilets, coin laundry, showers, dump, playground, beach, pay phone. Horseshoe pits, handicap accessible swimming pier, submerged ramp for wheelchairs, handicap accessible fishing area, boating(l), fishing, swimming, basketball, volleyball, biking/hiking trails, waterskiing. Pets & ORV prohibited. Group picnic shelter $45. (304) 872-3459. NRRS (MD-LD).
GPS: 38.22167, -80.90972

⑥ SUTTON LAKE
GPS: 38.6617, -80.6933

A 1,440-acre lake located 1 mile E of Sutton off US 19, NE of Charleston in central West Virginia on the Elk River. It has 40 miles of shoreline. Visitor Center, interpretive program. Day use facilities: Downstream Park -- picnicking, group shelter, playground, fishing pier; South Abutment -- boat ramp, group shelter, beach, hiking trail; North Abutment -- hiking trail. Non-campers pay $3 at boat ramps. Lake information, (304) 765-2816. Resource Manager, Sutton Lake, P. O. Box 426, Sutton, WV 26601. (304) 765-2816.

BEE RUN CAMPGROUND

From near Sutton on I-79, at exit 67, 1 mi E on SR 4; 1.2 mi E on SR 15; turn right. About 4/1-12/6; 14-day limit. 12 primitive pull-through sites, $10 ($5 with federal senior pass). 20-ft RV limit. No shoreline camping. Tbls, toilets, cfga, drkg wtr, beach. Swimming, boating(l), fishing. **GPS: 38.667539, -80.677658**

BAKER'S RUN CAMPGROUND

From exit 62 of I-79, 2 mi NE to Sutton; 4 mi S on old US 19 (CR 19/40); 12 mi E on CR 17. About 4/20-10/15; 14-day limit. 79 sites, some pull-through. Sites without hookups, $20; elec sites, $30 ($10 & $15 with federal senior pass). 58-ft RV limit. Tbls, flush toilets, showers, dump, cfga, drkg wtr, beach, playground. Basketball, horseshoe pits, volleyball, biking trails, swimming, waterskiing, fishing, boating(l). (304) 765-5631.
GPS: 38.619520, -80.684441

GERALD R. FREEMAN CAMP

From near Sutton at I-79 exit 67, 1 mi S on SR 4; 12 mi E on SR 15. About 4/23 to close of deer hunting season; 14-day limit. 54 non-elec sites, $16 base, $18 at premium locations; 104 elec sites, $18 base, $26 at premium locations ($8, $9, $9 & $13 with federal senior pass). Tbls, flush toilets, dump, coin laundry, cfga, drkg wtr, showers, pay phone, playground, beach. Boating(l), fishing horseshoe pits, hiking trail, ball courts, biking, waterskiing. ORV prohibited. (304) 765-7756. NRRS during MD-LD. **GPS: 38.670718, -80.547724**

WISCONSIN

Superior

St. Croix River

Flambeau River

Wisconsin River

51

Eau Claire

Green Bay

43

94

Lake Winnebago

90

41

3

Mississippi River

Milwaukee

94

Madison

90

43

4

WISCONSIN

STATE INFORMATION:

CAPITAL: Madison
NICKNAME: Badger State
STATEHOOD: 1848 - 30th State
FLOWER: Wood Violet
TREE: Sugar Maple
BIRD: Robin

WI

STATE TIDBITS:

• The first practical typewriter was designed in Milwaukee in 1867.

• The first Ringling Brothers Circus was staged in Baraboo in 1884.

• The National Freshwater Fishing Hall of Fame is in Hayward.

WWW.TRAVELWISCONSIN.COM

Toll-free number 800-432-8747.

Wisconsin Department of Tourism Development, PO Box 8690, Madison, WI 53708; 608-266-2161

WISCONSIN LAKES

To find campgrounds operated by the U.S. Army Corps of Engineers, match the lake's numbers on the preceding map page with numbered lake entries on the following pages. Campgrounds are listed alphabetically under the appropriate lakes. The following Wisconsin impoundments have Corps of Engineers campgrounds.

Eau Gall Lake. A 150-acre lake 45 miles SE of St. Paul off I-94; exit 24 S; 2 miles S on CR B; 2 miles N on CR N; 2 miles S on CR NN; 0.5 mile N of Spring Valley (40 miles W of Eau Galle).

Lock & Dam 3, Mississippi River. Pool extends upstream from the dam near Hager City to Lock & Dam 2 near Hastings, Minnesota.

Lake Winneshiek. Located 30 miles S of LaCross off SR 35 on CR B1 (3 miles S of Lynxville), the lake extends from Lock & Dam 9 to about 4 miles S of Lansing, Iowa.

Lock & Dam 11, Mississippi River. Located on the river just N of Dubuque, Iowa, this is the first of a series of locks extending between the point where Iowa, Wisconsin and Illinois join borders and 11 more southerly pools.

❶

EAU GALLE LAKE
GPS: 44.8583, -92.24

A 150-acre lake 45 miles SE of St. Paul off I-94; exit 24 S; 2 miles S on CR B; 2 miles N on CR N; 2 miles S on CR NN; 0.5 mile N of Spring Valley (40 miles W of Eau Galle). Electric motors only are permitted on the lake. Lake surrounded by two day use areas, a beach, two boat ramps, one campground and several miles of hiking and equestrian trails. Day use facilities: at Main Day Use Park, accessible restrooms, boat launch, hiking trail, horseshoe pits, interpretive trail, playground, swimming beach, phone, volleyball court, group picnic shelter with elec $40; at Lousy Creek Access, boat ramp, bridle trail; at Northwest Area, group picnic shelter, bridle trails. Park Manager, Eau Galle Lake, P. O. Box 190, Spring Valley, WI 54767-0190. (715) 778-5562.

HIGHLAND RIDGE CAMP
EAU GALLE RECREATION AREA

From Spring Valley, 2 mi NE on SR 29; 2 mi E on 10th Ave; 1 mi S on CR NN; at NE shore of lake. 4/1-10/22; 14-day limit. RV/tent sites

without hookups, $16 base, $18 at premium locations ($8 & $9 with federal senior pass); 35 elec sites, $20 ($10 with senior pass); 7 walk-to tent sites, $16 ($8 with senior pass); 10 equestrian sites without hookups, $14 ($7 with senior pass). 65-ft RV limit. Tbls, flush & pit toilets, dump, coin showers, playground, beach, cfga, drkg wtr, picnic shelter. Horseshoe pits, free movies or interpretive programs on weekends, hiking trail, interpretive trail, boating, fishing, swimming, (715) 778-5562. NRRS during 4/29-9/31.
GPS: 44.872534, -92.243268

LOCK & DAM 3
MISSISSIPPI RIVER
GPS: 44.3635, -92.3637

Pool extends upstream from the dam near Hager City to Lock & Dam 2 near Hastings, Minnesota. Dam was built in 1938. The only Corps campground is Commisory Point, a free boat-in primitive tent area (inquire locally for best directions).

LOCK & DAM 9
LAKE WINNESHIEK – MISSISSIPPI RIVER
GPS: 43.31, -91.07

Located 30 miles S of LaCross off SR 35 on CR B1 (3 miles S of Lynxville). Completed in 1937. Lake Winneshiek extends from the dam to about 4 miles S of Lansing, Iowa; it has nearly 6,000 acres of backwater and is part of the Upper Mississippi River National Wildlife and Fish Refuge. The Corps plans to build two islands in the lake to improve wildlife habitat. Resource Manager, Blackhawk Park, E590 County Rd B1, DeSoto, WI 54624.

BLACKHAWK CAMPGROUND

From DeSoto, 3 mi N on SR 35, then SW on CR B1. 4/1-10/30; 14-day limit. 100 sites without hookups, $18 ($9 with federal senior

pass); 75 elec sites, $24 ($12 with senior pass); walk-to tent sites $16. 65-ft RV limit. Tbls, flush & pit toilets, coin showers, fish cleaning station, beach, playground, picnic shelters ($40). Interpretive programs, horseshoe pits, free movies on weekends, boating(l), fishing, swimming, volleyball.
GPS: 43.462206, -91.223833

LOCK & DAM 11
MISSISSIPPI RIVER
GPS: 42540279, -90.644294

Located on the river just N of Dubuque, IA, This is the first of a series of locks extending between the point where Iowa, Wisconsin and Illinois join borders and 11 more southerly pools. Near this lock, the Corps operates a popular recreation area. Boat landing at Bagley Bottoms. Project Manager, Pools 11-22, PO Box 534, Pleasant Valley, IA 52767. 309-794-4522.

GRANT RIVER RECREATION AREA

From Dubuque, Iowa, E across river into Wisconsin, then N on US 61; 2 mi W on SR 133, following signs (2 mi S of Potosi), then left (E) on River Lane Rd; right (S) on Park Lane to campground on N shore of Mississippi River. Fees 5/1-11/24 (free primitive camping off-season); 14-day limit. 10 tent sites, $10 ($5 with federal senior pass); 63 elec 50-amp sites, $20 ($10 with senior pass). No wtr hookups. 55-ft RV limit. Tbls, flush toilets, cfga, drkg wtr, showers, playground, dump, picnic shelter ($25), amphitheater. Boating(l), fishing. Campground: 608-736-2140, 800-645-0248. NRRS. **GPS: 42.651061, -90.7000432**

CFGA
CAMPFIRE GRILL AREAS

CR
COUNTY ROAD

D
DOCK

DRKG WTR
DRINKING WATER

E
EAST

ELEC
ELECTRIC

FH OR FR
FOREST ROAD

JCT
JUNCTION

L
LAUNCH (BOAT)

LD
LABOR DAY

MD
MEMORIAL DAY

N
NORTH

NRRS
NAT. RECREATION
RESERVATION SERVICE

ORV
OFF-ROAD VEHICLE(S)

PRIM
PRIMITIVE

RV
RECREATIONAL VEHICLE

SR
STATE ROUTE

S
SOUTH

US
UNITED STATES ROUTE

W
WEST

WTR
WATER

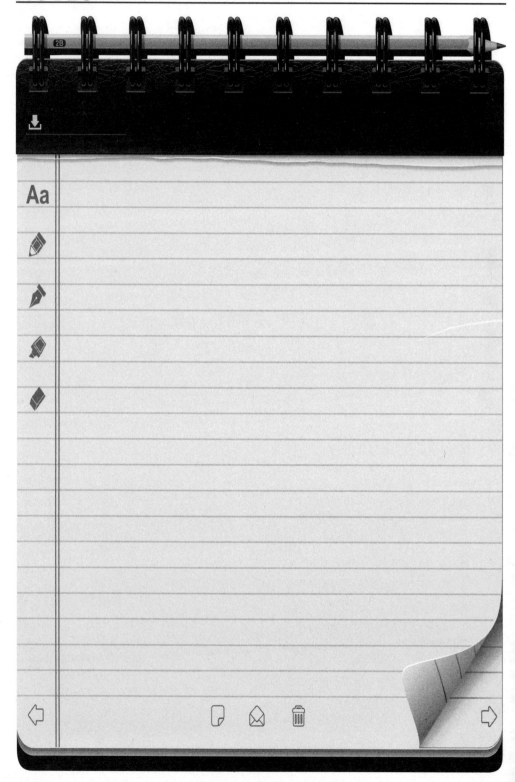